THE COUNTRY ROUND
SWARTH...

SCALE IN ...

0   1   2   3

F.M.H. = Friends' M...

········· Routes across ...

Rydal
Hall

• Ambleside

WINDERMERE

• Windermere

Sawrey

Graythwaite
Hall

Crosthwaite

Underbarrow

KENDAL
F.M.H.

Firbank
Fell

SEDBERGH

Brigg Flatts
F.M.H.

Newby Bridge
Staveley

Height
F.M.H.

River Kent

Levens
Hall

Preston
Patrick
F.M.H.

Lindale

Cartmel

Grange

Kents
Bank

Silverdale

Yealand Conyers
F.M.H.

River Lune

Over Kellet

Nether Kellet

CAMBE

Hest Bank

LANCASTER
F.M.H.

Pendle Hill
15 miles

MARGARET FELL

Mother of Quakerism

by

ISABEL ROSS

WILLIAM SESSIONS BOOK TRUST
THE EBOR PRESS, YORK, ENGLAND
1984

First published in 1949
(by Longmans, Green and Company)

Second Edition 1984

©

ISBN 0 900657 83 9

Printed in England by
William Sessions Ltd., York

PREFACE TO THE FIRST EDITION

IT is nearly three hundred years since Margaret Fell first heard George Fox speak in Ulverston Church. She was convinced of the truth of his teaching, and soon her home, Swarthmoor Hall in Furness, became the centre of Quakerism, and for the rest of her life she was a source of inspiration and guidance to the growing Society of Friends.

In this book I have attempted to portray this remarkable woman, set against the background of her time, within her family and among her friends.

Margaret Fell has always interested me, partly because she is an ancestor seven generations back, but the interest was quickened when my husband, William McGregor Ross, our two sons and I lived for five years at Swarthmoor Hall which had been her home for seventy years. I was then led to make a deeper study of her, through a wide research in the hundreds of old letters, Quaker minute books and other manuscripts still available. Through them a number of new facts came to light, and her portrait grew clearer and more vivid. Here indeed was an outstanding woman, a pioneer in thought, with grace of body and mind, a woman winning the love and respect of great numbers of men and women by her understanding sympathy, her wisdom and her power to encourage and inspire.

She had the spiritual qualities which revealed to her profound religious truths and in addition she had the practical ability which enabled her to manage a large household and estate and to help to organize the growing body of Friends into a coherent whole, resilient against the troubles of the time. She was both a Mary and a Martha.

In this story of Margaret Fell I have included much about her children, not only because the seven daughters were themselves women of character and achievements on their own account, but also because of their illuminating relationship with their mother.

The picture of the economic and social conditions of Furness in Lancashire which I have tried to give also comes from the records of this family. *Sarah Fell's Household Account Book* is unique for a manor house of North Lancashire in the seventeenth century, showing as it does the commodities bought and sold and the labour employed on such an estate.

The records also show that Swarthmoor Hall was exceptional in that it received letters and visitors from all parts of the British Isles, from the continent of Europe and from across the Atlantic. At that time Furness otherwise was a part of England to and from which travellers were few.

A religious movement is probably on surer ground when it is founded and nurtured by a man and a woman in sympathetic partnership, than if by only one. And so it is with Quakerism. Margaret Fell's character and work have meant a great deal for Quaker women, and the position she held has coloured, whether consciously or unconsciously, the whole trend of the Society of Friends.

Perhaps the history of this great woman and of those around her has a particular significance for us to-day. For it illustrates the power that comes from a faith in the supremacy of spiritual values, a power which enabled her to resist persecution with courage and serenity and without bearing malice towards her persecutors.

ACKNOWLEDGEMENTS

So many friends, both here and in the United States of America have helped me in my task, that it is impossible to name them all, but to all I give my grateful thanks.

I would especially like to thank and acknowledge the great help given me by those who read my manuscript: Gerald K. Hibbert, T. Edmund Harvey, Robert Davis, Mrs. Mary Tout, Miss Janet McCrindell and my sons, Hugh McGregor Ross and Peter McGregor Ross. To the last named I am also indebted for the map and much valuable detailed criticism.

I wish to thank the Town Council of Barrow-in-Furness for permission to use a photograph of the portrait (reputed) of Judge Fell; the Librarian of Friends' House, London, for permission to photograph Margaret Fell's letter, and my son, Hugh McG. Ross for the four photographs of Swarthmoor Hall.

I am most grateful for the unfailing help of John L. Nickalls and Muriel Hicks of Friends' House Library, London, and for the loan of valuable seventeenth-century books both from that Library and from Tullie House, Carlisle, and for permission to examine and use MSS. at the Friends' Meeting Houses at Lancaster and Nottingham.

I acknowledge with gratitude also help and encouragement given me by Professor Henry J. Cadbury of Harvard University, Dr. Geoffrey F. Nuttall and Miss Elisabeth Brockbank, and last but not least I thank the Council of Woodbrooke, Selly Oak, Birmingham, for the grant of a Fellowship there, which gave me opportunity for some months for work in happy and indeed ideal conditions, with the use of a valuable library.

I am greatly indebted to Miss Margaret Cropper for kind permission to print her three little poems on Sunbreck.

Quotations in this book are taken wherever possible from the original or from contemporary copies. Omissions are shown by dotted lines.

Words in square brackets are additions made by the author for the sake of clarity.

Far Sawrey, Ambleside,   ISABEL ROSS
Westmorland.
   1948

NOTE TO 1984 EDITION

It is 36 years since Isabel Ross completed the recognised standard work on Margaret Fell. It is impossible to know in what ways she would have wished to revise the book were she alive. Up to her death in 1964 she kept a copy for annotation. This has been made available through the kindness of her elder son, Hugh McGregor Ross, and through Sylvia M. Ross, the widow of her younger son, Peter. Of the 80 amendments she recorded, about 50 are incorporated in this revision. The remainder were either notes for her personal use or comparatively minor points that could not conveniently be incorporated. We have added some 40 further corrections, mainly to clarify references or to move a few steps forward in the uniform treatment of dates. For clarity all changes of text, except for a few literals, are shown in bolder type.

The dating of letters and other documents, as also, perhaps, events mentioned in the text, is not one which admits of any easy solution. At the end of her 1948 'Acknowledgements' Isabel Ross wrote:

> Dates and punctuation and usually the spelling are modernised. If the original date is left, it is followed by O.S., indicating the old style of reckoning the calendar.

Unfortunately the matter is not as simple as that and a few words of elaboration and explanation are needed.

The introduction of the Gregorian calendar ('New style') to England & Wales in 1752 by Lord Chesterfield's Act (24 Geo 2 c 23) has two elements:–

  a the elimination of the error in the Julian calendar by the 11-day adjustment;

b the change of new year's day from Lady Day (25 March)
to 1 January.

It might have been assumed from Isabel Ross's words that,
except when O.S. was given after a date, she had made a
10-day adjustment for 17th-century dates and an 11-day
adjustment for 18th-century ones (1700, it will be recalled, was
a leap year in the Julian calendar but not in the more correct
Gregorian one).

In fact, Isabel Ross's 'new style' ran only to altering the year
for dates between 1 January and 24 March. This is a perfectly
logical position, providing that the words 'new style' are not
used. It has been our aim, therefore, to eliminate all references
in the original work where O.S. or N.S. have appeared. But
first we must outline the complications which arise from
Quaker usage.

Friends refused to use the heathen names alike for the days
of the week and the months of the year. Sunday was first day,
March first month, and February twelfth month: September,
October, November and December were acceptable until
1752 since they were simple statements of the seventh, eighth,
ninth and tenth months (after 1752 they were abandoned as
untruthful). The first 24 days of March were normally
double-dated (1677/8) but, if this were not done, the year given
was normally that which was to begin on 25 March: this,
however, was not universal, some Friends using the year that
was to end on 24 March (see p. 346).

It may be relevant to quote from the preamble to
Chesterfield's Act:–

> Whereas the legal Supputation of the Year of our Lord in
> that Part of Great Britain called England, according to
> which the Year beginneth on the twenty-fifth Day of
> March, hath been found by Experience to be attended
> with divers Inconveniencies, not only as it differs from
> the Usage of neighbouring Nations, but also from the
> legal Method of Computation in that Part of Great
> Britain called Scotland, and from the common Usage
> throughout the whole Kingdom, and thereby frequent
> Mistakes are occasioned in the Dates of Deeds, and other
> Writings, and Disputes arise therefrom . . .

Where 'the world's people' were involved in Quaker deeds, other mistakes were liable to arise. Francis Camfield's 1706/7 declaration of trust is dated 'the seventh of the elevnth[sic] month called February' – the scriveners in the office presumably having (with some logic) assumed that Quakers regarded 1-24 March as twelfth month.

Further difficulties may attend letters from Friends written from Scotland or the continent. While an English visitor or a person at sea might think and write in Julian terms (as, perhaps, at p. 394), a more settled inhabitant would be more likely to have used the Gregorian calendar. Isabel Ross dated the William Ames letter (p. 97) as 'From near Amsterdam. 13. 6. 1658[August]': it may more probably have been written in June, as suggested (though not asserted) in this revision.

In eliminating the use of O.S. and N.S. we have revised entries either by following the language of the original with the appropriate month in square brackets or by using the form '7 iii [May] 1682'. We have adopted roman numerals for the months, partly to avoid confusion for American readers (who may expect the month first) and partly to distinguish our changes from Isabel Ross's dating, where arabic numerals are used for months.

Since 1949 a number of books and articles have been published which Isabel Ross noted, or would have noted. Here we can mention but a few. *The journal of George Fox,* edited by John L. Nickalls (Cambridge 1952; London 1975) not only supplied a text based on the Spence MS rather than the Ellwood 1694 edition, but also in its footnotes made more certain a number of pertinent dates. The Henry J. Cadbury revisions of W. C. Braithwaite's *The beginnings of Quakerism* (Cambridge 1955; York 1982) and *The second period of Quakerism* (Cambridge 1961; York 1979) between them provide 110 pages of invaluable additional notes, pointing to information and interpretation since the original publication of these volumes. Hugh Barbour's *The Quakers in puritan England* (New Haven and London 1964) is the general study of 17th-century Quakerism that bears most closely on the life of Margaret Fell.

Geoffrey F. Nuttall's pioneering *Early Quaker letters* (privately printed 1952) provides a calendar of 563 letters up to 1660 in Swarthmore MSS vol. 1, 3 and 4. Craig W. Horle has produced working calendars (available at the Library of the Society of Friends, London) of the ARB MSS, Spence MSS vol. 3, Caton MSS vol. 3, and Abraham MSS. All these have helped with more precise dating and, though we have leant on them heavily, it may well be that Isabel Ross would have made further changes in the light of these aids which were not available to her. We are particularly sorry that Craig Horle's return to America has precluded our discussing the text with him, since he now probably knows more of Margaret Fell than any other living person.

It remains to add short notes on the legality of Quaker marriages (p. 294), the Women's Yearly Meeting (pp. 301, 370, 376), and the Affirmation Act difficulty (pp. 370–373).

Legality of Quaker marriages. It is not strictly true that 'the legality of Quaker marriages without the offices of a clergyman had been settled in 1661 by the ruling of a Judge of Assize at Nottingham' (p. 294). Leaving aside the position under the commonwealth, the restoration brought with it the new prayer book and the Act of Uniformity (13 & 14 Car 2 c 4), giving the liturgy the force of statute law. It also brought the re-establishment of church courts which, perhaps most relevantly as far as Friends were concerned, had the responsibility for the administration of wills. Non-Quaker relatives sought to claim that a Quaker marriage was void (and the children therefore illegitimate) so as to dispute inheritance. The Nottingham case before Judge Archer (8 August 1661) set an invaluable precedent in common law, but it was no more than that. The energies of Meeting for Sufferings and of local Friends for the rest of the century were engaged first in trying to remove any debates on the lawfulness of marriage from the church to the civil courts, and second in securing counsel's opinion and noting repeated civil law judgments in further cases of disputed inheritance. Quaker marriages were implicitly recognised in statute law in Lord Hardwicke's Act 1753 (26 Geo 2 c 33) and explicitly recognised in the Marriage Act 1836 (6 & 7 Will 4 c 85).

Women's Yearly Meeting. The Women's Yearly Meeting mentioned by Isabel Ross (note at p. 302) as ending in 1907 was started as late as 1785, having been authorised by Yearly Meeting 1784. Prior to this the meeting of the Women's Two Weeks and Box Meetings held at the time of Yearly Meeting in London was attended by women Friends from throughout the nation and frequently, as here, referred to as a Women's Yearly Meeting – being an effective body, even though lacking constitutional powers. For fuller information see 'The women's yearly meeting' by Mary Jane Godlee, in *London yearly meeting during 250 years* (London 1919), pp. 93-122; 'The women Friends of London: the Two-weeks and Box Meetings' by Irene L. Edwards, in *Jnl. F.H.S.* vol. 47 (1955) pp. 3-21. Brief notes will be found in Edward H. Milligan and Malcolm J. Thomas, *My ancestor was a Quaker: how do I find out more?* (London 1983), appendix E.

Affirmation Act. The form of words provided for Quakers, though not 'and others' (p. 371) under the Affirmation Act 1696 (7 & 8 Wm 3 c 34) was perhaps unacceptable to more Friends than Isabel Ross's 'a minority' (p. 371) suggests. All the particular and monthly meetings that made up Lancashire Quarterly Meeting were among the 'dissatisfied Friends' – a fact that may explain the vehemence of Margaret Fox's attack. For an account of the position as between the satisfied and the dissatisfied Friends from 1696 until the passage of the Affirmation Act 1722 (8 Geo 2 c 6), which received the royal assent 12 February 1721/2 ('1721', p. 371, being therefore not strictly correct), see *Second period of Quakerism*, pp. 181-206; N. C. Hunt, *Two early political associations* (Oxford 1961), pp. 49-61 ('The campaign for a modification of the Affirmation Act'). See also 'Lancashire Quakers and the oath 1660-1722' by Nicholas J. Morgan, in *Jnl. F.H.S.* vol. 54 (1980) pp. 235-254.

EDWARD H. MILLIGAN
MALCOLM J. THOMAS   *London, 1984*

CONTENTS

Contents

ILLUSTRATIONS

PRINCIPAL SOURCES AND BOOKS OF REFERENCE
with abbreviations used in this book (in order of mention)

While this reprint follows in the main Isabel Ross's wording and arrangement, entries have been amplified where there is later information or fuller details likely to be helpful to the reader. The standard symbol LSF is used for the Library of the Society of Friends, London (EHM/MJT 1984).

Jnl. F.H.S.   *The Journal of the Friends Historical Society* (London, 1903, in progress).

M.F. *Works*   *A brief collection of remarkable passages and occurrences relating to the birth, education, life, conversion, travels, services and deep sufferings of that ancient, eminent and faithful servant of the Lord, Margaret Fell, but by her second marriage, Margaret Fox, etc.* (London 1710).

Spence MSS.   Volumes I and II contain the autobiography dictated by George Fox to his stepson-in-law Thomas Lower in 1675 (or possibly beginning in 1674) interspersed with numerous letters, pastoral epistles and other papers: the contents of these two volumes were printed *verbatim et literatim* in 1911 as Camb. Jnl. (see below). Volume III contains principally letters and epistles by Margaret Fell (about 200 items). All these were preserved until 1759 at Swarthmoor Hall. They were mounted and bound when in the possession of Charles James Spence (1848-1905). They were purchased for London Yearly Meeting in 1920 and are now in LSF.

Camb. Jnl.   *The journal of George Fox,* edited by Norman Penney (Cambridge 1911, 2 vol.; New York 1973, 2 vol.). Prints, Spence MSS vol. I and II.

A.N.B. *Pers.*   *The personality of George Fox,* by A. Neave Brayshaw (London 1933). This enlarged and more widely available edition is to be preferred to the original edition (privately printed 1918; reprinted 1919).

Leeds Jnl.   *A journal or historical account of . . . George Fox* (Leeds 1836). 6th edition; for the 1694 Ellwood edition see below.

Life of W. Caton   *A journal of the life of Will[iam] Caton* (London 1689). Unless otherwise stated, references are to the 2nd edition, published as *Journals of the lives and gospel labours of William Caton and John Burnyeat* (London 1839).

Caton MSS. III   A volume of 168 letters (166 addressed to Margaret Fell by leading early Friends) copied in 1659–1660 by William Caton (1636–1665) with other MSS and some later editions. Added to LSF in 1935.

A.R.B.   *Letters, &c, of early Friends,* edited by A. R. Barclay (London 1841).

Swm. MSS.   Swarthmore Manuscripts, being 8 volumes of letters, epistles, etc. (about 400 items), originally preserved at Swarthmoor Hall. Volumes I, II, III and IV are chiefly letters addressed to Margaret Fell or George Fox: they were transcribed by Emily Jermyn 1866–9. Volumes V and VI formerly belonged to Robert Barclay (1833–1876) and were purchased for Devonshire House Library in 1895: they contain mainly religious epistles. Volume VII, mainly comprising documents emanating from George Fox, was in the possession of James Backhouse (1861–1945) was purchased for Devonshire House Library in 1907. Volume VIII was bequeathed by Isabel Ross. The collection is at LSF.

Croese   *General history of the Quakers,* by Gerard Croese, a Dutch writer (London 1696).

Webb, *Fells*   *The Fells of Swarthmoor Hall,* by Maria Webb (London and Dublin 1865); 2nd ed. (Philadelphia 1896).

B. Qism.   *The beginnings of Quakerism,* by W. C. Braithwaite (London 1912); 2nd ed. revised by Henry J. Cadbury (Cambridge 1955; York 1982).

F.P.T.   *The first publishers of truth,* edited by Norman Penney (Jnl. F.H.S. suppl. 1–5; London 1907).

Thirnbeck MSS.   A small collection of letters, originally preserved at Swarthmoor Hall, later in the possession of the Thirnbecks, descendants of Margaret Fell, and now at LSF.

Sewel   *The history of the . . . Quakers,* by William Sewel (London 1722, and later editions).

Rel. Bar. Reliquiae Barclaianae: correspondence of Colonel David Barclay and Robert Barclay of Urie and his son Robert (London 1870, lithographed from manuscript).

Abraham MSS. A collection of letters, deeds, etc., originally at Swarthmoor Hall, later in possession of Abrahams and Shackletons, descendants of Margaret Fell. Now at LSF.

Miller MSS. A collection of letters, etc., of which those of the seventeenth century were originally at Swarthmoor Hall. Destroyed by fire in 1940. A partial typescript of 17 letters from or to Margaret Fell or the family is available in LSF.

W. I. Hull, *Qism. in Amsterdam   Rise of Quakerism in Amsterdam, 1655-65*, by William I. Hull (Swarthmore, Pa., 1938).

Besse's *Sufferings   A collection of the sufferings of the people called Quakers from 1650 to 1689*, etc., by Joseph Besse (London 1753, 2 vol.). This folio should be distinguished from Joseph Besse's earlier octavo work, *An abstract of the sufferings* (London 1733-8, 3 vol.).

H. G. Crosfield   *Margaret Fox of Swarthmoor Hall* (London 1913).

Crosfield MSS. A collection of letters, etc., formerly in the possession of George Crosfield (1785-1847) and now in LSF. While mainly 18th century in content, the collection includes some papers from the Swarthmoor collection (*B. Qism*, p 540).

A.R.B. MSS. A collection of some 250 letters, etc., originally at Swarthmoor Hall. This collection was worked on by Abram Rawlinson Barclay for his *Letters, &c. of early Friends* (see above). It is now in LSF. The greater part of the collection has been printed (some in part, some *in extenso*) in *Jnl. F.H.S.* beginning with vol. 27 (1930).

Swm. Doc. in America   The Swarthmore Documents in America, edited by Henry J. Cadbury (Jnl. F.H.S. suppl. 20; London and Philadelphia 1940). Reprints 35 documents, mainly from the Etting MSS.

Spoore and Whiting MSS. A collection of letters of early Friends, chiefly from the north, copied by John Spoore and John Whiting in the seventeenth century. Now at Tullie House, Carlisle.

Short Journal   The short journal and itinerary journals of George Fox, edited by Norman Penney (Cambridge 1925).

Q. in A.C. The Quakers in the American colonies, by Rufus M. Jones (London 1911).

Extracts from State Papers Extracts from state papers relating to Friends, *1654 to 1672*, edited by Norman Penney (Jnl. FHS. suppl. 8-11; London, [etc.] 1913).

D.N.B. Dictionary of national biography.

Gibson MSS. A collection of Quaker MSS in 10 vol., formerly in the possession of George Stacey Gibson (1818-1883). Includes some 17th century material. Now in LSF.

G.F. Jnl., Ellwood Edn. Edited by Thomas Ellwood, this first edition of George Fox's Journal was published in 1694.

Second Period of Quakerism The second period of Quakerism, by W. C. Braithwaite (London 1919); 2nd ed. prepared by Henry J. Cadbury (Cambridge 1961; York 1979).

Cash MSS. A collection of manuscripts, including some 17th-century letters, formerly in the possession of A. Midgley Cash of Torquay and now in LSF.

S.F. Act. Bk. The household account book of Sarah Fell of Swarthmoor Hall, edited by Norman Penney (Cambridge 1920).

Luke Howard MSS. Manuscripts collected by Luke Howard (1772-1864), including 17th-century items. Presented to LSF by L. Violet Holdsworth in 1943. A partial summary listing is given in Jnl. F.H.S. vol. 38 (1946) pp 32-46.

Later Periods of Quakerism The later periods of Quakerism, by Rufus M. Jones (London 1921, 2 vol.).

Thwaite MSS. Now lost, but some were included in Maria Webb's *Fells of Swarthmoor Hall* and H. G. Crosfield's *Margaret Fox of Swarthmoor Hall.*

Chapter One

'Margaret Fell's personality is one of the glories of Furness.'
J. Brownbill, M.A., in his Introduction to *The Household Account Book of Sarah Fell of Swarthmoor Hall.*

LANCASHIRE North of the Sands has always been an iso-lated piece of England. Separated from the main body of the county by Westmorland, it lies to the north-west of the wide sands of Morecambe Bay. Seen from the Lancaster side the long, soft, grey line of its fells rises above sea and sand. Bounded on the south by the bay, on the west by the Irish Sea and hills of Cumberland, on the north and east by Windermere and the mountains of the Lake District, its only point of entry, until modern days brought coast roads and the railway, was by the hilly road from Kendal or by the dangerous crossing of the sands from Lancaster. A thousand years ago another means of entry had been used, from the sea. Then the Norsemen, sailing round the north of Scotland, and down the west coasts of Scotland and England found the sheltered bays of Lancashire a gateway to uninhabited valleys with rushing streams and well-wooded hillsides. Every dale in Furness[1] gives evidence in its place—and family—names to the settlements of the Norsemen; kirks, bys, and thwaites abound. On the high fells lived a dwindling folk, whose remains are still unearthed in ancient cairns and 'giants' graves.

Sixty years after the Norman Conquest, Stephen who later became king, founded Furness Abbey for Benedictines from Normandy. Later the Abbey became Cistercian, and the Abbot held lordship over the whole district still described as Furness. 'In wealth and importance Furness ranked second to Fountains, and its abbots enjoyed almost feudal power for centuries.'[2]

---

[1] The name 'Furness' is of Scandinavian origin. For=further, nes =a point or promontory. *Furness and Cartmel Notes*, by Barber, p. 45.
[2] *The English Lake District*, by M. J. B. Baddeley, B.A., p. 93.

The dissolution of the monasteries (1536) was the signal for the rise into landed independence of the former big tenants of the abbot. That is one explanation, among many, of the building in the reign of Queen Elizabeth, in Furness, as elsewhere in England, of solid stone houses, built and owned by gentle-folk, some of whom combined learning with the holding and using of land.

In the southern part of Furness, one of these families was that of Fell. A certain George Fell lived in the latter end of the sixteenth century at Hawkswell, near Broughton Beck, as the road climbs up from Ulverston over the fells dividing the estuaries of Duddon and Leven. He was an attorney at law, owner of an estate stretching from the Osmotherley Fells into Ulverston and to the edge of Conishead Priory, and being prosperous, he decided to build a large house for himself and his family at the other end of his property. Between 1600 and 1620 therefore he built Swarthmoor Hall. A mile to the south of the old market town of Ulverston, and on higher ground, midway between sea and fell and close to the 'black moor', this three-story hall still stands, its barns and stables grouped on the windward side. It is built of grey freestone, but in the course of time its walls have been plastered or pebble-dashed. The roof is of local slate, and from a distance the hall is hard to see, as it merges into the grey-green country around it. Outside, the plainness of the house is broken by stone-mullioned windows and their drip-stones, and one fine bay window which goes up throughout the three storeys. The house at present is little more than half the size it was when George Fell and his son Thomas were owners, but the rooms which remain, after the sad decay in the latter part of the eighteenth and throughout the nineteenth centuries, are large and high, beautifully proportioned and well lit from east, south and west. Originally the house was panelled throughout[1]—now only two bedrooms have the original panelling and carving left, while downstairs in the fine dining-hall and the parlour, leading from it through a little lobby where a doorway opens into the side garden, new oak panelling and beautiful carving have been added.[2] The dining-hall is floored with grey 'Cumberland flags'

[1] Letter from Wm. Forster of Tottenham. Jnl. F.H.S.

[2] Done by Emma Clarke Abraham (a direct descendant of Judge and Margaret Fell), who restored the Hall between 1913 and 1919.

and has a deep stone fireplace. No doubt it was the living room of the family, where mother and daughters spun their home-grown flax, where the children learnt their lessons and were taught to play the musical instruments of their day. The parlour was the study of the master of the house, originally a large room, looking east to Morecambe Bay and north to the fells and 'Old Man of Coniston'. Outside the parlour stand **six** ancient yews, **remaining from the eight** which tradition says were planted by the Judge for his **children.**

Lawns, gardens (including one for herbs), a large walled orchard of apples, pears, plums and damsons, woods to provide fuel for the great fireplaces, shelter from the storms and pleasant places to walk in, and a swift-flowing brook within twenty yards of the house, complete the picture of this old manor-house, which became during the latter part of the seventeenth century the centre and home of one of the most dynamic religious move-ments of our day.[1]

George Fell's son, Thomas Fell, was born in 1598–9. He was brought up to the law, and in 1631 became a barrister of Gray's Inn, London, and a bencher in 1651. In 1641 he was made a Justice of the Peace for Lancashire, and when Civil War between King and Parliament broke out in the next year, Thomas Fell was one of the gentry of the north-west who sided with Parlia-ment. In October 1645 he became a member, for Lancaster, of the Long Parliament.[2] He and his colleague, Sir Robert Bind-loss, Kt., of Borwick Hall, near Carnforth, took the place of their predecessors, who both lost their positions, one for bearing arms against Parliament, and the other for neglecting the service of the House and not appearing upon summons. Fell remained a member until 1647, when his name was among a great number who were reported as absent without cause, and a fine of twenty pounds was ordered to be levied.[3] He was therefore absent from

[1] Further description of the house is in Appendix I.

[2] 'At the end of 1645 and beginning of 1646, there had been fresh elections to fill up seats in the House of Commons, left vacant by Royalists expelled for taking the King's part; but though many Independent officers were chosen, there was still a decidedly Presbyterian majority.' *A Student's History of England*, by S. R. Gardiner, p. 551.

[3] From a letter to Robert Abraham, 1842, from Spencer Hall, Librarian, Athenaeum, Liverpool, **(LSF MS Box 1/13(3): copy).**

the House during those years (1647 to 1649) of increasing tension between the Parliament and the Army, leading at the end of 1648 to Pride's Purge, and the trial and execution of Charles. The fact was that Justice Thomas Fell disapproved of Oliver Cromwell's increasing assumption of authority. It was obvious now also that the Parliament was predominantly Presbyterian in sympathy, while the Army was Independent, and in favour of a measure of religious toleration, which was never for one moment envisaged by either the Royalist Episcopalians or the Presbyterians. Thomas Fell's sympathy was with the Independents and no doubt it was his authority, as Lord of the Manor of Ulverston, which instituted William Lampitt as Rector of Ulverston in place of an Episcopalian.

Although Justice Fell disapproved of Cromwell's increasing power, the period of his greatest public work coincided with the rule of the Protector. Charles I's execution in January 1649 was followed for ten years by a political experiment which, founded on violence, was forced by circumstances to maintain itself by violence, in spite of the noble yearning of Cromwell and some of his Puritan followers for freedom in state and religion. Even liberty of religion was to be granted to all forms of faith, 'save to Popery and Prelacy'—a 'liberty' which meant the possible persecution of large numbers of English people.

In 1649 Thomas Fell was appointed Vice-Chancellor of the Duchy of Lancaster and Attorney for the County Palatine. He also held the office of Chancellor of the Duchy Court at Westminster and was Attorney-General of the North Wales Counties. Two years later, he became Judge of Assize for the Chester and North Wales Circuit and held many other important offices.

Of his character, his widow Margaret Fell, wrote, 'He was much esteemed in his country, and valued and honoured in his day by all sorts of people, for his justice, wisdom, moderation and mercy; being a terror to evil-doers, and an encourager of such as did well, and his many and great services made his death much lamented.'[1] In Whitelock's *Memorials* he is described as 'a good lawyer and a good man', and as having served the Parliament as a soldier.[2]

[1] M.F. *Works:* p. 2.
[2] *The Welsh Judges*, W. R. Williams (1899), p. 58.

In 1632, a year after he had been called to the Bar, Thomas Fell, then thirty-four, married Margaret Askew, a girl of between seventeen and eighteen, living at Marsh Grange, on the Duddon estuary. Her home is now sadly reduced in dignity and beauty, but still has part of the fine early seventeenth-century front, the great grey stone gate posts, surmounted by the round stone 'gentility balls'. The roomy barns, large walled orchard, and fertile marshy fields are backed by the fells on which the Herdwick sheep find pasture.

Of Margaret Fell's ancestry little of certainty is known, beyond the facts in her own *Relation*. She wrote, 'I was born in the year 1614, at Marsh Grange, in the parish of Dalton, in Furness in Lancashire, of good and honest parents, and of honourable repute in their country. My Father's name was John Askew, he was of an ancient family, of those esteemed and called gentlemen, who left a considerable estate, which had been in his name and family for several generations. He was a pious charitable man, much valued in his country, for his moderation, and patience, and was bred after the best way and manner of persons of his rank in his day.'[1]

Nothing is known of her mother. In the Dalton Register is the note of the marriage in February 1613, of John Askew and Margaret Pyper—these may be her parents. On the other hand, Askew was, and is, not an uncommon name in Furness. She had one sister, and no brothers, and her father left his daughters a good portion of £3,000 each—a large sum, as money was then worth about ten times the present value. Marsh Grange and its estate was part of her marriage portion, and later in the seventeenth century was the home of her son George and his family, and after 1676 that of her daughter Mary and her husband, Dr. Thomas Lower, and their children, until they sold it in 1715.

During the nineteenth century, it was stated by Maria Webb in her *Fells of Swarthmoor Hall* that Margaret Fell was the great-granddaughter of Anne Askew, who for her insistence on reading the Bible in Lincoln Cathedral and elsewhere was by Henry VIII's orders tortured and finally in 1546 burnt at the stake in Smithfield.[2]

[1] M.F. *Works:* p. 1.
[2] Foxe's *Book of Martyrs*.

In many ways these two great women were alike, notably in their undaunted courage, but in spite of much research on the subject, the direct descent is still non-proven. There is however a strong tradition of the descent in one branch of Margaret Fell's descendants, and the reader may be referred to Appendix 3 for more information on this matter. Although the direct descent from Anne Askew is still but a tradition, the fact that Margaret Fell's son and his widow used the Askew coat of arms together with the Fell coat on their seal, shows that the Askews of Marsh Grange were of the same family as the Askews, who held estates in Lincolnshire, Yorkshire (Thirsk and Bedale), Nottingham, Cumberland (Seaton and Lacra), Northumberland, and elsewhere—a prolific family indeed, several of whose members held high office in Church and State.

The young Margaret Askew was as well educated as girls of gentle birth were in the seventeenth century, her handwriting was clear to read and beautifully formed, her style while sometimes wordy and involved, as was much of the writing of her time, is however frequently concise and fully expressive of her lofty ideals. The ability she showed in later life must have been obvious when as a girl of seventeen she married the barrister sixteen years older than herself, and became the mistress of a large estate and household.

Thomas and Margaret Fell had nine children, only one of whom they lost in infancy—a remarkable enough record in the days when families frequently reared only one out of four of their children. It was a happy marriage; 'he was a tender loving husband to me', she wrote, 'and a tender father to his children and one that sought after God in the best way that was known to him.'[1] She too 'was one that sought after the best things, being desirous to serve God, so as I might be accepted of him; and was inquiring after the way of the Lord, and went often to hear the best ministers that came into our parts, whom we frequently entertained at our house.' Some of these were 'serious and godly men', called 'Lecturing-ministers', and 'we had often prayers and religious exercises in our family'. These lecturing-ministers were the Puritan teachers, many of whom, not satisfied with even a purified Protestanism, were still seeking for a better

[1] M.F. *Works:* p. 2.

interpretation of the Scriptures. 'This I hoped I did well in', Margaret adds in her *Relation*, 'but often feared I was short of the right way: And after this manner I was inquiring and seeking about twenty years'—until there came to her home the man who changed her seeking into finding.

Chapter Two

GEORGE FOX'S FIRST COMING

'And Margaret Fell had a vision of a man in a white hat that should come and confound the priests, before my coming into those parts.'
George Fox's Journal—Cambridge Edition, I, p. 52.

ON a day late in June 1652, there was an air of expectancy at Swarthmoor Hall. The mistress, Margaret Fell, and her children had heard a few days before that a travelling preacher, George Fox, was at Kendal and Underbarrow, twenty miles to the north-east of Ulverston, their own near-by market town. This was their first news of the people called Quakers.[1]

For four years George Fox had been preaching in the Midlands and in Yorkshire. Born at Fenny Drayton (or Drayton-in-the-Clay, as it was then called), Leicestershire, in 1624, his father a weaver, and his mother Mary Lago, of a family of local gentlefolk, and 'of the stock of the martyrs', he had striven through years of doubt and dissatisfaction with the replies of the official religious guides of his day, and had come to the discovery of a personal experience of 'Christ within' which was for the rest of his life to fill him with a fire which no amount of persecution could quench.

He had a striking appearance and commanding personality. His eyes were penetrating—'Don't pierce me so with thy eyes, keep thy eyes off me',[2] pleaded a Baptist deacon at Carlisle. He had a fine resonant voice: at Carlisle, in the filthy dungeon, the jailer brought in a fiddler—'and when he played I was moved in the everlasting power of the Lord God to sing: and my voice drowned them and struck them and confounded them, that made them give over fiddling and go their ways.'[3] He dressed

[1] Spence MSS. III, 135.
[2] Camb. Jnl. I, 115.
[3] Camb. Jnl. I, 126.

8

in leather doublet and breeches, and although this suit was often criticized and derided, surely it was the best material for travel in all weathers. His linen, at any rate, was that of a conventional person, for once when he was searched for letters by a Justice, his accuser said 'he is not a vagrant by his linen'.[1] The courtly William Penn, who later became his friend and follower, wrote after his death, that he was in his behaviour 'civil beyond all forms of breeding'. This young man of twenty-eight had already met with much opposition from the clergy of the day, and had for long months been imprisoned both in Nottingham and Derby, but, especially in Yorkshire, he had turned many, both men and women, to the Light which he preached. So he came, on foot, to the borders of Yorkshire and Lancashire, to one of those high outcrops of limestone so characteristic of this part of the country, called Pendle Hill. This he climbed, and 'went on the top of it with much ado, it was so steep'. Here he was moved 'to sound the day of the Lord'. Here he saw westward to the Lancashire sea, and also had a vision 'in what places the Lord had a great people'[2]—a vision of the ingathering of the hundreds and thousands of men and women of Lancashire, Westmorland, West Yorkshire and Cumberland, who were seeking for a more spiritual Christianity than they had yet found.[3]

He went north through the Dales of Yorkshire, and came to Sedbergh on Whit-Saturday, 5th June 1652. Here on Whit-Sunday he met Justice Benson, who with his wife became his true friends, and the large meeting of 'seekers' at his house were 'generally convinced'. 'This was the place that I had seen a people coming forth in white raiment; and a mighty meeting there was and is to this day, near Sedbergh, which I gathered in the name of Jesus.' This is the Brigflatts meeting, **a mile and a quarter** from the old market town of Sedbergh.

On the following Wednesday in Whit week, the great hiring

[1] Camb. Jnl. I, 31.

[2] A.N.B. *Pers.*, p. 25.

[3] In George Fox's own short description of this spiritual experience on Pendle Hill, following some days of fasting, he used the expression 'atop of it', or 'atop of the hill', five times, and in many letters and epistles he used that same phrase in exhorting his friends, and even his wife, in their trials and anxieties, to keep atop of things.

fair was being held, where young men and maidens came in great numbers to be hired for farm and house work.

George Fox preached to large crowds with power and conviction, and on the following Sunday he preached again to more than a thousand people gathered on the craggy hillside above Sedbergh, called Firbank Fell, where was a chapel of the Seekers. Here he won some more followers, Francis Howgill, John Audland, John Blakeling and others.

Thence he came, still on foot, into Westmorland, to Preston Patrick, a few miles to the south of Kendal, the gateway to the Lake District. Here again was a chapel of the Seekers, and here again Fox preached 'the word of life and the everlasting Truth', 'that their bodies were the temples of God and that Christ was their teacher'.

Next day he came to Kendal, where he had a meeting in the town hall, and so, on over the fell westward, to the village of Underbarrow, where he met and won Edward Burrough, a youth of nineteen, who became one of his greatest followers, to die later of plague in Newgate gaol; and again he went, ever in a south-westerly direction, to the southern end of Windermere, where at Staveley the men were incited by the minister, Gabriel Camelford, to mob George Fox and throw him over a wall.[1] Then he went on over the low fells of Furness to Ulverston. Here from a friend, he heard of Swarthmoor Hall, the hospitable home of Judge and Margaret Fell. On his arrival there, towards the end of June 1652, he found the Judge was absent on the Welsh circuit, and the mistress away for that day, but her son and six daughters, varying in age from nineteen years to two, were there, also the rector of Ulverston, 'Priest' Lampitt. The rector was an Independent,[2] and receives short shrift in *George Fox's Journal*, as a 'Ranter', 'for he would talk of high notions and perfection and thereby deceived the people'.

The discussion that day caused the rector to leave the house in anger and distress, for was not there serious danger of his losing the support of one of his most influential parishioners, the wife of the Lord of the Manor of Ulverston?

On her return in the evening, Margaret Fell met him who

[1] Jnl. F.H.S., Vol. 31, 11.
[2] Nightingale, *Quaker Movement in Lancashire*, p. 21.

'opened us a book that we had never read in, nor indeed had never heard that it was our duty to read in it (to wit) the Light of Christ in our consciences, our minds never being turned towards it before'.[1] In George Fox's own description of that first meeting, he wrote, 'her children told her that Priest Lampitt and I disagreed; and it struck something at her because she was in a profession with him, though he hid his dirty actions from them: so at night we had a great deal of reasoning and I declared the truth to her and her family.'[2]

That night George Fox spent at the Hall, the first of many visits. Next day the anxious reverend William Lampitt came again to the Hall, and had much talk with Fox, in the presence of Margaret Fell. A day or two later, on Thursday, July the first, it being a 'lecture day' at the parish church, Margaret Fell invited her visitor to go with her and her children. He however explained he did not feel free to do so, and spent some hours walking about in the near-by fields. During the singing before the sermon he came in. The singing ended, he stood up on a seat, and asked liberty to speak—a proceeding entirely legal in the Commonwealth period. The rector gave him permission. His first words were: 'He is not a Jew that is one outward: neither is that circumcision which is outward: but he is a Jew that is one inward; and that is circumcision which is of the heart'. And so he spoke of his own great spiritual experience, of the inwardness of true religion, of the indwelling Light of Christ, of the Light that would gather every man to God. 'I stood up in my pew', wrote Margaret Fell, 'and wondered at his doctrine, for I had never heard such before.' Then he went on to rebuke those who understood the Scriptures only of themselves, without the illumination of the Spirit of Christ. 'This opened me so, that it cut me to the heart; and then I saw clearly that we were all wrong. So I sat down in my pew again, and cried bitterly; and I cried in my spirit to the Lord, "We are all thieves; we are all thieves; we have taken the Scriptures in words, and know nothing of them in ourselves".'[3] She was so stirred that she was hardly conscious of his further speech. When he went on to denounce false

[1] Spence MSS. III, 135.
[2] Camb. Jnl. I, 48.
[3] Leeds Jnl. I, lxii.

teachers, priests, and all who taught in words un-illumined by the Light of Christ, the minister grew angry and set the church-warden to hale George Fox out. 'But', wrote Margaret many years later, 'I stood up in my pew and looked at the church-warden, and he stood behind G.F.; and he let him alone, and G.F. spoke on a great while till at last they were so angry that one John Sawrey,[1] who was a justice, caused G.F. to be hailed out.' After that, he continued to speak to the people in the churchyard, and then walked back through the little market town, and along the footpath through the fields, to Swarthmoor Hall.

There that evening he spoke to the household. The homes of the gentry in the seventeenth century, especially if the master was a professional man, frequently away from home, had a large number of servants, a clerk, a tutor, agent, men and maid ser-vants for both house and estate.[2] Many of Margaret Fell's house-hold were convinced by George Fox. There was William Caton, then about fifteen years old, who had for the last year lived with the Fells as the friend and companion of the son George; there was Thomas Salthouse, one of the four brothers whose home was at Dragley Beck, less than a mile from the Hall, and who was the Judge's agent; there was Leonard Fell who like Caton was in a higher social position than the other servants, and whose father was a small landowner at Baycliffe, a nearby fishing village. There was Mary Askew whose service to the family was remembered by Judge Fell in his will—'twenty pounds, for her faithful and careful service performed unto my wife and chil-dren in all their extremities', and there was Ann Clayton who later joined other Friends in Barbados, and eventually became the wife successively of two Quaker Governors of Rhode Island.

These and several other servants, unnamed, were convinced that day.

But the mistress was in a dilemma—'I was struck into such a sadness, I knew not what to do, my husband being from home.

[1] Of Plumpton Hall, two miles **east** of Ulverston; a member of Barebones Parliament, 1653, representing Lancaster.

[2] Many servants were real friends of the family and in fact the word 'family' is used to include servants, at that time.

I saw it was the truth, and I could not deny it; and I did as the Apostle saith, "I received the truth in the love of it"; and it was opened to me so clear, that I had never a tittle in my heart against it; but I desired the Lord that I might be kept in it; and then I desired no greater portion.'[1]

Thus began a half-century (1652–1702) of work for the Quaker fellowship, a work in which there was a remarkable co-operation between the founder (till his death in 1691) and a woman who was frequently addressed as 'our nursing mother'. By her own personality, her social position, her education, courage, genius for friendship, and the gift not only of seeing essentials but of holding on to them even against the pressure of her friends, she gave stability to the movement especially in the early days before any organization had been created by George Fox himself.

But to return to that momentous first week in July 1652. Her visitor began now a series of journeys on horseback to villages and towns in the district.

First he went on the Sunday to Aldingham, a hamlet on the very edge of Morecambe Bay, a few miles from Swarthmoor, where he preached to the people. Then at the end of the service that afternoon, on to the extreme south of the peninsula, Rampside, where Thomas Lawson was minister. He was a learned man, a Hebrew scholar and a botanist, the son, it is thought, of Sir Thomas Lawson, Bart. He had told his congregation in the morning that George Fox was expected that afternoon and had desired them 'to be generally there to hear him',[2] and he went a mile to meet him on his way.[3]

Back to Swarthmoor he came and then next Sunday he passed to Dalton, the chief town of Furness, and on a few miles to the south-westerly end of the peninsula, and across to Walney Island, a long stretch of wild shingle bank facing the Irish Sea.

[1] Leeds Jnl. I, lxii.

[2] Account in Jnl. F.H.S., Vol. 31, p. 7, from Lancaster Minute Book.

[3] This kindly priest became a Friend, sacrificing a good income, and was later one of the band of 'First Publishers of Truth'. In later years, when suffering imprisonment he wrote to Margaret Fell asking for money to buy a Hebrew Lexicon, and in the Swarthmoor Hall account book is the record of his receiving money in return for the education of the Swarthmoor daughters in the knowledge of the herbs, both medical and culinary.

George Fox then returned to Swarthmoor where he found Margaret and her daughter Sarah, a child of ten, were now fully convinced, together with several of the household.

More villages were visited—Baycliffe, the home of Leonard Fell, and Gleaston: and on returning to Swarthmoor it was found that still more were convinced. What a ferment was working there during Fox's absences! Then back he went to Kendal, where he found that 'Priest' Lampitt had poisoned the minds of his fellow-ministers against him. But George Fox sat up all night in talk with the people, and they came to believe in him and see that Lampitt had deceived them. Then he revisited his friends at and near Sedbergh, and strengthened them.

While Fox was at Kendal and Sedbergh, his teaching in the Fell family was being greatly reinforced by his friends James Nayler and Richard Farnsworth who had followed him and 'enquired him out, till they came to Swarthmoor, and there stayed with me', Margaret says, 'at our house, and did me much good, for I was under great heaviness and judgment'.[1]

While Fox was at Sedbergh, he had a message from Margaret Fell, begging him to return at once.

It was now three weeks since that first visit to Swarthmoor at the end of June. News came to Ulverston that Judge Fell was returning home, from London.[2] He crossed the wide and treacherous sands of the bay, from Lancaster to the Cartmel peninsula and then across the last four miles of sand and watery channels and the deeper swift-flowing channel of the Leven River to Ulverston. As he was nearing the shore he and his men noticed a small body of men approaching him. Here were the rector, and the gentlemen of the neighbourhood, their faces clouded with anger. They hastened to explain to the Judge that during his absence a great disaster had happened at his home, that his wife and children and household had been bewitched by a travelling preacher and 'that he might either set them away, or all the country would be undone'.[3] A serious enough charge, in the days when witches were still believed in, and laws against bewitchment had been passed only in the reign of James I dealing

[1] Leeds Jnl. Testimony to G. Fox, by M. Fox.
[2] M.F. *Works*, p. 2.
[3] Leeds Jnl. Testimony to G. Fox, by M. Fox.

terrible punishment to the guilty. The Judge rode home in sadness, alongside the beck flowing through his fields. At the hall
he was met by his wife; 'and any may think what a condition
I was like to be in, that either I must displease my husband, or
offend God.'[1]

Nayler and Farnsworth were fortunately still at the hall, and
they, assuring the Judge that they came in love and goodwill to
his house, spoke to him very moderately and wisely. They
offered to leave, but the mistress begged them to stay; she needed
their support. Let us return to Margaret's own words. 'And
then was he pretty moderate and quiet; and his dinner being
ready, he went to it; and I went in, and sat me down by him.
And whilst I was sitting, the power of the Lord seized upon me;
and he was struck with amazement, and knew not what to
think; but was quiet and still. And the children were all quiet
and still, and grown sober, and could not play on their music
that they were learning: and all these things made him quiet
and still.

'At night George Fox came: and after supper my husband was
sitting in the parlour, and I asked him if George Fox might
come in; and he said "Yes". So George came in without any
compliment, and walked into the room, and began to speak
presently; and the family, and James Nayler and Richard Farnsworth came all in: and he spoke very excellently as ever I heard
him; . . . that if all in England had been there, I thought they
could not have denied the truth of those things. And so my husband came to see clearly the truth of what he spoke, and was
very quiet that night, said no more, and went to bed.'

The next morning Mr. Lampitt came up, and for long the
Judge and he paced up and down in the garden in earnest talk,
'but', wrote Margaret, 'my husband had seen so much the night
before, that the priest got little entrance upon him'.

Later in the day, the few Friends at the hall were discussing
how they and others in the district could meet to worship as
they wished, and Judge Fell, overhearing them, at once and with
a remarkable tolerance, said, 'You may meet here, if you will'.
Two days later, on Sunday, in the large hall of Swarthmoor, a
Meeting of Friends began, which then met there every Sunday

[1] Leeds Jnl. Testimony to G.F. by M.F.

until 1690, when George Fox gave the Society a small meeting
House nearby, for their use for ever. But the kindly Judge went
that first Sunday to the parish church, with his clerk and his
groom only, 'and the priest and people were all fearfully
troubled; but praised be the Lord, they never got their wills
upon us to this day', Margaret wrote nearly fifty years later.
Judge Fell continued to attend Mr. Lampitt's church for a year
or two, but some time before his death in 1658, he gave up going
to church and used to sit in the parlour and have the two doors
left open between his room and the large hall where the Meeting for worship was being held. 'He came to see', wrote Fox, 'by
the openings of the Spirit of God in his heart, over all the priests
and teachers of the world and did not go to hear them for some
years before he died; for he knew it was the Truth that I declared, and that Christ was the teacher of his people, and their
Saviour.'[1]

[1] Leeds Jnl. I, 188.

Chapter Three

THE FAMILY AND HOUSEHOLD AT SWARTHMOOR

By the end of July 1652 George Fox had won over to agreement with his beliefs a number of 'seekers' and others spiritually near to him, men and women of varied ages and education. Of great importance for the future of Quakerism was the fact that he had met and become friendly with a family and household, of whom the father was a man of outstanding position in North-West England, and of remarkable tolerance in an age of intolerance, and the mother was a cultured woman whose whole mind and soul became dedicated to the belief in and following of the 'Light of Christ'. Margaret Fell and her family threw themselves into the Quaker movement with utter selflessness. 'Her name is almost as intimately bound up with it as is that of Fox himself,' writes Professor Rufus M. Jones in his **study,** *George Fox, Seeker and Friend.*

Of the life of the family, William Caton has left a loving description in his Journal. He relates how at the age of fourteen, a year before George Fox's first visit, his father took him to Judge Fell's, there to study with a relative (a clergyman) who was tutor to the Judge's son George. He behaved himself so well as to find favour from the greatest to the least of them, and 'was in due time promoted to be a companion night and day to the judge's son, and did eat as he did eat, and lodged as he lodged, and went after the same pleasure which he went unto, as to fishing, hunting, shooting, etc.' He expresses gratitude to 'Providence [which] had cast me into such a noble family, where there were such sweet children, with whose company I was more than a little affected; and in much pleasure, ease and fulness, I lived with them as my heart could well desire.' Young Caton was a serious-minded and sensitive boy—'there remained an integrity in my heart towards God, and often did I call upon his

17

name: to that end, I would linger in the chamber, until the
judge's son, with whom I lodged, was gone down, that afterwards I might go to prayer alone.'[1]

Soon, the two boys were sent to Hawkshead Grammar School,
a few miles away, near Windermere. This was one of the very
few schools in Furness, having been founded in 1585 by Edwin
Sandys, Archbishop of York, a native of Hawkshead, to teach
Latin, Greek, and some science. In a later century, William
Wordsworth was a pupil there. The young Caton pays no high
compliment to the school, and was glad he and young George
left soon, when William was but fifteen.[2] It was then that he
met George Fox on his first visit to Swarthmoor Hall. The boy
at first wondered at the young man's non-conformity to the
fashions, customs, and salutations of the day, for Fox from the
beginning of his work had made a stand against the compli-
ments paid to social superiors, basing his action on the belief in
the equal value and dignity of every human being, irrespective
of race and class and sex, all in his view being equally capable
of possessing the Light of Christ within. But Caton adds 'something in me did love him, and own his testimony'. Slowly but
surely, the boy came to acknowledge the truth of the inner
religion he saw in others around him, and then his school studies
became a burden to him—'I was so much the more incapable of
making themes, Latin verses, etc., neither could I well give unto
the master the trivial compliment of the hat, for I was then convinced in my conscience of the vanity of it.'

Then it was that his 'special friend, Margaret Fell, the Judge's
wife', noticed his change, and allowed him to leave school and
not proceed to college, as her son might soon be doing; she
arranged for him to stay at home to teach her children, and to
go about with her on her visits, and to become her secretary.
He also wrote in his neat handwriting and perfect spelling many
letters and dissertations on the new teaching, which exist to this
day; and some years before his early death, he spent much time
during one of his return visits to Swarthmoor—in 1659—in
copying out over a hundred and sixty of the letters written to

[1] *Life of W. Caton*, p. 3.
[2] Further information on Hawkshead Grammar School is in Appendix 6.

Margaret by the men and women carrying Quakerism throughout the country.[1]

William Caton grew more and more to see the love and unity
so characteristic of the early Friends at Swarthmoor and elsewhere. Fellowship one with another had always been one of the
essential by-products of any religious movement, and decay of
true fellowship is inevitably a sign of the decay of the spirituality
of the beliefs. The way in which the barriers of education, class,
and individual peculiarities were overcome by the spiritual
fellowship among these early Quakers brought many a comment
from the outside spectator. Caton himself wrote, 'Oh! The love
which in that day abounded among us, especially in that family!
. . . the nearness and dearness that was amongst us one towards
another! . . . Truly willing we were to sympathise and bear one
with another, to be helpful one unto another, and in true and
tender love to watch one over another. . . . And hence came that
worthy family to be so renowned in the nation, the fame of
which spread much among Friends; and the power and presence
of the Lord being so much there with us, it was as a means to
induce many, even from afar, to come thither; so that at one
time there would have been Friends out of five or six counties;
all which tended to the augmenting of my refreshment; for by
reason of my much writing, it came to pass that I especially was
much conversant with them, and thereby I had a privilege beyond others of my fellow-servants; for I was frequently with
dear George Fox, who, as a tender-hearted father . . . sought to
nurture me up in all wisdom, faithfulness, and righteousness . . .
and on the other hand was I cherished, and encouraged in the
way of life by my entirely beloved friend Margaret Fell, who
as a tender-hearted nursing mother cared for me, and was as
tender of me, as if I had been one of her own children. Oh! the
kindness, the respect, and friendship which she showed me,
ought never to be forgotten by me.'[2]

When William Caton was seventeen or eighteen years old, he

---

[1] This manuscript collection, lost for over a century, was found in 1935,
and now is in the possession of the Library at Friends' House, London. It is
one of the original sources used in the writing of this book. It is known as
Caton MSS. III.

[2] *Life of W. Caton*, pp. 7–10.

left this loved home, to 'publish the Truth' where he felt moved;
the parting was against the will of the Judge, but Margaret
reconciled herself to it in that she knew it was not for the purpose
of serving another family, but to take the message further
afield.

Anthony Pearson has also left a description of the Swarthmoor household. Pearson, whose home was Rampshaw Hall,
Co. Durham, was a justice of the peace in three counties, and
while he was on the bench at Appleby, in 1652–3, he was 'convinced' during the trial of Fox's friends, James Nayler and
Francis Howgill. Up till that time he had been a great persecutor
of Friends. Fox in his journal said that 'over his head they carried
a sword when he went to the bench'.[1] After his convincement,
but while he was still in troubled doubt, he visited Swarthmoor
Hall. George Fox was at that time staying with Colonel West,
whose home was probably near the modern seaside town of
Grange-over-Sands on Morecambe Bay. Colonel West was, like
Judge Fell, a 'friend of the Friends', and on his hearing that
Justice Pearson was at Swarthmoor, he said to Fox, 'Go, George,
for it may be of great service to the man'. Fox adds, 'And the
Lord's power reached him'. After Anthony Pearson had returned home, he wrote a letter, dated 9th May 1653, to a Quaker
friend, showing the agony of a sensitive soul struggling to win
to the Light he had seen, and facing the loss of worldly prestige
he had always held. In the letter also is expressed profound
gratitude to his new-found friends:

Dear Friend,
   I have long professed to serve and worship the true God, and as I
thought (above many sects) attained to a high pitch in religion; but
now, alas! I find my work will not abide the fire. My notions were
swelling vanities without power and life: what it was to love enemies,
to bless them that curse, to render good for evil, to use the world as
using it not, to lay down life for the brethren, I never understood; . . .
all my religion was but the hearing of the ear, the believing and talking
of a God and Christ in heaven or a place at a distance, I knew not
where. Oh! how gracious was the Lord to me in carrying me to
Judge Fell's, to see the wonders of His power and wisdom,—a family
walking in the fear of the Lord, conversing daily with him, crucified

---

[1] Camb. Jnl. I, 108.

to the world, and living only to God. I was so confounded, all my knowledge and wisdom became folly; my mouth was stopped, my conscience convinced, and the secrets of my heart were made manifest, and that Lord was discovered to be near me, whom I ignorantly worshipped. . . .

What thou told me of George Fox, I found true: when thou seest him or James Nayler, (they both know my condition better than myself) move them (if neither of them be drawn this way) to help me with their counsel by letter; they are full of pity and compassion; and though I was their enemy, they are my friends: and so is Francis Howgill, from whom I received a letter full of tenderness and wholesome advice. Oh! how welcome would the faces of any of them be to me; truly I think I would scorn the world, to have fellowship with them. . . .

Dear Friend, there is a carrier comes from Kendal within a mile of my house every fortnight, and he shall call at Peter Huggin's to bring any letter that shall be left there for me; it will much refresh me to receive any lines from thee;—but be thou faithful. . . .

I am afraid lest the orders we made at Appleby, cause some to suffer, who speak from the mouth of the Lord; I heartily wish they were suppressed or recalled. I have seen at Judge Fell's, and have been informed from that precious soul his consort, in some measure what those things mean, which before I counted the overflowings of giddy brains. Dear heart, pity and pray for me, and let all obligations of former friendship be discharged in well wishes to the soul of your old familiar friend, that he may partake with you of your heavenly possessions.

A. Pearson

Ramshaw, near West Auckland, 9th May 1653.[1]

The reference to the orders made at Appleby is of course to the occasion of the trial of James Nayler and Francis Howgill, when Pearson was one of the judges.

Something has already been said about Judge and Margaret Fell's children. In 1652, when the Friends came first to their home, there were seven children, one son aged about thirteen and six daughters, the seventh daughter, Rachel ('Dear Rachel', she is generally called in the letters) being born in 1653. One other child had been lost in infancy. The young son, George, had at first been 'somewhat convinced of the Truth',[2] and in

---

[1] A.R.B. 10–12 and Swm. MSS. I, 87 and III, 33.
[2] *Life of W. Caton*, p. 5.

fact on one of George Fox's early visits to Ulverston the boy running to see what the people were going to do with Fox had suffered the indignity of having been thrown by the riotous mob into a ditch, and of hearing them cry out, 'Knock out the teeth of his head'.[1] Perhaps this did something to cure the boy of this religion which sometimes proved so unpopular, for Caton tells us that 'for a season [George] was tender and hopeful but afterwards meeting with many temptations, his heart was drawn aside from the truth, and his mind ran after the delights and pleasures of this present world'.[2] However, in December 1652, we find a Friend (Thomas Killam) sending his 'tender love to thy son George Fell, desiring and beseeching the Lord that they [he and his sister] may be faithful servants in His vineyard'.[3] George Fox, in the postscript to a letter to Friends, delivered at Swarthmoor, and dated 1652, wrote, 'George, be watchful and low that the tender plant may grow in thee'.[4]

About this time George Fell was admitted a student to Gray's Inn, London, the Inn of which his father was Bencher, and in 1655 he was apparently readmitted as 'George Fell of Gray's Inn'. He must therefore have gone to live in London, in term time, from early in 1653 until some years after his marriage, which occurred in December 1660, when he was about twenty-two years old. During this time, although absent from home by a distance of about 270 miles, he was still in the thoughts of several Friends, but he caused his mother much anxiety, as she learned of his sympathy with the worldly conventions around him, and of his getting into debt.[5] In 1657, the anxious mother at Swarthmoor wrote to her son in London, George then being eighteen years old.

George,

My dear love, take heed of wildness, lightness and vanity, and take heed of pride getting hold of thee. My dear heart, keep in the fear of the Lord thy Creator, who hath created thee and brought thee forth, and preserved and kept thee all thy lifetime until now. Now beware

[1] Camb. Jnl. I, 58.
[2] *Life of W. Caton*, p. 8.
[3] Swm. MSS. IV, 85.
[4] Swm. MSS. VII, 37.
[5] Jnl. F.H.S. Vols. 29, 30, 31, articles on Geo. Fell and S. Hall.

that thou require Him not evil for good in sinning against Him and transgressing against that in thy conscience which tells thee thou shouldest not do evil nor wickedly and so sin against God.

My dear babe, if thou mind the Lord and fear Him thou will be with me as present, and there thou will be kept safe from all dangers. If thou keep in the fear of the Lord thou wilt be kept from all temptations and be delivered from all evil, but if thou depart from the fear of the Lord, then thou lies open to the temptations and will be drawn away with the enemies of thy soul.

My dear love, all the ways of the wicked will come to naught and perish though never so delightful for the present, yet woe and misery will be the end of all sin and wickedness; therefore, my dear love, turn from evil and sin and take heed of rashness and forwardness and headiness. Keep these down and strive for patience, and thou will see the blessing of God will be upon thee. My dear one, I cannot forget thee; my cries to my Heavenly Father is for thee that thou may be kept and that the measure of Him in thee may be preserved.

So my dear love, the Lord God of power be with thee and keep thee in His fear. Read this often and as thou readest thou will be with me.

Thy sisters who are at home is all [well] and remembers their dear love to thee and let us hear from thee as often as thou can. We received thine.

M.F.[1]

Sometimes his mother asked a Friend to visit him—Thomas Rawlinson of Graythwaite Hall was one of these, a man who had been disowned, for turning Quaker, by his father, a well-to-do gentleman of Furness. He reported from London in March 1657, 'I went this day to George Fell, being 26 of the 1st month. I was with him 3 or 4 hours in his chambers. We spake of many things. The spark is not quite out.'[2]

The further story of George Fell will be told in later chapters.

The eldest daughter of Judge and Margaret Fell was Margaret, who was probably nineteen years old in 1652. She and all her sisters saw 'Truth' as George Fox preached it, and from then to the end of their lives, they, and the husbands they later married, were loyal supporters of George Fox and of their Mother, and wise leaders of the first generation of Friends.

[1] Spence MSS. III, 60.
[2] Swm. MSS. III, 11.

Margaret was a beautiful girl. Quite early on she had an experience of the spiritual power of Fox which must have made a deep impression. In 1653 when he was returning to Swarthmoor from Cumberland, he was accompanied by young Margaret and William Caton—perhaps they had gone to meet him. They came to Hawkshead, and rested a while at a Friend's house. There they found an eleven year old boy lying crippled in a cot. Fox told the maid-servant to wash the little boy—twice, for she failed to cleanse him properly at first. Then, 'I was moved of the Lord God', he records, 'to lay my hands upon him and speak to him: and so bid the lass take him again and put on his clothes: and after we passed away.' Three years later, the grateful mother, seeing him at Hawkshead again, told him of their joy at finding their only son, who they believed could not live long, playing in the streets just after Fox's earlier visit. 'He was grown to be a straight full youth then; and so the Lord have the praise.' Several times Fox showed a remarkable power of spiritual healing, and sometimes a kind of natural osteopathic knowledge—a gift which was so little understood in the late seventeenth century that when his Journal was edited in 1694 these stories were omitted. What an experience for those two young people, Margaret aged twenty, and William Caton only sixteen!

These Fell sisters did not shirk travelling in spite of the discomforts and perils of the road. In 1654, a Friend (Thomas Aldam) in York prison wrote, 'There was two of Judge Fell's daughters came to us in prison and did stay with us a pretty while. They was very solid and loving; we was moved to speak some words to them to which there was no gainsaying.'[1]

In that same year (8.6.1654) John Audland wrote to George Fox from Bristol or thereabouts, 'Judge Fell's daughters is gone North this day'.[2]

Early next year, two of the sisters travelled as far as Reading, where George Fox records in his Journal that they attended a Meeting in a Friend's orchard.[3] In August of that year young Margaret was visiting a Friend prisoner in Chester gaol, Thomas Holme, a weaver of Kendal. That he much appreciated the visit

[1] Jnl. F.H.S. Vol. 28.
[2] Jnl. F.H.S. XVI, 135, from a book of letters at Friends' House Library.
[3] Camb. Jnl. I, 185.

is shown in this letter to Margaret Fell, the elder (in a style almost of Biblical rhapsody, not uncommon in that century):

In the Life of God do I dearly salute thee, and thy daughter Margaret, who in me hath stuck fast since her face I did see, truly in the life and power of the living God of life, she is dear and near to me, by her my soul was refreshed when she came this away, truly she is glorious comely and beautiful, in that which is eternal and never fades away. Her countenance preached unto me, and she as a sweet-smelling savour was unto me; verily the glory of all nations is with you, and you do I honour with my life and soul and not with feigned words, for in the fear of the Lord do I write unto you, for I know the presence of the glorious God is with you and before you can no deceit stand, yea glorious daughters of Sion whose faces shine like the sun at noon day.

A nursing Mother thou art who feeds the hungry with good things, but the fat with judgment, who kills and stays the living and raises the dead. Judgment is committed unto thy hands, and judgment thou gives to whom judgment belongs, and mercy to whom mercy belongs, power in heaven and in earth is given unto thee. . . .[1]

In 1656, when Margaret was twenty-two or twenty-three years old, there was evidently some talk in the family of her marrying 'with the World', namely, a non-Friend. There are still preserved, among the Spence MSS, two curious letters,[2] one from the Mother, the other from the daughter. They are both addressed to Colonel West, that kind 'friend of the Friends', who was George Fox's host when Justice Anthony Pearson first visited Swarthmoor. The mother's is a gently worded letter beginning 'Dear Heart', pleading with her friend to follow God's law, and so win peace, even through suffering, and ending, 'And so the Lord God of power and life enlighten thy understanding that thou may clearly see the ground and rock on which we stand, . . . and this is from a friend of thy soul who desires thy eternal good and peace with God which is better than all the treasures of Egypt'. The younger woman however writes with some passion, and half is addressed to her father, and half to Colonel West. To both, she repudiates any suggestion of marriage with one who is not 'come into the Unity of the Spirit'—'if we should sell the Truth of God . . .

[1] Swm. MSS. I, 197.
[2] Spence MSS. III, 42 and 43.

for a fading inheritance . . . we should lose that peace which the whole world cannot purchase for us.'

The cause of such letters, one of which is endorsed by George Fox, 'The trial of M.F. and her children concerning her children's marrying with the World', can only be surmised. Did Colonel West want to marry the lovely daughter of his friend? and was her father backing his suit? At any rate, mother and daughter had their way, and Margaret remained unmarried for another five years, and then chose a Quaker for her husband, as did all her sisters.

The second daughter was Bridget. The dates of the births of all the children except the youngest are unknown owing to losses in the Ulverston Parish Registers, but Bridget was probably born in 1635, which made her seventeen at George Fox's first visit. Little is known of her until she takes charge of the household in 1660, during the absence of her mother and elder sister, but she was most probably the 'other sister' who accompanied young Margaret on her journeys to York and Reading already mentioned.

Perhaps something can be seen, in the following note which brought gifts, of the kindness shown by one at least of the many new-found friends. In 1652 Thomas Killam of Yorkshire wrote to the mistress of Swarthmoor, 'Here are some knives of a Friend's making sent for you, one for George Fell with an Inkhorn, one for each of thy daughters Margaret and Bridget, and one for thyself, with an inkhorn for my dear brother James Nayler'.[1]

The third sister was Isabel, born about 1637. Probably at fifteen she gave promise of the love she later aroused in others—she married twice and had at least one other love affair, her brother named one of his children after her, and in later years she is described as having had a curious voice, and a pleasing and 'free'[2] way of expressing herself.

The only son George probably came next, three sisters older, and four younger.

Of the younger set of children, Sarah came first, a child who even at ten showed such a religious sensitiveness that Fox men-

[1] Swm. MSS. IV, 87.
[2] Croese, quoted in Webb, *Fells*, 300.

tions her especially, bracketed with her mother, as having been convinced in 1652. She developed into the ablest of the seven daughters, a woman who combined great spiritual gifts with the ability to manage the Quaker Women's business meetings, and to govern a large estate and household.

The three youngest were Mary, Susannah and Rachel. Mary was delicate, and possibly passionate in childhood, for early on George Fox sends a message to her in a letter to her mother— 'Mary, take heed of thy will, else it will cover thee.'

The little sensitive girl, living in a home where she knew her loved ones were suffering persecution, and the contempt of their former friends, felt one day in 1655 that she had had a message sent to her for 'Priest Lampitt', the rector of Ulverston. This message is recorded in Fox's Journal, and also on a little scrap of paper, brown with age, preserved at the Library of Friends' House in London. It reads:

Lampitt,
  The plaiges of god shall fall upon thee and the seven viols shall bee powered upon thee and the milstone shall fall upon thee and crush thee as dust under the Lords feete how can thou escape the damnation of hell.

> This did the lord give mee as
> I lay in bed.
>
> Mary Fell.

When she was eight years old in 1655.[1]

The youngest, when Fox first came, was Susannah. She grew later into the daughter who was the helpmeet of her sisters—she is found staying with them when they were having babies, though she never had children of her own. She was the last of the sisters to marry. Few of her letters survive, and they show a large straggling handwriting, as if to write was more of an effort than to do the kindly practical things of everyday life.

Rachel, born in 1653, grew up to be her mother's constant companion. In later years, her sister Sarah handed over the management of the household and estate into her capable hands, and she followed Sarah in the clerkship of the women's Meetings. Even when a girl of sixteen, and possibly younger, she was travelling with her mother, visiting Meetings and Friends in

[1] Swm. MSS. VII, 24 and Camb. Jnl. I, 231.

prison. But her writing is poor, and her spelling erratic—perhaps she suffered from the lack of a tutor, in those years following the coming of Quakerism to her home, when this took precedence over everything else. No doubt the two youngest daughters suffered from the lack of tuition in writing when Will Caton left Swarthmoor on his travels. He was an excellent writer.

Of members of the household who later became conspicuous for their service for Quakerism, several have already been mentioned. There were others however who also became Friends, but not travelling 'Publishers of Truth'. Loving messages were often sent by the travellers to these faithful servants; there was little Mabby, there were John Taylor, Bet Drinkall, Peg and her sister, 'Old Jane'; and there was James Parke, who many years later rode all the way to Cornwall to visit his old master's daughter Mary recently married to Thomas Lower. There, at St. Austell, 'an old informer being sitting in an ale house drinking with others his pot companions, he looked out at the window as James Parke rid along; and supposing him to be a Quaker and riding upon a good horse, he said unto his companions I will warrant that is a preaching Quaker, and I will have the horse he rides upon the next first day.' The informer however was foiled by Thomas Lower sending the horse out of his reach. James Parke was cruelly treated by the Cornish magistrate, but the chairman of the Assizes, being appealed to by Thomas and Mary Lower, repudiated the 'inhuman and unchristian act to use a stranger so hardly that was come into the country as much to visit his old master's daughter as to preach', so James Parke 'was freed from that snare and had his liberty also to travel on as he found freedom'.[1]

[1] *Record of the Sufferings of Quakers in Cornwall*, p. 89. (Friends' Historical Society. London, 1928.)

Chapter Four

MARGARET FELL'S WORK FOR QUAKERISM, 1652–60

'*The Truth is one and the same always, and though ages and generations pass away, and one generation goes and another comes, yet the word and power and spirit of the Living God endures for ever, and is the same and never changes.*'

Margaret Fell, *Works*, p. 47.

'*The Light Within is that principle within us which shows us what is evil. And secondly the Light Within is that principle within us which brings us into unity, unity with God and unity with men.*'

From Rufus Jones's Foreword to *George Fox and the Light Within*, by Rachel Hadley King.

WITH the coming of George Fox to Swarthmoor in June 1652, that home became the centre of the Quaker movement for many years.

When Judge Fell had invited the Friends to keep their Meeting at his house, George Fox stayed on a little time to 'settle it'— to train it to be able to sit under the leadership of Christ instead of an outward human leader—and then he left, to travel for the next year and a half in Lancashire, Westmorland, Cumberland and West Yorkshire, with frequent returns to his base, Swarthmoor Hall.

During one of these visits he attended Ulverston Parish Church, where an uproar was caused when Justice John Sawrey of Plumpton Hall forbade Fox to speak, though he had a moment before told him he might, if he spoke according to the Scriptures. The brutality used against Fox may be read in his Journal, and the courage and serenity with which it was borne. Dragged, shaken, beaten with hedge stakes and willow rods, he fell down at last on the wet common, 'and when I recovered myself again and saw myself lying on a watery common and all the people standing about me, I lay a little still, and the power

of the Lord sprang through me and the eternal refreshings refreshed me that I stood up again in the eternal power of God
and stretched out my arms amongst them all, and said again
with a loud voice, "Strike again! here is my arms, my head and
my cheeks", and there was a mason, a rude fellow, a professor[1]
called, he gave me a blow with all his might just atop of my hand
as it was stretched out with his walking rule staff, and my hand
and arm was so numbed and bruised that I could not draw it in
unto me again; so as [that] the people cried out he hath spoiled
his hand for ever having any use of it more. And I looked at it
in the love of God, and I was in the love of God to them all that
had persecuted me. And after a while the Lord's power sprang
through me again and through my hand and arm that in a
minute I recovered my hand and arm and strength in the face
and sight of them all.'

But this treatment only made him the bolder, and he went
again through the town and the market and so back to Swarthmoor, where Margaret Fell and her daughters and servants were
'dressing the heads and hands of Friends and friendly people that
was broken that day by the professors and hearers of priest
Lampitt'.[2]

A fortnight's rest in the peace and protection of this home,
and Fox began to preach in the villages to the south-west of
Swarthmoor. Crossing the narrow sea channel to Walney Island (near the modern town of Barrow-in-Furness) he was again
mobbed, nearly drowned and badly beaten. Here, on the shingle,
he made a new friend, James Lancaster who, when George was
thrown down, lay on top of him to protect him from the stones
and blows of his wife, who had been told that George had bewitched her husband. This latest treatment was so severe that
when the horse arrived from his Swarthmoor friends who had
indeed been agitated to hear of his venture, George could hardly
mount or ride. When Judge Fell came home again, in a few
days, he asked Fox for the story of the Walney attack, but Fox
refused to prosecute—'I told him they could do no otherwise,
they was in such a spirit; . . . and so he told his wife that I made
nothing of it and spoke as a man that had not been concerned.'[3]

---

[1] Professing Church member or communicant.
[2] Camb. Jnl. I, 58.   [3] Camb. Jnl. I, 61.

Shortly afterwards George Fox was summoned to Lancaster Assizes, on a warrant issued by Justice John Sawrey. Judge Fell and Colonel West were among the judges who examined him. There is a human touch in the story of the journey across the sands, when the Judge and the Quaker were riding together, and the Judge asked Fox what he (the Judge) should do at the trial, for it was a trial for blasphemy, one of which he had had no previous experience. George Fox advised him to let those speak first who brought these charges, and then that he would stand and answer them, like Paul before Festus and King Agrippa.[1] This the Judge did, the forty priests who were Fox's accusers were confounded, the warrant proved false, and Fox was acquitted, and allowed to preach then and there in the court.

During 1653 Fox travelled again in Furness, and then on horseback through Cumberland—Bootle, Pardshaw, Cockermouth, Caldbeck, Wigton, and to Carlisle. He had audiences sometimes of a thousand and more, and several Meetings grew in this county. When he was at Carlisle, news reached Margaret Fell that he was imprisoned in the filthy dungeon of the castle. She at once appealed to her friend Colonel West, not only on behalf of George but of Friends who were in many of the northern prisons, in York, Carlisle, Appleby and Lancaster—in prison because they were preaching 'the everlasting Gospel', and at a time when the rulers themselves had promised religious toleration—a mockery in practice. 'Dear heart', she wrote to the Colonel, 'I cannot but let thee know the cruelty of these tyrants; Oh these acts and pretences that they have to act by, is odious to all that hath but common honesty.'[2]

When he was set at liberty, Fox returned to Swarthmoor, where he had a visitor who became the leader of Quakerism in North Wales, and whose converts later migrated in large numbers to America, specially to Pennsylvania where the Welsh names of Bryn Mawr, Merion, Haverford and many others still bear witness to these first Welsh settlers. He was John Ap John, a prominent member of an Independent congregation at Wrexham, sent with a friend by their minister Morgan Lloyd, the celebrated mystical preacher, to hear and see George Fox and

[1] Camb. Jnl. I, 62.
[2] Camb. Jnl. I, 116-20, and M.F. *Works*, p. 43.

his friends. Twenty years later he wrote a touching little account of his visit in July 1653—'This time 20 years ago was the time I John Ap John was at Swarthmoor with George Fox, in Lancashire. That was the first time I saw George Fox. How in this 20 years I have received much and done but little; and it was thee, O Lord, that was my upholder all this 20 years. I never lost the feeling of thy power since then in Swarthmoor I received it and felt it; and I believe I never shall lose it if I wait for it and fear thee, and if thy fear be before my eyes. This fear will keep me from offending against thee, the God of my life.

'The 9th of the 6th month 1673, were these things seriously considered and pondered upon, how the Lord hath been dealing with me and many more this 20 years, and upwards.

'My evening meditations after sun setting.'[1]

By the beginning of 1654, Fox felt that the Meetings in the north were 'settled under God's teaching and the glory of the Lord shined over them', so that he might safely leave Swarthmoor.

Accordingly he travelled south, to London, and many other parts of England and Wales and Scotland, often to towns where already some of his followers had preceded him and sown the seed. There for the present we must leave him, and return to Swarthmoor and to the story of Margaret Fell's work in spreading the message and building the Church.

The first great missionary campaign of Quakerism, from 1652 to 1660, showed those characteristics which the best work of the Society of Friends has shown ever since, namely, the union of corporate organization with individual action based on personal concern, and an intense belief in the guidance of God in the moral decisions of life.

In this campaign George Fox was the acknowledged leader; when he came into a room full of Friends, others remained silent to await his ministry; and he kept himself free for travelling, preaching, advising, writing epistles, dealing with countless individuals in their difficulties, and slowly building up the organization as need arose.

Margaret Fell did a different kind of work, which was complementary to his in an amazing way. She was for the first few

[1] *John Ap John*, by W. G. Norris, p. 6.

years tied to her home and her family, but by her hospitality,
her writings, her wide correspondence and her wisdom, she not
only spread the knowledge of the Quaker interpretation of
Christianity, but gave unity and fellowship to a scattered company of men and women of very varied background and
experience.

Margaret Fell's writings show over and over again how well
she understood the fundamental Quaker belief in the Inner Light,
and how anxious she was to bring understanding of it to others.
It is the Light of Christ which is 'our teacher, leader and guider',
which can preserve 'us out of sin and transgression', and as we
obey the Light, and follow it in our hearts and consciences it will
lead us out of sin and iniquity. 'And so as we waited and dwelt
in it, we came to witness a washing and cleansing.'

In a preface to a collection of a few of her epistles to Friends
(her first was written in 1653, only a few months after her
convincement) she wrote 'when we came to this sight, and
knowledge, and discerning, then we became very zealous for
God, and for his Truth, and for the preservation of his people in
the Truth; and our hearts became tender, and we had a pity for
all people's souls, that remained in the darkness. And we were
moved of the Lord to write often to Friends, and our testimony
was very much to the Light of Christ in the conscience; because
we saw that, *that* was the Way, and there was no other: for
Christ Jesus said, "I am the Light"; He also said, "I am the Way,
the Truth, and the Life; and there is none that can come to the
Father, but by me".'[1]

This belief in the Light of Christ given to every man, which
came to be known as the Inner Light, was from the beginning
of George Fox's teaching, and still is, the basis of Quakerism. It
has, of course, been the teaching of the great mystics and many
of the great religious prophets and saints down the centuries. It
became for the early Friends first of all an inward experience and
worked itself out in the practice of Life. In seventeenth-century
England there were many men and women who had missed the
inwardness of religion by dwelling too much on words and outward forms—theological discussions about notions largely man-
made. To them the sudden understanding of the new teaching

[1] M.F. *Works*, p. 46.

of the early Friends was a revolution in their lives. It brought a
new conception of the relation of God and man, a peace of mind
while suffering barbarous persecution; it turned quiet home-
loving men and women into travellers over the earth, and it led
them to emphasize the supreme importance of every individual,
and so to denounce war, and later slavery, unjust economic and
social conditions, and capital punishment, as well as the more
personal evils of drunkenness, thieving, lying, and dishonesty.
But in the seventeenth century it also frequently brought them
into trouble with the State and with both Puritans (under Cromwell) and Episcopalians (under Charles II). One outcome of
their beliefs was their refusal to take any oath whatsoever, for
they said that to swear was contrary to the direct command of
Christ. To reinforce their arguments they were not slow in
pointing out to both the magistrates and Charles II himself how
frequently the oath was merely a cover for hypocrisy and disloyalty—a truth which was peculiarly irritating to magistrates
and judges who had found it convenient to be loyal to both
Cromwell and Charles II. William Penn, in his Preface to Fox's
Journal, explained the Quaker position thus: 'They uphold the
sufficiency of Truth—speaking . . . from Christ's express prohibition to swear at all. And for that, they being under the tie
and bond of Truth in themselves, there was no necessity for an
oath, and it would be a reproach to their Christian veracity to
assure their Truth by such an extraordinary way of speaking:
but offering at the same time to be punished to the full, for false
speaking, as others for perjury, if ever guilty of it.' Their per-
sistence and suffering finally had its reward and the Toleration
Act of 1689 began a movement for the abolition of oaths and
the right of affirmation which was completed by the Oaths Act
of 1888. Another principle was their refusal to pay tithes, because they would not support a Church which they believed
had fallen away in many important respects from pure Christian
teaching, nor help to pay the salary of a minister who they
believed ought to give his teaching freely. Their belief in the
brotherhood of man, and equality of all before God led them to
refuse the convention of raising the hat. When extravagance of
good manners often was a cloak for hypocrisy, and when men
only removed their hats to those socially their equal or superior,

this Quaker protest was of great value, but it led them into
much trouble, and even imprisonment. Then again the Quakers
believed that God called them to spread their knowledge to
others, and in an attempt to stop this, the old law against
vagrancy passed in Elizabethan times to prevent migration of
labour from one parish to another, was used against them. For
non-attendance at the parish church, and (after 1664) for holding their own Meetings for Worship, the Quakers were equally
at variance with the laws of the land.

In these ways and in others, the early Friends with remarkable
consistency held to what they believed were the inevitable
effects of their central belief of the Spirit of God dwelling in
every man. Their form of Christianity is without ritual or outward ceremony, without a paid ministry or complicated
theology, and when their members come together to worship
God they meet in the plainest and simplest of buildings, waiting
in silence for the message through the Holy Spirit. So it was
that when Margaret Fell had made the Quaker beliefs her own,
she could not remain silent or inactive. Particularly must she
try to make their enemies understand, and their persecutors
cease from persecuting. She herself explained her work of these
early years in the following revealing statement. 'That sight and
convincement that God had opened in me continued with me,
and I grew in it, and many more was convinced besides me, and
a great astonishment there was in the country. But the Truth
grew, and increased amongst us, and the Lord's eternal power
seized upon many, and many was moved of the Lord to go to
the steeplehouses to cry against the priests, so that it raised such
a bitterness, and envy amongst the priests and professors, that all
was on a fire, and being that they had never heard nor known
of such things before, they all concluded it was of the Devil, and
that it was sorcery and witchcraft, and that they gave us bottles
to drink, and tied strings about our arms, and fearful lies, and
stories they raised up against us. But the Lord preserved us
faithful to him, and we kept our integrity and met together at
our house at Swarthmoor with my husband's consent. And he
being the chief magistrate in the country, they could not fall
upon us in persecuting of us, as their hearts desired, and so that
tormented them worst of all, because the Truth did spring and

spread and increase, and they knew not how to get it suppressed. . . . The highest priests and professors were and are our greatest enemies. . . . When the high priests of our times saw that the Truth struck at their foundation and root, and turned them out of their place of teaching, and brought the Light to be people's teacher, that so there would be no need of them to teach, . . . and thereby turned them out of their maintenances and benefices; they seeing that the Truth struck at all this, and that this would be the end if the Truth prospered, this made them all mad. So that they joined hand in hand against the Truth, and they petitioned the Parliament and petitioned Cromwell, and Richard Cromwell; and the priests and professors in our parts began to write against us. And George Fox being gone out of the country, Friends brought things to me, and I answered them. And I was but young in the Truth, yet I had a perfect and a pure Testimony of God in my heart for God and his Truth. And I believe I could at that day have laid down my life for it. And I was very zealous in it.'[1]

Perhaps her zeal for the new teaching showed in the very early days a little too much emotionalism, as the following letter may indicate, but this soon deepened and passed away. This letter may however show also a sensitiveness to the feelings of their new friend, whose teaching at their house was being repulsed by someone, unnamed, who they had hoped would receive it at once. This explanation is prompted by the fact that the letter is endorsed by George Fox himself, who many years later added 'This was sent to G.F. and he came back again to them that sent for him, and he that he shaked the dust of his feet against, was not long after convinced'.

The first part of the letter is jointly written by Margaret and several members of the family and household. 'Our dear father in the Lord, for though we have ten thousand instructors in Christ, yet have we not many fathers, for in Christ Jesus thou hast begotten us through the Gospel, eternal praise be to our father. We thy babes with one consent being gathered together in the power of the Spirit, thou being present with us, our souls doth thirst and languish after thee, and doth challenge that right that we have in thee. O thou bread of life, without which bread

[1] Spence MSS. III, 135, **124.**

our souls will starve. O, for evermore give us this bread, and take pity on us, whom thou hast nursed up with the breasts of consolation. O our life, our desire is to see thee again that we may be refreshed and established and so have life more abundantly, and let not that beastly power which keeps us in bondage separate thy bodily presence from us, who reigns as King above it, and would rejoice to see thy kingly power here triumph over it. O our dear nursing father, we hope thou wilt not leave us comfortless, but will come again, though that sorrow be for a time, yet joy comes in the morning. O our life, we hope to see thee again that our joy may be full, for in thy presence is fulness of joy, and where thou dwells is pleasures for evermore.

'O thou fountain of eternal life, our souls thirsts after thee, for in thee alone is our life and peace, and without thee **have we** no peace, for our souls is much refreshed by seeing thee, and our lives is preserved by thee, O thou father of eternal felicity.'

The members of the household who sign this letter are Thos. Salthouse (who comes next after Margaret Fell herself), Ann Clayton, Mary Askew, then Margaret and Bridget, and finally William Caton.

Then Margaret herself writes:

My own dear heart, though thou hast shaken the dust off thy **feet** at him, who would not receive thee, nor is not worthy of thee, which shalt be a testimony against him for ever, yet thou knows that we have received thee into our hearts, and shall live with thee eternally, and it is our life and joy to be with thee, and so my dear heart let not the power of darkness separate thy bodily presence from us which will be a grief and trouble to us, and especially through him, whom thou knows can call nothing his own but the plagues and woes.

My soul thirsts to have thee to come over, if it be but for two or three days to strike down the deceit in him for the truth's sake.

And if thou do not come, it will add abundantly to our sorrow, and strengthen the beastly power. I know it is a burden and suffering to thee, but thou hast borne our burdens and suffered for us, and with us, and now dear heart do not leave us nor forsake us, for our life and peace is in thee.

M.F.

Little postscripts are added by the other daughters—Susan, aged two, adds: 'O my dear father, when wilt thou come'; Sarah, aged eleven, 'Dear father, pray for us'; Isabel, aged fifteen,

'Oh my dear heart, shall we not see thee once more', and the five year old Mary, 'Thou art the fountain of life'.[1]

This over-emotionalism of Margaret Fell and her household never recurred, and perhaps it may have given her a valuable insight into the working of the human mind under a sudden joy of spiritual release and the influence of a man of prophetic personality. It probably fitted her to be able to deal later on with others who had become over-excited.

Now and again her friends sent her women who were proving a trial to Meetings through their lack of balance or unwise behaviour. Of two such women, a man Friend wrote to her in 1654: 'Take heed of receiving [them] in amongst you hastily, lest you take a burden of which I do you forewarn of.'[2] Of another, she was told: 'There is little service for the Lord in her ministry, but rather hurt.' And of Sarah Knowles we have these two little pictures, from opposite sides; one is in a letter to Secretary John Thurloe from Timothy Langley at Leith, Scotland, 19th September 1658, in which he writes about the spread of Quakerism in South Scotland, and adds: 'Sarah Knowles, wife of Captain Knowles of this regiment, is gone on her feet as it were, on pilgrimage to one Margaret Fell, who lives about Lancashire, who, they say, is Judge Fell's wife, and that she is one that is past the cloud, and hath liberty to wear satins, and silver and gold lace, and is a great gallant.'[3] But William Dewsbury, also in Scotland, four days later, writes to Margaret: 'This I lay before thee, that care be taken to send Sarah Knowles with a man and a horse as soon as way is made for her to return to her family; the Truth is under suffering until she be in her family again.'[4]

In the rapid spread of new religious ideas, such as was occurring at this time, there was bound to be the appearance of some individuals who made difficulties and disunity. So to them, as well as to persecutors, Margaret Fell wrote Epistles, as did George Fox and others. As early as 1653 she wrote to Friends, begging them to mind 'That of God in your consciences', to let 'the candle of the Lord . . . search you and try you and mind whether

[1] Spence MSS. III, 24–6.
[2] Swm. MSS. IV, 113.
[3] *State Papers of John Thurloe*, Jnl. F.H.S. VIII, p. 165.
[4] Swm. MSS. IV, 146.

you have received the new Covenant which is the law written in the heart, which law is pure,—spiritual, just and good'.[1] When disunity appeared in the Meetings already gathered, she begged Friends not to strive against each other, nor to grow proud, but to be faithful to their 'growth in the eternal, in the inward man, according to your measures'.[2]

Margaret Fell spent much time and energy in writing pamphlets and letters, both to those in authority and to her friends. In public affairs she believed in trying to reach those responsible, and not only their underlings. Thus it was that four times she addressed the Protector Oliver Cromwell. He had promised religious toleration, but he did not prevent persecution by his servants. Her first letter to Cromwell was written in 1653, a few months after her convincement. Two years later she wrote again, and in 1657 she wrote twice, once at great length. After Cromwell's death in 1658, and during the unsettled rule of Richard Cromwell and the increasing power of the Army, dreaded by all, she wrote to the Council and Officers of the Army and every Member of Parliament.

Although Oliver Cromwell's second daughter, Lady Claypole, was sympathetic with Friends, and in spite of the presence of two Quakers in his household, Cromwell all through his Protectorate was unable to prevent wide persecution of Friends. No doubt he faced great difficulties, but Margaret Fell boldly declared against his hypocrisy, appealed to him to follow the Light of Christ in his conscience, and warned him of his overthrow if he disobeyed it. She accused the clergy of his time of corruption and covetousness, and their savage persecution of innocent people, stealing their goods and destroying their liberty. She reminded him frequently of his unfulfilled promise to give religious toleration. Once indeed, not long before his death, Cromwell did send orders to his magistrates that they should deal tenderly with 'such poor deluded persons' as those who refused to remove their hats in court.

In fact, the severe persecutions of this period were the work chiefly of local authorities, and it is perhaps an interesting comment on the dictatorship of Cromwell that he was in this respect

[1] M.F. *Works*, p. 47 *seq*, **abridged.**
[2] M.F. *Works*, p. 53 *seq*.

at any rate unable to have his more tolerant views obeyed by his people.

When Margaret Fell wrote to the persecutors themselves, she wrote with passion. It was an age of frank speech, and one who told a lie was plainly called a liar, and those who beat and imprisoned men and women whose aim was to beg people to return to Christianity in thought and deed were called false deceivers and worse.

She was particularly severe with the local Justice of the Peace, John Sawrey. His persecuting zeal continued, added to which he made malicious and slanderous remarks against her and her friends. She rebuked him in three letters, in forceful language, calling him 'A catterpiller, which shall be swept out of the way',[1] and charged him with taking bribes and doing injustice. One of her letters was sent consequent to a meeting with him at the parish church, as the following note added to the letter by a later writer will show: 'This aforesaid paper was written to John Sawrey . . . a Justice **a** great persecutor, one of the first in the North, that set the rude multitude to beat Friends, who set many in the stocks **and** put in prison, and M.F. was moved to go to the steeplehouse to speak to the priest of the parish, where she and he lived, and when she was in the steeplehouse he came to her, and said, "Good Mistress Fell, go into your own pew, or else go your way", and he took her by the arm and offered to pull her away, but she said, hold thy hands off me, and she spoke to the priest, what she had to speak and afterwards she spoke to him [viz. Sawrey], and she charged him to do Justice, and not to wrong or oppress the poor people, whereupon he was vexed, and writ a letter to her and sent it to her husband, and charged her to prove what injustice he had done; so this letter is an answer to his, and within a few years after [he] was drowned in water upon the road coming from York.'[2] Justice John Sawrey, Member of the Nominated Parliament of 1653, was indeed drowned as he was crossing the treacherous sands of Morecambe Bay.[3]

[1] Spence MSS. III, 144, 146 and 147. [2] Spence MSS. III, 146, 147.
[3] His home, Plumpton Hall, **two miles from** Ulverston, on the edge of those sands, is now a farmhouse, but its fine old staircase is there still to remind one of its former dignity.

But not every Justice of the Peace persecuted the Quakers. Her own husband was one who did not. Another was Colonel West, M.P., whose service to Fox and other Friends was great, though he never joined them completely.

Another Justice who was helpful to Friends was Anthony Pearson whose letter[1] has already been quoted, after his first visit to Swarthmoor Hall. A few months later Margaret wrote to encourage him in his seeking—'my dear heart, wait upon the Lord in the light of God in thee . . . and it will bring the seed of God out of prison if thou hearken to it and be obedient to it. . . . Be low and watchful, and mind that which keeps thy peace . . . it will lead thee to another Kingdom which is not of this world, which is righteousness and peace and joy in the Holy Ghost, and then thou wilt see the vanity and emptiness of these vanishing things, which all the world is busying themselves about, for the very fashion of this world shall pass away.'[2] She asked his legal help for an imprisoned Friend, John Lawson of Lancaster, who had been cruelly beaten and stoned and set in the stocks four hours before he was sent to prison.

Sometimes specially against 'priests and professors' was her pen used. At great length she would explain the meaning of the Light within, and appeal for a true understanding of an inward religion, in contrast to one of outward words, and ceremonies, and 'notions'. 'Turn to the Light, wait in the Light, keep your minds within to the Light, and walk in the Light, which checks you, and convinces you of sin and evil, and discerns the thoughts of your hearts, and lets you see the outgoings of your minds, and discerns every sinful lust, even in the very appearance and rising of it.' 'If ever you come to know the living God, you must turn your minds to the Light which is in you.' Quakers have never of course denied the presence of sin, but in the seventeenth century they protested vehemently against the Puritan over-emphasis on sin and their denial of the presence of the perfect Light in man, for they found in actual practice that the turning to the good, will of itself expel the evil—a practical application of St. Paul's command to overcome evil with good.

There was one minister against whom both Margaret Fell

[1] See pp. 20–21.
[2] Spence MSS. III, 28.

and George Fox issued several letters—Gabriel Camelford, of Staveley in Cartmel. It was he who had instigated his congregation to throw Fox over the church wall on his first visit to the district. His theology as well as his behaviour was particularly obnoxious at Swarthmoor. In one of her letters to Camelford, Margaret told him that for his attacks on the innocent he would be turned out of his church. Her prophecy came true, for seven years later, in 1662, he and about seventeen hundred more of the Puritan clergy were ejected from their livings.

The 'Independent' minister of Keswick, James Cave, collected all the Quaker books which appeared in his parish, not to read them himself, but to prevent others from doing so.[1] The priest of Aldingham, near Ulverston, Thomas Shaw, was described as 'that great persecutor . . . one of the first in England that put Friends in prison for tithes, and so continued till he died'.[2] This is the first mention of Friends refusing to pay tithes—a refusal which lasted for a couple of centuries, and which led them into impoverishment and imprisonment. In fact, when the Rev. Thomas Shaw sent Richard Ashburner of Gleaston (a hamlet in his parish) to prison for non-payment of tithes, he was left in Lancaster Castle till he died in 1655.[3]

Persecution for the non-payment of tithes became so savage that a petition with 15,000 signatures against this oppression was presented to the Rump Parliament in June, 1659. The petition was supplemented in the next month, bearing the signatures of 7,000 women Friends, who called themselves 'handmaids and daughters of the Lord'. At the head of the list are the signatures of Margaret Fell and her seven daughters, Rachel the youngest being then but six years old! This extensively signed Petition of women seems to have been the first uniting of Quaker women for action against a national wrong.

While there were many cases of cruel and unjust imprisonments and considerable violence done during these early years (1652 to 1656), they were not characteristic of every part of the country. In London and the south generally Friends had much freedom, and in fact the years 1654 and 1655 were times gener-

[1] Spence MSS. III, 142.
[2] Spence MSS. III, 137-9.
[3] Camb. Jnl. II, 475.

ally of widespread and joyous publishing of Truth. They were
followed however from 1656 by years of persecution throughout
the country. In August 1656 George Bishop of Bristol, formerly
a captain in the Parliamentary Army, described to Margaret Fell
the arrests, sufferings, trials and imprisonments of numerous
Friends in Devon, Cornwall and Somerset, chiefly on the charge
of vagrancy, and he added, 'The day is passing over, the night is
coming, iniquity gathers up all its powers of darkness against the
seed . . . that so it may be cut off'.[1]

Bishop's prophecy of troubles and trials was true, and his tale
of imprisonments can be multiplied almost endlessly in the
letters sent to Margaret Fell from all parts of England, Scotland,
Wales, Ireland and the Isle of Man. From early in 1656 until
September George Fox lay in the terrible Doomsdale at Launceston, and the cruelty and injustice to him and his fellow prisoners
roused William Caton to write to Margaret 'if all their trans-
gressions were numbered for which they suffer, and laid upon
the head of one, they would not be a sufficient transgression to
cause one to suffer deservedly'.[2] 'Surely, surely', adds this sensitive youth, 'the Lord will not always hold his peace, but he will
arise, and plead the cause of the innocent. . . . These sufferings is
for the perfecting of the body of which Christ is the head, who
through sufferings was made perfect.'

And the persecuted were the victors—they refused all offers
for freedom which had conditions attached, they refused to
promise to preach no more, they refused to promise not to
travel where the Lord moved them to go, they refused to doff
the hat in reverence to man, they refused to pay the jailer's fees
and they were finally released from Launceston, George Fox
and his friends, early in September 1656, free men.

It was the same elsewhere. One Friend was released from
Carlisle, who had been kept in prison for the jailer's fees, 'yet
the Lord so ordered that he hath through suffering, conquered
them all, and come forth with victory over the deceit and
without paying them one penny; for the mayor's officers after
a little temptation . . . said to him, "Look whatever here is, that

[1] *The Swarthmore Documents in America:* Jnl. F.H.S. Supplement 1940, p. 22.
[2] Swm. MSS. I, 313, 23.5.1656.

is thine, and take it and go thy way." Pharaoh was wearied with the Israelite.'[1]

This unconquerable spirit was well expressed by George Fox as he lay at Launceston. In an Epistle to Friends, those going forth to all parts at home and abroad, and those suffering imprisonment, he wrote: 'Let all nations hear the sound by word or writing. Spare no place, spare no tongue nor pen, but be obedient to the Lord God; go through the work and be valiant for the Truth upon earth. . . . Be patterns, be examples in all countries, places, islands, nations, wherever you come, that your carriage and life may preach among all sorts of people, and to them; then you will come to walk cheerfully over the world, answering that of God in every one.'[2]

From her home at Swarthmoor, Margaret Fell sent out many letters of appeal and encouragement to her suffering friends. 'Be nothing terrified at their threats of banishment, for they cannot banish you from the coasts and sanctuaries of the living God', she wrote.[3]

To Margaret Fell's appeals to the Protector and his Councillors, other leading Friends, both men and women, added theirs. However, in the political confusion, unrest and disillusionment of the last years of the Commonwealth nothing was done to relieve the Quakers. By April 1659, Friends told Parliament that about 2,000 of their number had suffered imprisonment during the last six years, twenty-one of whom had died as a result. A few days later, 164 Friends offered to lie in prison in the place of the 144 suffering then. Their appeal however was in vain.

Before the Restoration early in 1660, the number of those who had suffered for conscience' sake had risen to 3,170, and there were still 700 Quakers lying in the jails of the country.[1]

---

[1] Swm. MSS. I, 257. Letter from Geo. Taylor of Kendal to M.F. at Swarthmoor. 11.8.1655.
[2] B. Qism. 239.
[3] Jnl. F.H.S. V, 148.
[4] Camb. Jnl. I, 385.

Chapter Five

MARGARET FELL'S WORK FOR QUAKERS, 1653–8

'Thy care, thy watchings, thy diligence, thy prayers and breathings into the everlasting fountain for the seed, I know and feel in the eternal, and the desire of thy soul and all who with thee in the spirit are joined, is the Lord satisfying.'
Richard Hubberthorne to Margaret Fell in 1655 (Caton MSS. III,342).

'A nursing mother to all the babes which are tender and young.'
Thomas Salthouse to Margaret Fell in 1653.

'My dear counsellor and comforter.'
John Stubbs in 1657.

WHILE Margaret Fell felt impelled to appeal for justice from rulers, magistrates and ministers and to enlighten them on Quaker beliefs, yet the greater part of her large correspondence was with individual Friends, specially with many of those seventy to a hundred men and women, all from the north of England, who from 1653 were the 'First Publishers of Truth'.[1] Between her and them was a constant two-way flow of letters. The love and admiration which were felt and expressed to her in these letters are indeed remarkable. They always begin and end their letters to her with praise and expression of gratitude so fervent that one wonders if it was part of the seventeenth-century habit. But a glance at other letters of that time soon shows that it was not the custom to write in such a style. Evidently these expressions of affection were genuinely felt by these early Friends when they had experienced Margaret Fell's love and care for them.

These messengers of Quakerism included the scholar, the well-to-do landowner, the farmer, the schoolmaster, the weaver, the maid-servant, the soldier, the former minister, the shopkeeper, the craftsman, the ploughman, and 'a haberdasher of small

[1] This is the title given to the itinerating Friends who spread the Quaker message.

wares'.[1] For long months, and sometimes for years, they left family and friends, and usually in couples they journeyed throughout England, to Scotland, Ireland, Wales and the Isle of Man, and to the Continent and America. To their 'nursing mother' they wrote, to tell her of their experiences, to beg her for her prayers that they might have strength and courage, to thank her for help received by them or their families during their absence, to implore her to write to them. Few of her letters to them, alas, remain, but, largely owing to her own good sense, to the love of William Caton for her, the historical foresight of George Fox, and the loyalty of Margaret's grandson, John Abraham, many hundreds of their letters to Margaret have been preserved, either in their original, or as contemporary copies.[2]

We have already seen how, during 1652 and 1653, several Meetings in the north of England, notably Brigflatts (near Sedbergh, W. Yorks.), Preston Patrick and Swarthmoor, were settled. For the most part the next period, from 1653 to 1658, was a time of seed-sowing, of a great missionary campaign in these islands and overseas, Meetings being gathered one by one in the homes of sympathizers, and it was not till after 1666 that there was an effort made by George Fox to create an organization for the movement. The seed-sowing time however was not an

[1] It has often been thought that the early Friends came entirely from the less educated section of the nation. This is a mistake, for a number were men and women of education and wealth. George Fox himself had had little education in his youth (he remained a very bad speller all his life), but he was a writer of powerful and pungent English as can be seen in his Journals and Letters, and he became such a student of the Bible that a contemporary said of him that if the English Bible were lost it could be re-written from Fox's memory. He had a good library of books, of wide variety of subjects and he insisted on Friends founding schools for their children. He even wrote a spelling book for the pupils!

[2] Housed until the middle of the eighteenth century at Swarthmoor Hall, together with George Fox's Journal and Margaret's own Library, they are known as the Swarthmoor Manuscripts, the Abraham MSS., the Thirnbeck MSS., the Spence MSS., the A. R. Barclay MSS., the Miller MSS. and the Thwaite MSS. The greater number of them are now in the possession of the Library of the Society of Friends in London. Most of them were endorsed by George Fox himself, probably during one of his long visits to the Hall in his later life, and are part of what he himself so expressly desired to be preserved, as they with others would 'make a fine history'.

unrelated wandering of inspired individuals; it had Swarthmoor Hall as its base, and Margaret Fell as its guiding mother, providing also spiritual and material help. The travellers reported to her in what towns and counties they were working, and where they believed God was leading them to go next, and they frequently reported the movements of their fellow-preachers. It was Margaret at Swarthmoor who seemed to keep a plan of their movements, so that there was no overlapping, and so that all places could be covered. The news too was constantly being passed on to George Fox and other leaders.

Fox in his Journal relates how towards the end of 1653 and during 1654 'when the churches were settled in the north, and the Lord had raised up many and sent forth many into his vineyard to preach his everlasting Gospel; as Francis Howgill and Edward Burrough to London; John Camm and John Audland to Bristol through the countries; Richard Hubberthorne and George Whitehead towards Norwich; and Thomas Holme into Wales; that a matter of 70 ministers did the Lord raise up and sent abroad out of the North countries.'[1]

How faithfully these men and women did their work may still be read in a volume entitled *The First Publishers of Truth*, a collection of the adventurous beginnings of Meetings all over the country, collected years later, at the beginning of the eighteenth century, but not published till 1904. Their own accounts however live still in the letters addressed chiefly to Margaret Fell.

A sense of fellowship was essential for the support and encouragement of all. Frequently she was asked to have copies made (by hand of course) of general epistles to be dispatched to the Northern Meetings. Sometimes she received shorthand notes as was the case at a General Meeting held at Scalehouse in Yorkshire,[2] where Alexander Parker told her that George Fox had 'bid me write to thee to certify thee, that they are going on with the like work in those parts'. She was told also that General Meetings were about to be held at Cambridge for the Eastern counties, at Bristol for the Western, and another for the Midland counties 'as the Lord orders'.

Thomas Salthouse, Judge Fell's agent, wrote to her, 'I have

[1] Camb. Jnl. I, 141.
[2] Caton MSS. III.

thoughts this day to pass towards Shrewsbury and so on towards
the West (as I see the way opened). It would have been much
refreshment to me to have seen thy face before I had passed.
The work that thou gavest me to do, I have cheerfully been
carried through. In Cheshire since I passed with my dear
brother Leonard Fell, I have had six Meetings.'[1]

Thomas Taylor (once the priest of Skipton in Yorkshire) in a
letter to James Nayler asking him to come to Manchester and
Lichfield, as Friends were weak and needing help from 'a grown
Friend' added, 'Margaret Fell was speaking to me of some that
are drawn forth into the ministry to come this aways shortly, so
thou may send her word that it will be well so to do, as the Lord
makes any willing and free, for hereabouts as in other places is
work to do.'[2]

John Slee of Cumberland had been visiting Margaret before
starting on his travels and sent a loving expression of gratitude—
'Dear Heart, after I departed with thee as I passed over the sands,
the Lord's love to me did much appear that day, and thy dearness in his sight to me did much appear, and how thy prayers did
much prevail with him for his dear ones'.[3]

'Dear Sister', wrote William Dewsbury when he was in Scotland, at Leith, 'as thou art free, let me hear from thee how it is
with the dear children abroad, and what [news] comes to thee of
John Stubbs and the rest of Friends that is in the countries where
the Lord hath sent them.' (John Stubbs then, in 1658, was in
Holland.) Then he adds a further request, 'Sarah Welsh wants a
Friend to be servant with her. I lay it before thee, let not any
come but whom thou sees unmovable [in] the power of truth
to be an example. I leave it with thee.'[4]

The women ministers showed, equally with the men, their
love of and reliance on Margaret Fell. Early in 1655, Ann Audland, whose husband John was ministering in Bristol with John
Camm (all three coming from Westmorland) was imprisoned
at Banbury, Oxfordshire. From there she wrote beseechingly
to Margaret, 'Oh, that I could hear from thee, let me feel thee

[1] Caton MSS. III, 75.
[2] Swm. MSS. III, 31 (1655).
[3] Swm. MSS. IV, 110. 8.9.1655?
[4] Swm. MSS. IV, 146. 23.7.1658.

in the eternal that my life may be refreshed by thee, for my sufferings hath been great since I saw thee. Dear heart, pray for me that I may be kept in the eternal wisdom of God. . . . My joy is full, when I see thee present with me, near me even in my very heart, and there is my life refreshed, and with thee and in thee I am bound up, and sealed for evermore. My dear and near and eternal mother, by thee I am nourished. I see and feel thy care over all the lambs of my Father.'[1] Later, but still in Banbury jail, she could write, 'Thou hast been strength unto me when I was weak, and pure refreshment have I found in thy presence. . . . This is a place of joy indeed, and eternally doth my soul rejoice in the Lord.'

For these men and women to be sure that she knew of their struggles and their suffering, as well as their joys, was a comfort to them, often in their intense loneliness.

How rejoiced the family must have been to read in the letters which came so frequently to them, that 'great boldness and courage is given to friends in those parts [Yorkshire in 1653] that makes them mighty valiant for the Truth',[2] and 'Here [from Norwich Castle in 1654] are tender lambs of God coming daily to us out of the country, and our soul rejoiceth in the prosperity of the Lord's work',[3] and again, from Richard Hubberthorne, working in London and Kent, 'The Truth got much dominion amongst them', 'The magistrates in that county is generally quiet' (this early in 1657), and 'The Truth was ministered unto them—[the Justices, Colonels and Captains of the Cromwellian Army, of which Richard had once been an officer]—and the ground of prejudice stopped and brought under, and a love and an acknowledgement of the Truth raised in some of them.'[4]

Great news came to Swarthmoor from London. The capital was first visited by Quakers early in 1654, by two women from the north, Isabel Buttery[5] and her unnamed companion, who distributed an Epistle of George Fox, and had private meetings with Robert and Simon Dring in the City, but they did not

[1] Caton MSS. III, 431. 8.12.1654.
[2] Swm. MSS. IV, 83.
[3] Swm. MSS. I, 340.
[4] Caton MSS. III, 372.
[5] A.R.B. p. 4.

preach, except to say a few words now and again. It was in July of that year, that five of the ablest Quaker ministers reached London, Francis Howgill and Edward Burrough, John Camm and Richard Hubberthorne, and Justice Anthony Pearson.

In their first letter to Margaret, written on 10th July, they look back with affection and joy to their recent Meetings with her and her family at Swarthmoor, which they had left but a week before. Indeed during the two years, 1652 to 1654, these and other men and women (mostly young) starting off to preach, had met there many times, building up their own spiritual strength and working out the implications in their daily lives and in their relationship with Church and State.

From London this group of five, gradually reduced to four and two, wrote to Margaret every week or fortnight. Their long letters full of vivid details told her of the exhausting work in the great city, of the discussion meetings for the spreading of their message—'threshing and ploughing, reaping and gathering in'—and of the quiet evening gatherings for themselves where they could refresh their spirits. They told Margaret that in London were 'the highest and subtlest that we have to deal with', and they warned her that only mature and skilful Friends should be sent there.[1]

When two of her chief correspondents, Howgill and Burrough, moved on to Bristol in October 1654, where two other north countrymen, John Audland and John Camm, both of Preston Patrick, had already been working with great success, she continued to hear of their adventures.

On their return to London in a few months' time (March 1655) she heard how they had met George Fox on his first coming to the city since his religious work began, brought up as he was on a charge of blasphemy. The Protector however set him free 'to go whither he pleased. . . . Oliver Cromwell was very loving to him, and wished him to come again to him.'[2]

A very widespread attack on the 'rude world' in London was now being made by the many Friends there. But Burrough and Howgill reported to Margaret that Friends were also going

[1] Caton MSS. III, 181–5.
[2] In a letter from Alexander Parker to M. Fell from London, 10.1.1655 (March 1655). Caton MSS. III and A.R.B. 24.

further afield—some to Norwich and Suffolk, others to Dover, Plymouth, Bedfordshire and Bristol, so that they themselves were now being left alone in London. 'We two', they added, 'are too few in this city for this service, for truly it is very great; at present many come in daily to the acknowledgment of the Truth. Friends are so many, that not one place can hold them on the First days [Sundays], where we can peaceably meet for the rude people; for since we came, they have been very rude, . . . very oft to pull us down when we have been speaking. George was at the great meeting place two First days before we came; and his voice and outward man was almost spent amongst them.' Friends generally were thankful for the freedom from persecution which they were enjoying. But there was soon to be a change.

In April 1655, after a Royalist insurrection, a proclamation was issued requiring persons suspected of Roman Catholicism to take the oath of Abjuration, abjuring the Papal authority and belief in transubstantiation. Frequently in the public mind, Quakers were believed to be Jesuits in disguise, and were accordingly ordered to take the oath, and on refusal were imprisoned.[1] From now on, in spite of the known liking of the Protector for George Fox, the Quakers were widely persecuted. Sometimes it was under the old laws against vagrancy, sometimes it was because they refused to remove their hats before a magistrate, or because they insisted on their legal right to speak in churches, or because they journeyed on Sunday.

Margaret Fell had already in 1653 and 1654 helped to comfort prisoners in the north—in Carlisle, Appleby and Lancaster. Now in June 1655, she heard from Francis Howgill of the persecutions in the south. 'Dear heart', he wrote from London, 'thy letters I received which was to Oliver and to the rest of the brethren, which I shall convey so soon as I can. And those to O. Cromwell are both delivered unto his hand, but he is full of subtlety and deceit, will speak fair, but hardens his heart, and acts secretly underneath.

'Dear Heart, the rage of the heathen grows high and subtle, and traps arise everywhere and every way laid to ensnare.

'Dear heart, our army is almost scattered, and broken and

[1] *F.P.T.* Penal Laws affecting Friends.

cast into prisons by the Devil. I know none almost at liberty, but
George and Alexander, Edward and I and Gervase—except
John Stubbs and Will Caton and John Wilkinson and John
Story, and it is like they cannot be long out.'

Yet he writes triumphantly.

Five or six meetings every First day of Friends, beside two great
places for a threshing floor, and we have got up a Meeting a little
beyond Whitehall, near Westminster, and many are coming in, and
many enquiring, and many convinced daily. Friends grows in the Life. [1]

Then he gave her news of other of these Northern Friends who
were all her 'children' and recently arrived in London and the
south. Richard Clayton, brother of her servant Ann, and
Richard Hubberthorne of Yealand were in prison, but George
Whitehead of Westmorland and Dorothy Waugh, a serving-
maid of John Camm's, had been released. Two, Myles Halhead
and Thomas Salthouse, were imprisoned in Exeter. James Lancaster of Walney Island was in prison at Bedford, seven others
in prison at Northampton.

In spite of persecution, all through 1655, Truth was spreading
and flourishing in London, James Nayler then becoming the
great preacher, 'a great love being begotten for him'. [2]

Early in July both Burrough and Howgill felt called to cross
over to Ireland. It was possible for them to leave London now,
for George Fox and James Nayler were both ministering there.

They travelled first to Swarthmoor, to gain refreshment for
the difficulties before them. Quaker teaching had only reached
Ireland the year before when an old Cromwellian soldier of
Westmorland, now a settler in Ireland. William Edmundson,
founded a Meeting at Lurgan. He had been convinced in 1653
when, during a business visit to the north of England, he had
heard James Nayler speak.

Ireland at this time was suffering from the results of a rebellion, which had been repressed with ferocity by Oliver Cromwell. Here were a hunted Celtic people, proscribed and persecuted Roman Catholics, ruled by English garrisons who were
chiefly zealous Baptists, Independents and Presbyterians. Cromwell's general, Fleetwood, was in command.

[1] Caton MSS. III, 176–8, also A.R.B. 35–6.
[2] Caton MSS. III, 295–8, also A.R.B. 37.

The two friends, Burrough, then aged twenty-one, and Howgill thirty-seven, reached Ireland in mid-August, and their letters
to Margaret began again. From Swarthmoor they had travelled
to Dublin by Warrington, Ormskirk, Liverpool and Chester,
holding meetings at each place, and visiting Quaker prisoners.
In Dublin they had met General Fleetwood, and had meetings
with the Baptists. 'But they are a careless, dissolute, proud
people,' they explain. After three weeks together in Dublin, the
two friends felt they must part for a time, a great cross 'in so
strange and barbarous a nation', Francis Howgill to go to Cork,
and Edward Burrough to stay in Dublin. Howgill begs Margaret to write to his wife left at home at Grayrigg, Westmorland,
for she was ill.[1] A little later she died before her husband was
free to return home to their children. She was one of the many
wives who willingly shared with their husbands loss of income
and social position, and long separation.

Edward Burrough missed the help and companionship of his
older friend very sadly. But in October he told Margaret that
he had met Elizabeth Fletcher, just come over from England.
'Truly I suffer for her', he added, 'she being as it were alone,
having no other woman with her in this ruinous nation, where
it is very bad travelling, every way afoot, and also dangerous.'[2]
This intrepid traveller was from Kendal, not more than seventeen years of age at this time, who had already suffered cruel
indignities and persecution in Oxford. She and an older woman,
Elizabeth Leavens, had in 1654 been the first Quakers to visit
that city 'where they suffered by the black tribe of scholars—
for they dragged them first through a dirty pool, afterwards
had them to a pump, and holding their mouths to the pump,
endeavoured to pump water thereinto with other shameful
abuses; after threw the said Elizabeth Fletcher down upon a
grave stone in a steeple house or graveyard, and bruised her so
sore that she never recovered it, but complained thereof to her
lives end, as a principle cause of her lingering weakness afterward.'[3] She was a 'very modest, grave young woman', 'innocent and comely', 'a virtuous maid, and of considerable family

[1] A.R.B. 260-2.
[2] A.R.B. 262-4.
[3] *F.P.T.* 258 and 259.

in the world'. The magistrates, not content with the riotous cruelty of the students, ordered Elizabeth to be 'severely whipped'. Even in spite of this treatment, she travelled in Ireland in the following year, and alone, until at Burrough's request, Elizabeth Smith of Gloucestershire came to be her companion, a fact reported with joy to Margaret in January 1656.

Burrough and Howgill remained in Ireland throughout the winter of 1655–6, the former leaving Dublin after a time to travel to Kilkenny and Waterford. Their letters to Margaret not only express the great love and admiration they felt for her, but give vivid pictures of Ireland. Of Dublin they write: 'It is a bad place, a very refuge for the wicked', and of the rest of the country: 'our service lays only in great towns and cities, for generally the country is without inhabitant, except bands of murderers and thieves and robbers which waits for their prey and devours many', and again: 'This is a rebellious people, and uncircumcised wholly, even they are the scum of England and other nations: they defy our God and saith who is He that they should obey him and hear his voice', and 'The rulers are seated in darkness and takes their ease in the flesh, upon their lofty mountain, and have turned their victory into their own exalting'.

Burrough asks Margaret to send some books to Ireland, and tells her that he had only received two letters from her since he had left England, six months before. He is thirsty to hear 'how the war prospers in England'.[1]

Howgill reported to Margaret that many influential people in Cork had been convinced, and by them he had been protected against the more persecuting Dubliners, when Cromwell's second son, Henry, was the Governor of Ireland. One of them, Colonel Phayre, Governor of Cork, said that more had been done by the Quakers than all the priests in the county had done in a hundred years.[2]

Leaving Ireland in March (1656) the two friends made a short visit to the north—Francis to see and arrange for his motherless children—then they returned to their work in London and the south. How arduous that work was in 1656 may be seen from

[1] Swm. MSS. Dated 5.11.1655 (Jan. 1656) from Waterford.
[2] A.R.B. 268.

a letter written to Margaret Fell by Francis Howgill: 'Oh, my dear, we are even almost spent in the service, it is so great, beyond declaring the harvest is almost lost in many parts for want of reaping; even the least who could but handle any instrument for God would be serviceable in the countries about. If there be any in the camp thereaways, send out. . . .

'Great is our care. Friends from all quarters comes daily. From Holland is come over from Amsterdam four Friends who is convinced and pretty. We speak to them by an interpreter. Four from London and 4 from Bristol are gone towards New England.'

George Fox was no longer there, with his powerful personality, his wisdom, and spiritual vitality; he was lingering most of that year (1656) in the foul dungeon called Doomsdale at the Cornish town of Launceston. So terrible was that imprisonment that during those eight months (Jan. to Sept. 1656) three Friends, Humphrey Norton, Joseph Nicholson of Bootle and young Richard Hubberthorne petitioned Oliver Cromwell to be allowed to lie there in place of their leader.[1] Each one was refused, though George Fox tells us in his Journal that the offer of Norton 'so struck him (O.C.) and came over him that he said to his great men and his Council, "which of you would do so much for me if I was in the same condition?"'

Whether Margaret was able to send any more Friends from the North to help Howgill in London is not recorded, but this year 1656 was a critical one in many ways, for in addition to the anxieties just related, there was serious trouble caused by James Nayler, a story told in a later chapter.

That Friends had faith in Margaret Fell's judgment and never-failing sympathy is shown in the variety of requests asked of her, and advice sought, and there was very great confidence in the efficacy of her prayers.

One day she would be asked to give her opinion on the wisdom or otherwise of a marriage, and then her help was appealed to as to how a Quaker marriage should be performed.[2] Here one

[1] Caton MSS. III, 360. Letter from R.H. to M.F. from London, 2.7.1656. See Camb. Jnl. I, 247.
[2] Swm. MSS. I, 357 and I, 358.

of the customs of the Commonwealth was helpful to Friends. At that time it had become legal for a Justice of the Peace to perform the marriage ceremony instead of the clergyman. Friends having no paid ministry, and being convinced that marriage was made by God, in the very early years of their movement decided on the means by which a marriage could be solemnized. In a Meeting for Worship called for the purpose, with as many witnesses and as much publicity as possible, both beforehand and at the time, the bride and bridegroom promise before God to take each other in marriage, and to be loving and faithful till death. Careful records in writing were to be kept, and in Commonwealth days the witness and signature of the Justice of the Peace. No marriage was to be contracted until the consent of parents or relatives had been given, and until the man and woman had appeared personally before their Meetings, though this last only became customary after 1666 when Monthly Meetings for the discipline or government of the Society were established. Indeed one important reason for the creation of this organization was because there had been some irregularity of marriages earlier. Margaret Fell herself,[1] and George Fox a little before, wrote a letter to Friends as early as 1656 to impress on them the need for orderly and legal marriage. Her suggestions for this machinery are in essence what is done still in the Society of Friends, and it says much for the wisdom of these seventeenth-century Friends that their simple but very exact procedure, coupled with a deeply spiritual background and careful preparation, have helped to produce marriages which so rarely result in unhappiness or divorce.

Another day Margaret would be told of dissensions and difficulties between Friends, 'a rebellious spirit [is] in many at Grayrigg, and it is stronger since Thomas Wilson came home than it was before'.[2] And three years earlier, Richard Hubberthorne had told her he had found troublesome spirits at Kendal, a special grief as such fine 'First Publishers' were already coming from that Meeting. 'This lay upon me from the Lord', he added, 'to declare it unto thee; dear sister, pray for me that I in the

[1] MSS. formerly in possession of Alaric Richardson, Ambleside, now of Isabel Ross.
[2] John Camm to M.F. 1656. Swm. MSS.

wisdom and power and life of God may be kept and preserved. If thou be moved to write to friends that ways, that that spirit may be kept down which judgeth the appearance of the life and motion of God in one another, and that they may wait in silence in their conditions who are not come to know the life nor motion of God, lest they judge the life and do harm to the prophets of the Lord.'[1]

Judging, and an over-abundance of words were creators of trouble then as now.

One of the many letters asking for her prayers was written by Josiah Coale on the eve of his voyage to the American Indians. He was the first of a long line of Quakers who befriended those people.

'Dear heart,' he wrote, 'when I was with thee I saw little of my going to Virginia with Thomas Thurston, but since I have been made sensible of the groanings of the oppressed seed in that place, unto which my soul's love dearly reaches, and I am much pressed in spirit to go there; and so to pass through the Indian's country amongst them and so to go into New England; and it is so upon my dear brother Tho. Thurston to go through with me. Dear, let thy prayers be that in unity and love we may be preserved and kept together faithful to the Lord, in his power and wisdom to stand continually, that so wheresoever the Lord calls us, we may have a good savour unto God in all his servants which shall come after us, which is the desire and breathings of my soul; that so the Lord alone may be honoured and glorified who is worthy. Dear heart, we have gotten promises of passage from Bristol, but it is like it will be near six weeks from this time before the shipping will be ready; glad and much refreshing would it be to me to receive a few lines from thee before we go, if thou art free, who art dear and my life is in thee, so my dear mother I bid thee farewell and am thine begotten again by the word of life,

Josiah Coale.

My dear and tender love is to thy daughter M.F. and to the rest of thy children and to Ann Clayton and the rest of thy servants who loves the truth.[2]

[1] Swm. MSS. I, 341.
[2] Swm. MSS. I, 377.
Josiah Coale was the Friend who helped William Penn with his father, the Admiral, when the young man first became a Quaker. As long as J. Coale was

Very few of Margaret Fell's letters to individual Friends have been preserved. One which she sent to John Camm during his last illness was described by him as 'full of marrow and fatness . . . it was like balm unto my head'.[1]

Some were felt to be important enough to have copies made at Swarthmoor before dispatch, Such was the case with one she wrote to Justice Anthony Pearson and his wife, and George Fox who was staying with them. It is given here as being probably typical of many of her own letters, written to enhearten her friends and to keep them faithful to the inwardness and spirituality of their religion. This letter was written in 1654, soon after Fox had left Swarthmoor on his journey to the Midlands and the South. It expresses her belief in Fox as specially chosen of God, and looking to the speedy triumph over the powers of darkness. Then to the Pearsons she continues: 'My dear hearts, wait upon the Lord and be faithful to him in that which is made manifest in you, and be not troubled about many things, but be constant and faithful in that one thing which is necessary, and you shall see the Lord present, and near; for he is not a God afar off, but where he is a God it is where he is near at hand and where something of him is witnessed and possessed there he is a God, but to them that look at him afar off, and without them, there he is not known and so they ignorantly worship the unknown God.

'And dear brother Anthony, thou hast been serviceable to the Lord since thou was called, thou shalt not lose thy reward; if thou wilt thou shalt see the treasure of infinite riches open to thee, and the inheritance which never fades away, but runs and streams out afresh; the Lord God of power preserve you and keep you faithful, waiting in the pure [Life] which will lead you up to God, who is pure and eternal, and to him be eternal glory and praise for ever.'[2]

Perhaps Margaret in her wisdom sensed in the character of

---

present, the father 'kept his temper', the old account tells us. (Jnl. F.H.S. XXXII, 24.)

J. Coale died in 1668. The only piece of verse written by Margaret Fell was an elegy after his death. (From the *Works* of J. Coale, at the Bevan Naish Library, Woodbrooke, Birmingham.)

[1] Caton MSS. III, 482.
[2] Swm. MSS. III, 100.

Anthony Pearson something of a weakness or inconsistency which seems to appear in a letter[1] dated May 1657 from John Lilburne to Margaret Fell. Lilburne, the Leveller and formerly a lieutenant-general in Cromwell's Army, had become a Quaker, and in 1657 had a serious dispute with Anthony Pearson about some land in Durham. The letter beginning 'Dearly beloved friend Margaret Fell' explains the whole complicated case to her. Lilburne in his faith in her capacity both to understand the legal position as well as the justice of the case, told her, 'Thy clearly judged by me preciousness and clearness of understanding, hath in no small measure filled me with desires at this present time to acquaint thee'. Whether Margaret and Fox and other leaders who had also been appealed to by Lilburne, were able to help in the case is doubtful, for very soon afterwards Lilburne died, and probably the quarrel was never resolved. Perhaps however it was a cause of Anthony Pearson's giving up his Quakerism soon after the Restoration.

While Margaret Fell was an encourager of the humble, she was a fearless critic and denouncer of the hypocrite, the vain, the spreader of disunity, the selfish. She called upon such men and women to test the Light they felt within them by their deeds and the effect of those deeds on their Meetings and on their families and neighbours. If they led to ill-will then their Light was not the Light of Christ. It was of course this also that George Fox taught, from the beginning of his public teaching. It was the fall from this consistency of inward emotion and outward behaviour which lay at the back of the 'fall' of James Nayler (Chapter 8). It was to create and make permanent this balance of mysticism and practice that George Fox drew up the organization of the Society step by step in these and following years.

Hospitality was the custom at Swarthmoor Hall from the beginning of the married life of Judge and Margaret Fell. After George Fox's first visit, its warm welcome extended to such numbers that, as William Caton tells us, 'at one time there would have been Friends out of five or six counties'.[2] Sarah Fell told the historian Sewel that once when her father returned with his

[1] Thirnbeck MSS. 2.
[2] *Life of W. Caton*, p. 9.

servants from his judicial circuit he found in the stables so many horses of strange guests (though his wife had cleared the stable where they first stood, to make room for her husband's own horses) that he told his wife that they would be eaten out of their provision of hay. But Margaret replied in a friendly way, that she did not believe that by the end of the year they would have the less for that. And so it proved, that they had so much hay that they had much to sell.[1]

Scattered about in the letters to Margaret are constant references to her hospitality and what refreshment it gave. 'It was good to be there,'[2] wrote Caton on one of his return visits, and again, 'After my great travels I always found it a place of refreshment to me, both for soul and body'.[3] Not only did she give them spiritual food, but well-cooked food from the busy kitchen, home brewed cider and drinks made from country plants. They had soft feather mattresses in the big carved oak four-poster beds, and large airy panelled bedrooms, and they listened to the gentle murmur of the brook which ran through the garden, and the voices of happy children and busy people— a peaceful comfortable home to live in.

Much of her help was given to the wives and children left behind when the husbands had gone to carry the message. The wife of Myles Halhead once complained that she would rather have married a drunkard, for then she would at least have known she could have found him at the ale-house. She lived however to change her mind, and become a true supporter, like the others. The sturdy independence of these wives is remarkable; they were left to carry on the farm, or the shop, or the estate, often caring for little children as well. Letters from their husbands were rare, for a penny post, for one folded sheet without an envelope, was only introduced in 1680 and then only for London, though a postal system had been established in 1635 by Charles I.[4] Off the main post road, carriers would take the letters. The Fells employed a man, John Higgins, and others, to bring their letters across the sands from Lancaster, or over the fells

---

[1] Sewel, I, 142.
[2] *Life of W. Caton*, p. 41.
[3] *Life of W. Caton*, p. 47.
[4] *Early Friends and the Post*, by S. Graveson, Jnl. F.H.S. XXXII, p. 27.

from Kendal. Even as late as 1678 it took twenty-three days for a letter from Robert Barclay of Ury, near Aberdeen, to reach Sarah Fell at Swarthmoor; the letter having been posted at Edinburgh, travelled to London and then to the distant north-west.[1]

Sometimes Margaret would arrange to look after the children, when both father and mother were away, as was the case when John Stubbs and his wife were together in London. John Stubbs, scholar and formerly soldier, was convinced by George Fox's imprisonment in Carlisle in 1653, and later travelled extensively, in Holland, Ireland, Scotland, Italy, Egypt and America. He was many times in danger of the Inquisition. Sewel tells us that he was a man skilled, not only in Latin, Greek and Hebrew, but also in Oriental languages. He was very helpful to Margaret in arranging for a translation into Hebrew of her books for the Jews (a story related in another chapter).[2]

The Stubbs had come to live for a time at Ulverston, no doubt to be near Margaret and the Swarthmoor Meeting, while the father was travelling in the ministry.

In September 1657, John Stubbs having recently returned from Scotland, went to London on his way to Holland. His gratitude for Margaret's friendship and for her letters was intense. He told her that he had heavenly visions of her which had brought great peace to his weary soul;[3] and a little later he wrote to her as his 'dear counsellor and comforter', adding, 'The truth is I have none now in England that I know of that I have so much freedom to impart my secret intent as thou and my wife, neither do I judge any so fit (who now is in the nation as I know) as thyself to determine upon my present condition, for all hath not the spirit of knowledge and wisdom and discerning,

---

[1] *Rel. Bar.* p. 45.

[2] He was part author with George Fox and Benjamin Furly of Amsterdam of a remarkable book called 'The Battledore' (the full title was *A Battledore for Teachers and Professors to learn singular and Plural, &c*), published in 1660, written to prove that the insistence on the use of 'thee' and 'thou' to an individual, whatever his social standing (a Quaker custom which was extremely irritating to the seventeenth-century Englishman) was justified by the presence of singular and plural for that personal pronoun in thirty different languages. Examples from those languages, and printed in their own characters, make the book a unique specimen of the printers' art.

[3] Abraham MSS. 3.

or rather not the spirit of pity, compassion and love to mourn with those that mourn, and to have a fellow-feeling of another's misery, and so cannot mourn with them. This gift is not given to all, but blessed be the Lord for it. I have experienced it often from thee, that many times I have admired it, but it hath been revealed unto me, that the Lord had made thee, as it were, an interpreter one of a thousand, for truly I could write if it were lawful to utter, great and weighty things in this particular, of thy appearance to me since I saw thee last in the outward, but silence flesh for ever.'[1]

When the 'Publishers of Truth' went forth to preach, they travelled chiefly at their own expense. They went on foot, walking along footpaths and bridle paths, fell roads and high roads; or on horseback. In Cornwall at any rate they became known as being well-horsed, their beasts a temptation to the greedy informers. Many of these men and women however were poor in this world's goods, and Margaret Fell was the first to help to lighten their burden. She founded a fund, giving generously to it herself. She appointed two Friends of Kendal, Thomas Willan and George Taylor, to be her agents, primarily for disbursements and later for collection also.

Collection was not always easy—one critic, while giving a donation, doubted if such financial help was truly according to the teaching of Christ.[2] The enemies of Quakerism sometimes took the same attitude, and tried to make capital out of such a fund existing among a people who denied a paid ministry, and who scorned the 'hireling priest'. One only has to read these accounts, carefully preserved for nearly three centuries among the Swarthmoor MSS. to see how little justification there was for the jibe.

The first accounts begin in June 1654, soon after the Publishers of Truth set out from the north to the south, though the agents record that earlier payments had already been made. Before the year ended, Margaret appealed to all the Meetings in Lancashire, Westmorland and Cumberland.[3] Later similar

[1] Swm. MSS. I, 92. 19.8.1657.
[2] Letter from M.F. to Ambrose Appleby, 1654. MSS. Box, 10, 7, Library, Friends' House, London.
[3] Thirnbeck MSS. I, and M.F. *Works*, pp. 56-9.

Judge Thomas Fell of Swarthmoor,
Margaret Fell's first husband

(*from reputed portrait at the Town Hall, Barrow-in-Furness*)

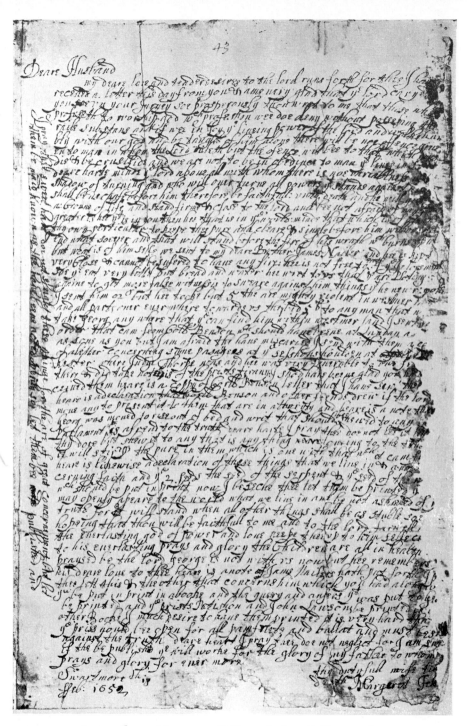

*Letter from Margaret Fell to Judge Fell in 1653
in her own handwriting*

collections were made in Bishoprick, under the leadership of Anthony Pearson, and in Yorkshire, through Thomas Killam.

Several times Margaret sent epistles to the meetings, between 1654 and 1658, appealing to their generosity. She was careful to base her appeal on the need for unity and fellowship, 'so you may come to be one with them (the brethren) in their sufferings, in their travails, troubles, buffettings, whippings, stebings [=scoffings], prisonings, beatings in the synagogues, hailings before magistrates, who is sent as lambs among wolves, among whom there is no mercy'. 'Oh dear hearts', she wrote to them, 'put your hands to this work, and be not slack but up and be doing in the name and power of Jesus and in the fear of the Lord offer freely to his service that in your freeness and willingness . . . your brethren may be refreshed.' She told them that the collections were needed to provide necessities for those Friends called 'into several nations, as Holland, Barbados, Ireland, Scotland and Flanders, Denmark and Germany, all these within this month, and a great part of them North country Friends. So the Lord God of peace open your hearts. . . . So let [every man] give, not grudgingly nor of necessity, for the Lord loves a cheerful giver.'[1]

Next year she made a special appeal for some North Country Friends 'that are poor in the outward', and who yet wished to go to New England, that home of Puritans whose fathers had fled from persecution, but who themselves were savage persecutors of Friends. Passage across the Atlantic was to cost five pounds a-piece (fifty pounds in modern money), and there were four or **five** of them, giving up 'all for the service of Truth'.[2]

That George Taylor and Thomas Willan held a difficult position at Kendal, there is no doubt from their remarks in several of the large number of the letters they wrote to Margaret. 'Truly sister, this service lies heavily sometime, and especially how to supply the faithful and truly serviceable, and miss or avoid the maintaining of deceit, but our ends being for the truth it is made lighter.'[3] Sometimes the cost of postage was unreasonably changed, the charge of 3/– being raised to 4/–, as the

[1] Miller MSS. 65. About 1656.
[2] Spence MSS, III, 10.
[3] Swm. MSS. I, 255.

postman 'doth but play upon us here',[1] it would be better to use the weekly carrier who only charged 2d. 'for what now costs 2/– or 3/–'.

Sometimes the calls on the purse were so many and insistent, that the 'public stock' (as the fund came to be called) was low, and the two agents were 'out of purse at present'. Then in 1658 there were murmurings against the administration of one of the Kendal agents, and some Kendal Friends went so far as to attack the whole conception of supplying money to the ministering Friends who were travelling even in England.[2]

However, the fund continued and developed and soon the south had a fund collected and administered by its own Meetings, the north-eastern counties also had a separate one, specially for the work in Scotland, while the north-western counties were still under the care of Margaret and her agents. This financial organization was the first step to the Yearly Meeting Fund and all its ramifications which is the financial basis of the modern British Society of Friends.

The old accounts themselves throw flashes of light on the life of a wandering Friend. John Story of Westmorland had £1.4.9. given him for 'clothes making and furniture and mending', Edward Burrough when he went to London had a 'kase of knives' given him which cost the fund 3/6, Thomas Holme, a weaver of Kendal had to be supplied with shoes and a pair of 'britches', at the cost of 10/6, Elizabeth Leavens who later became his wife, had to have £1.3.0. worth of clothing provided for her. Elizabeth Fletcher's hat cost 2/4, which compared with a pair of shoes 'to a friend poore' at 1/10, sounds as if it was a very good hat; let us hope it kept out the rain. It cost 1/– to send Francis Howgill's forgotten cloak after him, and John Browne received clothes costing 7/8, a pair of 'britches' 2/8, and 6/– for 'bringing and carrying B. Fletcher's horse to and again'.

Little Alice Birket, a servant maid, who had been put into the House of Correction in Kendal, and there kept for three days without food or drink, received 4/– during her imprisonment, a pair of shoes (2/6), and on her release 3/– 'at her going for Cheshire'.

[1] Spence MSS. III, 7.
[2] Swm. MSS. I, 317 and IV, 80.

Prisoners are often mentioned—£1.3.0. for those at Appleby in 1654, and 18/– spent on books for George Fox when a prisoner at Carlisle. Prisoners at Norwich, Cambridge Castle, Lancaster and Bedford, had both money and books sent to them.

In 1655 there are larger disbursements to Friends abroad, in Ireland (£1), £2 for a Friend to go to New England, £1 for Wm. Caton to help him to go to Holland, and 10/– for Elizabeth Coward travelling to Venice. The visit to Scotland by several Friends in 1655 cost the fund £16. 'A Bible and other necessaries' cost 7/6. Elizabeth Coward was given a waistcoat and petticoat, the 'making and furnishing' of which came to 19/2, and then she had 3/– to take her into the south.

It is not surprising that there are frequent payments for mending of shoes.

One month the postage on letters and the carriage of parcels for Friends amounts to as much as £1.5.8. Total disbursements varied from £3 to £10 for a month, considerable sums for those days.

Nor were the prisoner's families forgotten, as the entry of 3/– for a cheese for T. Taylor's wife shows.

Prisoners paid fees to the jailer, so Jane Waugh had 4/6 sent her 'for charges in prison, 18 days'.

The last entries are of the 8th month (October) 1658:

To Anthony Pinder that he and Thomas Taylor borrowed to relieve Richard Bennett that was like to famish in Appleby Gaol	6.	8
To Ambrose Rigg for cloth for a pr. of britches	10.	0
To Jo. Braythwaite p. Thos. Atkinson for a pr. of boots	10.	0
For John Stubbs at his going towards Jerusalem	£2. 14.	2

Sometimes letters reached Margaret setting out the need for help; Thomas Holme wrote from prison on behalf of eight prisoners who were forced by the tyranny of the jailer to pay twopence a night for each of their beds.[1] Another time she was asked to send up £20 to London 'for printing books'.[2] Later on, in 1668, even after the fund had expanded into a national affair she still received requests for help 'in the outward'. Henry Woods, arrested at a Meeting in Bury, Lancashire, was one of

[1] Swm. MSS. I, 189. Dated 1653.
[2] Caton MSS. III, 480.

several Quaker prisoners in Lancaster Castle where she herself
was still a prisoner. From one cell to another he wrote to tell her
that they lacked some necessaries, and asked her 'if thou have
any such at Lancaster to lend us a while, as something to keep
a little drink in, something to fetch a little water in, or such odd
things, and we will carefully look unto and restore back when
thou pleased'.[1] Sometimes the travellers refused the proffered
aid. 'We could get honest Richard Hubberthorne to take no
money',[2] wrote the Kendal agents to Margaret in 1655, and
Mary Howgill, sister to Francis Howgill, bravely wrote once to
Margaret, 'The burden hath been great to many, and as for me
I can follow my calling as without me, or otherwise I have of
my own. I shall not be chargeable to any.'

This chapter cannot end without mention of the valuable help
given from the fund to Thomas Lawson. Scholar and botanist,
he had, as we have seen, relinquished the living of Rampside in
Furness at Fox's first visit to his church. He became one of the
'First Publishers', travelling in Sussex and elsewhere for some
years with John Slee of Cumberland. In 1657 he stayed at
Swarthmoor, but the mistress was absent. He therefore left a
note for her on her return when he moved on across the sands
to visit Robert Widders at Kellett (near Carnforth). He wanted
her to know that when he was at Newcastle, he met a relative
who was an excellent Hebrew scholar, from whom he had
bought a Hebrew Lexicon, but only by borrowing ten shillings.
He asks Margaret if she could pay back this debt from the fund.
He had also bought for five shillings a Greek dictionary so as to
be able to study the New Testament. 'If it please the Lord to give
me an abode in the earth', adds the homeless man, 'I know I may
do service therewith.' Evidently he hoped Judge Fell might
help him to establish himself in Ulverston. Two years later
Lawson was a schoolmaster near Penrith, 'as the first of the
distinguished line of great Quaker schoolmasters'.[3]

Hats, shoes, breeches, Hebrew Lexicons, Greek dictionaries,
Bibles—all these and much else were the necessaries of the First
Publishers of Truth, supplied by the Swarthmoor Fund, part of
the tender care practised by Margaret Fell.

[1] Swm. MSS. I, 130. Dated 13.2.1668.
[2] Swm. MSS. I, 252. Dated 17.7.1655.   [3] B. Qism. p. 370 and note.
The accounts of the Kendal Fund 1654-7 are printed in *Jnl. F.H.S.*
vol. 6 (1909) pp. 49-52, 82-85, 127-128.

Chapter Six

MARGARET FELL AND MEMBERS OF SWARTHMOOR MEETING, FROM 1652

'*In the same year 1652, in the Government of Oliver Cromwell, the Word of the Lord came unto me, saying, Go thy ways to Swarthmoor, where my lambs and babes, and Children of Light will be gathered together to wait upon my Name: I will feed them with the finest of wheat, and with honey out of the rock; and with the Dew of Heaven I will refresh them, that they may grow as plants of my right hand planting, that above all the families of the Earth I may rejoyce to do them good. So I freely gave up, and took my Journey towards Swarthmoor, . . . So I parted with her, and went to Swarthmoor, where I found the Lord's People gathered together, to wait upon his Name, and the Lord was very good unto that family in feeding them according to his promise.*'

Myles Halhead, *Sufferings and Passages*, p. 4 seq. 1690.

'*And when I thus behold thee in the invisible, if I be in sufferings, I am comforted, if weary and heavy laden I am eased and refreshed, seeing thy hand stretched forth to me, to draw me nigher and nigher unto thee, that thou mayest take part with me of my sufferings. . . .*'

From a letter to Margaret Fell from William Caton in 1657.

(Swm. MSS. I, 316.)

DURING the Commonwealth years, the Meeting at Swarthmoor Hall suffered comparatively little from persecution, owing to the protection of Judge Fell. What violence there was, was against a few individuals by over-zealous justices or vicars; the chief members were left in peace enough to be able to establish the Meeting in strength. There is a curious reference in a letter of Humphrey Norton to George Fox in April 1656 (while the latter lay at Launceston), to 'many speakers and prayers' at Swarthmoor Meeting 'and such a singing as the like I have not heard and likewise a lightness amongst them which I saw',[1] and so he offered himself to be imprisoned instead of Fox, as he was

[1] Camb. Jnl. I, 245.

convinced that Fox's presence was needed in the meetings. This
accusation drew forth a spirited reply from Margaret Fell, who
utterly denied that the meeting had a 'lightness' in it.

Whatever lies behind this criticism, Swarthmoor possessed
enough spiritual vitality to send forth ten of its own members
(other than Margaret and her daughters) to many parts of the
world to win over to Quakerism many men and women. In
their absence these missionaries looked back to their fellow-
members, especially to Margaret Fell, with deep love, knowing
that they in turn were in constant remembrance. These men and
women of the Swarthmoor household and meeting were particularly indebted to Margaret for the nurturing of the new
truth which had come to them. They, even more than the
Friends of the north-west mentioned in the previous chapter,
were indeed an important part of her life.

Even those who remained behind were kept busy, for it was
at Swarthmoor Hall that letters were constantly being copied
out by hand and sent forth to Meetings. One instance of this
will suffice: in 1656 George Bishop of Bristol enclosed with a
letter to Margaret a packet of letters received from the imprisoned George Fox, which were to be duplicated at Swarthmoor and then sent on to Meetings in Scotland and Northern
England. Bishop himself had undertaken to make copies and
send them to the Isle of Man, Ireland, Wales and London. George
Bishop also asked that copies of some writings which George
Fox had dictated earlier should now be sent by Margaret to him
in Cornwall to be dispatched thence to France.

Many of the copies of letters sent to individuals were made by
Will Caton and Henry Fell, before they left for their travels or
on their return visits. The other copyists are unknown, but one
was named Stephen for he wrote on his copy 'Copied over by
me Stephen for I am but weak and not strong in the Lord'.[1]

One of the first members of the Meeting to leave Swarthmoor
was Ann Clayton (mentioned already in Chapter 2). Before
sailing for Barbados, Boston and Rhode Island she was in
prison in Lancaster Castle both in 1654 and 1655[2] (where on
both occasions she tells of Colonel William West's great kind-

---

[1] Swm. MSS. IV, 171.
[2] Swm. MSS. I, 310 and Swm. MSS. I, 380.

ness to prisoners). She is frequently mentioned with affection in the letters of other members of the Swarthmoor household. She was a woman of intrepid courage.

Possibly the next to leave Swarthmoor was William Caton. Friend, companion, tutor and secretary, there can be no doubt that his travels throughout England and later to Holland were directly inspired by talks with Margaret Fell.

His experiences in England were a valuable training for the more difficult work abroad. He left Swarthmoor in January 1655, at the age of eighteen, and went southwards, and eastwards. 'Oh! The tears that were shed among us at our parting; oh! the prayers and intercessions that were made to the Lord', he wrote some years later in his Journal, 'so exceedingly were we united and bound up together, that it was very hard for us to part one with another.'[1] He travelled through several counties, and came after two or three weeks to Norwich. 'It being in the depth of winter, and we travelling altogether on foot, it was something hard to the outward man; but the Lord was with us, and his mighty power upheld us, and carried us through all, and through mercy we got finally well to Norwich, where there were several of our north country Friends in prison, whom we visited, and with whom we were sweetly refreshed.'

Eventually he came to London, where, as we have seen, some Friends, notably Edward Burrough, Francis Howgill, and George Fox himself, were already having large meetings among the Baptists and Independents, often with great success. Soon there came also James Nayler from Yorkshire, whose dynamic personality and powerful preaching did great service for a time. Throughout 1655 Caton with John Stubbs travelled in the south, chiefly in Kent, meeting often with opposition and cruelty, but sometimes with kindness and sympathy. One of their converts in Kent was Samuel Fisher, the Baptist scholar. At Maidstone, Caton visited the meeting of the Independents, and Stubbs the Baptists, after which they were both arrested 'and the day after'[2] he wrote to Margaret, from London, 'we were brought before the magistrates, examined, and sent to the house of correction, and there we were searched, and had our

---

[1] *Life of W. Caton*, p. 13.
[2] *Life of W. Caton*, pp. 26–7.

money and our inkhorns and a Bible and such things as we had
in our pockets, taken from us; and then had to the stocks, and
there we were stripped and whipped, and then had irons and
great clogs of wood laid upon us; and in that manner with such
cruel using of us, they would have compelled us to have
wrought,[1] but we did see our calling that it was at that time to
suffer for the testimony of the Truth, and not to be subject nor
slaves to their wills.' The two Quakers refused to give in. 'By
the entreaty of some soldiers and others we had only a little
water once a day, which was all they would suffer us to have for
several days together; some there was that privately would have
given us meat, but we were not free to take any man's bread for
nought.'

Many other extracts from his letters to Margaret might be
quoted, showing the courage and faithfulness of this young man
from Swarthmoor. He kept her fully informed of his ventures.

During his travels in Kent, he met with Dutch people for the
first time, at their church at Sandwich. In June 1655 he made
a short visit to Calais where he had a meeting with several of the
important people, a Scottish lord acting as interpreter. After
further travelling in the Eastern counties of England, Caton,
together with John Stubbs, sailed for Holland in September.
Owing to delays, the two men were forced to come as far north
as Sunderland to get passage, and while waiting there for a ship,
Caton could not resist walking across England—a matter of
over a hundred miles, over the Pennines—to see his friends at
Swarthmoor again. 'Oh, the refreshment which we had at our
meeting', he wrote in his Journal, '. . . and dear M.F. (who had
been as a tender-hearted nursing mother unto me) was refreshed
to hear how the Lord had been with me.'[2] After a short stay,
Caton recrossed England, met Stubbs again, and the two men
sailed for Holland. To encourage them on their way, Margaret
sent a little letter of love and joy after them, addressed to them
at 'Sunderland or Newcastle, or if they have taken shipping,
with the first messenger . . . to Holland'.[3]

On this short visit, their first, both men being ignorant of the

[1] Wrought = worked.
[2] *Life of W. Caton*, p. 32.
[3] This letter now is in the possession of Isabel Ross.

Dutch language, they concentrated almost entirely on the English and Scottish people living in Holland, but they had little success amongst them. The courage of these two men is even more appreciated when we read that during this time, September 1655, the plague was raging there, 13,287 people dying of it in Amsterdam in the latter half of that year.

On their return to England Caton again visited Swarthmoor —for refreshment—and in mid-winter, he and Stubbs walked to Scotland, where early in 1656 they had great success, being in friendly contact with both Colonel William Osborne, and General Monk who was at that time Commander-in-Chief of the English Army in occupation of Scotland.

During the next few months, this indefatigable traveller journeyed on foot, often alone, through Northumberland and Durham, Lancashire and Cheshire, Leicestershire, Cumberland and into Scotland again in June 1656—that 'dark and barbarous country'[1] as he called it, and again 'that barren and rude country'—comments on the devastation of General Monk's campaigns. Back through Cumberland where many were turning to Quakerism, to Swarthmoor they came again, then on his travels to Bristol, Devonshire and Cornwall, where he visited George Fox and several other Friends imprisoned in Launceston Castle, then eastwards to Kent and London. As he journeyed, this twenty year old man preached in churches, in market-places, in houses, ignorant beforehand of what he was to say, relying on the gift of words when he spoke. 'Yet hath the Lord been pleased to give me his word so plentifully, that through him I was enabled to speak two or three, yea, sometimes four hours in a meeting with little or no intermission.'

In September (1656) William Caton, in spite of bodily ills owing to his strenuous travels, was drawn to visit Holland again. He went to strengthen the work of John Stubbs and William Ames, who had recently returned from that country. It was during this visit that he first made contact with the Jews. 'I was also at the Jews' Synagogue at Amsterdam',[2] he wrote in his Journal, 'upon one of their Sabbath days; and staying most of the time of their worship, I beheld the manner of it, which was very strange in divers respects.'

[1] *Life of W. Caton*, p. 46. [2] *Life of W. Caton*, p. 56.

William Caton continued for the rest of his short life (he died in December 1665) to devote his energies to Holland, Germany, England and Scotland. Sometimes his travelling companions were also of Swarthmoor—John Stubbs, Bridget and Isabel Fell. Of all Margaret's correspondents, Caton was the most affectionate and grateful. She was so much a part of his life that he had vivid visions of her which he delighted to describe to her—he saw her sitting 'spinning flax most joyfully, being clothed with honour and beauty . . . arrayed like a lily of the field';[1] another time she was 'fruitful in a glorious plantation'.[2] At the reading of her letters to him, 'the very power of the Lord did spring up',[3] he wrote once from London.

In Holland, Caton sometimes had much discouragement, partly because the Meetings were small, partly because of the extravagant behaviour of some who came in, but he occupied himself a good deal with publishing and spreading Quaker literature, not only amongst the Jews but also amongst the Dutch. This he did at Margaret Fell's desire.[4]

He and his colleague William Ames had Quaker books translated into German also, so that they could be dispersed in the territory of the Palatinate, whose Prince was very tolerant and friendly to William Ames.

In 1658 Caton told Margaret that a Friend had gone to Denmark, had talked with the King and given him books.[5]

Caton was the author of three books in Dutch and several pamphlets, and he translated some Epistles. His book in English was an abridgement of *The Ecclesiastical History of Eusebius Pamphilus*, with as an introduction a charming treatise on education called *General Epistle for Young Scholars and Little Children*, in which he gives some details of his spiritual struggles in his schooldays. He wrote the book so as to bring home to his readers the similarity of the persecution of the Quakers with that of the early Christians.

In 1661 Caton went into Germany with William Ames, and

[1] Caton MSS. III, 31.
[2] Caton MSS, III, 32.
[3] Caton MSS. III, 16.
[4] Caton MSS. III, 39 and 40.
[5] Caton MSS. III, 509.

had valuable talks with notable people. At Heidelberg Caton had many hours on several occasions with the Prince of the Palatinate; at Frankfort he met the Jews in their synagogue, and had discussions (in Latin) with Roman Catholic priests who were so angry with him that they beat him furiously and left him bleeding on the floor of the cathedral; at Worms he had a long talk with the head of the Jesuits' College. At Kreisheim, where was a small group of Friends, Caton and Ames helped them to gather their grapes, as on another occasion he had helped with the harvest at Swarthmoor. Once at Heidelberg, when Caton was alone, he met John Stubbs and Henry Fell, on their return home from Alexandria and Italy, after they had failed to reach the Far East. All three men visited the Prince and discussed with him the question of tithes and Friends in his dominions. Henry Fell reported to their friends at Swarthmoor that Caton was much loved and 'is and hath been a good savour to Truth'.[1]

A month or two before he died he visited and took relief (including shirts and other necessaries) to the English prisoners of war in Amsterdam, following the war between the Dutch and the English. Such was the respect felt to Caton by non-Friends in Holland that he was personally helped by the Burgomaster who was also Lord of the Admiralty, who gave him complete liberty to do this relief work.[2] He was the first of a long line of Quakers who have helped prisoners of war.

Three years before his death (at the age of twenty-nine), Caton married a Dutch Friend, Anneken Dirrix, and before doing so he wrote long letters both to Swarthmoor Meeting and to Margaret Fell and George Fox, asking for their loving approval and blessing. His was the first Quaker marriage in Holland.

There were four Salthouse brothers, of Dragley Beck, Ulverston, Robert, William, Thomas and John, all Friends. Thomas was a 'mercer or shopkeeper',[3] and steward to the Fell family. William was a shoemaker, Robert travelled in the Isle of Man, Scotland and elsewhere (sometimes with Leonard Fell and at other times with Will Caton), and John was employed by Friends

---

[1] Swm. MSS. IV, 171.

[2] Swm. MSS. I, 350 and W. I. Hull, *Qism. in Amsterdam*, p. 174.

[3] *Original Records of Sufferings*, p. 290, MS. at Library, Friends' House, London.

in London in 1671 and was servant to George Fox during his bitter imprisonment in Worcester in 1673.[1] Thomas was the most gifted of the four. Convinced in 1652, he became a noted preacher, travelling from Meeting to Meeting in Devon and Cornwall and other parts of S.W. England. In 1670 he married Anne Upcott, daughter of the priest of St. Austell.[2] He seems to have left Swarthmoor in 1655, travelling to the south-west where he and his companion (Myles Halhead) met with an imprisonment worse than that of the criminals, due to their refusal to take the Oath of Abjuration, and further punishment due to their refusal to promise to return to their own county, 'choosing rather to suffer imprisonment or banishment out of the land than to purchase outward freedom by making a covenant with death and so bring ourselves into inward bondage'.[3] Besse in his *Collection of the Sufferings of the People called Quakers*, described this charge of vagrancy 'an illegal proceeding against men of substance and reputation, who travelled on horseback, lodged at the best inns, and paid punctually for what they had there'.[4] Then Besse adds, 'In their passage between Taunton and Bridgwater, the officer charged with them was suddenly seized with a kind of apoplectic fit, which disabled him from going any farther; they returned to Taunton, and informed a Justice of the Peace of what had happened, desiring to know his pleasure concerning them. He thereupon suspended any farther execution of the warrant, and set them at liberty, wishing that the Lord might be with them.'[5] That Thomas longed to go home, and only stayed in the south from a stern sense of duty is seen in a loving letter to Margaret Fell from Bristol, in which he wrote, 'Our life is in the North, but a weight is laid upon us, that we see no way of our return at present. . . . A word from thee I long for, for truly my life is in thee. Remember my dear love to all Friends, to all thy dear children, plants of the Lord's renown, growing in his garden which thou dost water daily.'[6]

[1] Letter from Geo. Fox to Margaret Fox, 21.11.1673, now in Philadelphia.
[2] *A Quaker Saint of Cornwall*, by L. V. Hodgkin.
[3] Caton MSS. III, 86.
[4] Besse's *Sufferings*, I, p. 146.
[5] Ibid.
[6] Caton MSS. III, 73. 27.2.1655?

A little later, Thomas's companion was able to report to Margaret that their sufferings had not been in vain, for many people 'of outward importance' had been convinced by them, and that their enemies had at last become loving and even serviceable to them.[1] In fact, soon the two men experienced a victorious release—'Yesterday', he wrote in a letter to Margaret, 'we were freed from outward bonds by order of the Major, who is governor of this city. He sent the Cornet of his troop to bid the keeper of the prison release us. So the keeper said he was glad of it with all his heart. And he bade us take our time and go forth when we would. So as we find drawings we shall go, that the power and presence of the Lord may go along with us.'[2]

To write to Margaret was a joy to him. In a letter from Durham he fills a page with his expressions of love and admiration, and then adds, 'Dear heart, it's my unfeigned love to thee, that causeth this ink and paper; for I have no extraordinary thing to acquaint thee of.'[3] In another he writes of her 'wisdom, innocency, singleness of heart, humility and integrity'.[4]

Leonard Fell was one of the 'family' convinced in June 1652 (see Chapter 2). His exact position in the household is not known, but he was a retainer of some education, his father being a small landowner (yeoman) of Baycliffe, a grey-stoned village on the edge of Morecambe Bay, some three miles from the Hall, and close by the old Quaker burial ground of Sunbreck. He travelled in many parts of England and Scotland, sometimes in the company of George Fox, and of Margaret Fell and her daughters. On one occasion he was sent by Fox to establish the organization of Monthly Meetings in Westmorland (1667).[5]

In the Commonwealth time he was one of several of Swarthmoor Meeting imprisoned in Lancashire for speaking to the priests. Besse in his *Sufferings* writes, 'As they esteemed it their Christian duty to exhort both priests and people to repentance and amendment of life, they discharged that duty through many afflictions, knowing that as the sufferings of Christ abounded in

[1] Caton MSS. III, 94–6, 1656, from Exeter Gaol.
[2] Caton MSS. III, 103. Exeter.
[3] Caton MSS. III, 109, etc., 1658 or 1659.
[4] Caton MSS. III, 118.
[5] Camb. Jnl. II, 113.

them, so their consolation also abounded in him.'[1] On one occasion (in 1654) to emphasize the illegality of his sentence he refused to leave the prison unless he was put out by authority, who had put him in, but who had ceased to guard him.[2] After the Restoration of Charles II he was many times imprisoned, for being in Meeting at Swarthmoor, or for refusing to pay tithes. For preaching at a Meeting at Windermere he suffered the loss of twenty pounds' worth of malt.[3] In the old Minute Book of Lancaster Monthly Meeting and Lancashire Quarter Meeting, Leonard Fell's name appears as representative from Swarthmoor, or as trustee to a fund for the care and apprenticeship of Quaker orphans. Even at seventy-one, 'dear ancient Leonard Fell . . . once again [has] come to visit and encourage [Friends] in the ancient spring of life',[4] as the records of some Scottish Meetings relate. A number of his letters to Margaret Fell are still extant, filled with love and affection both to her and the Swarthmoor Meeting.

Another member of the Swarthmoor Meeting to go forth to preach was Richard Clayton, who suffered imprisonment in Norwich and Lancaster.[5] He travelled in Cornwall and North Ireland, and tried, apparently in vain, to go to Norway[6] with James Lancaster. He was probably a brother of the adventurous Ann Clayton.

Henry Fell, like Leonard, was no relation to Judge Fell, but was a member of the household, and perhaps the Judge's clerk. Possibly he was acting in that capacity when the Judge crossed the sands in June 1652, to be met by Priest Lampitt and his friends with the news of George Fox's visit to his family. Henry was convinced, and by 1655, when he was twenty-five, he had set out to publish 'Truth'. He was an educated man, as his beautifully written and correctly spelt letters show.[7] In a long series of remarkable letters to Margaret Fell, he told of his work and

---

[1] Besse's *Sufferings*, I, p. 303.
[2] Swm. MSS. I, 116.
[3] Besse's *Sufferings*, p. 321.
[4] Jnl. F.H.S. XII, 143.
[5] Swm. MSS. I, 344. Swm. MSS. I, 56.
[6] Caton MSS. III, 30 (**pp. 49-50**).
[7] We are told that he was of 'middle stature . . . with brown curled hair'. Luke Howard MSS. Jnl. F.H.S. Vol 38, p. 38.

his travels, in England and overseas. In 1656 he felt drawn to go
to Barbados. He sailed from Bristol, where the Friend, George
Bishop, saw to the booking of the passage and provision of all
necessaries for him. Henry Fell made his last-minute arrangements for the long voyage, in a letter to his friend and former
companion, Thomas Rawlinson of Graythwaite in Furness, who
was then in Exeter prison with James Nayler and some twenty
other Friends. To him he wrote: 'I leave my little mare here,
either to be sold or else sent into the North to Swarthmoor to
be disposed of as Margaret Fell sees fit, (and my saddle, and bridle
I would have saved if I could).[1] . . . As for money of mine, which
is out, is there £5 left with M.F., 40/- more which thou had,
and £4/10 to Leonard Fell, 14/8 to young Mt. Fell, and 14/- to
Richard Waller, and 10/- to Joseph Nicholson. My brother
Thomas Fell hath £5, and 40/- which I brought with me. And
sugar and 2 rolls of tobacco left with John Stubbs's wife, and
two rolls of tobacco left with William Milner at Dalton[2] to sell
for me. John Stubbs' wife hath a note of the sugar what it is, one
roll of tobacco to Neddy Cowper and one roll left with James
Clegge which I was to have 7d. for, but less will serve. And the
mare cost me 48/-. I do not remember any more, so if the Lord
order it so as that I do not return (for I am not my own but to
him I commit all) let it be disposed of as in wisdom dear M.F.
shall see cause. Thus I was free to acquaint thee concerning this
thing in regard thou was speaking of it when we were together.'[3]

Arriving in Barbados in October, Henry Fell went to 'Indian
Bridge', where he found that Peter Head, John Rous (son of
Lieutenant-Colonel Rous who owned a large sugar plantation
in the St. Phillip's parish in the Island), and Mary Fisher were
waiting for a boat to take them to the Leeward Islands—Nevis
and Antigua.[4] In his letters to Margaret, Henry Fell told her of
the amazing courage of this young woman, Mary Fisher. She
and an older friend Ann Austin were the first Friends to reach
the American hemisphere; they came to Barbados at the end of

[1] Part in brackets was crossed out by the writer, when he changed his mind.
[2] A town between Ulverston and modern Barrow-in-Furness.
[3] Swm. MSS. I, 42. **19 vi [Aug] 1656.**
[4] It is interesting to notice that Fell spells Antigua as it was and is still pronounced—Antego.

1655, a year before Henry Fell met them there. After they had for some six months published their message in this rich tropical island, with the resulting conversion of Colonel Rous and his son John, and the creation of three Meetings, with many convincements, they were drawn to go to New England. In July 1656 the two women found a captain in Barbados who took them in his ship to Boston, Massachusetts. The Puritans of New England were determined, if they could, to keep Quakerism out of their colonies; the Quakers were equally determined to defy the rigours of religious persecution and go where they believed God meant them to carry their teaching.[1]

Mary Fisher and Ann Austin on their arrival at Boston were put into prison, very cruelly treated, searched for signs of witchcraft on their bodies, their books were taken and burnt, no one was allowed to visit them in prison, and a fine of five pounds was laid on any who should come to see them. In spite of the threat one brave man offered to pay the fine, so as to be allowed to visit them, but in vain. The women were then put in the ship again, and returned to Barbados. 'Truly Mary Fisher is a precious heart', added Henry Fell, when he related this story to Margaret, 'and hath been very serviceable here', as had also the young John Rous and Peter Head. The Quakers in Barbados, which Henry Fell said was an 'exceedingly wicked place', were not then suffering persecution, as the Governor, a friend of Colonel Rous, was a moderate man who restrained the colonists.[2]

Four months later Henry Fell told Margaret that Mary Fisher had sailed from the Windward Islands to Holland, while John Rous had returned to Barbados.[3] (This John Rous later became Margaret Fell's first son-in-law.)

In his letters to her, Henry Fell always sent loving messages to her family and the Meeting, not forgetting his former master,

---

[1] An enlightening account of the 'invasion' of the American Colonies by the Quakers is given by Rufus M. Jones in *The Quakers in the American Colonies*, specially Book I, Chapters 2, 3 and 4.

[2] Swm. MSS. I, 66.

[3] Swm. MSS. I, 69. Mary Fisher re-visited the West Indies in 1657-8, and in 1660 courageously and alone undertook successfully a journey to the Court of the Sultan Mahomet IV at his camp near Adrianople (Sewel, I, Besse's *Sufferings*, Bowden's *History of Friends in America*, and M. R. Brailsford's *Quaker Women*).

Swarthmoor Hall in 1938

*The staircase, showing the
unusual newel*

The 'Great Hall' where Quaker meetings were held from 1652 to 1690.
The panelling and carvings are part of the restoration of 1914

A bedroom with the original panelling, carved fireplace and porch

Judge Fell. In his exile, he longed for her letters—'verily a few words from thee would be now more welcome than a spring of water to a thirsty man in a dry and barren wilderness'.[1]

This letter crossed one from her to him—it took three months for a letter to pass from Swarthmoor to Barbados—and in his immediate reply he told her how he had longed to hear her voice, 'for thy words to me are spirit and life'.[2] He would let her know if he needed financial help, 'but as yet there is no want'. He begged her to remember him in her prayers.

Six weeks later Henry Fell wrote to Margaret to tell her that John Rous and he were hoping to go to New England, there to challenge the claims of the Puritan ministers and rulers. They knew that two days after Mary Fisher and Ann Austin had, in the summer of 1656 been turned away from Boston, a new group of English Friends had sailed in, four men and four women. Examined by the magistrates and imprisoned, these Friends were effectually prevented from winning freedom to travel in Massachusetts, and the ship's captain was forced to take them back to their native country. But the seed of Quakerism had been sown, and one or two New Englanders came out courageously for the new teaching.

So in May 1657 Fell and Rous in Barbados tried to reach the new battleground. Henry Fell however failed to find a captain to take them, and two months later sailed for home. John Rous stayed on in Barbados, though he was longing to meet Margaret Fell; he was bent on going to New England; 'the rage of the magistrates there is very great', he told Margaret, 'but many are discontented at their dealings with Friends.'[3]

The journey to England took Henry Fell over three months, for as their ship neared home it was captured by Spaniards and taken to Spain. They escaped from the hands of 'those unreasonable men', and travelled through part of France by land to Rochelle, thence by boat to Lynn in Norfolk and so to London.[4] To see Margaret Fell and her family again as soon as possible was his great desire, and he quickly left London, and spent the winter at Swarthmoor.

[1] Swm. MSS. I, 69. 14.2.1657.
[2] Swm. MSS. I, 67. 19 Dec. 1656.
[3] Swm. MSS. I, 79. (Dated 22nd July 1657.)   [4] Swm. MSS. I, 71.

In April 1658 however he started off again to visit Barbados. 'Oh, dear one', he wrote to Margaret on his departure, 'my love is larger towards thee and all the faithful with thee, than can be expressed with tongue or pen.'[1]

In July he is on board *The Supply* in the Downs and writes— his farewell letter: 'To many hast thou been a nursing mother, whose souls have cause for ever to bless the Lord that ever they saw thy face or heard thy voice.' Ann Clayton and two companions are with him, trying to reach New England. He begs her to write to him 'as often as thou sees freedom. There are some ships or other passing to the Barbados once in six weeks or two months all the year long.'[2]

On his arrival in Barbados he wrote to George Fox, telling him of the terrible sufferings of Friends in Boston, Massachusetts.[3]

To Margaret he wrote in September an account of the voyage, full of dangers such as the travelling Friends risked continually. For eleven weeks they had been aboard, among 'a perverse generation and ungodly'. But God had made them bow before the Quakers, and had also visited the ship with a plague, which killed twenty-five or -six people, specially those who had been most hostile to them (comments Henry Fell). Scarcely any on the ship had escaped the illness, including the Friends, none of whom however had died. 'It was good for us', he told his friend, 'for the Lord hath tried us by it.' As for Quakerism in Barbados, he had found it had progressed in numbers and in quality.

Three weeks later, in October 1658, he writes again to Margaret, as he finds a ship is about to leave for England. 'It is likely after I go from hence to Surinam [now Dutch Guiana, formerly English], I may not have the opportunity of writing so often.' He gives news of Ann Clayton, and other Friends. Then follows a story of a case of apprenticeship which must have been very akin to slavery, but that of white man to white man. Poor emigrants sold themselves into a four-year servitude to pay for their passage across the Atlantic. On completion of their service they received a suit of clothes, tools and a sum of money.[4] Henry Fell

---

[1] Caton MSS. III, 226.
[2] Caton MSS. III, 252. 12.5.1658.
[3] Swm. MSS. IV, 182.　　　　　　　　[4] Jnl. F.H.S. VII, 142.

had found that one of his fellow-passengers on the long Atlantic voyage was a nephew of Gervase Benson of Kendal, where the boy had been apprenticed to a barber. He had crossed from England as a servant to one of the passengers who intended to sell him on arrival in the West Indies. Henry Fell therefore offered to buy him, so that the young man could serve his four years' slavery in the house of a Friend where conditions would be better than another's. Fell found a Friend in Barbados to buy him, the price being 1,600 pounds of sugar. Fell asked Margaret to inquire of Gervase Benson if he would release him or leave him in his servitude.[1] The story is a curious one, in that Gervase Benson, besides being a well-known Friend in the north, was a man of some wealth and social position. We are never told why this unfortunate nephew suffered this form of slavery in the West Indies.

In Henry Fell's letter to Margaret Fell, written on 8th May 1659, we again have news of the good progress of Quakerism in Barbados, and 'that the Governor is pretty moderate and noble and loving to Friends'. 'The last week' he adds, 'he did release two of our Friends out of prison, who were committed by the Justices (so called) for refusing to bear arms, they having gotten an Act here in the country lately made, that who did so refuse bearing arms, should pay 500 lb. of sugar or go to prison, which fine of a thousand pounds of sugar the Governor did freely pay himself, and so released the two Friends, saying he could not release them otherwise except the fine were paid. This Act it is like was made a purpose against Friends to ensnare them, which now the Governor perceives, and sees their envy, and it is like he intends to have the Act repealed, so that the enemies will not have their wills.'[2]

This possibly is the first reference to the Quaker stand against military conscription.

Six months later Henry Fell was back again in England, and at Swarthmoor again. He was passing through a time of temptation (it is not known what this was) and begs George Fox to pray for his deliverance from it, 'For truly at present I am much under, and as one without strength, but not altogether without

[1] Swm. MSS. I, 72. 7.8.1658. O.S.
[2] Caton MSS. III, 232 *seq.*

hope, but am waiting to see the issue of all this, and the end and cause, which as yet I do not clearly see'. He hopes that George Fox will feel free to give him advice, and sends the letter by a trusted Friend who 'may give thee a more particular account of things'.[1] And he adds, 'I am at present in a fast for 14 days.'[2] This fast in the Swarthmoor household is also mentioned in a letter written three weeks before, from William Caton to George Fox: 'Friends here are well, and great and marvellous is the work of the Lord in this family where several have been exercised and yet are in fasting; Bridget Fell fasted twelve days, Isabel hath fasted about seven and is to fast nine; little Mary hath fasted five, and a little maid that is a servant in the house, called Mabby, hath fasted twenty. . . . And two more in this family are exercised in the same thing. And blessed be the Lord, they are and have been generally wonderfully preserved, and some of them are come very well through it, and others are kept in the faith and patience, and all is pretty well, blessed be the Lord. . . . Thy dear and precious presence is longed for by many, and some are in hopes of seeing thee in these parts this winter; the dear and unexpressable love wherewith thou art beloved in this family is never to be forgotten. A line or two from thee to it would now be very seasonable and acceptable.'[3]

Fasting was not unknown among the early Quakers, for in 1652 James Nayler was under a fourteen-day fast when he first visited Swarthmoor,[4] and George Fox fasted at the time of his examination before the Lancaster Sessions, when Judge Fell and Colonel West openly protected him from the malice of the priests.[5] A little later Richard Hubberthorne fasted so strictly that he nearly died,[6] and Francis Howgill fasted for eight or ten days—'God is doing him good, and raising up his own to praise and serve Him',[7] added James Nayler. In 1653 while George Fox was again visiting Swarthmoor Hall, he fasted for ten days,

---

[1] Swm. MSS. IV, 181. 14.9.1659. [Nov.]
[2] One wonders if this fasting at Swarthmoor was prompted by the knowledge of Fox's serious illness at Reading at that time.
[3] Swm. MSS. VI, 52. 23.8.1659.
[4] Camb. Jnl. I, 51.
[5] Camb. Jnl. I, 72.
[6] Camb. Jnl. I, 105.
[7] Swm. MSS. III, 66.

and as Judge Fell and Colonel Benson were there also, he was moved to tell them that before a fortnight was gone the Long Parliament should be 'broken up and the speaker should be plucked out of his chair'. And so it came to pass.[1]

Three months after Henry Fell had fasted at Swarthmoor, he was again in London, apparently well in body and mind, for he writes to Margaret a vivid description of the effect on Friends of the political excitement of the months immediately preceding the Restoration of Charles II.

London, **the 7 of the 12 mo 59** [Feb **1659/60**].

M.F. my dearly beloved in the Lord, my soul greets thee, and honours thee. . . .

G.F. and Friends here are generally well; but General Monk's soldiers begin to be rude concerning Friends' Meetings. John Scafe is come to town, and went yesterday to the meeting in the Palace-yard at Westminster; but soon after he began to speak, they began to pull Friends out of the house violently, and beat them very sore, and would not suffer any of them to stay in the house; yea, they beat and abused Friends exceedingly in the streets. I came there when they had hailed almost all Friends out, and scattered them; and they pulled me out, and beat me much, and knocked me down in the street, and tore all my coat. Edward Billing and his wife were much abused, he especially. I hear he went presently [=immediately] and wrote to the Parliament [=the recalled residue of the 'Long Parliament' known as the 'Rump'], and acquainted some of them with their usage, and that he would endeavour to lay it before General Monk and the rest. . . . Great distractions and disaffections there are in people, as things now stand: but to them that fear the Lord and wait upon him, all things will turn to their good.

Thy brother,

Henry Fell.[a]

Pepys in his diary mentions the same incident: 'Feb. 7.1660. To the Hall [Westminster]; when in the Palace [Yard], I saw Monk's soldiers abuse Billing and all the Quakers, that were at a meeting place there; and indeed the soldiers did use them very roughly, and were to blame.'[3]

Margaret Fell had several Friends telling her of these puzzling

[1] Camb. Jnl. I, 107.
[2] Caton MSS. III, also in A.R.B.
[3] *Diary of S. Pepys*, I, 13, quoted by A.R.B. p. 75.

and chaotic months, Thomas Salthouse, William Caton, William Dewsbury and others.[1] How thankful she must have been when she received in her far-off home this letter from Richard Hubberthorne, written in London on the 20th of March 1660:

Dear Sister,

Our meetings at present are peaceable and quiet, though we have had rudeness by some soldiers and disturbances. I was moved to write something to Monk about it, upon which he gave out a few words as an order to the officers and soldiers, which did stop them for the present from their rage. I intend to stay in the city about two weeks, and then pass towards Suffolk and Norfolk, and then towards Yorkshire. F.H. [Francis Howgill], Samuel Fisher and John Stubbs, are in the city.

Thy dear brother,

Richard Hubberthorne.[2]

The order of General Monk ran thus:

St. James, 9th March.

I do require all officers and soldiers to forbear to disturb the peaceable meetings of the quakers, they doing nothing prejudicial to the Parliament or Commonwealth of England.

George Monk.[3]

The Government of the country was by this time in the hands of General Monk and the Council of State, and the negotiations of the former with the exiled Charles and his advisers culminated in the signature early in April of the Declaration of Breda, one of the clauses of which gave liberty of conscience in religion, so long as the peace of the kingdom was not disturbed. At the same time a new Parliament was being elected midst great excitement, and on 29th May Charles II entered London. Richard Hubberthorne described the entry in a letter to George Fox who was than on a month's visit to Margaret and her household: 'This day did King Charles and his two brethren James and Henry come into this city: Charles is of a pretty sober countenance, but the great pride and vanity of those that brought him in, is inexpressible; and he is in danger to be tempted to those things, which he in himself is not inclined unto.

[1] *B. Qism.* Chapters 17 and 18.
[2] Caton MSS. III, quoted by A.R.B. 79–80.
[3] A.R.B. 80, note.

The great excess and abomination that hath been used this day in this city, is inexpressible.'[1]

Hubberthorne's reading of the signs on that day was only too true—all over the country constables and magistrates combined to attack the Quakers. While George Fox was taken from Swarthmoor, Henry Fell became a prisoner at Thetford in Norfolk. By the Mayor's order he was taken from a Friend's house where a meeting was being held. Accused of vagrancy, he was sentenced to be whipped at the town cross. As the order made no mention of his having to be unclothed preparatory to the whipping, he refused to remove his own clothes and the men would not do it for him. On the second time of being taken to the cross, the constables 'stood looking upon one another as before, a good space and none could do it, so even shame struck them before the people; at length one of the constables did it gently as if he had been handling a young child; and put my hands fast (but I told him they need not) and when the beadle came to whip me, at the second blow his whip broke, the lash from the stick, and so I had no more, at which the people were glad.' He spoke some words to the people and later was sent away. But he was moved to return to the town and was at once imprisoned,[2] and only released a month later, on which he returned to London (August 1660), there to meet Margaret Fell and her eldest daughter. (See Chapter 10.)

At the end of the year Henry Fell was holding meetings throughout the Eastern counties, where he found 'a great calm'.

This calm which came a few months after Charles II's restoration was rudely ended by the Rising of the Fifth Monarchy Men on 6th January 1661. Believers in the literal interpretation of Scripture, and in the near approach of the millenium, these men only resembled the Quakers in their refusal to pay tithes and their plea for the simplification of the lives of Christians. However their rising 'caused a furious persecution of the pacific Quakers'.[3] George Fox relates in his Journal what happened to Henry Fell that day in London. There was such great excitement, that as 'Henry Fell was going to a general meeting at

---

[1] Swm. MSS. IV, 18 and A.R.B. 82 (corrected).

[2] Swm. MSS. I, 73.

[3] Trevelyan, *England under the Stuarts*, p. 336, quoted in Camb. Jnl. I, 468.

Major Beard's the soldiers knocked him down and he had been killed if the Duke of York had not come. And all the prisons were soon after filled with Friends, and many inns, both in cities, towns and country, and it was hard for any sober people to stir for several weeks' time.'[1]

About this time Henry Fell told Margaret of George Fox's suggestion that he should travel in the Truth to the East Indies, a still harder adventure than to the West Indies. Under the year 1661, George Fox in his Journal refers thus to this ambitious plan: 'John Stubbs and Richard Scosthrop and Henry Fell was moved to go towards China and Prester John's country: and so no masters of ships would carry them, and so at last they got a warrant from the King, and the East India Company would not obey it nor the masters of their ships. And then they went to Holland and would have got passages there: but no passage there they could get; and then they took shipping to go to Alexandria in Egypt: and so to go by the Caravans from thence. . . . But John Stubbs and Henry Fell came to Alexandria in Egypt: and the English Consul banished them from thence: though they gave forth many papers and books concerning of truth (to the Turks and Grecians). And they gave the book called *The Pope's Strength Broken*[2] to an old friar to give to the Pope; and he clapped his hand to his breast, and confessed it was true, but if he should confess to it they would burn him, but he said it was truth, what was written therein; and they returned to London again: And John Stubbs had a vision, that the English and Dutch would fall out, who had joined together not to carry them; and so it came to pass soon after.'[3]

The English consul at Alexandria wrote to an English merchant at Leghorn, 'The Quakers did throw pamphlets about the streets in Hebrew, Arabic and Latin, and if they staid a little longer, it might have set them aburning.'[4]

The East Indies, China and Prester John's country—what a picture those names give of the indomitable spirit of these 'First Publishers of Truth'; the whole world, east to west, was their parish, for God's Spirit dwelt in every man.

[1] Camb. Jnl. I, 386.   [2] A book not yet identified.
[3] Camb. Jnl. II, 8. This was the First Dutch War of 1665 to 1667.
[4] Besse's *Sufferings*, II, p. 420.

Prester John's country suggests romance and myth. Until the fourteenth century it was believed in Europe that Prester John's country was in Asia. Two centuries earlier Prester John appears as an Eastern priest-king, with a wide dominion in Central Asia, beyond Persia and Armenia, a Nestorian Christian. He was said to be of the ancient race of the Magi, and had a sceptre of solid emerald. His letter to the Emperor of the West in 1165 spoke of great wealth and grandeur and splendour, and a 'sea of Sand'— the great desert of Central Asia. Marco Polo, exploring Central Asia in the thirteenth century, spoke of Prester John's kingdom. In the fifteenth century Prester John's country came to be regarded as Ethiopia in Africa, owing to a curious confusion of India with Ethiopia, 'but the Asiatic tradition still held sway among the more educated circles of the West.'[1] It is clear from George Fox's writing quoted above that he and Henry Fell were among those who believed that Prester John's country lay in Asia and not in Africa.[2]

Fox also wrote a letter to Presbyter (Prester) John in 1660, and Stubbs and Henry Fell addressed one to him in Latin in the same year.[3]

John Stubbs and Henry Fell never reached the Far East. It was because the English Consul at Alexandria feared to offend the Mohammedan rulers that he refused to give them their passports. So they returned home, via Turkey where they distributed literature, and Germany where they met William Caton, and together had a friendly interview with the enlightened Prince Elector Palatine of the Rhine at Heidelberg.

By early February 1662, Henry Fell and John Stubbs were back again in England.

Four years later Henry Fell, now married, was again in Barbados. He and Margaret were still corresponding with each other, though the Dutch war was delaying the letters. Things were not going well with Friends in the island—John Perrot

---

[1] Article on Prester John from *Encyclopaedia of Religion and Ethics*, ed. by J. Hastings, 1918. Article by Th. Barns, M.A. (Oxon.).

[2] It will be seen that the name 'Prester John' was used as the title of the ruler of this Eastern country throughout the centuries.

[3] Stubbs and Fell also knew Arabic and Hebrew well enough to translate Quaker books into these languages.

had caused some disunity. Henry Fell was considering going to settle in New York,[1] but he evidently decided against such a plan though he went there for a visit, for in December 1672 he was back again in Barbados, where apparently he had been living for some time. George Fox and others had recently arrived there to strengthen the large number of Friends on the island. It is sad to find that Henry Fell had in some way transgressed, and also had fallen into debt. But his letter expresses not only his continued love for Margaret but his deep gratitude for her spiritual help to him, and his acknowledgment of her wisdom in foretelling that he would come into a 'better condition than I ever yet knew, if I did but return unto the Lord with my whole heart, and come down in the humility of my mind, and lay all before Him; and forsake my sins, and wait upon Him.' Already he was feeling restored and healed. He had written before to tell her of his recovery, but he feared the letter had been lost in a shipwreck. He speaks of the value of George Fox's visit to Barbados and tells Margaret that his wife had recently gone to visit Friends at Bermuda.[2]

Margaret received the letter, and replied to it in March 1673 in one full of tender love and advice, to which the sorely tried man replied in great gratitude for Margaret Fell's never-failing care for him, and for the knowledge that the Light of God had shown him his sin and the way out of it to return to Him.[3]

Nothing further is heard of Henry Fell, and it is thought that he died in America. His life was one of the most adventurous of the men and women of Swarthmoor Meeting, a Meeting which sent out more of its members than any other in the first twenty years of Quakerism.[4]

[1] Thirnbeck MSS. 4.
[2] Abraham MSS. 20, also in Webb, p. 281, and Jnl. F.H.S. XI, 160.
[3] Camb. Jnl. II, 256 *seq.*
[4] See Appendix 8 for list of ministering Friends of Swarthmoor Meeting.

Chapter Seven

MARGARET FELL AND THE JEWS, 1655–77

MARGARET Fell was the first Quaker to show an interest in and sympathy for the Jews.

Early in 1656, the year in which after centuries of exile Jews were once more allowed to settle in England,[1] Margaret Fell wrote the first of her five books addressed to the Jews. In that same year in July George Fox also wrote a book entitled *A Visitation to the Jews*. This was the first of three he wrote and was published in London, but seems never to have been printed either in Latin or German or Dutch.[2]

These books, written for the conversion of the Jews to Quakerism, were carried to Holland by the first of the 'Publishers' to visit that country, William Ames and William Caton. Others who helped for shorter periods were John Stubbs and Samuel Fisher, an M.A. of Oxford, and one of the most learned men who became Quaker ministers.[3]

By 1656 Holland had become the home of many of the persecuted Jews, notably from Portugal. One of the leading Rabbis in Amsterdam was Manasseth-ben-Israel, whose father had belonged to a Jewish group in Portugal who professed Christianity, but secretly practised Judaism. Manasseth himself, a scholar and a linguist, had many friends among the Christians of his adopted city. He was one who believed in the imminent fulfilment of the Messianic prophecies, and as a young man had worked to improve the condition of his race in Europe, and was specially anxious that England should allow the Jews to re-settle there. Since Edward I's edict in 1290 no Jews had been allowed by law to live in England, though a number of well-to-do Jewish merchants were in London before 1656, but only as foreigners.

[1] *B. Qism.*, p. 427.
[2] W. I. Hull, *Qism. in Amsterdam*, p. 59, note.
[3] Ibid., p. 179.

Manasseth was particularly interested in the struggle in England for liberty of conscience, as seen in the Civil War: and after the death of Charles I, he petitioned Cromwell to allow the Jews to settle in England freely and openly. In spite of the presence of sympathetic friends in England, he was unable to visit the country until October 1655. He came with his son and some influential Jews of Amsterdam. Cromwell then appointed a Council to consider the petition, and gave it such sympathetic treatment that the Jews were admitted.[1] During 1656 and 1657, Manasseth and his son stayed in London helping in the establishment of their friends, and both died within a few days of each other in November 1657.

Following the wise principle that to convince a man in a key position is of great value, Margaret Fell appealed to Manasseth. Her book was published in February 1656, very shortly after his people were admitted to England, and was entitled *For Manasseth-Ben-Israel; the Call of the Jews out of Babylon, which is good tidings to the meek, liberty to the captives, and of opening of the prison doors*. In this book she makes an impassioned appeal for men everywhere to turn to the Light of God, as it is in the heart, to turn away from formal outward religion to the inner Spirit. There is ample quotation from the Old Testament. There is no mention of Christ, except as implied in the sentence 'And if ever you come to know the true and living God, you must hearken to this prophet which calls your minds to within, for by this doth the living God teach his people himself.'[2] 'Now the free grace of the everlasting God is offered to you this day', she wrote, 'and therefore return to the pure Light and Law written in the heart, which is spiritual, just and good, and by that let your minds be guided and led up to God, who is Light, who hath said I will be a Light to Israel'.[3]

Margaret Fell addressed Manasseth as one 'who art come into the English nation, with all the rest of thy brethren, which is a land of gathering where the Lord God is fulfilling his promise'.[4]

[1] Evelyn in his *Diary* wrote on 14th Dec. 1655, 'Now were the Jews admitted'.

[2] M.F. *Works*, p. 107.

[3] Ibid., p. 115.

[4] Ibid., p. 105.

She charged him to send her book to be read and published amongst his brethren wherever they were scattered.

She wished to have this book translated into Hebrew, and another, probably a book for Christians, entitled *A Testimony of the Touch-Stone for all Professions* also published in 1656, she wanted to be in Latin or Greek. She knew of the recently convinced scholar Samuel Fisher,[1] but she had not met him. However in March 1656 she wrote to Fisher asking him if he would make these translations.[2] Presumably Samuel Fisher was unable at that time to do the work, but a year and a half later John Stubbs reported to Margaret (in September 1657) that Fisher had translated into Latin her book for the Jews called *The Second Call to the Seed of Israel*, and also an Epistle. He was then engaged on translating the first of her Jewish books into Hebrew also, namely, *To Manasseth*, but finding the task difficult.[3]

Caton, Ames and Stubbs had great veneration for Margaret's books, and Caton told her that her writings were more liked by the Jews than were those of other Quaker writers. In October 1656, he wrote that the Jews were 'hungering' for the publication of her book for them. It had now been translated (apparently into Dutch), and he hoped it would be printed shortly. Caton had little respect or liking for the services of the synagogue, and disliked also the prohibition of disputes (such as the Puritans in England permitted), 'but' he adds in his letter to Margaret, 'in one of their houses, we had three or four hours' discourse with some of them, and a good principle in the conscience they owned in words, but they could scarce endure to hear Christ mentioned. They are a high, lofty, proud and conceited people, far from the Truth, yet there is a seed among them, which God in the fulness of Time will gather into his garner.'[4] A few months later he writes, 'I have understood that there are some among them that would willingly become Christians, but that they fear intolerable persecution, and that specially from their brethren.'[5] In November 1656 Caton, who

---

[1] *Life of W. Caton*, pp. 23, 24.

[2] Spence MSS. III, 37.

[3] Abraham MSS. 3.

[4] Caton MSS. III., **11(p. 25)** Dated 29.8.1656. [**probably Aug. but possibly Oct.**]

[5] Caton MSS. III.,**16 (p. 35)** 5.4.1657. [**probably April but possibly June**].

had just reached London after terrible experiences on a man-of-war,[1] was able to tell Margaret that her Epistle[2] to Friends with her book to the Jews[3] had both been translated and he doubts not 'but that it is in its service before this'.[4]

Margaret Fell's second book for the Jews was entitled *A Loving Salutation, to the Seed of Abraham among the Jews, where ever they are scattered up and down upon the face of the Earth . . . wandering up and down from mountain to hill, seeking rest but finding none.* It was first published in 1657, and had a later edition in 1660.

In spite of the respect shown for her books by Caton and Stubbs and Ames, and the Dutch Jews themselves, these books appear to us nowadays as very wordy, and with much repetition, but throughout is the constant plea for an inward religion, a turning to the Light of God, and sometimes Margaret expresses these ideas with real beauty. 'The Covenant of the Lord is given for a Light to open blind eyes, which brings salvation to the ends of the earth, which Light lets you see the thoughts of your hearts, that they are vain, which Light lets you see when you do amiss, when you bear false witness, when you tell a lie, when you do wrong to any man; which Light will lead you unto justice and equity; which Light will teach you to fulfil the law of Moses, and to do to all men as ye would they should do to you; which Light will lead you unto righteousness, by which ye may fulfil, and answer to the righteousness of the Laws and statutes and commandments of God, which ye can never do, your minds being from the Light.'[5]

Margaret sees in the Light the Spirit which would unite all peoples—Jew, Gentile, barbarian, Scythian, bond and free. She begs them not to turn away from her plea, because it comes from the Gentiles—'Therefore start not aside, nor cast not this behind you, as ye have done all the gracious tenders of the Lord's love formerly, but come to the Light that is in you. . . .

[1] Caton MSS. III, **3 (p. 13)**. (Letter to M. Fell describing the voyage.)

[2] This Epistle to Friends is not extant (W. I. Hull, *Qism. in Amsterdam*, p. 270).

[3] Presumably this was her book to Manasseth, and the translation was into Dutch, which Sewel (in his *History* II, 624) says was done by William Ames.

[4] Caton MSS. III, **3 (p. 13)**. **Probably ix [Nov.]1656 (W.I. Hull,** *Qism in Amsterdam,* **pp. 120-1).**

[5] M.F. *Works*, pp. 153-4.

Come into the Covenant of Light and Love and partake with us of the everlasting riches and inheritance that never fades away.'[1]

These two books for the Jews having been written, Margaret and her friends had then to arrange for their translation into Dutch and Hebrew, and for their publication in those languages and also in English. We have seen already that she asked Samuel Fisher to translate her book to Manasseth, into Hebrew, and her *Testimony of the Touch-stone* into Latin or Greek, but that apparently he did not do it.

The translation into Dutch of the book for Manasseth and the *Testimony of the Touch-stone* was by William Ames who knew the language well, and the former was translated from Dutch into Hebrew by a Jew of Amsterdam, who had been met with by Ames. In a letter to Margaret, from Utretcht, dated 17th April 1657, he tells her that there was a Jew in Amsterdam, who had been cast out of the synagogue by the other Jews 'because he owneth no other teacher but the Light, and he sent for me and I spoke to him and he was pretty tender and doth own all that is spoken. . . . I gave order that one of the Dutch copies of thy book[2] should be given to him, and he sent me word he would come to our meeting.'[3]

It is an exciting thought that possibly, indeed probably, this excommunicated Jew was the famous philosopher Benedict Spinoza, then a young man of twenty-four years, who had been condemned as a heretic by the Jews of Amsterdam in the preceding year, July 1656. This suggestion, first made by Helen G. Crosfield in her book *Margaret Fox of Swarthmoor Hall*[4] (1913) has been repeated by William I. Hull in his exhaustive study of *The Rise of Quakerism in Amsterdam, 1655–65* (published in 1938) and corroborated by Professor Henry J. Cadbury of Harvard University. Spinoza was in 1657 living quietly a few miles out of Amsterdam in the home of some Collegiants, whose pure morality and simple-minded piety attracted Spinoza, who already had friends amongst a similar body, the Mennonites.

[1] M.F. *Works*, p. 188.
[2] The book to 'Manasseth', presumably.
[3] Swm. MSS. IV, 28.
[4] P. 50, note.

Incidentally it is known that Spinoza could speak no English, though he knew several other languages.

It seems probable to the present writer that it was Spinoza who also translated, from Dutch into Hebrew, Margaret Fell's second book to the Jews, *A Loving Salutation*. The following letters seem to prove this.

William Caton wrote from Amsterdam on the 18th November 1657 to Margaret, 'The principle cause of my present writing to thee, is to give thee to understand that I have been with a Jew, and have showed him thy book [*The Loving Salutation*],[1] and have asked him what language would be the fittest for them. He told me Portuguese or Hebrew, for if it were in Hebrew, they might understand it at Jerusalem or in almost any other place of the World. And he hath undertaken to translate it for us, he being expert in several languages.'[2]

In the following March (1658) Caton wrote from Leyden, Holland, to Margaret: 'As touching thy book (titled *A Loving Salutation*) I have gotten it once translated into Dutch, because the Jew that is to translate it into Hebrew could not translate it out of English. . . . He hath it now under hand, and is translating of it, like as he hath done the other [the book for "Manasseth"],[3] which Samuel Fisher and John Stubbs have taken along with them. The Jew that translates it, remains very friendly, in his way.'[4] The rest of the letter adds an interesting comment on the Jews of Holland. 'Samuel Fisher was in their synagogues at Amsterdam, and among them at Rotterdam. They were pretty moderate towards him: (I mean they did not abuse him) but assented to much of that which he spoke: he had some discourse with two or three of their doctors in private at Amsterdam, and they seemed to own in words the substance of that which he declared, but they are in bondage as people of other forms are.'

On his return to London from Amsterdam, Caton, in May 1658, wrote 'Thy dear letter I received the same day I came from Holland, and I had done according to thy request about thy

---

[1] I. Ross's suggestion.
[2] Caton MSS. III, 48.
[3] I. Ross's suggestion.
[4] Caton MSS. III, 507.

book [*The Loving Salutation*]¹ which is forth in its service. The
night before I came from Amsterdam I got them from the press
and the same day that I came from thence I got about 170 of
them dispersed among the Jews who willingly and greedily
received them (they being in the Hebrew tongue). I purposed
to have brought half a hundred of them with me to England,
but I disposed of some of them in Zeeland, there being several
Jews.'²

It would be interesting to find proof—but it has not so far
come to light—both that some Jews were persuaded of the truth
of the teaching of the Light within and joined the new Quaker
movement, and also that Spinoza found it in line with his own
philosophy. In his great books, written later in his short life, he
claimed complete freedom of expression for thought and belief,
and also that no speculative nor scientific investigation could
put religion in jeopardy³—certainly both inherent in Quaker
belief. He also declared—'Christ was the temple of God, because
in him God has most fully revealed himself.'⁴

Margaret Fell wrote three more books for the Jews, *A Call to
the Universal Seed of God*, in 1664 while she was in prison; *A Call
unto the Seed of Israel*, in 1668 (together with an Epistle and
twenty-five queries); and *The Daughter of Sion Awakened*, in
1677. All three make a strong appeal for the Jews to acknowledge the supreme importance of Jesus, and of an inner
religion, and to come to the knowledge of the Light within. *A
Call unto the Seed of Israel* and the Epistle were translated into
Latin.⁵

The faith that William Caton had in the concern that Margaret felt for the Jews (together with several other Friends, notably George Fox, Isaac Pennington, John Perrot, in addition to
those we have already noted) is lovingly expressed in the following letter, written in 1657—'As touching the Jews, it is no
marvel if thou (with whom the secrets of the Lord are) be
sensible of something among them, for I believe there is a spark

---

¹ I. Ross's suggestion.
² Caton MSS. **III, 24(p. 40), 21 iii** [May] 1658.
³ *Encyclopaedia Britannica*, 9th edition. Article on *Spinoza*.
⁴ Quoted by C. F. Andrews in *The Sermon on the Mount*, p. 33.
⁵ Abraham MSS. 3.

in many of their bosoms, which in process of time may kindle
to a burning flame.'¹

When Caton was travelling in Germany in the winter of
1661–2 he distributed Quaker literature, including Margaret
Fell's books for the Jews. These he gave to them in their synagogue at Frankfort and he told Margaret that, being in Hebrew,
hers were more appreciated than Isaac Pennington's which were
in German.² In a letter from John Stubbs to George Fox, probably written in 1660, there is a proposal which throws valuable
light on this story of Quaker contacts with the Jews, particularly
as it suggests that Friends believed that the Jews newly arrived
in England should have Quaker beliefs laid before them as had
the Jews of Holland and Germany. Stubbs suggested that Margaret Fell's book should be translated again into Hebrew, this
time by a Jewish Rabbi lately come to England from Poland,
very poor but very perfect in Hebrew, and interested enough in
Quakerism to be attending Meeting.³ This was done, and the
third edition of *A Loving Salutation* was published that year in
London, each page having one column in English and the other
in Hebrew. It is printed with the beginning at the end of the
book, in honour of the Hebrew.

George Fox himself evidently believed that these contacts by
visits and literature between 1656 and 1679 had had some effect,
for in a letter to Robert Barclay in April 1679, he wrote, '[I was]
glad to hear of something stirring among the Jews, and it would
be very well, if some weighty Friends did give them a visit in
Holland, this Yearly Meeting that is to come, and to see what is
stirring among the Jews and among the Collegiants and the
Ministers which we had the discourse with.'⁴

Difficulties there were to contend with, not only in the hardness of heart of the visited, and in the risks of travel, but in the
publishing and translating of the books. There is more than a
hint that one of Margaret's difficulties was that one of her books
might be vetoed by Judge Fell—'let it come forth speedily and be
sent abroad, before my husband come up to London, lest he

¹ Caton MSS. III, 35. 5.4.1657. [O.S.]
² Swm. MSS. I, 327.
³ Crosfield MSS. 7.
⁴ *Rel. Bar.*, p. 48. Dated 8.2.1679. [O.S.]

light of it and prevent the service of it.'[1] Her book on this occasion seems never to have been published, so perhaps Judge Fell did light on it, and prevented its being printed! Even if sometimes her husband's judgment did not accord with her own, her Quaker friends who helped her in this work had an unfailing trust in her, and this chapter of her contact with the Jews may end with the following letter from William Ames, the indefatigable traveller in Holland, Germany, Bohemia and Danzig.

From near Amsterdam. 13.6.1658 [August].

Dear Margaret,

Thou knowest I love thee and great cause I have to love thee above all others that ever I yet saw, because such an overflowing of wisdom and love (in which my soul hath been refreshed and my life strengthened) which is in thee, I never yet in such a measure could be sensible of in any other, for in weakness thou hast strengthened me, and in affliction thou hast comforted me, and hast borne my infirmities in patience and wisdom, and when other friends (of great account) have been no small trial to me, even then have I felt thy love supporting, therefore my soul loves thee, for wherever I am and under what trial soever, the virtue of thy love I can feel which is refreshment and strength unto me.[2]

[1] Spence MSS. III, 49. 21.8.1657 (Oct.).
[2] A.R.B. MSS. 4.

Chapter Eight

MARGARET FELL AND JAMES NAYLER, 1652–60

*'Now search with the Light, which is eternal, whether ye be established
in righteousness and purity; if ye be not, ye deny the teaching of the Lord.*
From an Epistle to Friends, from M. Fell, probably 1655.
(Caton MSS. I, 60)

JAMES NAYLER was not a member of Swarthmoor Meeting,
as were the Friends whose story and relationship with Margaret
we have followed in a previous chapter. He had, however, come
into her life very shortly after George Fox had, for, as we saw
earlier, Nayler and Richard Farnsworth arrived at Swarthmoor
a few days after Fox, in June 1652, and were largely instrumental in persuading Judge Fell to consent to meet Fox. The
life and tragedy and glory of Nayler have been described by a
number of writers; in this chapter it is his contacts with Margaret Fell that will be our particular concern.[1]

A Yorkshireman, an educated farmer of a small estate, Nayler
had fought in the Civil War in Cromwell's Army, rising to
become Quartermaster in Lambert's Regiment of Horse, which
bore the brunt of the fighting at the defeat of King Charles II
at the Battle of Worcester (1651). When he left the army that
year, broken in health, he joined a progressive church of Independents, but soon after he eagerly welcomed George Fox
and his teaching on his first journey into Yorkshire. He was six

---

[1] Sewel in his *History of the Quakers*, Braithwaite in *Beginnings of Quakerism*,
Chapter XI, Mabel R. Brailsford, *A Quaker from Cromwell's Army*; *James
Nayler*, published by the Swarthmoor Press, Ltd., 1927, and Emilia Fogelklou,
James Nayler; the Rebel Saint, published by Ernest Benn, Ltd., 1931. The two
last authors, while giving much valuable information, are in their anxiety to
sympathise with Nayler less than fair to Fox. See articles by E. Brockbank in
Jnl. F.H.S. 26, p. 11 and by Prof. H. J. Cadbury in Jnl. F.H.S. 27, p. 33 and 28,
p. 67, and A. N. Brayshaw, *Personality of G. Fox*, pp. 86, 87, and *The Quakers,
their Story and Message*, p. 134.

years older than Fox. After his first visit to Swarthmoor he
travelled widely in the northern counties for three years, and
wrote frequently to Margaret Fell, giving her news of his
journeys, blessing her for her care of the growing fellowship,
and exhorting her to faithfulness to the Light as she was receiving it. Often his letters are written in a picturesque style; in one
he wrote: 'Thou art sealed in my heart, my sister, thy care for
the babes is pleasant, and in it thou prospers.' His trust in her
power to guide is shown in that he tells her he has sent a woman,
new to the Quaker teaching, to see her and talk with her. 'Judge
the death', he told her, 'but save the little thing, which I have
seen moving in her. Let her stay awhile with thee, and show
her the way of Love, which is much lost in the height.'[1] What
a picture of emotional extravagance needing to be brought to
earth!

In his letters to Margaret, Nayler always sent messages of love
to her children and family, specially to Judge Fell, for whom
from the time of their first meeting he seems to have had a great
affection.

In 1653 James Nayler, together with Francis Howgill, was
imprisoned at Appleby, after a trial where their words had
reached the consciences of several of their hearers, notably one
of their judges, Anthony Pearson, who then joined the Quakers.
When Margaret heard of their imprisonment (Nayler's 'crime'
was preaching, refusing to remove his hat, and addressing those
who thought themselves his betters, as 'thou') she sent them a
spirited letter of encouragement. 'I do see the secret work of
God going on in People's minds', she wrote to them, thinking
perhaps of their influence on Anthony Pearson, 'look not at the
hard rocks, nor look at briars, nor look not at the thorns, nor at
the mountains, nor the coldness, for well it may be so; for there
have been no vine-dressers, nor no ploughmen; there's none to
dress the ground, no seedsmen to sow the seed, and therefore
these seedsmen sowed in vain. The true seedsmen must not
regard the weather, the winds that blow, they sow the seed
before the winter. There is a winter, and there is a summer;
there is a time to sow the seed, there is a time to reap; so the
Lord give thee an understanding in all things.' She assures them

[1] Swm. MSS. II, 829. 1652.

that they have in them what is eternal, which will withstand all the earthly plotting of their enemies. 'Look at the Lord alone, see him present with you, in his Spirit and Power lifting up your heads above all your enemies.'[1]

During this imprisonment Nayler fasted for a few days, as he had done once before, for fourteen days, at Swarthmoor. In the prison, he seems to have done it as a 'sign' or protest, against the loose living of those around him.[2]

Nayler was released from Appleby jail in the spring of 1653, and continued his journeys through Cumberland, Durham and Yorkshire, preaching to crowds and discussing with individuals and small groups. He was equally successful with both and was already acknowledged to be a leader of the new movement, almost equal to Fox himself.

At the beginning of 1655 he came to London, where Edward Burrough and Francis Howgill had been working since the previous July, having been joined later, not only by George Fox, but also by such men as John Audland, John Camm, Richard Hubberthorne, James Lancaster, Miles Halhead, Alexander Parker, Anthony Pearson, John Stubbs and Will Caton, all men of the North.

Nayler, by his outstanding personality, his power of preaching and his success in disputing with Puritan theologians, soon attracted many to the Meetings. Within a few months of his arrival, Alexander Parker was writing to Margaret Fell that 'James is very serviceable here, and his fame begins to spread in the city, seeing that he hath had public disputes with many', and again, 'James is fitted for this great place, and a great love is begotten in many towards him'.[3] But popularity, the unwise adulation of a small group of men and women Friends, added to constant overwork, and a draining of his spiritual emotions without time to refresh himself from the Source—all combined to create unbalance. It was as if a great spiritual darkness was overwhelming his light. The very tenderness and sensitiveness

---

[1] M.F. *Works* (published in 1710), p. 51, where however all mention of James Nayler is omitted, owing to the events of 1656 *seq.* A contemporary copy, mentioning J.N. is in Swm. MSS. III, 27.

[2] Brailsford's *James Nayler*, p. 67.

[3] A.R.B. 37 and note. July and September 1655.

of his nature made it impossible for him, for a time, to withstand flattery; he forgot, when praise came his way, to give God the glory; it was as if the tool took credit for its efficiency when it was the power behind and beyond it which was the cause of the wonders performed. Some years later, when strength returned to him, he described his action thus: 'I reasoned against [the Spirit's] tender reproof, and consulted with another and so let the creatures into my affections. And his pure Spirit was grieved and he ceased to reprove, and he gave me up, and his Light he withdrew and his judgment took away.'[1] The influence of Martha Simmonds, a hysterical woman, almost drove Nayler, even as early as 1655, to quarrel with Howgill and Burrough, and cause a split in the ranks. The breach was temporarily closed, as Howgill was able joyfully to report to Margaret Fell.[2]

At the end of June Fox was in London, but only for a short time, and soon afterwards Howgill and Burrough left on a visit to Ireland. Thus in July (1655) Nayler alone was left to cope with the heavy demands in London. Fox had his misgivings: 'As I parted from him', he wrote in his Journal, 'I cast my eyes upon him and a fear struck in me concerning him.'[3] In November 1655, James Nayler wrote to his friend at Swarthmoor, telling her of a meeting he had had at Lady Darcy's, where many 'from the Court' attended, lords and ladies, officers of the army, 'some of the highest priests in the city', how many he did not know as 'they got behind a ceiling,[4] and came not out till I was gone.' Sir Harry Vane, republican and leader of a religious group, was also there, 'drunk with imaginations'.[5]

In the following year (1656) trouble was increasing and letters to Margaret Fell told her of the growing disunity. One north-country Friend, Richard Roper of Cartmel, North Lancashire, on his visit to London in October 1656, told her very clearly what was happening:

It's like there is an evil thing begot amongst Friends in that city, the

---

[1] Nayler's *Works*, p. xli, quoted by Brailsford, *James Nayler*, p. 96.

[2] Caton MSS. III, 293, and quoted in Fogelklou, p. 130, from Swm. MSS. I, 86.

[3] Camb. Jnl. I, 200.

[4] Ceiling is a screen of tapestry or panelling (*Oxford English Dictionary*).

[5] A.R.B. 39. (3rd Nov. 1655.)

same as was amongst the church at Corinth, divisions and strife and
contention, one saying I am of James, another saying I am of Francis
and Edward: and so it's like that Truth will suffer by them. Truly
Friends in the North are rare and precious, very few I find like them,
yet this I declare to thee, not to them, lest they should be puffed up.[1]

Other letters told her of the foolish uncontrolled behaviour
of these few women and their husbands, who frequently inter-
rupted the Meetings.

Sometimes when one of the leading preachers like Howgill or
Hubberthorne was speaking, these women would chant or call
out incessantly, so as to drown the speaker's voice. When rebuked they appealed to Nayler, who though he at first reproved
them, later, most unhappily for all, gave way to them and
therefore became dominated by them. Richard Hubberthorne,
in his letter to Margaret Fell on 26th August 1656, wrote concerning Martha Simmonds: 'And now an exceedingly filthy spirit
is got up in her, more filthy than any that yet departed out of
the Truth, and with it labours to break and destroy the Meetings if it were possible.'[2]

These women—Martha Simmonds, Hannah Stranger, 'Mildred' and 'Judy'—were, as Nayler should have recognized,
behaving as Ranters. The danger of Ranterism in the latter half
of the seventeenth century was great. It showed a mental and
spiritual lack of balance existing in certain individuals among
the mystical sects, which led to extravagance and even immoral-
ity of behaviour. It believed in the infallibility of the individual,
in that he was entirely possessed of the Holy Spirit, and that
therefore his actions could be independent of the judgment of
either the Church or the community, and were above the usual
moral distinctions of right and wrong. These misguided friends
of Nayler's not only brought disunity and confusion into the
Meetings, but they attacked the very foundation of Quaker
teaching. Their lack of self-discipline and Nayler's compliance
and subsequent fall showed the dangers in the doctrine of the
Inner Light. If the Holy Spirit dwelt in each man and woman,
they argued, had *they* not as much Light as Fox, Burrough,
Howgill and the rest? And was not their own conduct as much

[1] Swm. MSS. III, 131. 20th Oct. 1656.
[2] Caton MSS. III, 364–8.

the result of the indwelling spirit as theirs? The answer given by Ranters was 'Yes', and any action which they felt urged to do was therefore good and inspired by the Holy Spirit. But Fox and Margaret Fell knew otherwise. They held to the true teaching of Christ, that by our fruits we shall be judged. The indwelling Spirit must be manifested in right behaviour.[1]

Margaret Fell took part in the struggle against Ranterism not only in her efforts with Nayler himself but also by writing a book in 1656. This, the second book which she published, attacked with vigour the spirit and deeds of the Ranters. She told them that their view that 'God is darkness as well as light' was blasphemy, as was their belief that whatever they did was God's will. She charged them with calling evil good, and good evil, darkness for light, light for darkness. She attacked their claim to unlimited individual freedom, for they said they could swear, lie, be drunken and cheat, because all was done in the light, in faith, and therefore without sin. They did not know, she told them, the true liberty of God—their liberty was but bondage. She claimed that the Quakers 'utterly deny thee and all thy principles and all the Ranters is by us denied; and your practices we abhor. In the eternal light which never changes do we see you and know you.'[2]

The Quaker movement in four years had had great successes—many had welcomed its teaching and it had spread far and wide. Now, in 1656, came this unlooked-for attack on its very basis. It was no wonder that Fox and his friends were alarmed at the defection of Nayler, and in letters and interviews fought for his soul and his sanity. It was largely this struggle in 1656 and 1657 which caused Fox a few years later to create an organization,

---

[1] See *Studies in Mystical Religion:* chapter on Seekers and Ranters, by Professor Rufus M. Jones, and article on the Ranters by the same writer in the *Encyclopaedia of Ethics and Religion*, and also his *Mysticism and Democracy in the English Commonwealth*, pp. 132–3.

[2] This book is not included in M.F.'s *Works* published in 1710, possibly because by that time Ranterism was no longer a dangerous movement. It appears, bound with *Trial of False Prophets* and *A Testimony of the Touchstone* in the Edward Cadbury Collection, Vol. 2, at Woodbrooke, Birmingham. It is interesting to find from Smith's Catalogue of Quaker publications that this book against Ranterism was translated into Dutch, a necessity, as in Holland a number of Ranters appeared and disturbed Quaker Meetings.

simple but strong, which stressed the importance of submitting the 'concerns' of the individual to the judgment of the meeting, so that they might be considered in a spirit of Truth and humility. Two non-Quaker contemporary writers stated that if God had not raised up the principle of Light and Life which George Fox preached, the nation would have been overrun by Ranterism, and all the justices could not have stopped it with their laws.

Always the news of the struggle with Nayler and his friends was sent to Margaret in the north. Her sufferings must have been great; she knew that from the end of December 1655 until 13th September 1656, George Fox was imprisoned at Launceston in Cornwall, one of the most terrible of his many imprisonments. Margaret knew as others did, what a loss his inability to visit Meetings was in this year of disunity. Indeed, as mentioned earlier, three of his friends petitioned Cromwell to allow them to lie in Doomsdale, Launceston, instead of Fox, as they recognised the harm his absence was doing. While Fox was at Launceston, Margaret heard from Howgill and Burrough of the crowded Meetings at Bristol at the end of July where Nayler's friends had been exceptionally unruly, then she heard of Nayler's imprisonment at Exeter in August, as the result of a wide campaign by the authorities to try to prevent Friends travelling about the country, in particular on visits to the imprisoned George Fox.

Thomas Rawlinson of Graythwaite in Furness shared a room during this imprisonment at Exeter with Nayler, and in a long letter to Margaret, he told her, 'James Nayler is here with me, standing in the will of God, waiting in his own way, for he is precious and dear with God and is willing to bear reproach. He hath been in a fast, he ate no bread but one little bit, for a whole month, and there was about a fortnight when I came to him, he took no manner of food, but some days a pint of white wine, and some days a gill mingled with water.'[1]

Nayler, in spite of the severe fast, was reported in September by John Stubbs as strong and loving, though he was still incapable of rebuking his unruly friends.[2] A fortnight later, Hubberthorne told Margaret that Nayler's condition was 'pretty low

[1] Bowden MSS. Friends' House, London.
[2] Swm. MSS. III, 455.

and tender, and dear and tender love from my soul flowed forth
to him. After a little time his heart was opened towards me, and
he let forth himself to me, but there came Martha Simmonds
when I was there, and when at any time we were together she
would have called him away, and he was so much subject to her.
She remains in her filthiness still.' Hubberthorne explained how
she had just come from Fox at Launceston, where she had been
vain and impudent and had almost created a scandal.[1]

A week later, Fox, having just been released, came to see
Nayler at Exeter. Long interviews between the two men, with
other Friends present, followed. In them much patience and
tenderness were shown by Fox, and sometimes Nayler had a
return of his old humility and spiritual sanity, but always his
loyalty to Fox and his teaching was destroyed by the extravagance and adulation of Martha.

Leaving Nayler in Exeter gaol, Fox travelled in Wiltshire and
to Bristol during October, and when he reached Reading, he
wrote two important letters to Nayler, in the effort to make
him see where his actions would lead him. 'James, thou must
bear thy own burden, and thy Company's with thee, whose
iniquity doth increase, and by thee is not cried against.' Then he
describes Martha's behaviour to him at Launceston and adds
'Many would not expect that thou wouldst have been an encourager of such as do cry against the power and life of Truth,
but wouldst have been a nourisher of Truth, and not have
trained up a company against it.'[2]

Shortly afterwards, Fox referred to his visits to Nayler at
Exeter—'And I saw thee at Exeter, a cloud of darkness would
rise up against me, which was entered into thee, and wickedness
I told thee was growing to a mountain which would have be-
trayed the just.'[3] And in another letter he wrote: 'And James it
will be harder for thee to get down thy rude company than it
was for thee to set them up (if ever thou come to know and own
Christ) whose impudence doth sport and blaspheme the Truth.'[4]

In the meantime letters had been passing between Nayler and

---

[1] Swm. MSS. III, 153. **16 vii** [**Sept. 1656**].
[2] Swm. MSS. III, 193.
[3] Port. 24, 36, Library, Friends House, London.
[4] Swm. MSS. III, 195.

Margaret Fell. As early as August, before Martha's mischievous visit to Fox at Launceston, Margaret had written to Nayler in her anxiety, telling him that she had heard news of him which 'made her heart to ache', and begging him to confide in her.[1]

As the weeks passed, and the news became worse and more damaging both to Fox and Quakerism generally, she wrote a long appeal to Nayler, on 15th October (1656), which most unfortunately did not reach the distracted man, as he had been released from Exeter on 18th or 20th October, before the letter could have covered the distance from Swarthmoor. In places the very incoherence of the writing shows the feeling of acute anxiety felt by Margaret.[2]

She gives Nayler credit for having expressed subjection (to Fox) and love and unity in words, but accuses him of want of practising such virtues. He had shown the vice of jealousy 'where thou saith George is burying thy name that he may raise his own'. His claim that he would not let Truth suffer had been belied by his rebellion against Fox. 'Oh dear heart, mind while it is called to-day what thou art doing, lest thou walk naked and be a stumbling block to the simple.' 'And I could lie down at thy feet that thou might trample upon me for thy good, or so I know would he whom thou hath resisted, though to that spirit that rebels it cannot be, for that is not one with your Father.'[3]

If only this letter had reached him it might have prevented further tragedy, but on his release his physical weakness due largely to his weeks of fasting gave full rein to the influence of his misguided friends. Fox's last letter to him, together with two from Margaret, he put into his pocket as he left the prison, but at about the same time he received letters from his admirers which savoured of blasphemy. Martha's husband, Thomas Simmonds, addressed him as 'Thou King of Israel and son of the Most High' and 'Thy name shall be no more James Nayler, but Jesus'. Another wished she could present him with gold, frankincense and myrrh, while a third called him 'Son of Zion, whose mother is a virgin, and whose birth is immortal'.[4] Nayler never

[1] Brailsford, *James Nayler*, p. 108.
[2] For complete letter, see Appendix 9.
[3] Spence MSS. III, 38.
[4] Brailsford, *James Nayler*, pp. 109, 110, 114.

made those claims himself, but he did not now have the strength to reprove those who did. He would have destroyed the letters if he could, but he put them into his pocket, where on his arrest later they were found.

From Exeter, Nayler and his friends walked to Bristol, in those last days of October. As they neared the city, they formed into a procession in imitation of the entry of Jesus into Jerusalem; Nayler, in a dream, riding on horseback, led by a young man, with a woman walking on each side, trudging in the mud and crying in a chant 'Holy, holy, holy, Lord God of Israel'. This extraordinary entry into the city was followed by various meetings, where much confusion was caused by the extravagant behaviour of the women, all unrebuked by Nayler. He and his party were arrested, searched, charged with blasphemy, and sent to London. Howgill, writing to Margaret at the end of October, while Nayler was on his way to London, told her, 'They have made Truth stink in those parts, and truly my dear G.F. bore it so long, and stood so off us, that it's become a mountain; and he sees he suffered it too long now. I saw thy letter which James sent thee, and I saw it full of cunning subtlety, and repented I had sent it thee; but standing to thy own, nothing without can hurt. . . . Do not write to J.N. till thou hear further, lest his deceit grow stronger.'[1]

In November, Richard Hubberthorne, after a visit paid to Nayler at their inn in London where they were kept prisoners, wrote to Margaret, 'That power of darkness in the women rules over him, as I wrote to thee at the first.' The women were kneeling to James, and 'my heart was made to pity his condition', but Hubberthorne's advice was scorned.[2]

Then began the trial of Nayler for blasphemy, by Parliament. It was the last and shortest-lived House in Cromwell's day, packed with only 'godly' men who could be relied on, so he thought, to support him. Almost its first work was the trial of Nayler, in November and December 1656.

In spite of his weakness, Nayler answered the mass of questions put to him with care and wisdom, denying that he had

[1] Etting Early Quaker Papers, Philadelphia, 30. Quoted in full in *Swm Doc. in America:* pp. 28–30.

[2] A.R.B. **pp.** 45–6, dated **25 ix [Nov.] 1656**.

been guilty of blasphemy, but regretting that he had not prevented his friends from claiming too much honour and glory for
him. At length he was adjudged guilty, and the dreadful punishment was given—to stand in the pillory (this in the depth of
winter), whipping through the city, at the cart-tail, a second
stand in the pillory, with the boring of his tongue and branding
of his forehead, all to be followed by further whipping at Bristol
and a lengthy imprisonment. The barbarity of the sentence and
the amazing courage of the man shocked and subdued the
thousands of spectators. Afterwards he lay ill in Bridewell
Prison, London, visitors being kept from him for several months.

Among the Meetings, the strife, disunity and extravagance of
behaviour of his followers continued, though as Hubberthorne
explained to Margaret 'sweetly doth the water of life flow, and
pleasant streams are drunk of by those who keep patient in the
will of God.'[1]

A month later Hubberthorne told her that Oliver Cromwell
in his declaration to the City had said that the Quakers were
enemies of the State—a hardening due to the Nayler affair.

By February 1657, however, Hubberthorne was able to tell
Margaret that the power of the unruly spirits was lessening,
meetings were large and pretty quiet, 'the power of God having
come over those airy spirits'. He related how he had frequently
been moved to go and speak to them, and in tender love show
them wherein they misunderstood the Truth, for they were
simple people and weak. They were now coming to see their
errors.'[2] Two months later he again assured Margaret that the
'work of the Lord' could not 'be hindered by all the offences that
rise up against it'.[3]

Throughout 1657, while Meetings in London were large,
sometimes there were still disturbances. George Fox himself
was during this year rarely in London—he was chiefly travelling
in Wales, North-West England and Scotland, and did not return
to London until June 1658.

By the autumn of 1657 James Nayler, from the depths of his
suffering, physical and spiritual, had come to a most touching

[1] A.R.B. 48–9. Feb. 1657, quoted from Caton MSS. III.
[2] Caton MSS. III, 377 *seq.*
[3] Caton MSS. III, 356–9.

repentance. In September he was writing frequently to his old companion Richard Farnsworth, 'whereby it appears that he is in a great sense of his condition, and very loving, humble, tender and low; he also expressed that his love is great to all the faithful flock.'[1] Four months later Richard Hubberthorne wrote to tell Margaret that he had been with James Nayler three times lately and had found him loving 'and his love doth increase'.[2] Nayler's great desire now was to be reconciled to Fox. For a year and a half, Fox refused to be reconciled. Perhaps this hardness was due to the way in which this defection of Nayler had threatened a split in the infant Society, and a misunderstanding in the outside world, which had been of immense danger.

As Fox expressed it in his Journal—'After I had been warring with the World, now there was a wicked spirit risen up among Friends to war against.'[3]

George Fox and Margaret Fell, from their wide correspondence with Friends scattered in many nations, had heard how the claim made by Nayler's followers of Messianic power for him had harmed their work. In Holland, for instance, a large number of books were written or translated from English into Dutch, attacking Quakerism on account of the Nayler case, or refuting the lies in those attacks. Specially widely read in Holland was the book by a clergyman, John Deacon, entitled *The Grand Impostor Examined; or the Life, Trial and Examination of James Nailer, the seduced and seducing Quaker*. It had been published in London in 1656, and its Dutch translation was published in 1657. Deacon followed with a second book, after Nayler's punishment. Both books were widely read in Holland as in England, and in Professor Wm. I. Hull's view, 'the Dutch version of the first . . . created one of the chief obstacles to the successful planting of Quakerism on the Continent.'[4] Other difficulties met with by Caton and Ames in Holland, and mentioned in their letters to Margaret Fell, were created by certain women from England who were as unruly and extravagant as the Ranting women, Martha Simmonds and Hannah Stranger.

---

[1] A.R.B. pp. 52–3. **18 vii [Sept.] 1657**.
[2] A.R.B. from Caton MSS. III.
[3] Camb. Jnl. I, 244.
[4] *Qism. in Amsterdam*, W. I. Hull, p. 241.

Henry Fell, recently arrived in Barbados, reported to Margaret that their enemies had been more active since hearing reports of Nayler from England.[1]

The news even was sent out to Turkey by a Turkish spy who lived undiscovered in Paris for many years. In his letter (published in 1770) he speaks of Nayler as being the 'ringleader' of the Quakers, professing to be the Messiah; he describes his entry into Bristol, and suggests that all Quakers are equally extravagant in their claims, though very patient in their sufferings.[2]

In England, a number of Friends besought Margaret to pray for Nayler, and to write to his followers to show them how they were wresting wrong meanings from the Scriptures and so deceiving their hearers. 'It could not but be very serviceable', wrote Thomas Lawson to her, 'to scatter an answer to these things up and down the nation, for with their swelling words they catch several.'[3]

As Nayler regained his former power and humility of spirit, he and others turned to Margaret for her help. From Bridewell, probably early in 1657, he sent her a letter of gratitude for her love which had strengthened and comforted him—'for this my soul loves thee unfeignedly'. He wanted her to know that he was able to bear everything which came to him, and that he loved the Truth and its people. 'I beseech thee', he concluded, 'cease not to share with me in my tears before God, until the end.'[4]

On another occasion in 1657 or 1658 he wrote to her—'Thou hast been a Mother not willing to cast off compassion, nor part from pity. . . . I wait suffering, and am not without hope in the end to attain an everlasting unity. . . . My love to G.F. who is dear to me in the love of God which all the subtle workings of the enemy I know shall never break.'[5]

In June 1658 Alexander Parker on his visits to Nayler found him fully repentant, and anxious to make reparation. He wrote to Margaret from London on 15th June 1658:

[1] Swm. MSS. I, 69. **14 ii [April] 1657.**
[2] Jnl. F.H.S. VIII, 25–7.
[3] Swm. MSS. I, 242 and III, 86.
[4] Crosfield MSS. 9.
[5] Brailsford, *James Nayler*, p. 166, quoted from Swm. MSS. III, 83.

My dearly beloved sister,

[After relating the extravagance of 'Mildred' and others, and the efforts of Fox to control them]

I have been with J.N. in the prison three times since I came to this city, and true love and life are springing up in him; he is made willing to lie under all, and would do anything that might in the wisdom of God be seen convenient, for taking off all occasion, as much as in him lies, either by public recantation (which I do not judge serviceable) for exalting the Truth, or any other way; he is made willing to bear all, and to come under all, and hath passed through true judgment. . . . James hath written a few words with much subjection, desiring to be reconciled; and I know that George [Fox] is dearer to him than ever, as by his words I have heard. My dear sister, as thou hast been tender and of large compassion unto the sufferer, I beseech thee make intercession for him; that in the spirit of meekness, as a brother, he may be restored again. I am plain unto thee, dear one, having no other thing in my heart, but the glory and advancement of the Truth in this thing, and peace and unity amongst brethren . . . As thou seest in the wisdom of God, I shall leave it to thee, to do as thou art moved. I know it lieth wholly now in G.F. but to the Lord I leave it, and in patience I shall wait to see the Truth advance over all, for I have great hopes that all things will be well.

Thy dear brother in the fellowship of the Gospel,

Alex. Parker.[1]

Margaret was told in this letter that there was a group of Friends who were so strongly against Nayler that they were trying to publish a pamphlet to raise the whole controversy again and prevent his being received back into fellowship. Parker had 'besought G.F. even with tears to be tender in this thing and that he would stop that paper'. Later this group was repudiated by Fox,[2] but this threat mentioned by Parker probably explains one cause of the delay in reconciliation between the two men.

Next month Parker was telling Margaret that Nayler had been fasting in prison, eating occasionally a little bread and water, and was so weak that many did not expect him to recover.[3]

[1] Caton MSS. III, 315–17. Largely quoted in A.R.B. 57.
[2] Camb. Jnl. I, 343.
[3] Caton MSS. III, 321. 13th July 1658.

On various occasions this year Nayler wrote loving letters to Friends confessing his grief for the wrongs he had done them, 'whose sufferings is my greatest sorrow that ever yet came upon me'. To Margaret Fell he wrote a touching letter of appeal. In his time of heavy burdens he was comforted when he felt her sympathy, and he believed there were many Friends who felt mercy for him, 'but truly for the hardness and unreconcilableness which is in some, I am astonished and shaken, lest the spirit of Christ Jesus should be grieved and depart, for if I know anything of it, or ever have done, that is it which naturally inclines to mercy and forgiveness, and not to bind one another under a trespass till the uttermost farthing, though this may be just, and I do not condemn it. Yet I have felt a spirit which delights more in forgiving debts: . . . and by this spirit I have been able to bear all things. . . .'[1] He is not complaining for himself, but he fears these unforgiving people are doing harm to themselves and Truth. He is probably referring here not to George Fox as is suggested by E. Fogelklou (p. 258), but to the group of un-forgiving Friends mentioned in Parker's letter of June. Then he adds, 'Dear friend, thou mayest feel my heart by what I have written to thee, which I fear to do to others, for I have found the adversary watching what might come from me, to pervert for evil, which hath kept me much from writing what is before me. Yet to thee I am bold, having known thee near me in all things, even ever since I see thy face, and have been strength-ened in thee, often in the work of God, before this present condition.'[2]

Nayler continued to lie in prison (he was free for a short time in the winter of 1657–8, apparently for health reasons) until he had his final release in September 1659, after nearly three years' imprisonment. He at once went to see George Fox who was at Reading. Throughout 1658 and 1659 there had been bitter persecution of Friends. After the death of Oliver Cromwell, in September 1658, there followed the weak rule of his son Richard, a time of chaos and confusion. By the late summer of 1659 Fox was worn out with his travels and particularly with the sense of sin and suffering in the country and disappointed hopes, and for

[1] In Spoore and Whiting MSS.
[2] Swm. MSS. III, 84. Undated, but probably **spring** 1658.

ten weeks (probably from early July until mid-September) he lay at Reading between life and death.

Nayler came to see him towards the end of his illness, but he was not allowed to see Fox. In his distress Nayler wrote to Margaret:

Dearly beloved Sister,

Thou art often in my remembrance and my heart is to see thee when God wills; in whose counsel and life I desire to walk, to his praise alone, who hath thus far redeemed me out of deep adversity; and doth still work with me and for me, (as I abide in his patience and obedience,) making my way through many oppositions and trials. In his will alone I desire to rest and be still; who in the needful time hath still appeared. . . . I suppose thou may have heard of my going to see our beloved G.F. at Reading, which in tenderness of love I did, as soon as I was set out of prison, hearing he was not well: but I was not permitted to come where he was; which my adversary rejoiced at, that thereby he might add sorrow to affliction: . . . but my spirit was quieted, in that simplicity in which I went, in that to return; and [He] gave me His peace therein, as though I had had my desire. . . .

My dear love to thee and to thy family . . . I am refreshed when I feel thee near me, or hear from thee, in that in which we cannot be separated.

James Nayler.[1]

On his return to London, Nayler attended Meetings, and began to minister again, many being convinced by him.[2]

After Fox's recovery from his illness, William Dewsbury, fellow Yorkshireman with Nayler, and old friend, persuaded Fox to meet Nayler, and their full and public reconciliation came about at the end of January 1660. Joyfully Dewsbury wrote to tell Margaret.

Much the Lord laid it on me, that dear George Fox and J.N. might meet together, my travail was great in the spirit, until the Lord answered, which in the day he determined were done. Mighty was his majesty amongst his people, in the day he healed up the breach which had been so long to the sadness of the hearts of many. The Lord clothed my dear brethren G.F., E.B. [Edward Burrough], F.H. [Francis

---

[1] A.R.B. p. 58 and Port. 41, 22, at Friends House, London.

[2] A.R.B. pp. 60-1 and Caton MSS III 124 (pp. 392-3). Letter from Richard Hubberthorne to M.F. dated by A.R.B. 22 viii [Oct.] 1658 and by Isabel Ross as apparently 1659. C. W. Horle, however, argues from internal evidence for 1655.

Howgill] with a precious wisdom. A healing spirit did abound within them, with the rest of the Lord's people there that day, according to their measure, and dear J.N. the Lord was with him, and ordered him by his spirit. . . . With gladness of heart then was I set free to pass from London through Surrey and so Bristol.[1]

There are no further letters to Margaret Fell either from Nayler or about him. Soon after the reconciliation, he went to Bristol to beg and receive with gladness the forgiveness of Friends in that great city which had been the scene of his former tragedy. For the next few months he was in or near London, and in Yorkshire in May and June, writing a loving letter to Fox when he heard of the latter's imprisonment at Lancaster. In October he left London again for the north, and in Huntingdon he was found dying by the roadside, but 'in the peace of God'.

Margaret did not forget her friend, for she speaks lovingly of him in her testimony to George Fox which she wrote thirty years later. She, in whose compassion and wisdom he had trusted, had striven with him when, as he later confessed, he had failed to rebuke those who had claimed for him greater spiritual power and eminence than he really had, and had thus fallen into grievous spiritual darkness; and she must equally have rejoiced when he found that God had given him back the Light, and he was able fully to repent, and be as fully received back into loving fellowship with his friends. Indeed it was the beauty and wonder of his repentance and the victory over darkness which made the glory of this man whose suffering of mind and body had been so deep.

'There is a spirit which I feel that delights to do no evil nor to revenge any wrong, but delights to endure all things, in hope to enjoy its own in the end.'[2]

---

[1] Swm. MSS, IV, 134.
[2] J.N.'s dying words, *B. Qism.*, p. 275.

Chapter Nine

JUDGE FELL, 1652–8

IN the first chapters of this book Judge Fell's professional life and important public services are described, and also his tolerance and hospitality to George Fox and his friends. He was 'mighty serviceable to Truth', wrote Fox in one of his Journals.[1] This was his mature judgment, but in 1652 Fox wrote twice to the Judge in almost violent terms, because he did not come out entirely for Quakerism.[2]

In the early days there were one or two other Friends equally concerned to win the judge over openly to their side, and sometimes their letters were more conspicuous for outspokenness than for tact. But those who knew him best—Farnsworth and Nayler who had seen his wise kindliness at Fox's first visit to his home, and his servants Henry Fell and Thomas Salthouse—loved him and frequently sent messages to him in their letters to his wife. Although the Judge never became a Quaker, he gave considerable help to individual Friends, sometimes in money, and at other times in matters of law.

Robert Widders, for example, wrote from Lancaster Castle where he was imprisoned in 1654 that his discharge had been brought from the sheriff for their liberty, but that he was a little doubtful as to taking his liberty thus, and would Margaret consult Judge Fell or Colonel William West.[3]

While Robert Widders was still in Lancaster Castle, Judge Fell and Colonel West visited him, before they travelled up to London, and they were 'very loving and tender'. Widders wanted George Fox to see them in London, and gave George their addresses—West lodging 'at the Angel on the back of St.

[1] *Short Jnl.* p. 26.
[2] Swm. MSS. VII, 73 and 74.
[3] Swm. MSS. IV, 102.

Clements, at Mr. Stanton's house, and Judge Fell at his chamber
in Gray's Inn in Holborn Court'.[1]

Another Quaker from his prison in Derby asked Margaret to
remind her husband that two friends of his had become bond
for his appearance at the coming Assizes (perhaps in Lancaster),
but that he should see they do not suffer from his lack of attendance if he were still in prison.[2]

When Thomas Salthouse, lately the Judge's agent, was suffering imprisonment in the south-west the Judge sent a man to inquire if he needed any financial or other help, which the man was
ordered to supply, 'so I wrote to him', said Salthouse, 'to satisfy
him I had no want for the outward, but to see his love [which]
I received as from the Lord, I was refreshed'.[3] It says much for
both the Judge and his agent that their affection and respect for
each other survived the relinquishing of a business agreement
for the sake of the new work of spreading Quakerism.

During the Judge's stay in London in 1655, he was so friendly
to Quakerism that he attended part of a General Meeting held
there. Alexander Parker described the incident thus in his letter
to Margaret: 'Towards the latter end thy husband came with
Giles Calvert into the meeting, and as George [Fox] was
passing forth he took George by the hand and a pure love was
raised up in him; afterward James Nayler and I passed down to
Giles Calvert's, and we found him there: was exceeding
tender and loving towards us'.[4]

In other letters to Margaret, Alexander Parker remembers his
love for the Judge, and prays that he may have 'courage to stand
up for Truth',[5] and 'wisdom and courage to rule for God, to be
a terror to the evildoers and a praise to them that do well'.[6]

Twice at least did Judge Fell find himself on the Bench at
Chester (one of the cities of his circuit), trying Friends. In one
case two Quakers were arrested by Sheriff's writ for non-payment of tithes and 'steeplehouse leys' in Chester, and one of

[1] Swm. MSS. IV, 41.
[2] Swm. MSS. IV, 67.
[3] **Swm. MSS. I, 112. 8 xii 1655 [Feb. 1655/6].**
[4] **Caton MSS. III, 91. 10 iii [May] 1655.**
[5] Swm. MSS. I, 166.
[6] Swm. MSS. I, 167.

them hoped that if Margaret saw it 'meet in the Light' she would tell her husband about their case, as he might be concerned in their trial 'we desiring nothing but Justice'.[1] The other case concerned the Judge's former clerk Henry Fell. He had already pleaded successfully with the Judge, on behalf of these two Friends, and they were not imprisoned, and then he told Margaret of his own trial: 'The Judge [evidently Judge Fell] was loving to me. But as for Bradshaw he uttered forth abundance of enmity against the Truth in his charge which I perceive thy husband was not well pleased with.'[2] Judge Bradshaw, who in January 1649 had presided over the High Court of Justice which tried and condemned Charles I, was later the colleague of Judge Fell in the Chester and North Wales Circuit. Judge Fell remembered him in his will thus: 'I likewise give and bequeath unto my very honourable and noble friend the Lord Bradshaw, ten pounds to buy a ring therewith, whom I humbly beseech to accept thereof, as all the acknowledgment I can make, and thankfulness, for his ancient and continued favours and kindness undeservedly vouchsafed unto me since our first acquaintance.'[3] Henry Fell's criticism of Judge Bradshaw is not corroborated by William Penn who many years later ranked Judge Bradshaw, Judge Fell and Colonel West as courageous friends of Friends.[4]

Judge Fell's relations with Friends are best summed up in the words of both his wife and of George Fox himself.

In the preface to the Journal of William Caton, which Fox edited thirty years after Judge Fell's death, Fox wrote: 'Judge Fell was very serviceable in his day and time, to stop the edge of the priests, justices and rude multitude, who often fell upon Friends, beat them and persecuted them. For when I was laid for dead by the beating of the rude multitude, near Ulverston, and afterwards in Walney, when the people rose upon me, and thrust me into the sea, and after beat me down, and laid me for dead, and all this for Truth's sake. And after warrants were granted out against me, and I was had to a sessions in Lancaster, and many priests appeared against me and Friends; Judge Fell

[1] Swm. MSS. I, 149.
[2] Caton MSS. III, 251.
[3] Webb, *Fells*, p. 142.
[4] Penn's *Works*, Vol. I, 880. Printed 1726, written in 1694.

and Justice West stood up nobly for us and the Truth, and our adversaries were confounded; so that he was as a wall for God's people against them. And afterwards he came to see beyond the priests; and at his latter end seldom went to hear them in that parish: and let a meeting be in his house from '52 to his death, and so there has been to this day; a testimony of his sense of the Truth of God in his people, for which he has his reward of the Lord.'[1]

And Margaret, whom he called in his will 'my dear careful and entirely beloved Margaret Fell my wife', wrote in her old age as she looked back at the early years of spiritual struggle and awakening, and specially at the first meeting of these two men: 'At night [in the parlour at Swarthmoor Hall] G. Fox spoke so powerfully and convincingly, that the witness of God in his [her husband's] conscience answered that he spake Truth; and he was then so far convinced in his mind that it was Truth, that he willingly let us have a meeting in his house the next first-day after, which was the first public Meeting that was at Swarthmoor, but he and his men went to the steeplehouse (our Meetings being kept at Swarthmoor about 38 years, until a new Meeting House was built by G. Fox's order and cost near Swarthmoor Hall), and so through the good power and word of God, the Truth increased in the countries all about us, and many came in, and were convinced, and we kept our Meetings peaceably every first-day at Swarthmoor Hall, the residue of the time of his life. And he became a kind friend to Friends, and to the practicers of Truth upon every occasion, as he had opportunity. For he being a magistrate, was instrumental to keep off much persecution in this country, and in other places where he had any power.

'He lived about six years after I was convinced: in which time it pleased the Lord to visit him with sickness, wherein he became more than usually loving and kind to our Friends called Quakers, having been a merciful man to the Lord's people. I, and many other Friends were well satisfied the Lord in mercy received him to himself.'[2]

Although Judge Fell's public work was of great importance

---

[1] *Life of W. Caton*, **1689 ed., p. [iv]**.
[2] M.F. *Works:* p. 3.

and influence, and his toleration was remarkable, perhaps the most outstanding aspect of his character is revealed in his relationship with his wife.

At their marriage, Margaret was only seventeen while her husband was double her age—perhaps, near neighbours as they were, he had waited patiently for her to grow into womanhood —but, in spite of this difference in age, his trust of her judgment and actions is most conspicuous. He might so easily have been jealous of her, but he obviously never was; their deep love for each other was not endangered by the affection felt and expressed by her from 1652 onwards for Fox and countless other Quakers, and their almost extravagantly expressed love of her.

Probably the only letter still existing which is entirely in Margaret's own handwriting—beautiful and clear—is one to her husband in London in February 1653, seven months after she had been convinced. It is given here in full.

18 xii 1652 [Feb. 1652/3].

Dear Husband,

My dear love and tender desires to the Lord runs forth for thee. I have received a letter this day from you and am very glad that the Lord carried you on your journey so prosperously. Thou wrote to me that those which professed to worship God which profession we do deny without possessing the real substance, and if we enjoy the living power of the Lord and walk humbly with our God and be taught of him alone, there will be no offence given unto man in whom the Lord ruleth, but the offence will be to that which must die and be crucified and we are not to be in obedience to man that lives in [sin?]. Dear heart, mind the Lord above all with whom there is no variableness nor shadow of turning and who will overturn all powers that stand against him; [they?] shall be as chaff before him. Therefore be faithful unto death and he will give thee the crown of life, and stand firm and close to the Lord and be not afraid of man. Greater is he that is in you than he that is in the world. Mind that which is of [life] in thy own particular to keep thee pure and clear and single before him without end whatsoever, and that will stand before the fire of his wrath which burns up all but what is of himself.

We sent to my dear brother James Nayler and he is kept very close and cannot be suffered to have any fire; he is not free to eat of the jailor's meat so they eat very little but bread and water. He wrote to us that they are plotting again to get more false **witnesses** to swear against him things that he never **spoke**.

I sent him 20 shillings, but he took but 5. They are mighty violent in Westmorland and all parts over everywhere towards us. They bid £5 to any man that would take George anywhere that they can find him within Westmorland. I sent [thee an] order that came from Colonel Benson which should have been at London as soon as you but I am afraid they have miscarried. I sent with them a copy of a letter concerning some passages **at** the sessions holden at Lancaster where Judge Thorpe was, and he was very favourable to our friends there and did take notice of the priests' tyranny. I should have been glad you had received them. Here is a copy of Colonel Benson's letter that I have sent thee, and here is a declaration that Colonel Benson and other friends drew; if the Lord move any to present it to them that are in authority; and here is a note that George was moved to rise out of bed and write that should be showed to any in Parliament that is a friend to the truth. Dear heart, I pray thee do not let it lay at thy door but show it to any that is anything loving to the truth. It will stir up the pure in them which is one with that which it came from. Here is likewise a declaration of these things that we live in and a note concerning faith and the two seeds, the seed of the serpent and the seed of the woman, which should be put in print. Now I beseech thee let them be printed [that they] may openly appear to the world what we live in, and be not ashamed of the truth for it will stand when all other things shall be as stubble, so hoping that thou will be faithful to me and to the Lord, farewell. [May] the everlasting God of power and love keep thee up to himself [?] to his everlasting praise and glory.

The children are all in health, praised be the Lord. George[1] is not with us now but he remembered his dear love to thee. Here is a note James Nayler hath put forth, [I pray] thee let this and the other that concerns him which you had along with you be put in print in a book, and the query and answers that was put to George be printed and the priest's petition and John Lawson's be printed in another book. I much desire to have them printed. It is very hard that the press should be open **for** all pamphlets and ballads and must be shut against the truth.

Dear heart I pray thee do not neglect, for I am sure if they be published they will work for the glory of my Father, to whom [be] praise and glory for evermore.

Thy dutiful wife till death,
Margaret Fell.

An addition, along the side of the letter:

[1] Probably their son, not George Fox.

I pray thee sweetheart do not slight these things for they are of great concernment but let them be made known, as they have been acted openly, so let them be published.[1]

Five years later, early in October 1658, Judge Thomas Fell died, aged about sixty. Although he had ceased for some time to attend the parish church of Ulverston, he was buried there beneath his pew. He had the honour of a torchlight procession.

To his family his death was a serious blow financially, for his salary as Judge of Assize was now lost to his widow and large family of seven daughters between the ages of twenty-five and five years, and a son undergoing expensive training for the Law in London.

A month before the Judge's death, the Protector Oliver Cromwell had died, on 3rd September 1658. While the growing political and social confusion under the weak rule of Richard Cromwell caused an increase of persecution of Friends throughout the country, the death of Judge Fell removed the protection which he had been able to give to a large extent to local Friends in North-West England.

Writing forty years later, William Penn, courtier and founder of Pennsylvania, looked back to the Judge as a 'check' to the rage of the priests in their legal proceedings against the Quakers, and as one who 'countenanced this people'. 'For', he added, 'his wife receiving the Truth with the first, it had that influence upon his spirit, being a just and wise man, and seeing in his own wife and family a full confutation of all the popular clamours against the way of Truth, that he covered them what he could, and freely opened his doors, and gave up his house to his wife and her friends; not valuing the reproach of ignorant or of evil-minded people; which I here mention, to his or her honour, and which will be, I believe, an honour and a blessing to such of their name and family as shall be found in that tenderness, humility, love and zeal for the Truth and people of the Lord'.[2]

Judge Fell's will is characteristic of the man, showing wisdom, generosity, and a careful appreciation of the character of those who were to benefit by it or administer it. (The full text is in Appendix 10.) He appointed two yeomen, his trusted servants,

---

[1] Abraham MSS. 1.
[2] Penn's *Works*, I, p. 880.

non-Quakers, as his executors, men who had no scruples as to taking the oath of administration, and two Friends of good standing, Anthony Pearson of Durham and Gervase Benson of Yorkshire, to act as trustees, to see that the will was properly administered by the executors. After leaving legacies to friends, faithful servants both at Swarthmoor and Marsh Grange, the aged poor and destitute at Ulverston (of which the Judge was Lord of the Manor) and at Dalton, he left thirty pounds (about £300 in value of modern money) to found a school for poor children in Ulverston. Before the end of the year, the towns-people had appointed trustees, and a schoolmaster was chosen. In Furness there was only one grammar school existing in 1658, at Hawkshead (other than a small free-school at Urswick), and the school founded by Judge Fell's will later became known as the Town Bank School, and in modern times has grown into the Ulverston Grammar School. To his wife he left fifty pounds 'as a token and testimony of my dearest affection unto her', and for as long as she remained a widow he left her Swarthmoor Hall with all the buildings, stables, barns, orchards, gardens and fifty acres of ground. To his 'beloved son George' he left 'so many of my law books as will make those which he hath the complete body of the law, and wherein they shall prove defective, my executors shall sell so many of the rest of my law-books as will buy those that are wanting'. George Fell was at this time probably nineteen years old, and was living chiefly in London, having been first entered a student at Gray's Inn, his father's Inn, in 1652 at the age of thirteen and apparently readmitted three years later. The residue, and indeed the main part of the large estate, was left to the seven daughters. In the will this is described as the residue and overplus of all his real and personal estate. As Margaret wrote later: 'He left one son and seven daughters, all unpreferred[1]; but left a good and compe-tent estate for them.' We know from a letter from Margaret that she herself had wealth in her own right, for her father had left her half his estate, £3,000. Margaret also had an annuity from the Hawkswell estate, which now became the property of the son George. It is probable that the Judge left the chief part of his estate to the daughters, and not to the son, because he already

---

[1] Unpreferred = unmarried.

knew the strain of extravagance in the son's character, and he probably left the law books to the son as an incentive to hard work at his profession.[1] George Fell most probably was already the owner of two-thirds of Marsh Grange, his mother's birthplace. The oldest existing deed of this estate shows him to have been the owner of it in 1670.

The only son was far from being worthy of so fine a father. His unhappy history will be told in a later chapter.

The death of Judge Fell proved not only a loss to his family and the Quakers, but to the public. The wisdom and fair judgment which Judge Fell showed in his professional work sometimes led him to adopt a course of action unpopular to many of his influential contemporaries, and the courage with which he pursued what he felt to be right appears remarkable when one considers his worldly position and how much he stood to lose by doing so. Three instances can be given of his independence of mind in public affairs. One was his refusal to support Cromwell when the latter assumed arbitrary powers. Another case was when the Parliamentary Commissioners in the north-west demanded fines from tenants to pay the expenses of the Army and the Scots, but it was Judge Fell who gave a judgment which effectively protected the tenants from a grasping State.[2] Another occasion was, when, sitting with his colleagues on the Bench at Lancaster in October 1652, he courageously allowed Fox every opportunity to defend himself against the ignorant prejudices of his accusers.

It is interesting to speculate how seriously the early Quaker movement would have been handicapped without the tolerance

---

[1] This opinion is corroborated by a letter from Mr. J. Llewelyn Curtis of London, who in 1865 wrote to Mr. John Abraham of Liverpool, a direct descendant of Margaret Fell, in reply to a request for his view of the meaning of Judge Fell's will 'beyond what appears on the surface'. Mr. Curtis wrote, 'If the Judge's "beloved son George Fell" were not otherwise well provided for either by marriage settlement or by legacies from relatives, I should be inclined to suspect that his father thought he had already received and perhaps spent more than his fair share of the family estate and I think it is evident that Judge Fell thought it desirable that his daughters should be in some measure independent of their mother as well as free from any contest on the part of their brother.'

[2] *Social Policy during the Puritan Revolution*, by Margaret James.

of Judge Fell, the freedom of thought and action he accorded to his wife, and the kindness and unlimited hospitality shown to the numbers of Friends staying in his home or attending Meetings there, during the last six years of his life.

Chapter Ten

MARGARET FELL'S FIRST VISIT TO LONDON, 1660, 1661,
AND HOW SHE FREED THE PRISONERS

*'And as you tender your own souls, and your eternal peace and comfort, be
tender of tender consciences, which the Lord hath made tender, and which are
tender and dear unto him, and make not ye their hearts sad, which the Lord
hath not made sad; which if you do, sad and heavy will be your misery.'*

Margaret Fell, in a letter to 'the Clergy who are the men that go
about to settle religion,' M.F. *Works*, p. 211. 1660.

IN May 1660, while Charles II was being welcomed back to
his country and throne by his vociferous subjects in London,
George Fox was visiting Swarthmoor Hall.

One day he was sitting in the parlour with a friend and Margaret Fell when some of her servants came in to tell her that
some constables were come to search the house for arms. They
went up into some of the bedrooms, 'for pretence', as Fox said.
Fox at once went out of the room to meet them. They asked him
his name. On hearing it they laid hold of him and said he was
the man they looked for, and took him to Ulverston. There
they kept him at the constable's house all night, 'and set a guard
of fifteen or sixteen men to watch me; and some of them sat in
the chimney, they was afraid I would go up the chimney; the
Lord's power so terrified them, and they was very rude and un-
civil to me.'[1] Next day 'thirty foot and horse' took Fox to
Lancaster across the sands. They would not let him ride on his
own good horse, but put him on a 'little horse behind the saddle',
and beat the poor beast so that he kicked and threw Fox off.
Later when they reached the swift-flowing river channel which
crosses the sands, and is sometimes deep as well as swift, the
guard let Fox ride his own horse. They were mightily pleased
with their capture, but Fox records that he was 'moved to sing
praises unto the Lord in his triumphing power over all'.

[1] Camb. Jnl. I, 358.

So they came to Lancaster, where Fox was closely imprisoned in the castle, and charged with plotting against the King.

This treatment of her loved and honoured guest was more than Margaret Fell could bear, so she took immediate action to try to remedy it. Her daughters Bridget and Isabel had just returned with Will Caton and Thomas Salthouse from attending a General Meeting at Balby in Yorkshire, when within two weeks of the King's restoration, Margaret Fell left her home for her first visit to London. Her eldest daughter Margaret had been there for some months (her sister Isabel being with her part of the time), having medical treatment for her knee, and the mother seems to have taken her faithful servant and companion Mary Askew with her on this long arduous journey on horseback through England. In London they apparently stayed with Elizabeth Trott, a wealthy woman who had a large house in Pall Mall. Left behind at Swarthmoor were the other six daughters, Bridget now twenty-five years old, down to little Rachel aged but seven. In Fox's Journal there is an amusing comment on this journey of Margaret's: 'And when Margaret went to London', he wrote, 'this Justice Porter [the Justice who had recently treated him so uncivilly, and imprisoned him] vapoured that he would go and meet her in the gap[1]; and when he came before the King, he having been a zealous man for the Parliament, several spoke to him concerning the plundering of their houses, so that he soon returned again into the country.'[2]

As soon as Margaret reached London in June she appealed to King Charles and his brothers, the Dukes of York and Gloucester by letter and personal visits. 'I spake often with the King, and writ many letters and papers unto him,' she wrote in her old age, 'and many books were given by our Friends to the Parliament, and great service was done at the time. And they were fully informed of our peaceable principles and practices.'[3] Indeed, it was to explain these principles and make them known

---

[1] 'To meet in the gap' is given in Dr. Joseph Wright's *English Dialect Dictionary* as an expression, especially used in Devonshire, meaning 'to get even with' somebody. George Fox may have learned this expression while travelling in S.W. England.

[2] Camb. Jnl. I, 361.

[3] M.F. *Works*, p. 4.

to the rulers and the country generally that the Quaker leaders concentrated their efforts at this critical time. An exiled King returned, a nation weary of civil war and the alternate rule of an unrepresentative Parliament and an Army, violence and excitement were in the air. Some Quakers had been in Cromwell's Army, but had left it very soon after turning Quaker. George Fox himself refused the offer, made in his early days (1650), of a captaincy of the Parliamentarian Army, with his famous reply, 'I told them I lived in the virtue of that life and power that took away the occasion of all wars.'[1] Now, ten years later, something more had to be done to bring understanding to the people, and to bring justice and freedom to Fox and others imprisoned on the baseless suspicion of wanting to use violence against the King. Margaret Fell in her letter to the King and the Dukes reminded them of the goodness of God in restoring them to the throne and their estates without the shedding of blood, and begged them to keep their promises made at Breda to respect the consciences of their people. She asked them too to be carefully discriminating in their choice of advisers! She told them that the Quaker refusal to take oaths was based on Christ's command, and that many of those subjects who readily took the oath of allegiance felt little loyalty in their hearts. This letter she gave into the 'King's own hand' on the next Sunday after he was crowned[2]—an incident which shows the comparative ease of approach to Charles II. Of this, her first interview with him, we are given more details in a letter from Alexander Parker to George Fox. He wrote, '[She] had a full and large time to lay all things before him, of Friends' sufferings. He was very moderate and promised fair things, if he perform them it will be good for him; he also desires a particular account of all friends that are present sufferers here, and the cause of their sufferings and the names of the magistrates who sent them to prison and the time how long we have suffered, all which by the last post I sent him.'[3]

At the same time Margaret drew up another paper, entitled 'A Declaration and an Information from us the people of God called Quakers, to the present Governors, the King and both

[1] Camb. Jnl. I, 11.
[2] M.F. *Works*, pp. 17–19.
[3] Swm. MSS. III, 146. **21 iv [June] 1660.**

Houses of Parliament, and all whom it may concern.'[1] This, 'given forth' on the 5th of June 1660, was subscribed to by thirteen of the leading men Friends, including George Fox (still in prison at Lancaster), Richard Hubberthorne, Samuel Fisher, William Caton, Gerrard Roberts, John Stubbs, and Ellis Hookes. It was delivered into the King's hand on 22nd June, and Margaret added a postscript that she had left her house and family, and travelled two hundred miles to witness to the Truth, and to answer any who objected. After reminding her readers of the terrible sufferings endured by Friends from 1652 to 1660, she attacked the payment of tithes to support a 'hireling ministry', which Friends believed was contrary to Christ's teaching, and the prosecution for refusal to take oaths, or to remove their hats in homage to persons, holding all to be equal in the sight of God. She explained their loyalty to the presence of the Light of Christ within every man, and how if that Light were followed 'there would be a feeling of God's justice and righteousness'. She criticized the clergy of the last decade in that they taught the letter of Scripture instead of the spirit. 'We are a people', she wrote, 'that follow after those things that make for peace, love and unity; it is our desire that others' feet may walk in the same, and [we] do deny and bear our testimony against all strife and wars and contentions. . . . Our weapons are not carnal, but spiritual. . . . And so we desire, and also expect to have the liberty of our consciences and just rights and outward liberties, as other people of the nation, which we have promise of, from the word of a King. . . . Treason, treachery and false dealing we do utterly deny; false dealing, surmising or plotting against any creature upon the face of the earth; and speak the Truth in plainness and singleness of heart; and all our desire is your good and peace and love and unity.'

This was the very first document to be drawn up by Quakers to proclaim their firm belief in peace, and their denial of the use of warlike weapons for any purpose. It is a proof, if proof were needed, of the pioneering spirit and of the high position of Margaret Fell in the Quaker movement, that hers was the first public statement made on a subject which Friends for three centuries have believed to be an integral part of Christ's teaching. Six

[1] M.F. *Works*, pp. 202–10.

months later, in January 1661, George Fox and Richard Hubberthorne, supported by ten other Friends, published *A Declaration from the Harmless and Innocent People of God, called Quakers, against all plotters and fighters in the World*. This followed the Fifth Monarchy Men Rising, and went through several editions.

In July 1660 Ann Curtis of Reading added her efforts to Margaret's to have George Fox released from his imprisonment in Lancaster. Ann Curtis was the daughter of Robert Yeamans who, after having served as Sheriff of Bristol, was in 1643 hanged opposite his house for his loyalty to the Royalist cause. He had planned to hand over the City, which was in Parliamentarian hands, to Prince Rupert, but the plot failed, and Yeamans was tried and hanged. He left a widow Anne and eight young children, and a ninth was born posthumously. His daughter Ann married Thomas Curtis and they became prominent Friends at Reading, their home always being open to Fox and his friends. She had indeed nursed Fox tenderly in 1659 when he was for ten weeks in a 'great travail in my spirit',[1] brought on largely (as we have seen) by the persecution of his friends, and the hypocrisy of the rulers of the time. With her Royalist background, Ann Curtis was likely to be received by Charles II with consideration. Margaret's letter from London to George in Lancaster Castle, dated 17th July 1660, tells the tale:

My dear love and life everlasting, the last 7th. day Ann Curtis came hither about the 11th. hour, and I went with her to Whitehall and brought her to the King, and she made known to him whose daughter she was and how that her father was executed for him or in his father's cause, whereupon he showed much love to her. And she said she had now a request to him. He asked her what it was. She said she had a dear friend in Lancaster Castle whom she had been to see, and she desired her person might be accepted for his or else that he might be brought up with his accusers too before him, and he might be judge in the cause. And he gave command to his Secretary to issue forth an order to that purpose, but the subtlety of the Secretary gave out order to the Judge to [that George should] be brought up by Habeas Corpus [the letter is in the writing of Margaret's daughter Margaret, and she spells the Latin words 'Horposs scorpions'] and to appear before the Judges, so that she was disappointed of her request to him and of what he had granted. If the Secretary had proceeded

[1] Camb. Jnl. I, 341.

according to order, we might have had it, to have sent down this day, but being it was contrary we could not send it. We was with the King this day about it and he appointed us to come to-morrow, so what the effect will be we know not. The Presbyterian party is exceeding mad that he should admit us so to come to him and in any measure hearken to us, and I do believe doth incense him that if he answer our desires the whole nation will be against him. But the man is moderate and I do believe hath an intent in his mind and a desire to do for Friends if he knew how and not to endanger his own safety. He is dark and ignorant of God, and so anything fears him, but we have gotten a place in his heart that he doth believe we will be true to him and so doth many of his own party. And truly the power is exceedingly over them, and over the City, meetings are all quiet and peaceable and many saith they never saw them so full. . . . My return to me is yet uncertain. How thou may come up we know not, whether they will give us way to bring thee up or they will send for thee up by order, but we shall not neglect anything. They that have to do with these people must be contented to wait.[1]

A week later (24th July 1660) Margaret wrote again to George:

My dear eternal love and Life: I gave thee an account the last week, how far Ann Curtis had gone in the business concerning thee, and according as I wrote we went the next morning, but before they would suffer us to go in to speak to him, General Monk did come, I believe on purpose to prevent us; and we were with him a pretty while before we were called in. And we were called in while he was there, and while we spoke to him, he stood by, and before we could get anything spoken to him to any purpose, they took him away from us, and the most that he said to us was that he would speak to the Judges and they should set Friends at liberty.

She explains that by the law of the land the King can only have George brought up by Habeas Corpus—a sidelight on the constitutional position won in the seventeenth-century political struggle. And she continues:

The last seventh day [Saturday], after Ann was gone I was with the King in his bed chamber and spoke to him about the oath which Friends could not take, and spoke to him about all the prisoners and he promised me that the Judges should take order concerning Friends and that he had given them order to that purpose, but being that he is

[1] Camb. Jnl. I, 372–3.

prevented of doing what he promised, he shames and will not stay, when one speaks to him.[1]

A week later Margaret wrote again to Fox, telling him that the day after Ann Curtis's visit to the King, she herself had gone again, and had won a promise that he would give a special order to the judges to release Friends, 'but what he would do, he cannot'. She had explained to him Friends' objection to swearing an oath, even those who were about to take up service for their country, and begged him to exempt them. 'It puts him to a stand', she added, 'and he said he knew not what to do in it; they that were about him gave answer and said, the King could do nothing but according to law, and if we would not be subject to the laws of the nation, then we might suffer by them—so at that time they took him away from me.'

A few days later she had still another interview with the King, and presented him with a paper which she had written for him. To three of his courtiers, a Friend with her gave copies of *The Battledore* and answers to the *Phanatic History*, a book attacking James Nayler, who had replied to the charges, taking blame on himself and absolving Friends.[2]

Nevertheless Margaret's and Ann's work with the King was not in vain, for shortly after (in September) George Fox was released by the King and his Council. The Sheriff at first proposed to send him to London with a guard of horse soldiers, but the expense of that deterred them. Then they suggested that Fox should give bail that he would be in London by such a time, and so could travel with his own friends. As a staunch believer in his innocence, he refused to give bail—nor to pay silver to the jailer of Lancaster Castle. He then suggested to his former persecutors that he would go up with one or two of his friends at his own expense and be in London on such a day 'if the Lord did permit'. They consented, and he was a free man. He first crossed the sands to Swarthmoor for a short rest, then re-crossed them, and came to London, visiting and preaching on the way, a three weeks' journey.

While Fox was in prison letters passed between Margaret Fell and her daughter Bridget, now the head of the family and

[1] Camb. Jnl. I, 373–5.
[2] MSS. copy at Friends' House Library, London, 23, 37.

household at Swarthmoor, letters which give vivid pictures of the life there and the relationship between mother and daughters.

[From Swarthmoor]   **22d of the 5th month [July] [16]60**
Dear Mother

My duty and dearest love is unto thee dearly remembered. By this thou may know of all the children's wellbeing, and that Rachel is very well—and no way wants thee, but is well contented. I have been weak in body since I came home, but I made a Gandess drink, and taken it and it seems I am much recovered, to my former health and strength, praised be the Lord.

Yesterday I came from G.F. at Lancaster, who was very well and desired to be remembered to Friends. He also bid me write to thee concerning a book which is mentioned in the Diurnell [=Journal] concerning the Quakers and Anabaptists, that some Friend might look for it, and answer it, and he also sent some papers and directed them to John Boulton, he would have them called for of him. We much did wonder that nothing should come from thee nor no other this post. G. did fully expect to hear from thee. Thou might do well to let us have a line or two from thee every week whilst thou stays there. It would be much satisfaction to us.

Here is report that Dobson is like to have his place again. Thomas Fisher hath spoken to me concerning the hog that was taken, whether he should stand to it or no. I bad him let the thing go on as it was concluded upon. The hog would be saleable enough. Thou might let us know if there be anything [to] do in it. My dear love to my sister and brother and Mary [=Mary Askew]. No news at present but that I am

> Thy dutiful daughter,
> Bridgett Fell.[1]

Over the page was a postscript to her sister Margaret, telling her of the rumour that their brother was one of the life guard, and 'thy being married with Tomlinson was almost in everybody's mouth'. Perhaps this Tomlinson was the Richard Tomlinson of Selby, Yorkshire, whose servant had been Mary Fisher who in this same year undertook the hazardous journey to the court of the Sultan Mahomet IV.

Bridget's letter crossed one from her mother who from London wrote on the 25th of July 1660:

[1] Spence MSS. III, 69

My dear Lambs and Babes of God, the Father of you all,

My dear love flows freely unto you, in the bowels of endless love be ye refreshed and nourished for ever, and there do you drink freely and eat abundantly and be satisfied. Dear hearts, my way and time of return is not yet manifested to me, but here I am set fast the will of the Lord to fulfill every jot and tittle which is the desire of my soul and therein shall I be satisfied. The last week we received a letter which made mention of Bridget not being well. I would have her to drink at least twenty days of her janesse drink and I would have her take a quantity of alice three mornings together, and keep warm and to [drink?] warm broth. I am told this is good for her disease. Let this be done shortly after the receipt of this; maybe we may send her some pills by Walter Miers when he comes. Let us hear from you as often as you can. . . .

Your brother is well, he was here yesterday and sealed the lease to his sister, but he hath not got his pardon[1] sealed yet, but he doth not fear but get it done. Keep all in the fear of the Lord God and there you will be preserved in His counsel and wisdom. The arm of the Almighty reach over you and His blessing rest upon you for ever. My dear love to all Friends. I have writ every week since you [we?] went, but we have received few from you.

> Your dear mother in the eternal life of Truth,
> Margaret Fell.

This letter was written for her by William Caton, but the anxious mother added a postscript in her own writing along the side of the letter:

Bridget my dear love, keep in the patience and be subject to the will of the Lord. My dear love to little Rachel and all the rest.

> M.F.[2]

'Gandess' or 'Janesse' drink means jaundice drink, a herbal medicine made from the common barbary. 'Alice' is 'Sweet Alice',[3] the plant name for one of the alyssums. Here we have an instance of the knowledge and use of valuable herbs, customary in all large households of that time, and advocated by George Fox when he gave advice on the education of Quaker children. In his library he had Culpeper's famous book on herbal medicines—*The English Physician Enlarged, or the Herbal*—published in 1653.

[1] This pardon from Charles II is referred to on p. 179.
[2] Spence MSS. III, 70.
[3] From *The English Dialect Dictionary*, by Wright, 1898.

A week later, Margaret was telling her daughters that the trial of the regicides and various Commonwealth supporters was about to start, and that this might delay her return home. But she exhorted them to love and unity and patience. 'And do not desire my return till the Lord that brought me hither give me back again, to whose will I stand committed if I had a thousand lives, and I doubt not but his arm and power will be over you, and his sweet love and presence will be with you.'[1]

Every letter from mother to daughter expressed this anxiety to return home, and a special concern for little Rachel and for Bridget's health. Sometimes requests are made by Bridget to her sister Margaret to make purchases in the London shops. A fabe or flounced petticoat is one such request. Nearly three months later Bridget is still without her flounced skirt, and begs Margaret to send it by the first messenger she can find.[2] In reply Margaret (junior) tells her that she had already sent a pattern for the skirt, amongst several things of theirs sent to Swarthmoor earlier. 'Blacks are very dear, they are so much worn', she added. She would like to know if their things had reached Bridget, for they had sent two trunks, a box, a hatcase with several things in it, three desks and other things.[3] At another time Margaret Fell asked Bridget to collect fifty pounds to repay a loan from Gerrard Roberts in London, partly for her own expenses, partly for a debt contracted without her knowledge by her son George now living in idleness and extravagance.[4]

Throughout July, August and September, Margaret was hoping and working for the release of George Fox, for until he had been able to come to London, she felt she was not free to leave.

In a letter[5] written to Alexander Parker and George Whitehead (who were prisoners) towards the end of July, Margaret related how in the last five or six weeks in London she had spoken to the King every week, sometimes twice or thrice, and

---

[1] Spence MSS. III, 71.
[2] Spence MSS. III, 76.
[3] Spence MSS. III, 82. Perhaps one of these desks is that still in existence, the property of Milner and Agnes Shackleton, both descendants of Margaret Fell. It is known as M.F.'s writing desk.
[4] Spence MSS. III, 73.
[5] Spence MSS. III, 56.

'both he and many about him carry fair and very loving towards us', but she realized how hard it was to get Friends out of prison, though the King did not want to put them in. 'Wicked bloody-minded men make light of it to take men's liberties from them', she wrote. The men about him were preventing the King from giving liberty of conscience, which he had promised only a few months before.

Her appeals however were not only for Friends. In August, when the King and his advisers brought to trial Lambert, Vane, Haselrigg and others of the Commonwealth statesmen and generals, Margaret wrote to the King, begging him not to show a revengeful spirit, but to remember how God had restored him without the shedding of any blood. She pleaded with him to put down wickedness, drunkenness, lightness and vanity.[1]

Indeed she wrote many letters to the King during these months; they have been preserved in full in the Spence Manuscripts, and in a shortened form in her *Works*, though this précis made in 1710 is in heavy eighteenth-century style, and does not do justice to the simpler and more direct English usually found in her letters. Sometimes she joins with one or more Friends in making her appeal to Charles. One such letter was by the scholar, Samuel Fisher, and herself, and their request was that Charles should summon some bishops to debate before him with some Quakers, 'for we do know that thou art of the most temperate, mild, meek spirit and reasonable and fit and able to judge in this matter of any one against them'. One wonders if this produced a smile from the King, but he arranged a debate. However, when the chosen Quakers—Richard Hubberthorne, George Whitehead, and Samuel Fisher—appeared at Court, one of the King's servants told them the bishops were not ready, and the debate never took place.

Margaret wrote also to other members of the Royal Family. To the Princess of Orange, the King's sister and the mother of the future William III, she wrote and delivered in person a loving greeting, appealing to her heart and mind and 'courage to answer His love that thereby thou might be blessed for ever'.[2] On the death of the Princess, and also on the death of the Duke

---

[1] Spence MSS. 104. M.F. *Works*, pp. 19–21.
[2] Spence MSS. III, 115. M.F. *Works*, p. 23.

of Gloucester, the King's brother, Margaret wrote notes of sympathy and admonition to the King.[1]

To the Dowager Queen Henrietta Maria, Margaret wrote about the Light within, and begged her that the sufferings of the Quakers should be ended. She had an interview with the Queen, and presented her letter and a number of Friends' books, and suggested a meeting between her priests and the Quakers, but in vain.[2]

To the Queen of Bohemia, daughter of James I, and aunt to the King, she wrote, referring to her long years of suffering living away from her native land. The Queen was now in England for a time. Margaret wrote: 'God is Light, and in Him is no darkness at all: the word is Light, which shines in thy heart; if thou turn thy mind to this Light within, thou wilt see from whence ariseth envy and strife and all that is evil, that proceeds out of the heart.'[3] The Queen of Bohemia had had a tragic life. She was married early and happily to the Protestant Frederick V, Count Palatine of the Rhine, and in 1618 her husband was invited by the people of Bohemia, who were Protestants and had been cruelly persecuted by the Roman Catholic, Ferdinand of Austria, to become their King. Frederick of Bohemia entered Prague in 1619, but Ferdinand, who had now become Emperor, rallied the Roman Catholics round him to stop the growth of Protestantism. So began the Thirty Years' War which, with its resulting starvation and typhus, devastated Europe until 1648. Frederick died sixteen years before the war ended, and his widow lived with her children on the Continent until her nephew was restored to the English throne in 1660. As she had known well what religious persecution meant, she willingly received Margaret Fell and heard her pleadings.

Margaret's freedom of address and outspoken courage are well shown in the letter she wrote to Charles and his brother the Duke of York (later James II).

Dear heart, the good and gracious God hath been merciful to you in preserving of you, and keeping of you in many dangers and trials. . . . Consider in time God have proved and tried you [the Duke of

---

[1] M.F. *Works*, pp. 23, 24.
[2] Spence MSS. III, 101. M.F. *Works*, p. 33.
[3] Spence MSS. III, 102. M.F. *Works*, p. 34.

Gloucester had died a few days before], and you have had a small time in this nation, which you have spent in wildness, in wantonness, in vanity, sporting yourselves in the day-time, and now your joy is turned into mourning: . . . that you might reign and prosper is the desire of my heart. . . . I do warn you to beware of hearkening to the counsel of the priests of the nations, of what sort soever, for God is departed from them, and his curse will be in their undertakings and counsels, whether you can believe it or no. (She foretells troubles to come.) Truly I stand admiring [=wondering] to see the Infinite goodness of God unto you, how He deals with you even as if He intended to do you good, for He chasteneth every one whom He loves, and the way to Him is through trials and tribulations. . . .

From one who cannot flatter, that is a true lover of your souls, and your eternal Good,

Margaret Fell.[1]

Let us return here to correspondence between mother and daughter still in London, and the six daughters left at Swarthmoor.

On 25th October Margaret wrote to her children to tell them the glad news of George Fox's release: 'G.F. is now freed . . . after he had appeared before the judge who sent for him up; then he appeared before the Lord Chief Justice of England in his chambers; and the next day he appeared before them all in open court, in the King's Bench; and all this after the King had granted out an order to set him free; but they would not set him free, till he had appeared in all these places to see if any thing would come against him. It was of great service to the Truth.'[2]

Every letter (and she wrote each week) still expressed the longing to return home, only prevented by the feeling that she still had work to do in London. Every letter showed the deep affection between mother and daughters, and the desire to have constant news of their welfare, specially of the three little ones. Sometimes Bridget would report pieces of business concerning leases, collecting of rents, or arrangements for sending money for Margaret's expenses in London.

The first mention of persecution is made in a letter from Bridget in November, where she tells her mother that though Swarthmoor Friends were well and being left alone, a great many

[1] Spence MSS. III, 103. M.F. *Works*, p. 23.
[2] A.R.B. 88–90.

in Cumberland were in prison for refusing the oath, and in Kendal also.[1]

A little later Bridget must have written a letter, now lost, to her mother, telling her that local gossip was whispering about her continued stay in London—possibly gossip about her friendship with George Fox. We have one or two other references, both in her own letters and in the writings of her enemies, that she was criticized and misunderstood for her friendship with Fox in these eleven years of her widowhood. It must indeed have been difficult in an age of such licentiousness for men and women to understand the true freedom of relationship of the Friends, based on the intensely strong belief in the equality of all in the eyes of God, and therefore of the true mental and spiritual co-operation of the sexes. Margaret's reaction to the gossip was to attack it in words when it was in the open, and otherwise rise above it.

I am so well used to them I know how to bear them, (she wrote to her daughters), but the Lord of Heaven and earth knows that if His hand had not holden me here, I had been with you ere now, but to that arm in which I stand and am preserved must I be subject.

Then she told them how the King and his Council had promised to free all the Quaker prisoners, which had been her chief task.

Thinking that their stay would now be short, she had begun to prepare for the journey home. It was now December, so they had bought a little coach, and hired a man and two horses to go either all or part of the way with them. They needed another horse which would be very expensive. She told Bridget that Thomas Coulton (the trusted servant who had acted as her husband's executor) should without delay bring up to London the deeds of the rents for some of their property, as she needed them for the settlement of a lawsuit concerning some of her husband's estate. He was to ride on horseback, bringing with him another horse, to be left at Coventry for their arrival from London. They were not certain whether they would use the coach only as far as Coventry, or take it through to Swarthmoor.

Her letter gives a vivid picture of the difficulties, and the need

[1] Spence MSS. III, 77.

for careful organization which a winter journey through England necessitated in the seventeenth century.[1] Three weeks later, on 1st January 1661, the daughter Margaret wrote again about the projected journey north, and gave the news that the King's expected granting of liberty had still not been fulfilled.[2]

Then almost immediately a fresh blow fell on the Quakers. The Fifth Monarchy Rising broke out in London. A band of religious fanatics who cried 'King Jesus, and their heads upon the gates', threw the city into a panic for four days, and led to a Proclamation on 10th January to prohibit meetings of Anabaptists, Fifth Monarchy Men and Quakers. It was both curious and outrageous that the Quakers were thought to be implicated, for though one or two of their views were identical, the Fifth Monarchy Men believed in violence and acted violently, while the Quakers had always advocated peace and consistently refused to carry weapons. The Rising gave occasion for magistrates to arrest and imprison Friends all over the country. In a few weeks 4,230 were in jail. In some counties no men Friends were left free. In Cambridge the prisoners included widows and fatherless children. But the Meetings were continued, even if only two or three were left to carry them on.

Three letters from Bridget Fell to her sister and mother in London relate the violence suffered at Swarthmoor during January and February:

23d of the 11th mo. 60 [Jan. 1660/1]

Sister M.

We have ever greatly longed to hear from my mother or thee, but hath not received one line this long time, neither do we know whether you be in bonds or at liberty, but yesterday we received letter from H.F. [Henry Fell] which had been long acoming; it was some satisfaction to us. Our friends in all parts here away is most part of them in prison, and men servants from all places is gone except John Taylor and a lad at Marsh [Grange], which we do expect may not be with us long, and we do expect shortly to be taken away, but that doth very little trouble us, if we could but hear from you. The soldiers told me there came letters from my mother which they said was suspicious, but I know not who kept them from us.

I would have thee to let us know the manner of my brother's

[1] Spence MSS. III, 78. 10th Dec. 1660.
[2] Spence MSS. III, 81.

marriage, what the woman is every way; compose as much as thou can in a little room.

Our dearest love to my mother, farewell.

Thy loving sister, B.F.[1]

The fact was that forty-three Swarthmoor Friends were taken in January 1661, some from their houses, others from the market, and some from their labour and employment, by a party of horsemen, and without any warrant. Without any examination by a magistrate, they were all imprisoned in Lancaster Castle. By March there were 270 Friends there, mostly for refusing to take the oath of Allegiance.[2]

Early in February Bridget wrote to her mother, from whom she had just received a letter after several had gone astray. She told her of the dangers of sending letters, as there were constables on the watch to confiscate them, and it was difficult to find anyone to bring letters to them. So they had had to be patient and to be content with the continued separation from her which 'was much more to us than the loss of outward liberty and enjoyments'.[3]

Bridget's next letter to her mother, written on 14th February 1661, gave her a more detailed account of their trials, a story she could not tell before because her earlier letter was being sent by the post. This letter was being carried by one of their servants or a Friend, so she could write freely, giving news of the persecution which early in the month had burst on to the Meeting and household. All letters were being opened on their way to Swarthmoor, and the news in them spread about untruthfully, causing Friends to be worse used. Eight men had come to the Hall, pretending to be soldiers, four were servants of Mr. Thomas Preston of Holker Hall, Cartmel, the others were servants of the Sheriff of Lancashire and of Sir Robert Bindloss, of Borwick Hall, near Carnforth, a Justice of the Peace, a continual persecutor of Friends. Carrying a warrant with them they searched the house and took the pistols and fowling pieces. The only man they met in the house they took without a warrant. They went

---

[1] Spence MSS. III, 80.
[2] Besse's *Sufferings*, Vol. I, p. 308.
[3] Spence MSS. III, 83.

on to search the homes of other Friends, and then they rode over the fells to search Marsh Grange. Here they were very rough, finally arresting the bailiff Joseph Sharp, and taking a mare from the stable. They also arrested the miller as he was working at his mill.

It was a very hard time for money, corn could not be sold, and they had no men left to carry the corn to market, wages had to be paid to workmen and servants, and several who had bought corn the year before had not yet paid for it. Bridget added that bees, horses and all sorts of commodities were very cheap, that money was leaving the district to pay the soldiers, and if they kept the men in prison who ought to be tilling the fields, it being the time of seed-sowing, it would not be possible to pay for their maintenance in prison, to hire other workers for the ploughing and seed-sowing, and pay what would be ex- pected from them later. 'Truly the burden of outward things hath been very heavy here; . . . if our comfort had been in out- ward things we had utterly been undone. . . . If this trial had come to some of us a little while ago it could scarce a been undergone, but now I can truly say that we are made partakers in measure of that which is able to bear all things.'[1]

These letters from the over-burdened but courageous young Bridget brought letters of comfort from her mother, who assured her that 'no outward thing' kept her in London, but only upon 'the Lord's account and Truth'. She begged her to do what they could well without much trouble to themselves, and to 'leave all things to the Lord'.[2] She was expecting Friends to be set free at the Assizes at latest—but this did not happen.

For at least two months the attempts to destroy the Meeting at Swarthmoor, and bend the Quakers to the wills of the local Justices, continued, though without success.

Towards the end of April Bridget wrote to her sister in Lon- don, the last letter of hers which we have. There was great rag- ing, she told her, among the local Justices, 'because we cannot forbear to meet together as our manner hath been, to worship God'; they were very offended, and said the Quakers were rebels, but, she added 'many of our Friends doth choose rather to suffer

---

[1] Spence MSS. III, 85, quoted by H. G. Crosfield, 87–90.
[2] Spence MSS. III, 87, quoted by H. G. Crosfield, 90–2.

what as may be inflicted upon the outward man than to do that
which may bring the spirit into bondage'.

At the last two Sunday Meetings there had been much disturbance from 'the rude fellows that came along with the constable', but they only took eight Friends into custody. Colonel
Richard Kirkby of Kirkby Hall, not far from Marsh Grange,
was the instigator of these disorders. He was about to go to
London where he might see her mother and tell her how
offended he was at Bridget. For he had sent a man 'out of love'
to warn her not to have a Meeting as the constables were coming, but she had replied that she accepted his love in sending
them word, but to forbid the Meeting she could not do.[1]

While these events were happening at Swarthmoor, Margaret Fell was still busy in London appealing to those in authority.
'Friends stood nobly in the Truth and valiant for the Lord's
name; and at last the Truth came over all',[2] wrote Fox in his
Journal. It is significant that George Fox was able to go about
the country during these months preaching, visiting and debating, while neither he nor Margaret Fell was arrested when they
attended Meetings.

She continued to write letters to the King. 'This is a sad day',
she wrote, 'that we should have the word of a King for the
liberty of our consciences and yet be hailed out of our Meetings
and had to prison.' She told of a hundred who were in prison for
refusing tithes. Friends had never taken any oath, for Christ told
them not to swear, but he told them also to be loyal. They had
suffered grievously under Presbyterian, Baptist and 'Professors'
of New England, and they pleaded now for liberty of conscience.
'And if you do cause us to suffer as others have done, the same
reproof you will receive for our sakes.'[3]

In another letter she remarked, 'Thou hast many enemies in
the nation, but we are thy friends'.[4]

Another time she sent to the King and his Privy Council the
'humble request of the oppressed people called "Quakers",
drawn up by six well-known men Friends, all in prison. They

[1] Spence MSS. III, 89, quoted by H. G. Crosfield, 92–4.
[2] Camb. Jnl. II, 8.
[3] Spence MSS. III, 106.
[4] Spence MSS. III, 108.

told him that thousands of them were in prison, loyal, law-abiding, payers of taxes, and good Christians. The prisons were so crowded and the jailers so cruel that many had no mat or straw to lie upon, no food to eat for days on end, and had become ill and weak. Twenty Quakers had recently died in prison, from disease and ill-usage.

Margaret also wrote to others in authority, who were responsible for cruelty to Friends at this time,[1] to the Justices of Lancashire, notably the persecutor Colonel Richard Kirkby, and to the Judges of Assize of Lancashire, and particularly to Judge Windham who had declared that the Light Within led to all manner of sin. To him she wrote a long letter showing that the Light Within of the Quakers was no other than the Light of Christ, which showed men the evil, and led them out of sin.[2]

In the Spence MSS. there are original copies of some twenty letters to Charles II and the Royal Family and his Council, written while she was up in London. Most of them she delivered personally, and had opportunity for talk. They were direct and clear in expression giving facts as well as appeals to the better nature of the person addressed.

At last her work bore fruit, and the King and his Council gave the word by which over four thousand Quakers were released from their prisons and restored to liberty. Then she 'had freedom in spirit'[3] to return home, and in September 1661, fifteen months after she had left it in the hands of Bridget, she and her daughter Margaret reached Swarthmoor again.

[1] Spence MSS. III, 122.
[2] M.F. *Works*, p. 39.
[3] M.F. *Works*, p. 5.

Chapter Eleven

MARRIAGES, PERSECUTION, JOURNEYS, 1661–3

'And so, my dearly beloved, be strong in the Lord, and in the power of his might, and be faithful and bold and true to your maker, and he will be a husband unto you, and set your feet upon the rock most sure, that if the storms beat, and the tempests blow, yet you will not be shaken, for he that keepeth you, is greater than all, and none is able to pluck you out of his hand.'

From an Epistle of M. Fell to Friends in Ireland, November 1661.
(Spence MSS. III, 19)

AFTER her return from London, where she had so often borne the 'weight of the vanity and naughtiness of a Court',[1] as Will Caton described it, Margaret Fell remained at her home for nine months. During that time, when she was busy with her household, including its varied business and finances, the Meeting, and her large correspondence, she also saw the marriage of her two eldest daughters, Margaret and Bridget.

Margaret, then about twenty-nine years old, was married in January 1662, at Swarthmoor Hall, to John Rous, son of Lieutenant-Colonel Rous of Barbados. As has been related in Chapter Seven both father and son were Friends—they were the first in the island to become so[2]—and the son had for some years been corresponding with Margaret Fell senior, before they had met. Possibly the young people had met in London, though there is no mention of John Rous in the letters which passed between mother and daughter during 1659. Young Margaret's letters gave news of Friends in London then, and persecution of Friends in New England, and the trouble she was having with her knee.[3] 'Baths made with herbs' were tried, and there was

---

[1] Swm. MSS. I, 327.
[2] Q. in A.C., p. 28.
[3] Spence MSS. III, 59, 61, 62, 63 and 64.

much discussion as to employing a Dutchman, and buying an instrument from him for the knee.[1]

John Rous first comes into the picture in a letter from Henry Fell who had just arrived in Barbados in the early winter of 1656 (see Chapter Seven). Not only was John Rous very 'serviceable to Truth', but his father and mother had been able through their friendship with the Governor of the island to moderate hostility to the Quakers.[2]

No doubt it was Henry Fell who had told his new friend all about the Fell family, and had inspired the young man to wish to meet them. Rous soon was travelling to New England, where he was persecuted as other Quakers were in that intolerant country. The attitude of the Puritan rulers of New England to Friends is a tragic comment on the intolerance mankind is capable of, even practised by those who had themselves fled from intolerance and tyranny in their own country. Not all the New Englanders shared the intolerance of their rulers, as John Rous recognized when he wrote to Margaret Fell just before leaving his home on 22nd July 1657: 'I wait to get passage for New England; I am free to go to any other place thereabouts whereby I may get among them; . . . they have fenced themselves strong, but a fire is kindling in their own bowels.'[3]

The month's coastal voyage to New England, preaching, debating, visiting, trial, imprisonment and flogging followed during the next few months, until in September 1658 John Rous wrote again to Margaret, this time from 'The Lion's Den called Boston Prison':

Dearly beloved Sister,—whom I honour of the true nobility wherewith the Lord God hath clothed thee, though thy face I have not seen in the outward, yet because of thy beauty in the Truth, is my heart enlarged towards thee beyond what words can express. . . . Often hath it been my desire to see thy face in the flesh and although hitherto the Father hath not given me my desire, having service for me in these remote countries, which hath prevented me, yet he hath not altogether denied me my desire, for one night as I was lying on my bed at Rhode Island, did God give me a lively sight of thee, and some

[1] Spence MSS. III, 65, 66, 67, and 68.
[2] Swm. MSS. I, 66.
[3] Swm. MSS. I, 80.

more of thy family which was no small refreshment to me; and I hope when I am clear of this land, and have spent sometime in Barbados, I shall according to the will of God go for England, and, as way is made, see thee. . . .

He then tells her the story of his travels. Leaving Barbados in August 1657, with another Friend of Barbados, he had in October landed at Rhode Island, which was the only colony at that time which allowed freedom of conscience, thanks to the courage and statesmanship of Roger Williams.

From Rhode Island, Rous and his friend went to Plymouth Colony, and to Sandwich, where there were sympathizers, then on to Connecticut where they had a great dispute with one of the leading Puritans. Returning to Rhode Island, then to Plymouth where they were whipped with rods, they went later to Boston where they had the most savage treatment, whippings with 'a threefold whip', bound 'neck and heels in irons', '117 strokes with a pitched [tarred] rope'. When he was writing this letter he and his companions were lying in jail, waiting 'to have each of us an ear off'. Yet the whole letter speaks of triumph, 'dominion', and of the spread of Truth, for the sufferings of these visiting Friends added strength to the local group.

Great have been the sufferings of Friends in this land, (he concluded,) but generally they suffer with much boldness and courage, both the spoiling of their goods and the abusing of their bodies. There are Friends few or more, almost from one end of the land to the other that is inhabited by the English. A firm foundation there is laid in this land, such a one as the devil will never get broken up. . . .[1]

When Rous was later released he sailed to England, and possibly visited the Fells at Swarthmoor in the summer of 1659, for in a letter to Margaret from Alexander Parker he may be the 'J.R.' who had just left London and might be with her even before the post could carry the letter to her.

The cruelty to Quakers in New England continued all through 1659, 1660 and 1661, and the story of their sufferings was sent, as we have seen, to George Fox and to Margaret Fell. In October 1659 William Robinson from London and Marmaduke Stevenson from Yorkshire were hanged on Boston Common; Mary Dyer, from the more tolerant Rhode Island, was hanged in June

[1] Swm. MSS. I, 82.

the next year; and William Leddra (John Rous's companion in 1657) from Barbados in March 1661.[1]

George Fox, 'an extraordinarily sensitive, sympathetic and even telepathic person', as Professor Rufus M. Jones calls him, was deeply moved by this suffering in North America. In his Journal he wrote, 'When they were put to death (in New England) I was in prison at Lancaster, I had a perfect sense of it as though it had been myself, and as though the halter had been put about my neck.'[2]

A little later Margaret Fell heard the additional story of the courage and persecution of Elizabeth Hooton, a landowner of Lincolnshire, and the first woman to become a follower of Fox. Elizabeth had been moved to go to Boston, **Massachusetts, to try to** find a small piece of land, on which to build a meeting-house, with cottage attached for the use of travelling Friends (since no one was allowed to give shelter to a Quaker, on pain of a fine of one pound a night), and a burial ground,[3] so that those hanged need not be buried at the foot of the gallows.

Stirred by this suffering in New England, Margaret wrote to the King once more. He indeed had already taken drastic action to stop the persecution, for, having read a book about it, *New England Judged*, by the Bristol Quaker, George Bishop, he had sent an order to the colonies that their rulers should cease persecu-

---

[1] The reader can be referred to the early chapters of *The Quakers in the American Colonies*, by Professor Rufus M. Jones, for more information of the Quaker 'invasion' of the New England Colonies. The reason for the persecution is dealt with in the following quotation, taken from Q. in A.C., by Rufus M. Jones, p. 35, and quoted from *Dutch and Quaker Colonies*, by Fiske, Vol. II, p. 112: 'The ideal of the Quakers was flatly antagonistic to that of the settlers of Massachusetts. The Christianity of the former was freed from Judaism as far as was possible; the Christianity of the latter was heavily encumbered with Judaism. The Quaker aimed at complete separation between Church and State; the government of Massachusetts was patterned after the ancient Jewish theocracy in which Church and State were identified. The Quaker was tolerant of differences in doctrine; the Calvinist regarded such tolerance as a deadly sin. For these reasons the arrival of a few Quakers in Boston in 1656 was considered an act of invasion and treated as such.'

[2] Camb. Jnl. II, 5.

[3] It is interesting to note that all the old Meeting Houses built later on in England—after 1670—followed this plan, of Meeting House, cottage and burial ground: e.g. Swarthmoor, Colthouse, Jordans and many others.

tion. He added ironic humour to the order, when he agreed with Edward Burrough's suggestion that it should be carried from England in a Quaker ship, and presented by Samuel Shattuck, one of the Quakers formerly banished from Massachusetts. But Margaret now wrote to tell him that his order was not being obeyed, for the colonists were still whipping, putting them into the stocks, imprisoning and banishing. She told him the aged Elizabeth Hooton could find no night's lodging because of their wicked law. They had put it about that Quakers had forged the King's letter, and that he was passing very strict laws against them in England. She begged him not to 'believe better of them than they deserved'.[1]

This then was the condition of New England which was the early experience of John Rous. It was no wonder that he was warmly welcomed at Swarthmoor, and won the love of the beautiful eldest daughter. After their marriage he settled in England, with their home at Mile End Green, London.

Soon after they were married they crossed the Atlantic to Barbados, where according to one of Margaret Fell's correspondents, they had 'a very pleasant place and a pretty house'.[2] But young Margaret Rous was very ill on the voyage out, and then she had a fall from a horse which brought on a miscarriage.[3] Their stay in Barbados was not for very long, for two years later they were in London again, and early in 1665 they went to stay at Swarthmoor, where their three eldest daughters were born in 1665, 1666 and 1667.

In business John Rous remained a West Indian merchant, and he crossed to Barbados on several occasions, later being accompanied again by his wife, together with several of their children.

Like all Margaret Fell's sons-in-law, Rous was consistently loving and helpful to her.

On the 26th of March 1662, just two months after her elder sister's wedding, Bridget, then twenty-seven years old, was married at Swarthmoor Hall. Her husband was John Draper of Headlam, Gainford, in Co. Durham. He was the son of Henry Draper, a well-to-do country gentleman, a Justice of the Peace,

[1] Spence MSS. III, 116, and M.F. *Works*, pp. 32–3.
[2] H. G. Crosfield, p. 98.
[3] Thirnbeck MSS. 3.

who had been convinced by George Fox in 1653.[1] His mother, who died while he was still a child, was Eleanor Birkbeck, only daughter and heiress of the owner of Headlam, and a member of an important family. John was the only surviving son of a family of nine children. Born in 1640 he was about five years younger than Bridget.

A little old book in the British Museum, Walbran's *Antiquities of Gainford*, described the house to which Bridget went as a bride. It lay at the east end of the village 'in a retired situation, shaded by tall and luxuriant trees'. John's and Bridget's old house was largely pulled down in 1730 by a later owner, but 'it seems to have been one of those delectable structures of the time of Elizabeth or James with a spacious and high-walled garden adorned with terraces and ornamental buildings, which seem to accord most naturally with English scenery, and are associated with a peculiarly interesting and romantic period of the past. Some slight terraces on the west, and one in front of the house adorned by four noble old yew trees, are still preserved; together with that liberal extent of garden so necessary an appendage to a country residence: but two ornamental turrets, or banquetting rooms, a little further down, at the extremity of the first division, and some ornaments at the entrance, were destroyed by the late proprietor. . . . An extensive lawn with fish ponds, and a shady walk by the side of the brook, complete the seductions of this most agreeable retreat. The eastern wall of the house and some neglected buildings behind, with square-headed, mullioned and labelled windows, are of the original fabric, and now used as a stable and other offices. The hall [about 31 feet long, by 18 feet wide] and the ample staircase have been included also in the modern mansion.' In 1939 several of the old yew trees still stood, and the original wall could be seen built into the eighteenth-century house. There was still the beautiful garden with its long, canal-like fish pond, and at one end of it there stood a stone bridge with a stone seat overlooking this most 'agreeable retreat'.

Bridget however enjoyed her new home for less than a year. Early in 1663 she and her baby Isaac[2] died, and were buried in

[1] Camb. Jnl. I, 135.

[2] Walbran's *Antiquities of Headlam*, quoted from Mr. Surtees who had the information from Mr. Sherwood.

the orchard to the east of the house. In all the Quaker letters extant there seems to be but one which refers to Bridget's death, and that is from the dear friend and companion of all the children, Will Caton. On the 13th of April 1663, he wrote from Amsterdam to Margaret Fell: 'Before my return out of England I had heard the sad and unwelcome news concerning the death and departure of dear Bridget, which thou may be assured came exceeding near me, but what shall I say? We must go after her, for here we have no continuing city. Oh that we always therefore may be found in that faith, life, power, and spirit, through which the entrance is made into the eternal inheritance.'[1] It is also from this letter that we know that Margaret Fell herself crossed England in the winter of 1662–3 to be with her daughter before and during her confinement. It was no easy task for a middle-aged woman to face the rigours of a winter crossing of the Pennine Hills. It is very possible that Bridget's early death may have been precipitated by the strain of the fifteen months in 1660 and 1661 when she was left to bear the heavy burden of household, estate and Meeting, following as it did on an attack of jaundice.

Bridget's young husband only survived her by eight years— he died early in 1671; he had by then left Friends, and was buried not in the orchard of his house but in Gainford churchyard. Bridget's estate went, after the death of her husband, to her sisters Sarah and Mary.[2]

In late May 1662, two months after Bridget's wedding, Margaret Fell left home again for London. In her own *Relation* she wrote: 'I stayed at home about nine months, and then was moved of the Lord to go to London again, not knowing what might be the matter or business that I should go for. And when I came to Warrington [South Lancashire], in my way to London, I met with an Act of Parliament, made against the Quakers for refusing oaths. And when I came to London I heard the King was gone to meet the Queen, and to be married to her at Hampton Court. At this time Friends' Meetings at London were much troubled with soldiers, pulling Friends out of their meetings, and beating them with their muskets and swords; inso-

[1] Swm. MSS. I, 330.
[2] Letters of Administration for her estate were dated 22nd May 1671.

much that several were wounded and bruised by them; many were cast into prison, through which many lost their lives; and all this being done to a peaceable people, only for worshipping God, as they in conscience were persuaded. Then I went to the King and Duke of York at Hampton Court, and I wrote several letters to them, and therein gave them to understand what desperate and dangerous work there was at London; and how the soldiers came in with lighted matches and drawn swords amongst Friends, when they were met together in the fear and dread of the Lord to worship Him; and if they would not stop that cruel persecution, it was very like that more innocent blood would be shed, and that would witness against their actions, and lie upon them and the nation. And within some certain days after, they beat some Friends so cruelly at the Bull and Mouth that two died thereof.

'The King told me when I spake to him, and writ to him, that his soldiers did not trouble us, nor should they, and said the City soldiers were not his, and they would do as they pleased with them;[1] but after a little time they were more moderate, and the King promised me that he would set those at liberty that were in prison; and when he brought his Queen to London, he set them at liberty.'[2]

The Act against Quakers for refusing oaths, news of which Margaret had heard at Warrington, had taken some months to pass through Parliament, and received the Royal Assent early in May. It began a period of severe persecution which only ended after ten years of struggle and resistance. Wm. C. Braithwaite sums it up thus: 'The bitter and barren persecution of Friends for the ten years from 1662 to '72 has a dramatic unity of its own. It began with a severe but futile Act directed expressly against the Quakers: it developed into a general attempt to root out Nonconformity, with Friends bearing the brunt of the attack: it died down for a time under the stress of the Plague [1665], the Great Fire [1666], and the Dutch War [1664–7], only to gather fresh strength with the Conventicle Act of 1670; and it ended with the signal triumph of

[1] An interesting sidelight on the constitutional independence of the City of London.
[2] M.F. *Works*, pp. 5–6.

the King's Declaration of Indulgence in 1672, and the Great
Pardon of Friends later in the year. The dominant notes are
always the same—the fears and prejudices of the authorities and
of Parliament, the tolerant worldliness of the King, the honest
dislike of the average Englishman to destroy his neighbours, and
the victorious heroism of the victims.'[1] Thus it was that when
Margaret Fell heard of this Act against the Quakers, she at once
approached the King, for she always believed in appealing to
the chief authorities. When she had arrived in London in June,
she wrote to him:

> King Charles, I desire thee to read this over, for it nearly concerns
> thee to search into these things.

She warned him of the punishment which invariably follows
evil-doing. She told how Friends in their Meetings were being
attacked, the soldiers 'beat them with their naked swords,
knock them with the butt-end of their muskets, and beat them
with their halberts and pikes, until some are wounded with
their swords, and others run in with their halberts'. Even in
court they were beaten 'openly in the face of the court, to the
terrifying of hundreds and many cried out, "Murder, murder"
. . . And if we must suffer the forfeiture of our estates to the
King' [many had been praemunired], 'and the loss of our liberty
all our days, and be out of his protection and laws, the will of
the Lord be done; it is for Him and His sake, and blessed be His
name who hath called us to it, and our estates and liberty will
add little to the King. . . . If we cannot have our liberty, we can
suffer for our liberty.'

Now that the King knew what was going on, he only could
stop it, she told him. She reminded him how they were paying
taxes—'poll-money, and chimney-money' [hearth-tax, an unpopular measure] 'and benevolence money, and all this to pay
soldiers to fall violently upon us in our own houses'. She
warned the King to consider these things before it was too late,
and before God's punishment fell upon him.[2]

When the King assured her that he was not responsible for
the City soldiers, she turned her attention to the Lord Mayor of

---

[1] *The Second Period of Quakerism*, Wm. C. Braithwaite, pp. 21-2.
[2] Spence MSS. III, 118. M.F. *Works*, p. 37.

London and the rest of the Justices on the Bench. 'Let your moderation appear unto all men', she wrote; 'ye profess Christ, and yourselves to be Christians; we are so indeed, and in Truth, as well as you. It is now your day. It hath been others before you, and it will be others when your day is passed away.' She denies that their Act gives them the right to use soldiers to break up their Meetings. 'Our Kingdom is not of this world, neither can the subjects of it fight; you need not bring swords and muskets amongst us. . . .What evil have we done? . . . that we should be taken by a company of soldiers and had to a gaol and never see the face of a magistrate? Is this Justice? . . . you have made void his law, to thrust poor innocent people into gaols on heaps, even till sickness and death overtake them. The Lord open your eyes to see these things in time before it be too late. M.F.'[1]

Towards the end of August, as we have seen, at a time of public rejoicing at the entry of the Queen to the Palace of Westminster, Charles II gave a limited order for the release of Quakers,[2] which discharged most of them from their overcrowded prisons. This general discharge however was not in time to save the life of young Richard Hubberthorne who in that month died of plague in the foul air of Newgate. He had been an indefatigable publisher of Truth, and like Margaret, had had interviews with many in authority, including the King and the House of Commons.

In September 1662 Margaret Fell, feeling her work accomplished for which she had travelled to London, returned to Swarthmoor.

Three times now, in the last two years, Margaret Fell, alone or with the help of others, had been able to persuade the King to release the Quakers. The tolerance of the King shines out brightly in a dark age of intolerance. Specially is that so when it is remembered that Margaret was the widow of a Judge whose friend and colleague, Judge Bradshaw, had been President of the Court which had passed sentence of death on the King's father. The interviews between her and the King show also the power which had been won by the Commons and Executive by the constitutional struggle of the previous twenty-

---

[1] Spence MSS. III, 122.
[2] *Extracts from State Papers*, p. 150.

five years. Charles's difficulty in granting permanent toleration
to the Quakers was but one sign of the political and constitutional weakness of the Crown.

Great credit for the success of her concern must go to Margaret herself. It is hardly possible to think that the worldly King
would have received her so often and in such a friendly way
unless she had been a woman of tact, beauty and charm. Though
we have no mention of her in any letter of the King's, nor of
that great gossip and diarist **Samuel** Pepys (his entry under 11th
Jan. 1664 in which he described a 'pretty Quaker woman' delivering a long paper to the King who 'Thou'd him all along'
cannot refer to Margaret, who then was imprisoned in Lancaster
Castle), we have many references to her beauty and loveliness
of character in the letters of Friends. 'I behold thy beauty, and
comeliness, and the pureness of thy love',[1] wrote one to her.
Another, 'My life is truly refreshed, . . . by thee are the tender
babes nourished, . . . thou art comely and glorious.'[2] A Friend
of Chester wrote to her, 'I am refreshed when thou comes into
my mind, as many times thou doth, and then I behold thee as if
I were present with thee in the body, and thy countenance is
many times fresh in me, and thy voice also, and I am sometimes filled therewith, and it is as the voice of a well-tuned
instrument, with which a man is overcome.'[3] The young man,
Josiah Coale, during his voyage across the Atlantic, wrote to
her, 'My love towards thee is exceeding large. I cannot open
myself to many more besides thee. My dear, let me not be forgotten, who am thy dearly beloved one in the Truth.'[4]

Another who had just left Swarthmoor wrote, 'I see thou
exceeded in the pureness of the life of what I heard of thee, and
truly I can speak it, that I did not receive a little refreshment, by
the seeing of thy face.'[5]

John Camm when he was travelling and preaching in the
south-west during the time of Cromwell had written, 'My love
is great unto thee; yea, greater than I can express or utter. . . .

[1] Swm. MSS. I, 210.
[2] Swm. MSS. I, 161.
[3] Swm. MSS. I, 141.
[4] Etting Early Quaker Papers, 47, quoted in *Swm. Doc. in America.*
[5] Swm. MSS. I, 371.

And for all thy care and labour of love to and for the servants of God, the righteous God will reward thee according to thy work, for he is and will be thy exceeding great reward and thy work will follow thee.'[1] His friend John Audland, who on one occasion told her that the more he saw her, the more he loved her,[2] wrote, 'Thy life reacheth me, I feel it, and I am sensible of thy breathings; thou art clothed with beauty, with glory and wisdom from on high. Oh thou fairest among women, blessed art thou for evermore. . . .With pen and ink I cannot utter that which I feel and enjoy of thee. . . . Thou art as a fountain in me, sealed in my very life.'[3]

Two of her own household loved her most deeply, Will Caton and Thomas Salthouse. Some of Caton's letters have been quoted earlier in this book, and mention made of his little manuscript book containing letters addressed to Margaret. He called her 'a precious jewel in the hand of the Lord, and in the eyes of His lambs. . . . It is not thy person that I do admire' [wonder at], 'but that glory, excellency, wisdom, knowledge, understanding, and manifest virtues, wherewithal thou art qualified, and these make thee amiable in my eyes, and in the eyes of the whole Israel of God that beholds thee.'[4] Another time he gave her thanks for her long-expected letter, for which he had waited, 'like unto the husbandman that waiteth for the former and latter rain', and how he now knew that she was 'as ready to nourish the tender plant after it be removed out of the nursery, as well as if it remained in it'. 'Hast thou not often eased me when I was burthened and heavy laden, fed me when my soul hath been hungry, yea clothed me when I was naked, and strengthened me when I was weak and feeble.'[5]

Thomas Salthouse from Somerset, when persecution fell upon Friends in the early days after Charles II's restoration, wrote frequently to her for help, for her prayers and her advice, for she was filled with 'a spirit of wisdom, meekness, sincerity, and supplication . . . which makes thee honourable among the

[1] Caton MSS. III, No. 8.
[2] Caton MSS. III, 425.
[3] Caton MSS. III, 415.
[4] Caton MSS. III, 506 (writing from Holland, 1658).
[5] Caton MSS. III, 27.

daughters as a lily among thorns or as an apple tree among the trees of the wood. Thy speech is pleasant and thy voice is delightful, thy prayer is powerful and in thy presence there is refreshment to the righteous and joy for the upright in heart.'[1] When he heard that she had gone to London to appeal to the King on behalf of the prisoners, he compared her with Esther, for, said he, 'I know the same princely deportment, spirit and carriage is with thee that Esther had, and therefore I confidently expect to hear of the like success and effects'.

Hardly had the King given liberty to the prisoners, when a fresh wave of persecution broke out, specially in London. The respite had only lasted for two months. The Lord Mayor was an old Cromwellian—perhaps his zeal to persecute Quakers and Baptists was part of his attempt to show zeal to the new Cavalier regime, to which he was now loyal.

News of the savagery was sent to Margaret at Swarthmoor by Ellis Hookes, who was Secretary to the Friends in London.

Towards the end of October 1662, while Friends were holding their usual Meetings, 'as innocently as ever', there came the Life Guards with their head-pieces and breast-pieces on, and there they stayed. In another Meeting, the Bull and Mouth, the train-band men came and took away a great many Friends. Some were driven along by the muskets of the soldiers, and others were very much beaten and abused. In all about one hundred and sixty Friends were arrested, ninety-six put into the Common Jail, including three women. Over a hundred Baptists also had been arrested, and taken to Newgate. Ellis Hookes could not say what the reason for this calamity was, except that he had heard there were rumours of a plot by Quakers and Baptists which had filled the authorities with fear. The falseness of such rumours, at any rate where Friends were concerned, was well known.[2]

A month later, Ellis Hookes again wrote to Margaret, a letter which never reached her, as it was intercepted and sent to Alderman Brown, Lord Mayor of London, this great persecutor. He told her of sad occurrences in London, disunity within as well as attacks from without. General Monk, now the Duke of Albe-

[1] Swm. MSS. III, 168.
[2] Swm. MSS. Quoted, but slightly inaccurately, in A.R.B. 114.

marle, and the Council had summoned six Friends before them, and had offered freedom to all innocent Friends if these six would sign a paper promising not to take up arms nor plot against the King, but they said they were not free to engage nor to promise anything because they were a free people. The Council reminded them that Margaret Fell and Richard Hubberthorne had formerly stated that Quakers would never plot against the King, whereas to promise half as much would be enough now, and they had replied that it was not a principle to promise any such thing. Hookes sadly reported that these Friends had threatened to cancel her and Richard's declaration of peaceableness (the one published in June 1660), and that thus many would be liable to suffer, and lie in prison, simply because these six Friends refused to promise what was in the hearts of most Friends to do. There was urgency in the matter, as twenty-three Friends were ill with fever, and near death, in the White Lion Prison, Southwark.[1]

This terrible trial through which Friends were passing was evidently driving some into a confusion or distress of spirit and consequent lack of wisdom. And thus they took up this unnecessarily negative stand. The trouble seems to have passed away later.

After spending the winter of 1662–3 at home, and in visiting Bridget, Margaret Fell in May 1663 set out on a long journey to visit Friends in their Meetings. It was a journey for their comfort and inspiration. From her own pen we have only the shortest account of this amazing journey: 'In the 3rd month 1663 I was moved of the Lord again to travel into the countries to visit Friends; and I travelled through the countries visiting Friends, till we came to Bristol, where we stayed two weeks, I, and some other Friends that were with me, and then we went into Somersetshire, Devonshire, and Dorsetshire, visiting Friends, and then came back to Bristol: from thence, we passed through the nation into Yorkshire, to York, and into Bishoprick and Northumberland, visiting Meetings all along amongst Friends, and then into Westmorland, and so home to Swarthmoor. . . . It was thought we travelled about a thousand miles; and in our

[1] *Extracts from State Papers*, pp. 153–5.

journey we met with G. Fox, who came to Swarthmoor with us, and stayed about two weeks.'[1]

This long journey apparently took from May until August— an average of over ten miles a day—for at the end of August she was writing a letter from Swarthmoor to the Judges at Lancaster.[2] In the most beautiful months of the year, leaving their home just as the fruit blossom was setting, the little party on horseback set out across the dangerous sands. Two of her daughters went with her, Sarah then twenty-two years old, and Mary only sixteen, Leonard Fell and Thomas Salthouse, and probably two or three servants who would act also as grooms. From Lancaster they travelled south through Lancashire, the long moors on their left, the flats on their right stretching to the sea, but all rural then before the days of industrialization. There were frequent stops, however, as Meetings in Friends' houses were held 'within eight miles one of another throughout all this country' (Lancashire, Westmorland and Cumberland), as Daniel Fleming of Kendal wrote in that very year.[3] Then they rode on through Cheshire, Staffordshire, beautiful Worcestershire[4] and Gloucestershire to Bristol, the centre of Quakerism in the south-west. George Fox had for some months been travelling and preaching in this district, and when Margaret Fell and her party went on into Devon he met them, some more Friends having joined them, and they travelled some weeks, 160 to 180 miles a week, and had meetings every day.[5] They rode on into Cornwall where one of their large meetings was at Humphrey Lower's house at Tremeere, and another at Loveday Hambly's at Tregangeeves, near Truro. Loveday made her home the centre of hospitality to Friends travelling in those counties.[6] As for Mary, this part of the journey was perhaps the most memorable, for now she first met her future husband Thomas Lower who travelled with the party as it went on from place to place—to Falmouth, Helston, Marazion, the tin mines, Land's End, Red-

---

[1] M.F. *Works*, p. 6.
[2] Spence III, 132.
[3] *Extracts from State Papers*, p. 177.
[4] F.P.T. mentions her as one who took Truth to them.
[5] Camb. Jnl. II, 26.
[6] *A Quaker Saint of Cornwall*, by L. V. Hodgkin.

ruth, Truro, and back to Humphrey Lower's. Thomas Lower and his father Humphrey came of an ancient family 'seated in Saint Winnow parish and at Clifton in Landulph'.[1] Thomas was at this time a widower, having recently lost his wife Elizabeth, eldest daughter of Sir John Trelawney, first Baronet. He was a nephew of Loveday Hambly, and lived at her home.

On reaching Devonshire, on their return, the party divided again—perhaps Thomas Lower stayed with Margaret and her daughters—but they met again at Bristol, and passed on together into Wiltshire where was held a very large meeting in a great barn. While George Fox next went north-west through Herefordshire into Wales, Margaret and her daughters rode through the Midlands in a north-easterly direction. This must have been a more leisurely progress, for Margaret's journey was shorter than George's, and they eventually met again in the Peak district, in the northern corner of Derbyshire. At Cinder Hill Green on the borders of Yorkshire and Derbyshire, a large meeting was held. They went together to a meeting at Balby, near Doncaster, South Yorkshire, and again went their separate ways, he along the coastal district of Yorkshire to York, while she probably went a more direct route to the same city. The only mention of this part of the journey of Margaret's, other than in George Fox's Journal and in her own *Relation*, is in a letter to Margaret from William Dewsbury, who with about one hundred and ten other prisoners was in bonds in York Castle. He wrote to her, 'We have liberty to meet together in this prison every day and the presence of the Lord crowns our meetings to our great comfort and the astonishment of his enemies. . . . Thy visiting of us was of much service to these tender friends in this place; the woman that had been a papist that run forth in words when thou was in York she is prettily stayed.'[2] (Did Margaret deal with her, one wonders?)

The whole party went on into Durham where they stayed with Bridget's father-in-law at Headlam, and into Northumberland, then turned west across the Pennines to Sedbergh, and so into Westmorland, and home to Swarthmoor, where they had a restful two weeks.

---

[1] Baring-Gould, *Cornish Characters and Strange Events*.
[2] Swm. MSS. IV, 150.

It was when the party had reached York that they heard of a plot. This was not only a rumour, but an organized—though badly so—plot of old Parliamentarians. It is known as the Kaber Rigg or the Derwentdale or Farnley Wood plot, and affected the whole of the north of England. (Kaber Rigg is in Westmorland, Derwentdale in Durham, Farnley Wood in Yorkshire.) The plot was to force the King to carry out the Declaration of Breda, abolish certain unpopular taxes, including the hated hearth tax, and restore a gospel magistracy and ministry. The rebellion was a small affair, Captain Atkinson the chief leader having only a following of some thirty men, who after one night's meeting on Kaber Rigg returned to their homes. In Mr. Francis Nicholson's view it was possibly nothing but 'a plot fomented by agents of the Government in order to cast further discredit on the Parliamentary party, which had so recently been ousted from power'.[1] The discussion of the plots had been going on for some months, and was well known to the authorities. Atkinson proved a double-dealer—an old Cromwellian, but in 1663 he was acting as spy for Sir Philip Musgrave, Governor of Carlisle, and leading loyalist and churchman of the district. He was also unfaithful to his pay-master. The plot resulted in the hanging of several men, and—as we shall see—the merciless persecution of Quakers, though the only man in the plot who had any connection with Friends was one Fawcett who had some years previously been disowned by Friends after only a slight relationship with them. This fact the authorities were fully informed of by Francis Howgill at Appleby. As soon as George Fox heard of the plot he wrote a paper against the whole principle of plotting against authority,[2] and as soon as Margaret Fell returned home she addressed the Judges at Lancaster on the same subject. Writing on the 29th of August she advised the judges to prevent jealousies, thoughts, doubts and misapprehensions of any, and reminded them that three years earlier Fox had been imprisoned by Justice Porter and later examined before the King's Bench and given a pardon on being proved innocent. She told them that he was now at her home at

[1] *Transactions* of the Cumberland and Westmorland Antiquarian and Archaeological Society, XI. N.S. 212.
[2] Camb. Jnl. II, 35.

Swarthmoor and that Quakers were a peaceable people. Then she told them how, as they had ridden north they had found all was peaceable until they had come into Yorkshire, and Durham, and Westmorland, and there they had heard report of a plot, 'but what it is we know not, but certainly there is wickedness in the hearts of some. . . . And this I write to you to prevent all false accusations which might be otherwise cast upon us, who are an innocent and an harmless people, and ye shall ever find us true and faithful.'

But the appeals of George and Margaret were unavailing, and the Quakers were believed wrongly to be implicated in the plot, and fear reigned among the sheriffs and justices. The resulting persecution was fierce, though at first, during the autumn, it did not fall on George Fox and Margaret Fell. Margaret stayed at home, while George Fox went visiting Friends and holding Meetings in all the northern counties, including Northumberland. Though the Meetings were contrary to the law, though there was a price of five pounds upon his head, he escaped over and over again from the men sent to arrest him, and returned in the early winter to Swarthmoor, unscathed and a free man.

Chapter Twelve

TRIAL AND SENTENCE OF PRAEMUNIRE, 1663-4

'*I am not out of the protection of the Almighty God.*'
M.F. at her Trial, 1664.

FREEDOM was not to be the lot of George Fox and Margaret Fell for very much longer. They were too important and too influential to be neglected or left at large. And they had enemies in the neighbourhood.

One of these was Justice Daniel Fleming of Rydal Hall, near Ambleside. He was in 1663 the head of a family whose ancestors had been feudal landowners since the time of the Norman Conquest, seated first at Gleaston Castle, between Ulverston and Barrow-in-Furness, then at Coniston Hall on the banks of lovely Coniston Water, and owning other estates in Cumberland and Westmorland. In the course of centuries the Flemings had become related to many of the most influential families of these counties, the Parrs, Lowthers, Curwens, Huddlestones of Millom, and Kirkbys of Kirkby Ireleth near Margaret Fell's birthplace, Marsh Grange. Daniel Fleming, born in 1633 (when George Fox was nine years old), was a student at Oxford and a Commoner of Gray's Inn, which he left late in 1653, a few months after young George Fell had begun his legal studies there. He was a genealogist and local historian, and left for future generations his memoirs and an account of Westmorland of the seventeenth century.[1] His advice to his son is a judicious mixture of loyalty to his church and worldly wisdom. His ideas on war specially make one regret that he was the persecutor of the Quakers instead of their friend, for he wrote to his son, 'Neither by my consent shalt thou train them [thy children] up to wars, for he that sets up his rest to live by that profession, can hardly be an honest man, or a good Christian; for every war

[1] *The Memoirs of Sir Daniel Fleming*, ed. by Collingwood (1924).

is of itself unjust, unless the cause make it just, besides it is a science no longer in request than there is use for soldiers; for in the time of peace, they are like to chimneys in summer.'[1]

In politics Daniel Fleming was a keen Royalist and he held a number of military and civil appointments in Westmorland as soon as Charles had been restored to the throne. As he was responsible for the good order of Kendal and district, he raised the train-bands on hearing of the Kaber Rigg plot, and by November 1663 he was able to report to Secretary of State Williamson in Whitehall that the plotters had been scattered. He added however that if any mischief were to arise it would chiefly be from the Quakers 'of whom we have too many, this part of the country joining upon that part of Lancashire where George Fox and most of his cubs are and have been for a long time kennelled'. He was sure that if any danger arose it would be from them, for they were the most numerous of any of those people against the authorities, with their meetings (usually only eight miles apart) in close correspondence with each other, and very obedient to Fox. The Quaker prisoners in Appleby and Carlisle were carefully guarded.[2]

Colonel Richard Kirkby of Kirkby Hall, and his brother, Justice William Kirkby of Ashlack Hall (both halls are now farm-houses), near the Duddon Sands, in Furness, were cousins of Justice Daniel Fleming, and similarly Royalist, Episcopalian,[3] and persecutors of Friends. So long as Judge Fell lived they were quiet, but as we have already seen, Friends of Swarthmoor Meeting in 1661 were disturbed by the Kirkbys and imprisoned while Bridget Fell was left in charge.

So it was that in 1663 the Kaber Rigg plot, with which the justices obstinately but erroneously connected the Quakers, set them off on an attack on George Fox and Margaret Fell, who in the winter of 1663–4 were both at Swarthmoor.

Fox having just returned from visiting Friends in the north-

---

[1] *The Memoirs of Sir Daniel Fleming*, p. 95. (He was knighted in 1681.)

[2] *Extracts from State Papers*, p. 177.

[3] Though Dom F. O. Blundell says Rd. Kirkby of Kirkby Hall was a Roman Catholic until 1678 I have not found any corroboration of this. However, there was a good deal of hiding of Roman Catholic sympathies in those days.

west was told that Colonel Kirkby had sent an officer to arrest him at the Hall, and had searched trunks and chests for him.[1] As he lay in bed that night Fox felt moved to go in the morning five miles over the fells to face Kirkby in his own home. There he found the Flemings and several other of the gentry come to take their leave of Colonel Kirkby who was about to go to London to attend Parliament. Fox was shown into the parlour, and soon Kirkby came in, and 'so I told him', wrote Fox, 'I came to visit him understanding that he would have seen me, and to know what he had to say to me or whether he had anything against me; and he said before all the gentry that was gathered together at his house that as he was a gentleman he had nothing against me, but said that M. Fell must not keep great meetings at her house for that they met contrary to the Act.' Fox told him that the Act was against those who plotted against the King, and that Kirkby knew that those who met at Margaret Fell's house were 'his neighbours and a peaceable people. And so after many words he shook me by the hand and said he had nothing against me, and others of them said I was a deserving man, and so we parted and I returned to Swarthmoor again'.[2]

At the same time Margaret Fell wrote her first appeal to Colonel Kirkby, whom she knew to be the prime mover of this attack on her and any Friends who worshipped at her house.

Colonel Kirkby,

I have never before this time presumed to write unto thee upon this account. . . . Although upon the Truth's account I have writ to many of the Heads of this nation, and now having this occasion that thou hast sent a warrant with the constables into our Meeting, I could not but certify unto thee our innocency and clearness upon any account of giving any just occasion thereof (God is our witness), and I know thou with many more of you are not ignorant, that we are no such people as are any way ill affected to either our King, State or Government, or to any man or person upon the Earth, but we desire the good and the peace of all men, and that under this Government we might live a godly and a peaceable life, and the King and many more about him are absolutely persuaded that we will never wrong nor injure him,

---

[1] A very graphic rugged description of this incident is given in George Fox's letter to Gilbert Latey in London in 1663. Latey is asked to show the letter to General Monk himself. Jnl. F.H.S. Vol. XI, 148, from Abraham MSS. 7.

[2] Camb. Jnl. II, 38.

and I am certain and dare engage both body, life and estate that you shall never find otherwise by me nor by any that we shall own to be of us. I do not doubt [=deny], but there may be some which may be called of us, that are not of us,[1] but my word goes for those that we own to be of us.

The last time that I spoke with the King, he said these words to me, 'I will not hinder you of your religion; keep it in your own house, God forbid that I should hinder you'. . . . Truly we have often many of us stood amazed to see your proceedings, that you should in the first place fall upon us, who wilt never do you hurt nor wrong, and by that means your enemies . . . goes free and shelters under our sufferings, but certainly these things are hid from your eyes, or else you would see this, and that the Lord's righteous hand cannot escape such things, that the innocent should suffer and the guilty is passed by. My desire is at this time to you that thou would be as favourable to these poor men that has families to maintain, and is innocent before God and all men, as thou can well. And now we hear that thou art agoing out of the country and it will be good and for thy peace and comfort to leave a good example, . . . to worship and serve the loving God, we are bound in our conscience to do; . . . and so the God of Power direct thy heart to do in this thing as thou wouldst be done unto.

From a true and faithful lover of thee and all men,

M.F.[2]

This noble appeal however failed to move the colonel.

Shortly after, while Colonel Kirkby was still in London, George Fox heard of a private meeting of the justices and deputy lieutenants at Holker Hall, the home, across the sands in Cartmel, of Justice Thomas Preston. He heard also that they had put out a warrant for his arrest. This mysterious piece of 'intelligence work' might have allowed Fox to escape, but he refused to, as he believed that, if he did, their fury would fall upon poor Friends. 'So I gave up myself to be taken and prepared myself against they came.'[3] Next day an officer, armed with sword and pistol, came to arrest him. Fox surprised him by telling him how he might have been forty miles away by

---

[1] Here she is thinking of the disowned Quaker, a very temporary adherent, who had taken part in the Kaber Rigg plot, and who had given an excuse to the authorities for all Quakers to be implicated.

[2] Spence MSS. III, 6.

[3] Camb. Jnl. II, 39.

then, but as he was an innocent man he had stayed. The officer
refused to show him his warrant.

George Fox and Margaret Fell then crossed the sands with the
officer, to Holker Hall. Here was a memorable scene—these two
spiritual leaders, innocent of intrigue and plotting, facing all
those in the district who held the powers of the State. In addition
to old Thomas Preston there were Justice Robert Rawlinson,
a lawyer, Sir George Middleton of Leighton Hall, near Yealand,
and many others.

They tried to implicate George Fox in the recent plot, whereas he had warned the authorities, even the King and Council, of
its being hatched; they chaffed him about his recent book, *The
Battledore*, which displays a knowledge of foreign languages, but
when they called him a rebel, he struck his hand on the table and
told them, especially Sir George Middleton whom Fox believed
to be a hidden Papist, that they knew he was no rebel and that
he had suffered imprisonment in the days of the Civil War
because he refused to take up arms against the King. 'But I have
more love to the King for his eternal good and welfare than any
of you have.' When they accused him of being against the laws
of the land, he denied it and reminded those justices that they
were for the punishment of evil doers, while he and his friends
were bringing people into the spirit of God so that their actions
would be good and not evil.[1]

Middleton was obviously tiring of this examination, so demanded that the oaths of Allegiance and Supremacy should be
put to Fox. He of course refused to take any oath, and they were
about to send him to Lancaster Prison, when they decided to
engage him to appear at the Sessions, and so for the time freed
him. Upon this he and Margaret Fell returned to Swarthmoor,
where soon afterwards their friend Justice West came to visit
them. A little later, on a Sunday, Justice William Kirkby with
a number of constables came to the meeting in the Hall at
Swarthmoor, and said, 'How now, Mr. Fox! you have a fine
company here'. 'Yes', answered George, 'we do meet to wait
upon the Lord.' Justice Kirkby took the names of many Friends,

[1] This scene at Holker Hall has twice been the subject of pictures. One by
John Pettie was painted in oils in 1864 and was the property of the late Major
Barclay at Bishop Stortford. The other is an etching by Robert Spence.

while others were handed over to the constables to be imprisoned.

Fox kept his promise made to Justice Kirkby and early in January 1664 went to Lancaster for the Sessions, Justice Fleming presiding. Offence at his wearing his hat before them,[1] questions as to the plot, tendering of the oaths of Allegiance and Supremacy, and much talk to a crowded court, filled the day, at the end of which Fox was committed to prison to appear before the Assizes in two months' time. The prison was full, as several other Friends were committed at the same time. Daniel Fleming proudly reported to Whitehall that they were proceeding 'smartly against the Quakers', they had praemunired one, had put George Fox into close confinement with ten others, for refusing the oath of allegiance, and had fined nearly sixty for 'unlawful meetings', notwithstanding that Margaret Fell had 'used her utmost endeavours with many of the Justices to prevent it.'[2] This is the only reference we have to the fact that Margaret accompanied George Fox on this occasion; she seized the opportunity of her freedom to try to prevent this cruel injustice to her friends. The justices had no peace either from the wives of the prisoners, for these very boldly told them that they kept their husbands in jail for nothing but the truth of Christ and for good conscience sake, and they would bring their children to the justices for them to maintain them. The prisoners themselves wrote to the justices. A number of these Friends had suffered much from having loyally supported the King during the Civil War, and had arrears of pay for their service due to them. They pointed out in their letter that the justices were refusing to carry out the promise of liberty of conscience, which the King had frequently given. It was this promise which upset Justice Fleming, as he explained at the end of his letter to Whitehall quoted above—'I doubt not but this proceeding against them here will break their meetings and other designs in a short time, if they procure not somewhat by way of favour from you at Whitehall, which will not a little encourage them, and discourage others.'

---

[1] The Chairman bade his officer remove the hat, but G.F. wrote in his Journal 'so a pretty space we looked at one another till the power of the Lord God arose over all.'   [2] *Extracts from State Papers*, p. 186.

George and Margaret were both shocked to be told by the justices that orders had been received by them from Colonel Richard Kirkby in London to prosecute Friends. They remembered his fair words on the eve of his going to London. Margaret therefore in January wrote for the second time to Colonel Kirkby, a letter which, by its inclusion in the State Papers, was presumably intercepted on its journey to London. She appealed to him as a neighbour—for God had given us a law to love Him and then our neighbour—and as a magistrate—for magistrates were supposed to be of service and help to their neighbours. Especially wrong was it of him to do such an ill to them in his absence—'It had been enough for thee to have laid thy rod upon us when thee was among us, and not to have encouraged others in thy absence. It was but a mean office', she added, 'for thy brother to be a witness against an innocent people for punishing them, for serving and worshipping the Lord.' Justice William Kirkby had also threatened her that worse was to come, that this was but a beginning of what she would find. Later in the letter she writes: 'I am sure it's without cause given by me or any that ever belonged to me, to thee, or any of thy family', a specific enough statement to contradict the suggestion made in *Margaret Fox of Swarthmoor Hall* that Kirkby's father had been deprived of honours and land through Judge Fell in the Cromwellian days, and that this present attack was taken for private revenge. However she had been told even by one of the other justices that no persecution of her household would have been taken but because of him, and adds, 'I . . . find that a professed enemy is a better friend that a professed friend and a secret enemy. This is no good character, neither is it a great conquest to get eight innocent men into prison by a snare.' She ends her letter by telling him that their persecutors will be judged and punished by God, and that they will never have a just cause against the Friends.[1]

How completely unsuccessful the persecution was, from the point of view of Fleming and the rest, can be seen from Fleming's letter to Secretary Williamson, written only a fortnight after the sessions:[2]

[1] *Extracts from State Papers*, pp. 187–8, and Spence MSS. III, **134**.
[2] *Extracts from State Papers*, pp. 188–9.

Sir,

I gave you an account in my last of our proceedings against the Quakers at Lancaster and Kendal, and notwithstanding the same, Mrs. Fell (Oliver's Judge Fell's widow, and now wife or I know not what to George Fox) had a greater meeting of them at her house than ever, the very next Sunday after the sessions, on purpose as 'tis generally thought to affront our authority, although near 40 of those that were tried at the sessions were for meeting at her house. If we receive any encouragement from you herein, we'll tender her the oath, and so praemunire her according to law, which will be the only way to take effectual course with her, who is the chief maintainer of that party in this country; I find a coolness in several honest justices to act against them by reason they several times have committed divers Quakers heretofore, and still when the judges came their circuit, they either picked some hole in their mittimus,[1] and so set them at liberty, or else fined them next to nothing, whereby they cast all the odium on those who committed them; but I hope we shall have no more of this, but that everyone will act heartily to his power in his proper sphere.

The next move in the drama came from Justice Fleming. On 18th February 1664 he was in Ulverston, meeting other justices enacting a variety of legal business, but his main concern was to capture Mistress Fell. He found he had to 'press' the justices to support him, and was glad to have with him Secretary Williamson's last letter supporting him in his attack on the Quakers. They sent for Margaret Fell to her house. When she appeared before them she boldly refused to promise to have no more meetings at her home, where for twelve years she had held them. They threatened that if she refused to promise they would offer her the oath of Allegiance. 'I told them', she wrote in her *Relation*, 'I should not deny my faith and principles, for anything they could do against me; and while it pleased the Lord to let me have a house, I would endeavour to worship him in it.'[2] She of course refused to swear, so they made a mittimus, and sent her across the sands to prison in Lancaster Castle.

George Fox and Margaret Fell waited in prison until the Assizes met on 14th March. Justice Fleming hoped that then the Judges would praemunire Margaret, which would mean imprisonment and poverty, as he believed that that would 'much

---

[1] Mittimus = a warrant of commitment to prison, given by a magistrate.
[2] M.F. *Works*, p. 7.

abate the interest of that faction in this country and no less encourage our Justices to act smartly against them'. He knew that his zeal against George and Margaret had made him very unpopular with Quakers in general, but he claimed he had only done his duty; however he warned the Government that Friends were not to be despised, as they were 'more considerable than many esteem them to be.'[1]

The story of Margaret Fell's trial at the March Assizes is given in her *Works*. At first, Judge Twisden, Justice of the King's Bench, showed consideration and even kindness to her. She was called to the bar, and the judge told the jailer to set a stool for her and a cushion for her to sit upon. She had with her four of her daughters, Isabel, Sarah, Susannah and Rachel (aged eleven), and the judge, seeing them standing at the bar with their mother, called out, 'Let not Mrs. Fell's daughters stand at the bar, but let them come up hither, they shall not stand at the bar'. 'So they plucked them up', the old record runs, 'and set them near where the Judge sat.'

The mittimus being read, Margaret stood up at the bar, and the Judge's first words told her that she had been committed by the local justices because she had refused the oath of obedience. 'I was sent for from my own house and family', she replied, 'but for what cause or transgression I do not know'. The Judge: 'I am informed by the Justices of the Peace in this county, that you keep multitudes of people at your house, in pretence to worship God; and it may be you worship Him in part, but we are not to dispute that.'

Margaret: 'I have the King's word from his own mouth, that he would not hinder me of my religion. "God forbid", said he, "that I should hinder you of your religion, you may keep it in your own house." And I appeal to all the country, whether those people that meet in my house, be not a peaceable, a quiet, and a godly honest people? And whether there have been any just occasion of offence given by the Meeting that was kept in my house.'

The Judge: 'If you will give security that you will have no more Meetings, I will not tender the oath to you. You think if there be no fighting nor quarrelling amongst you, that you keep

---

[1] *Extracts from State Papers*, pp. 189-90.

the peace, and break no law; but I tell you, that you are a breaker of the law, by keeping of unlawful meetings: and again, you break the law, in that you will not take the oath of Allegiance.'

Margaret desired liberty to answer these two charges. She told the Court that several of her neighbours were of the same faith as herself, and these were they who met at her house, and she could not shut her doors against them.

'Mistress', called the Judge, 'you begin at the wrong end, for the first is the oath.'

'I suppose', retorted Margaret, 'that the first occasion of tendering me the oath was because of meeting; but as for that, if I have begun at the wrong end, I shall begin at the other. . . . As for my allegiance, I love, own, and honour the King, and desire his peace and welfare; and that we may live a peaceable, a quiet, and a godly life under his Government, according to the Scriptures; and this is my allegiance to the King. And as for the oath itself, Christ Jesus, the King of Kings, hath commanded me not to swear at all, neither by Heaven, nor by Earth, nor by any other Oath.'

The Judge then called for the Statute Book and for the Grand Jury to be present.

Then one of the justices that had committed her reminded her that they had offered her not to tender the oath if she would promise not to have meetings at her house. The judge agreed with this.

Then Margaret appealed to the Judge, the Court and the rest of those present. She claimed that they met in her house in obedience to Christ's command that God should be worshipped in spirit and truth; and secondly, that Christ had commanded his followers not to swear at all. 'For obedience to Christ's doctrine and command', she added, 'am I here arraigned this day. So you being Christians, and professing the same things in words, judge of these things according to that of God in your consciences. I appeal to all in the country, whether ever those meetings did any hurt or prejudice?' The Judge replied: 'You are not here for obedience to Christ's commands, but for keeping of unlawful meetings. And you think, that if you do not fight and quarrel, or break the peace, that you break no law; but there is a law against unlawful meetings.'

Margaret asked: 'What law have I broken, for worshipping God in my own house?' The Judge replied: 'The common Law.' 'I thought', said Margaret, 'you had proceeded by a statute.' Here the Sheriff whispered to him, and mentioned the Statute of the 35th of Elizabeth. The Judge answered: 'I could tell you of a law, but it is too penal for you, for it might cost you your life.'

Bravely she replied: 'I must offer and tender my life, and all, for my testimony, if it be required of me.'

The latter part of the statute was then read to her, for the oath of obedience, and the judge told the jury and the prisoner what the punishment was for refusal. It would be the forfeiture of all her estate, real and personal, and imprisonment during life.

'I am a widow', replied Margaret, 'and my estate is a dowry, and I have five children unpreferred; and if the King's pleasure be to take my estate from me, upon the account of my conscience, and not for any evil or wrong done, let him do as he pleaseth.'

She asked to speak to the Jury, and the Judge tried to stop her, but she insisted she had the same rights as other prisoners, and proceeded to address the Jury.

Addressing them as 'Friends', she told them she was here on account of her conscience, and not for any evil done to any man, but for obeying Christ's doctrines and commands, for keeping meetings and refusing to swear. She told them the Statute was made to show up the Papists, and the oath was for Allegiance to the King, and were she and her friends the people aimed at? The Judge seemed to be angry and called out that she was not there on account of her conscience, and added that she had an ever-lasting tongue and that she was drawing the whole Court after her. She continued speaking on, and he still crying out: 'Will you take the oath or no?'

She refused to say 'no', but reiterated to the Jury that she was before them only on account of her conscience and not for any evil done. Then the judge was angry again, and told his clerk to tender her the oath and hold her the Bible. Three more times did he ask her 'will you take the oath or no?' until she finally answered 'if you should ask me never so often, I must answer to you that the reason why I cannot take it is because

Christ hath commanded me not to swear at all; I owe my allegiance and obedience to him.'

Then one of the justices, showing some conciliatory spirit called out, 'Mistress Fell, you may with a good conscience (if you cannot take the oath) put in security, that you will have no more Meetings at your house?'

'Wilt thou make it good,' she asked, 'that I may with a safe conscience make an engagement to forbear Meetings, for fear of losing my liberty, and estate? Wilt not thou, and all you here judge of me, that it was for saving of my estate and liberty that I did it? And should not I in this deny my testimony, and would not this defile my conscience?'

The Judge asked again, testily, 'This is no answer, will you take the oath? We must not spend time.'

To which Margaret replied: 'I never took oath in my life. I have spent my days thus far, and I never took an oath; I own allegiance to the King, as he is King of England, but Christ Jesus is King of my conscience.'

At this the clerk held out the Bible to her, and bid her pull off her glove and lay her hand on the book. To which she said: 'I never laid my hand on the book to swear in all my life, and I never was at the Assizes here before. I was bred and born in this county, and have led my life in it; and I was never at any Assizes before this time; and I bless the Lord, that I am here this day upon this account, to bear testimony to the Truth. . . . I do not care if I never hear an oath read; for the Lord mourns because of oaths.'

'Take her away,' cried the judge; 'will you give security to have no more Meetings?'

'Nay,' she answered, 'I can give no such security. I have spoken enough for that.'

And so they took her civilly away—the old record says.

George Fox was then called to the bar. The attempts of Judge Twisden to make him take the oath, George's outspokenness, the loudness of his voice ('I must call for three or four criers to drown thy voice, thou hast good lungs,' cried the angry judge), his protest against being called 'sirrah' and even the little exchanges of gentleness which passed between prisoner and choleric judge—are all in Fox's own story in his Journal. It is obvious from a letter written just after the trial, by Daniel Fleming to Secretary Williamson that Judge Twisden had qualms about the trial of these two leaders—Fleming had had to persuade him into it.[1] Fleming thanked Secretary Williamson for his last letter which cleared him and the local justices from the aspersions of acting against the Quakers upon private pique. The result of the trial was of course obvious; Fox refused to swear, and was sent to prison until the next Assizes, five months later.

Before the March Assizes ended, Margaret was again called from her prison cell before Judge Twisden. His heart seemed to be touched by the danger she was in, the danger of being praemunired, and both he and several in the court advised her to make a formal denial (a 'traverse') of the accusations made by her enemies, and so have liberty until the next Assizes. 'I would do you all the favour I can,' he told her. She replied: 'I acknowledge thy favour and mercy; for thou hast shown more mercy than my neighbours have done, and I see what thou hast done for me, and what my neighbours have done against me, and I know very well how to make a distinction; for they, who have done this against me, have no reason for it.'

'I have done you no wrong,' the judge said. 'I found you here.'

'I had not been here,' she replied, 'but by my neighbours.'

She went on to tell him that she had heard that people were saying that there was an order to prosecute her, which had come either from the King or the Council, and she demanded to have it read. This put the Judge in a fluster. His only reply was that she must believe what she had been told—and then he quickly went on to another subject. She was offered her liberty if she would not keep a Meeting in her house. 'But I answered the Judge that I rather choose a prison for obeying of God, than my liberty for obeying of men, contrary to my conscience.'[2]

Both George and Margaret were kept in Lancaster Castle until the next Assizes in August, when they both again appeared at the Bar, this time before Judge Turner, Baron of the Exchequer, who that same month tried Francis Howgill at Appleby, praemunired and imprisoned him for five years until he was

[1] *Extracts from State Papers*, p. 191.
[2] M.F. *Works*, p. 7.

released by death. George Fox defended himself boldly by pointing out to the judge several errors in his indictment, and also used the opportunity a crowded court gave him to 'publish Truth'.

Margaret again had with her her young daughters (only two this time as Isabel had now left for Bristol and Mary had gone to London), and for part of the trial she had counsel, although when she defended herself she showed great ability and considerable knowledge of the law. She denied their right to prosecute her, as she was no transgressor, for 'there is no law against the innocent and righteous'. Again there was talk back and forth about swearing. And then—'I am clear and innocent of wronging any man upon the earth, as my little child that stands by me here; and if any here have anything to lay to my charge, let them come down and testify it here before you all; and if I be clear and innocent, you have no law against me. You have work enough besides, if you do not meddle with the innocent, and them that fear the Lord.' 'Then', she adds in her own story, 'Colonel Kirkby and the sheriff whispered to the Judge; and I looked up, and spoke to Colonel Kirkby and said, "Let us have no whispering; I will not have so many judges, one of one side, and another of another: Here is one judge, that is to be judge." And the judge said, "No, I will not heed them". And then I called to Colonel Kirkby and said, "If thou hast anything to lay to my charge, or to speak against me, come down here, and testify against me". And I said, "The judge represents the King's person and his power, and that I own".'[1]

Later in the day Margaret Fell had an opportunity to complain to Judge Turner of the scandalous conditions of imprisonment at Lancaster Castle. As it was then raining she invited him to see for himself whether the rooms were fit for people to lie in, or not. Colonel Kirkby stood up, and gave excuses for the Sheriff, who was responsible for these conditions, and Margaret retorted to him, 'If you were to lie in it yourselves, you would think it hard; but your minds are only in cruelty, to commit others, as William Kirkby here hath done, who hath committed ten of our Friends, and put them into a cold room, where there was nothing but bare boards to lie upon, where they have lain

[1] M.F. *Works,* p. 287.

several nights, some of them old ancient men, above three score years of age, and known to be honest men in their country where they live'.[1]

When Willam Kirkby was asked why the prisoners might not arrange to have their own beds in prison, he replied that they were to commit them to prison, but not to provide prisons for them. He added that the King should provide them, if anyone did. The judge intervened, rebuking Kirkby for his callous behaviour, and saying that they should let them have prisons fit for men.

Before the trial finished, Margaret Fell's lawyers showed the judge several errors and defects, and 'places of contradiction and confusion in my indictment'. Though this made the judge pause, it did not sway him from passing the savage sentence of praemunire against her, which was that she should be out of the King's protection—an outlaw in fact—and forfeit all her estate, real and personal, to the King, and suffer imprisonment for life.

'But', she wrote many years later, 'the great God of Heaven and Earth supported my spirit under this severe sentence, that I was not terrified; but gave this answer to Judge Turner, who gave the sentence, "Although I am out of the King's Protection, yet I am not out of the protection of the Almighty God".'[2]

For over four years, from February 1664 to June 1668, Margaret Fell lay a prisoner in Lancaster Castle.

[1] M.F. *Works*, p. 288.
[2] M.F. *Works*, p. 8.

Chapter Thirteen

IMPRISONMENT IN LANCASTER CASTLE: I
AUG. 1664–JAN. 1665

EARLY in August 1664, while Margaret Fell lay awaiting the Assizes at which as we have just seen she received the heavy sentence of praemunire, she sent an appeal to the judges, to tell them that Fox had been in prison for seven months, she for six, and that their prisons were so wet with rain and snow that 'in the winter time it is not fit for neither beasts nor dogs to lie in'. Fox had hardly ever been allowed to leave the prison—and he was still an innocent man awaiting trial—'without a keeper', nor had she been allowed to go home to see her children and household. She charged the Kirkbys and their cousin Fleming with this injustice, as they had 'envy and prejudice against me'. Justice William Kirkby had acted unlawfully in fining Friends on an old Act against Conventicles, and also in condemning them to cruel imprisonment in addition to fines. And she added, 'And you all know that my estate is but a widow's estate, and it would not be very much advantage to my neighbours if they had it; and I have four daughters unpreferred; and what I suffer for, it is upon the account of my conscience, and for the Lord's sake, and I am freely given up to his will, and pleasure, what he permits, and suffers to be done unto me, in which doing I shall rest content, whether it be mercy or cruelty.'[1]

That the imprisonment of the two leaders did not stop the Meetings at Swarthmoor week by week is shown by the comment in a letter reporting his activities from Daniel Fleming to Secretary Williamson, in October 1664. 'There hath been lately' he wrote, 'two or three smart encounters betwixt Colonel Kirkby and some Quakers, who were conventicled at Mrs. Fell's house several Sundays since her being convict of a Praemunire;

[1] Spence MSS. III, 132.

which doth sufficiently demonstrate unto the world the great obstinacy of that sect.'[1]

While the courage of her own family and Meeting must have been of the greatest comfort to Margaret Fell, she had many anxieties and much business to deal with, which were a constant trial to her.

A disappointment which must have been hard to bear was that she was in prison when her daughter Isabel, then probably twenty-seven years old, was married to William Yeamans, a Friend of Bristol. Isabel had already, like several of the other daughters, done some travelling from home—in the summer of 1659 she was in London with her eldest sister Margaret, both not well in health.[2] The next year she and Bridget together with William Caton and some servants had attended the General Meeting at Balby in Yorkshire.[3] Now in the summer of 1664 she left Swarthmoor again, this time to make her home in Bristol. Her marriage is, curiously indeed, not in the registers of births, marriages and deaths, so carefully compiled since the early days of the Society, but from a letter of John Rous and from Margaret Fell's statements during her trial, we know that Isabel was married between June and August. Her husband, a Bristol merchant, came of an influential family,[4] one of whose members, a baronet, was one time Governor of Carolina, and resident in Barbados. William Yeamans's father, Robert, was the Sheriff of Bristol who was hanged for his Royalist sympathies, and one of his sisters was Ann Curtis, already mentioned in connection with her and Margaret Fell's visits to Charles II, pleading for the release of George Fox. William, who later married Isabel Fell, was four years old when his father died so tragically, and he was twenty-five at his marriage. He seems to have been a delicate man, for in one of the family letters it is hinted that his wife found it hard ever to leave him; he died in 1674 at the age of thirty-five, and of their four children, William, Rachel and Margaret died as little children, and their youngest son, also William, died probably of consumption in early manhood. The further story

---

[1] *Extracts from State Papers*, p. 221.
[2] Swm. MSS. I, 84. Letter from W. Caton to M.F.
[3] *Life of W. Caton*, p. 85.
[4] *D.N.B.*

of Isabel herself, and her service for Friends will be related in other chapters.

The daughter now left in charge at Swarthmoor was Sarah, a capable young woman of twenty-two, on whose shoulders the work of household and Meeting had largely fallen, while her mother was in prison.

The daughter next in age to Sarah was Mary, now a lively girl of seventeen. Very soon after her mother's arrest in February she had gone to London, where she stayed with her eldest sister Margaret Rous and John Rous, recently returned from Barbados and now settling into their house in Mile-End Green. She went to join them in pleading with those in authority to save her mother from being praemunired.

In addition to the threat of this terrible punishment, Margaret Fell was saddened by the behaviour of her only son George. Since his father's death in 1658 George Fell had been living in London, where at the end of 1660 he had married a young widow. During these two years before his marriage, George Fell was living an idle and extravagant life, which gave his sister Margaret and his mother considerable distress and anxiety, while they were in London (1659–60). For political reasons the young man was nervous at the time of the Restoration. A year earlier he had been authorized by Richard Cromwell's Government to raise a troop of horse mounted with riders who would be loyal to the Parliament.[1] As the Restoration came nearer, and the times grew more difficult, the young squire thought of going to Ireland for safety, or possibly back to Swarthmoor, but neither plan was carried out.[2] On the King's return, George Fell petitioned him for a pardon. 'His father', the frightened youth wrote, 'was a great malignant and purchased fee farm rents, value £220, but he, being only lately of age, has received none of the said rents, nor has acted in any way against His Majesty.' On 22nd June a warrant was granted to him 'of pardon for all treasons, misprisions of treason, etc., since 2nd Nov. 1640, with restoration of goods'.[3] Probably this pardon cost George a large sum of money.[4]

---

[1] *Extracts from State Papers*, p. 116.
[2] Spence MSS. III, 66, 25th Feb. 1660.
[3] Jnl. F.H.S. 29–58.   [4] Spence MSS. III, 69, 22nd July 1660.

Margaret Fell became increasingly anxious about her son's idleness and the 'profane company' with whom he mixed.[1] But affectionate messages were sent between him and his sisters at Swarthmoor, and there was at least one meeting with his mother at her lodgings in London.[2]

His wife, whom he married in December 1660 was Hannah Potter, daughter of a barrister friend, Edward Cooke. It was in London probably that their first child Sarah was born, for her birth does not appear in the Dalton registers, as those of their three youngest children do, though her death in 1669 is recorded there. There is no hint in any of the letters which have been preserved, that the young George did any business for his mother in the carrying out of his father's will—that was done by the two executors living in the neighbourhood, Thomas Colton and Richard Radcliffe. Nor in these six years (1658 to 1664) is there any suggestion that George Fell believed his father had left the Swarthmoor estate to him. But when his mother was being tried in 1664 for holding Quaker Meetings in her house—a practice which he deplored—he began to make a claim for the estate and Hall. One interpretation of this action is that he was anxious, when there was a possibility, even a probability, that his mother would be praemunired and have her property confiscated, to save the Hall and estate for the family, so that it should not be given to a new owner. Another interpretation is that it was the action of a man of weak character and extravagant nature, who with his wife had already run into debt; and who had not the slightest sympathy with his mother's religious beliefs.

Perhaps the most damning evidence of the weakness and disloyalty of George Fell lies in the fact of his friendship, and indeed co-operation, with the enemies of his mother, Richard and William Kirkby. In family letters of 1664, and in the petition for the estate, this collaboration is seen; what a heavy burden for Margaret Fell to bear!

If her own son was a sad disappointment to her, in spite of all her efforts to lead him aright, her sons-in-law were consistently loyal and helpful. John Rous was indefatigable in doing business

[1] Spence MSS. III, 68.
[2] Spence MSS. III, 73 and 75.

for her, legal and financial, in trying to persuade her son to re-nounce his claim against her, and in helping his wife and her sister Mary to interview the King.

In May 1664, between Margaret's two trials, John Rous re-ported to her what progress he and his wife and sister-in-law Mary were making in London. The two sisters had twice inter-viewed the King, who however would promise to do nothing for their mother, for, said he, if she did not keep meetings in her house, then she would not need to be in prison. John Rous and the two young women had spoken to a lawyer at Gray's Inn about their mother's estate if she were to be praemunired. It was clear that in court circles there were men, particularly one named Dobson, who saw to it that they had forfeited estates granted to them, by influence or in some more evil way. This was a very real danger to the Fell family.[1]

Then a month later, on 24th June, Mary herself wrote to her mother of still two more interviews with the King at Whitehall. Her letter with the charming description of Charles II is here given.

> Mile End Green, near London,
> 24th of 4th month [June] 1664.
> Endeared and tender hearted Mother,
> My duty and very dear love is freely given and remembered unto thee, as also my very dear love is to dear G.F.
> This is chiefly to let thee understand that yesterday sister and I were at Whitehall, where we spoke with the King and told him that if he would please to signify something to the judges, before they went their circuit, to release you, otherwise it would be past, for the time drew very near of the Assizes. He said he would release you, if we would promise you would not go to meeting. Sister said we could make no such engagements, for the meeting it hath been kept many years and never hath done any harm. He said, 'Cannot your mother keep within her own family, as she may have five more, but she must have such tumultous meetings'. We said, 'She hath no such meetings, they are only her neighbours that come'. The King said there were some Quakers in the last plot [Kaber Rigg Plot]. Sister said that could not be proved. He said he had letters of it and their names. So Chifines [the King's page] bid us come of the fourth day; we do intend to go to-morrow.

[1] Spence MSS. III, 161.

I was there about a week since and told the King that now the Assizes drew very near and said if he did not do something for thee, they would run thee into a praemunire and get thy estate from thee and thy children; and I desired him to take it into consideration. He was then very loving to me and as though he pitied me and said he would take it into consideration, and he said, 'They shall not have her estate from her'. He took me by the hand as soon as he came near me. And I spoke to Prince Rupert[1] and desired him to put the King in mind of it, and he said he would do what he could in it, and went then to the King and spoke to him. Prince Rupert hath always been very loving to Friends and hath often spoke to the King about you. . . .

I am thy dutiful and obedient daughter,

Mary Fell.

Remember me to sisters Susannah and Rachel.

P.S. When we was with Dobson last, he told us that it would be the best way for thee to remove all things from Swarthmoor to some place that be ours, for they say there is no repleaving [replevin=recovery of goods, C. O. Dict.] against the King.

As was usual with letters to Margaret Fell during her imprisonment, this letter was addressed 'for the hands of my very dear mother, Margaret Fell at Lancaster, leave this with Thomas Green, Grocer, at his shop in Lancaster, to be conveyed'.[2]

On 6th September[3] John Rous wrote two letters to Margaret Fell, which though long are included here, as they show the writer's deep admiration for Margaret's stand, and give news of the great sufferings of Friends under the new Conventicle Act. This Act of 1664 was the first to be passed in Charles II's reign to forbid all religious meetings except where the liturgy of the Church of England was used. Penalties for disobedience were extremely severe—fining, imprisonment and seven years' banishment to slavery in the American colonies (except Virginia and New England).

As the Puritan minister, Richard Baxter, noted, this Act fell more hardly on the Quakers than on any other Nonconformists,

[1] Cousin of the King, and son of the tragic Queen Elizabeth of Bohemia and Frederick V, Elector Palatine.

[2] Gibson MSS. V, 55.

[3] The date of this letter in Thirnbeck MSS. is 6.6.[Aug.] '64, but it must be 6.7 [Sept.], from comparison with dates in Besse's *Sufferings*, and from the fact that M.F. was praemunired on 29th Aug., and this letter is obviously written just after the news of that had reached the Rouses.

as the former continued their Meetings openly, while the latter hid them away as much as they could, or gave them up altogether.[1] The courageous stand of the ship's captain and sailors, as related in Rous's letter is notable. The second letter refers particularly to John Rous's own personal problem in face of this possibility of transportation. This letter was for Margaret's eyes alone, and in the first letter the hint is given that her eyesight was poor.

Mile End, the 6th. of the 7th. m. [Sept.] 1664.

Dear Mother,

In the unalterable and unchangeable truth, which is more precious than all changeable things, is my dear and entire love to thee, to whom my love is beyond what here I can express, who art honourable in the truth, and to be honoured by all that live in the truth, who hast not accounted anything too dear to thee to be parted with for the Lord and for his truth's sake, but hath stood to the hazard and loss of all rather than in the least to submit or come under anything that is contrary to the Lord or his blessed truth manifested in thy heart. Oh how happy are we thy children to have such a mother, who with such boldness in the power and spirit of the Lord stands up against the powers of darkness, and spiritual wickedness in high places; my desires are that as through thy faithfulness in the loss of all, thou hast obtained honour and renown, so we thy children in our several places may be found faithful in all trials that we meet with for the truth's sake, may add comfort to thy afflictions and may be no cause of grief or sorrow, for which cause we desire the help of thy prayers, which we know are heard and accepted by him who is mighty to save all those that trust in him.

He then refers to a letter just received from Sarah telling them of the hard and unjust dealings received by Margaret from the

---

[1] 'Here the fanatics called Quakers did greatly relieve the sober people for a time: for they were so resolute, and gloried in their constancy and sufferings, that they assembled openly, at the Bull and Mouth, near Aldersgate, and were dragged away daily to the Common Gaol, and yet desisted not, but the rest came the next day nevertheless, so that the gaol at Newgate was filled with them. Abundance of them died in prison, and yet they continued their assemblies still! And the poor deluded souls would sometimes meet only to sit in silence, when, as they said, the Spirit did not speak, and it was a great question whether this silence was a religious exercise not allowed by the Liturgy etc. . . , Yea, many turned Quakers, because the Quakers kept their meetings openly, and went to prison for it cheerfully.'

Richard Baxter, *Reliquiae Baxterianae*, Pt. II, 435–437.

judges at Lancaster, but he is certain of the eventual victory of good.

Then he continues with news of Friends in the south:

Last fifth day 7 Friends were brought from Hertford to London to be transported according to the sentence passed on them by Judge Bridgeman; the jailor some days before came up to London, and met with a master of a ship who was bound to Barbados and Jamaica, with whom the jailor agreed covertly (not letting the master know upon what account they went) to carry 4 of them to Barbados and 3 to Jamaica, and was to put them aboard last fifth day; but when the master heard upon what account they went, he was very sorry, and said he would not carry them if he could any way avoid it, and the chief owner said that he would set the ship on fire before it should carry them; the jailor next day after he came to town put them into a boat and carried them to the ship's side, but the master had ordered the seamen that if such came, except they were willing to go, they should not take them aboard, and told the jailor that his agreement was to have sent them aboard the day before, which he not doing, he had otherwise disposed of his ship, and now would not carry them if he might have 100 pounds a man. So the jailor was forced to carry them back, and that day went to Judge Bridgman to tell him what the master said, who advised him to arrest the master for his bargain. But on last 7th day the King and his Council set about it and Judge Bridgeman was with them, to consider what to do with the master, and in the afternoon two messengers were sent for the master to Whitehall where he was brought before one of the King's secretaries, who committed him close prisoner to the Gatehouse, not to be bailed, for refusing to carry them. I hear the master of the ship was very bold and answered very undauntly; there is none of the ship's masters that are going to Barbados, that I hear of, but are resolved they will not carry Friends except they are willing to go.[1]

John Rous then gives news of the Friends arrested and in prison, 17 likely to be banished, 199 men and women in Newgate and Bridewell, 12 men and 6 women from one Meeting and 60 from another. Some at Bristol had died in prison—the plague which raged in 1665 was already breaking out, and prisoners in their crowded quarters were among the first victims.

[1] The full story of the seven Hertford Quakers can be read in Besse's *Sufferings*, pp. 245–8.

Sending loving messages to George Fox and the three young Fell daughters, he ends his letter:

Dear Mother, if in anything we may be serviceable to thee, in speaking to anybody, or if at any time thou may have occasion for money, I desire thou would not spare to command anything that we are able to do, for I look upon it as mine and our duty to be as much assistant to thee in this time of thy suffering as may be, and in so doing to bear part of the burden with thee.

I have something in my mind concerning which I desire thy advice, which I intend to write on the other side, which I desire if thou cannot read, thou would reserve it till Sarah be with thee or some one whom thou art willing shall read it to thee, and I desire to know whether thou can read it thyself.

And so in dear and fervent love I rest,
Thy obedient and truly loving son,
John Rous.

I was with sister Fell last night but hear nothing of my brother Fell.

On the other side of the paper John Rous wrote the following letter, for Margaret's private view:

Dear Mother,

They [are] proceeding here very high in prosecuting the new act, which ends in banishment, which it's like if the Lord do not restrain them they will bring friends to, which I do not know how soon may be my portion from them, having been once in prison already; my desire is to know thy mind, whether in case I should be sentenced and come to be transported thou would be willing, my wife (being as she is) should go along with me, I am not unsensible of the sickness and illness she hath already gone through at sea,[1] which hath been very hard to her to go through, yet I believe the first time she was with child, if it had pleased the Lord she had missed the fall of the horse, she might have done very well, and in all probability might have gone out her time. And now, dear Mother, considering how hard it will be for us to part, and for me to go to sea, and leave her to follow with a young child, if it please God it live,[2] and to want me who was so great a help to her when she was sick, will be a thing that will be very hard to her, and if she goes to Meetings in the meantime she will be in danger of being banished so well as I, which considerations with others

[1] On the voyage in 1662.
[2] A daughter, Lydia, was born on 5th March 1665, at Swarthmoor. She lived only for a year, and was buried at Sunbreck.

and some inconveniences which may attend her not going with me, put me to a stand, that I do not know what to think, whether it may be better for her if I should be sent away to run the hazard of the seas and go with me, or to settle not to go with me, but stay behind, and run all the hazards and inconveniences which may attend her so doing. Dear Mother, I am given up freely in myself to bear my testimony amongst other Friends against this unjust law, and before I am imprisoned on the third account I would settle all as one that is ready to be transported, that if I do go I may go with clearness, or if I stay it may be with the same, and so desire that thou would seriously consider this, and let me know what thou thinks may be best for me to do, that so I may know how to order things. My wife hath been asking me whether I could not shun going to Meetings where Friends are taken, till such time as she might be up and in a condition to go with me, which I do not know at present I could with freedom do, and that would bring me under the judgment of Friends which I would willingly avoid. This is the substance of what I have at present to write in relation to this matter, thy answer to which I desire as soon as opportunity will permit. I am careful to avoid being imprisoned again as yet, my father having sent for divers things for his plantation which he cannot be without, which I intend to ship by a ship that may go away the latter end of this month, and till those things are sent away, I am not willing to go to prison, because the want of them will be a great prejudice to him, and he depends upon my sending them.

Farewell,
Thy dear son,
John Rouse.[1]

The letter in reply to this appeal has not survived the centuries, but we know that John Rous was not banished in these years of persecution, and we know from the old registers of Swarthmoor Meeting that his wife bore three children at her mother's home, Lydia in March 1665, Bethia in February 1667, and Margaret in February 1668. Possibly the Rouses gave up their home in Mile End Green early in 1665, Margaret coming to live in her old home while her husband divided his time between Swarthmoor and London where his business was.

Two more letters passed between Margaret Fell and the Rouses in 1664, showing the critical state of affairs connected with the estate, and other anxieties.

In November John Rous was able to tell Margaret that up till

[1] Thirnbeck MSS. 3.

then there was no record at Whitehall of the confiscation of her Swarthmoor estate. But the news given him by George Fell's wife that Colonel Kirkby was being 'very courteous' to her husband, did not add to his peace of mind. Rous had also found that George Fell owed thirty-six pounds to a Friend, who was now needing his money; for the reputation of the family, Rous had paid the debt for his brother-in-law, and he could be repaid later by rents coming in for George Fell at Swarthmoor.

John Rous had to report to Margaret a troublesome matter connected with the settlement he wished to make on his wife and children (if he had any later) in case of his death. He had asked his father Colonel Rous in Barbados to settle £20,000 on him and (if he died) on his wife and children. To this his father and mother objected as being too large a sum, and John Rous suggested to his mother-in-law that the sum should be reduced to £10,000 or £12,000, though he added, 'I would not have anything wanting to secure to my wife that which is already granted her; for I look upon it she very well deserves it if it had been more.'[1] No doubt the urgency of the settlement was aggravated by the present insecurity of the Swarthmoor estate. From a later letter (1671) it is seen that a settlement was made, a fortunate arrangement since about then Colonel Rous had remarried, and there was a danger of loss to the son and his wife.

In addition to financial anxieties, Margaret Fell now had news of the very serious illness of her daughter Mary, still visiting the Rouses. Mary had always been rather delicate, but this illness might have been an early case of plague[2] which swept through London in the following year.

On 1st **October** 1664 Margaret from her prison wrote a letter to comfort and thank John and Margaret Rous for their loving care of Mary.

My dear son and daughter,
    In the dear and infinite bowels of tender compassion of everlasting love, and in the everlasting life which never has end, do I write unto you, in which eternal life and power of the Godhead do I enjoy and possess my dear Mary, her spirit near and dear and present with me. Whether in the body or out, with the Lord and to the Lord of Heaven

[1] Abraham MSS. 9.
[2] A suggestion by Mrs. Webb in *Fells of Swarthmoor Hall*.

and earth she is given freely and His heavenly and holy will I freely submit to, that every jot and tittle thereof may be fulfilled to the glory and praise of His great and holy name.

And, my dear daughter, in the name and power of the Lord Jesus (who has all power of heaven and earth in his hand, who gives the life and breath of all his creatures, and takes away at His pleasure) keep over all visibles and in the invisible holy life of the holy God, which thou art made partaker of and has a rich portion in, solace thy soul in that, and in the life and power of Almighty God, which thou enjoys, rest satisfied and be content.

And, as I have said often to thee, give up to be crossed and that is the way to please the Lord and to follow Him in His own way and will, whose way is the best, and all those things are well, and blessed and happy are all they that is well with the Lord, and in His arm and bosom there's an enduring and eternal inheritance, where there will never be more change.

And let nothing enter thy mind concerning anything, for I am very well contented with the handiwork of the Lord and I know your care and tenderness was not awanting to her, and so be all satisfied in the will of the Lord God.

I hope in the Lord that you are all together[1] ere this come to you, and so in the name of the Lord Jesus Christ be all satisfied and content with the will of the Lord, and let neither murmuring nor repining enter none of your minds; nor let not sorrow fill your hearts, for we have all cause to rejoice in the Lord evermore, and I most of all, that bought her dear and brought her up for the Lord, whom I am sure is the true owner of her, and therein is my joy, and blessed be His holy name, who has given me her to the end that he might take her away at His pleasure. All your three sisters was here with me when we received thy letters and it was well it was so, and I intend they shall stay two or three days more till the Sessions be over, and so it has pleased the Lord to divide us equally, that if you be together there and we be together here it is well and blessed by His holy name.

I writ the last week concerning thy brother Fell, what my mind is, and I would desire to know his mind and intention, which he intends to do, as shortly as may be, for we intend to make a sale of some part of the goods however, but if he do intend to come and live in the country and take things into his own hands, we should make a sale of all and he shall have what as he sees fitting for him. I would have you to persuade him to come into the country as shortly as may be.

[1] Isabel Yeamans, with her husband, went up to London from Bristol, to help to nurse Mary.

Your sisters Sarah, Susan and Rachel, who are all here, remember their dear love to you and to their brother Fell, and their brother and sister Yeamans. No more but rest

Your dear mother,
Margaret Fell.

It is much satisfaction to me that you let me know all along how it was with her. It was very well done of you.

Colonel Kirby causes our bonds to be renewed and straightened more and more.

They lock up George Fox, under pretence of an order that came from London. . . . Get this enclosed letter of G.F.'s sent to Gilbert Latey that G. Whitehead and they may draw out what as they see convenient. The enclosed to brother Fell; deliver it to him thyself.[1]

Mary recovered from her illness, and early in 1665 returned to Swarthmoor, probably travelling with John and Margaret Rous.

As for George Fell, on the day the above letter was written by his mother, he sent to the King his 'humble petition' for her estate. It is signed by Sir Roger Bradshaigh and Richard Kirkby.[2] The former was one of the County Members of Parliament. It is curious that though in 1659 before the Restoration George Fell was authorized to raise a troop of horse and riders for the service of the Parliament, and the safety of his part of Lancashire,[3] in the petition five years later, his sponsors state that he was never in arms against the King. They even added that he 'before his Majesty's happy restoration expressed his great desire therefor'. They also said that he had absented himself from his old home because his mother refused to conform to the State Church, much to his distress. In January 1665 Margaret Fell's estate, both real and personal, was granted by the King's ministers to her son.[4] He did not leave London immediately to take possession, but left his sisters there, and there was no sale of goods, as hinted at in the letter last quoted. The fact was that George Fell never came to take possession of the Hall and surrounding land, which was his mother's right to hold as the widow of Judge Fell, which she had lost by being praemunired, and which her son had won

[1] Swm. MSS. I, 101.
[2] *Extracts from State Papers*, pp. 227–8.
[3] *Extracts from State Papers*, p. 116.
[4] *Extracts from State Papers*, p. 228.

by devious means. He and his wife and baby Sarah must have come north some time before 1667 and lived at Marsh Grange of which he already owned two-thirds, for the births of his other three children are all in the Dalton registers, Hannah born in 1667 who lived only until December, Isabel born in December 1668, who lived to grow up and marry James Greaves (or Graves), and Charles born in March 1670 a few months before his father's death, who also lived to marry and have one son who married a granddaughter of William Penn.[1]

[1] There are no direct descendants of Judge and Margaret Fell of the name of Fell, as Lieut.-Colonel Robert Edward Fell, only son of Charles and Gulielma Maria (née Penn) Fell, died childless in 1787. The majority of Judge and Margaret Fell's descendants are from their youngest daughter Rachel, who married Daniel Abraham.

Chapter Fourteen

IMPRISONMENT IN LANCASTER CASTLE: II
1665–8

'For the mystery of Faith is held in a pure conscience, that you may be led, guided, taught, and governed by this which cannot err, but is pure and eternal, and endureth for evermore.'

From an Epistle by M.F. written probably in 1668.

ALTHOUGH during Margaret Fell's four years of imprisonment in Lancaster Castle, she lived in a room where storm and wind and rain came in, she was not kept in solitary confinement. Twice she was given brief periods of liberty. Once in 1665, after twenty months' imprisonment, she was allowed to return home for a short time, and in 1667 she was given leave to visit a Meeting of Friends in Cheshire, to which George Fox (released from Scarborough in 1666) went,[1] and afterwards she returned to prison. In the early days when there was quite a party of Quaker prisoners in Lancaster, they used to meet in the daytime in a large room, and hold Meetings for Worship, and also long discussions with their Puritan fellow-prisoners. One such discussion which was as heated as these doctrinal arguments usually were in the seventeenth century, was with a Lancashire Baptist minister, John Wiggan, and books were published afterwards by both parties, Margaret adding a long appendix.[2]

Visitors came and went, notably her daughters, who took it in turns to stay in the town near their mother, though to reach Lancaster they had to cross the dangerous sands of Morecambe Bay, treacherous in summer from shifting river channels and quicksands, but in winter far more dangerous with storm or sudden mist or rain blotting out all sight of hills and guiding marks.

[1] Camb. Jnl. II, 114.
[2] Collection of Tracts, 2,202 in Bevan-Naish Library, Woodbrooke, Birmingham.

For the first eight months of Margaret Fell's imprisonment, George Fox was also in Lancaster Castle, though his final trial at which he was praemunired did not take place until March 1665, over a year after his arrest at Swarthmoor Hall. A month later he was removed to Scarborough Castle where he was kept for a year and four months under even worse conditions than at Lancaster. All this time Margaret from her prison, together with many Friends in London as well as Fox himself, was pleading on his behalf with the King. Late in August 1666, John White-head brought an order from Charles II for release, and the Governor of Scarborough Castle, the Roman Catholic, Sir Jordan Crosland, brother-in-law of Daniel Fleming, and at the beginning of the imprisonment as stern and persecuting as Fleming himself, gave Fox an honourable liberty. 'He is as stiff as a tree', said the officers and soldiers who had guarded him, 'and as pure as a bell; for we could never stir him.'[1]

Many letters reached her from London and elsewhere, giving her news of Friends and their Meetings, their writings and their severe sufferings in these years. The Conventicle Act of 1664 put thousands of Friends into jail all over the country, and especially in London. Then in 1665 the plague broke out, and the prisoners died in great numbers, 'thronged' as they were. Ellis Hookes was one of her most faithful correspondents. In April 1665 he was telling her of further arrests of Friends, and the possible confiscation of the large Meeting House at the Bull and Mouth. Next month he told her that the King had ordered that the judges should send no more Friends to Newgate Prison because of the plague, which was increasing rapidly, thirty having died of it the preceding week.[2] There were about 140 Quakers in Newgate. George Whitehead, faithful friend and letter-writer, recorded in his autobiography (*Christian Progress*) that 'It was a time of great calamity, sorrow and heaviness, to many thousands of all sorts; and that which added to our Friends' afflictions was the hardness of our persecutors' hearts, . . . their cruelty and barbarity in imprisoning and detaining so many of them in Newgate, and in the White Lion Prison in Southwark, after the plague was greatly broken forth, and many

[1] Camb. Jnl. II, 104.
[2] A.R.B. 147.

people swept away thereby'. He refused to leave the City, but attended Friends' Meetings (on Sundays he took his nightcap in his pocket when he went to Meetings, not knowing if he would be arrested and imprisoned!), and visited Friends, ill or well, in their homes and prisons.[1] He miraculously escaped the contagion. 'The desolation of the City is very great', wrote a non-Quaker to his friend, in September 1665, 'What eye would not weep, to see so many habitations uninhabited, the poor sick not visited, the hungry not fed, the grave not satisfied! Death stares us continually in the face, in every infected person that passeth by us, in every coffin which is daily and hourly carried along the streets. . . . The Quakers (as we are informed) have buried in their piece of ground a thousand for some weeks together last past.'[2] Although this is an exaggeration as regards the deaths of Friends in London, the records say that in that year nearly half the deaths (532 out of 1,177) were due to plague, the peak of the epidemic being in September (279 out of 502).[3]

In November, Ellis Hookes told Margaret Fell that Anne Travers (with whom he lodged in London) had buried three of her household in a month's time, and that her child had had the plague but had recovered. 'I have been preserved well,' he added, 'but as a brand is plucked out of the fire, so has the Lord delivered me, for I have often laid down my head in sorrow, and rose as I went to bed, and not slept a wink, for the groans of them that lay dying; and every morning I counted it a great mercy that the Lord gave me another day. . . . Last First-day they carried Esther Biddle and another woman to prison, for speaking in the street [the authorities having closed the Meeting House], and struck Esther over the face with their halberts.' He told Margaret that whereas there used to be sixteen or eighteen and even twenty Friends buried daily, for several weeks on end, now there was no more than one daily.[4]

In December Margaret heard from Morgan Watkins, a Herefordshire Friend who for attending a Meeting, had lain at the Gatehouse prison, near the west end of Westminster Abbey,

[1] A.R.B. 150.
[2] A.R.B. 152, note.
[3] A.R.B. 155.
[4] A.R.B. 153.

from early August until November. 'I suppose thou heard of
our releasement a while since', he wrote. 'I have been something
weak since I came out into the air; but through the great love
of my God I am wonderfully preserved to the praise of His name.
But the two imprisonments in Newgate, and the one at Gatehouse, in which I have had several battles with death, have much
weakened my body. But the power of my God arising gave me
dominion over the distemper, and weaknesses of the flesh. The day
was dreadful to all flesh, and few were able to abide it, and stand
in the judgment; but the Lord was very merciful to the remnant
of his people, and his blessed seed is arising in many vessels.

'Our Meetings are quiet, save only the Bull and Mouth,[1]
which is kept out; they are beginning to be very large, of strange
faces and good honest countenances that with exceeding hunger-
ings receive the Truth. . . . The work is very great. There is a
letter come to Walter Miers as I am informed, that William
Caton is out of the body. . . . The city doth begin to fill again
apace. I have an account of 920 Friends, and Friends' children
and servants that were buried in our burying-place since the
20th of the 1st month 1665, but I think not much above half
were Friends, so called. The ship in which the Friends are [await-
ing banishment], is yet in the River, and all in Newgate are
pretty well, and have much liberty. . . . The Bishop of Salisbury
is dead, and this day I hear that Canterbury was dead, but I am
not certain. . . .'[2]

To Margaret the saddest piece of news in that letter must have
been the death of William Caton, in Holland. Between her and
Caton, still a young man of thirty when he died, there had
since his boyhood at Swarthmoor, been the utmost affection.
The many letters that he wrote to her, and the few remaining
ones from her to him, breathe a wonderful spiritual understanding. His life's work, as we have already seen, had been the birth
and growth of Quakerism in Holland, but he had also travelled
into Germany where he had met and talked with the Elector
Palatine, Jesuits, and men of many creeds.

---

[1] In Aldersgate Street and near St. Paul's Cathedral. It was the first and most
important London Meeting-house. Its name was from an ancient inn. (*The
London Friends' Meetings*, Beck and Ball, p. 134. *seq.*)
[2] Swm. MSS. II.

Plague had also ravaged Amsterdam in 1663 and later, and thousands had died.[1] Yet Caton testified to the courage of the Dutch Friends who willingly visited the sick, watched with them, and tended them. Though the woman of the house where the Meeting was held, fell ill of the plague, and some in the house died of it, yet they continued to meet there, and not one Friend absented himself.[2] Shortly before he died he wrote of the lack of persecution of sects in Amsterdam,[3] and of the grievous plague in England. 'Methinks it is very commendable for to see, as I have often seen in this city [Amsterdam], how that Calvinists, Lutherans, Papists, Baptists of divers sorts, Jews, Friends, Armenians, etc., go in peace, and return in peace, and enjoy their meetings in peace, and all are kept in peace in the city; and that without any trouble to the rulers of the city; who I think have it manifold better, and are much more at peace and quietness than the magistrates in England, who first are troubled with making of laws to take away liberty of conscience, and then more than a little with executing those laws.'[4] This freedom had brought an increase of population and prosperity to the city, owing to the increase of trading and merchandize. He and others feared however that a spirit of intolerance would spread from England.

No longer would Margaret Fell and her children be able to receive the little gifts which Caton had loved to send them on his travels. To Margaret he had once sent 'one of the largest maps that are here to be gotten', to the children 'a little thread, with some other small necessary things for their use, which I suppose they cannot there procure for money', to 'dear' Mary some powder about which she had written to him,[5] and to Margaret 'a seal made by a friend in Amsterdam' which he begged her to accept and 'think it not strange, but first see the use and service of it; it is not to carry about with thee but to continue where thou resides, to be of use and service to thee, not only,

[1] In 1664 over 24,000 died in Holland of plague, and nearly 10,000 in Amsterdam alone. W. I. Hull, *Qism. in Amsterdam*, p. 170.

[2] Ibid., p. 172.

[3] This tolerance did not extend throughout Holland, as W. Caton described in an Epistle to suffering English Friends in 1661 (*Life of W. Caton*, p. 107).

[4] Swm. MSS. I, 350, and *Life of W. Caton*, p. 139.

[5] Swm. MSS. I, 331.

when thou puts up one letter, but especially when thou puts up more than one together'.[1]

No longer would his letters reach her, whether she was at Swarthmoor or in a prison, his letters which in their beautiful handwriting told her again and again of his deep love and gratirude to her, and which were treasured and preserved at the old home.

Margaret was to hear of still other calamities as she lay in her prison. Early in September 1666 was the Great Fire of London. The plague and the fire were regarded by Friends as God's punishment of the wicked, especially of the persecutors. Ellis Hookes early in October told her that people in London were still in great confusion, and that the fire had brought destruction and ruin. Such was the devastation that Justice Daniel Fleming's son who was living in London at that time told his father that the ruins of London reminded him of the fells of his homeland, with their great grey rocks jutting out among the hillsides. Individual Friends under concern approached the King to warn him of further judgments if he allowed the persecution to continue. 'I came to this sad ruined city,' wrote Alexander Parker to Margaret, 'the sight whereof did sadden my spirit; considering that the end of woes are not yet come.'[2] He had heard talk of a 'bloody massacre intended by the Papists', which had filled thousands with great fear.

During her imprisonment, Margaret Fell spent much of her time in writing, not only to her friends, but for a wider public. The obstinate misunderstanding by the authorities of the peaceable and religious intentions of Friends was a constant spur to her. In 1664, her first year in Lancaster Castle, she sent broadcast a moving appeal to magistrates and the people of England to stop persecuting harmless Christians, and making unjust laws against them.[3] 'What is the matter with the Christians of our age,' she asked, 'and of our English nation, that hath been looked upon to be a garden and a nursery in Christianity and religion beyond all other nations? . . . and are they turned persecutors and law-makers against Christianity?'

[1] W. I. Hull, *Qism. in Amsterdam*, p. 148.
[2] Swm. MSS. III, 137.
[3] M.F. *Works*, p. 290.

On the same day she wrote also to 'The Flock of God',[1] scattered throughout the world, to encourage them in their sufferings, to remind them to prize their liberty of conscience for which they fought by suffering. 'Therefore keep faithful to the Lord God, and his truth, and make war in righteousness, and give your backs to the smiter and your cheeks to them that pull off the hair; it is but for an hour, stand it out, the Lamb shall have the Victory.'

In January 1665 she sent a long Epistle to imprisoned Friends in London and Bristol and elsewhere,[2] especially remembering those who were threatened and condemned to banishment. 'My dearly beloved, in the entirest love,' she wrote, 'be strong in the mighty God, and nothing terrified with your adversaries . . . nor with their laws, and threats of banishment; for they cannot banish you from the coasts and sanctuary of the living God, as you abide in God's Covenant of Light and Life and Peace, and in the unity of the Eternal Spirit.'

When she had been in prison for two and a half years, she wrote again directly to Charles II. First, in simple strong words she accused Charles of having allowed bitter cruel persecution on God's people for six years since his restoration. Some had been banished, many imprisoned. 'When it was asked in open court, whether it was now become a transgression or a crime in England to worship God; he that was then the Chief Justice of England answered: "Yes, yes." Oh wonderful! Let this be chronicled in England for after ages, that all magistrates may dread and fear so to affront the Almighty, except they dare say, they are stronger than He.' She begged him to consider the fruits of this persecution—it had brought hundreds of God's people to their graves; it had rendered the realm cruel in its own eyes and that of other people. God's judgment was already seen in the plague, the Fire of London and in the Dutch War.

She reminded the King of her visit to him on his restoration when she told him their people were an 'innocent, harmless, peaceable people', and his reply, 'If they be peaceable, they shall be protected'. She had later written to him telling him of their beliefs and how they must worship God. Many of their books

[1] M.F. *Works*, p. 293.
[2] M.F. *Works*, pp. 299, 303.

they had sent to him, and also to Parliament, bishops and ministers, both ecclesiastical and civil. They had asked for a meeting
with the bishops to 'try' them, and he had consented, but the
bishops had refused—they 'feared that their cause would not
hold stitch with the rule of the Scriptures'. Instead the bishops
got the civil rulers to persecute the Quakers.

She reminded the King that she had promised they would
render to Caesar the things of Caesar's, and would 'give unto
God also the thing that was God's'.

She had begged him to remember this was a 'brittle people',
also to beware of the counsel of the bishops, for it was their
counsel which had ruined his father.

All this with much more I wrote to thee, and warned thee of; I can
truly say in the fear of the Lord, in much love and tenderness to thee;
and now I may say unto thee, for which of these things hast thou
kept me in prison three long winters, in a place not fit for people to
lie in; sometimes for wind and storm and rain, and sometimes for
smoke; so that it is much that I am alive; but that the power and
goodness of God hath been with me. I was kept a year and seven months
in this prison, before I was suffered to see the house that was mine, or
children or family, except they came to me over two dangerous sands
in the cold winter; when they came with much danger of their lives;
but since the last Assizes I have had a little more respect from this
Sheriff than formerly from others. And in all this I am very well
satisfied; and praises the Lord who counts me worthy to suffer for his
sake.

For I never did thee nor any other man in the nation any wrong
and so I may say for many more of our Friends that have suffered even
until Death; and all that we would write or speak we were not believed,
and all the warnings that we gave of judgments; and told you plainly
we had done so with other Governors before you; and how the Lord
had overthrown them; and desired you many times to beware lest the
Lord's judgments came over you also; but all was to no purpose, for as
long as there was peace in the Land the main business of the Parliament
was to *invent laws to punish and persecute Quakers*; but to make laws to
punish vice, sin, and wickedness and lasciviousness, we had but a little
of such laws.

And now after all my sufferings, in the same love that I visited thee
in the beginning, I desire thee once more to fear the Lord God *by whom
Kings rule, and Princes decree justice, who sets up one and pulls down
another at his pleasure.*

And let not the guilt or the burden of that word that passed from thee at Breda lie upon thy conscience, but as thou promised when thou wast in distress, and also renewed it many times since, that thou would give liberty to tender consciences: in the fear of the Lord perform it and purge thy conscience of it, and hearken not to wicked counsellors that hath stopped it in thee all this time, for they will bear none of thy burden for thee, when the Lord pleads for breach of covenant with him and his people; I know it hath been often in thy heart to perform it, and thou hast seen what fruit the want of it have brought forth.

So if thou lovest thy eternal peace and comfort with the Lord, try what the performance of it will bring forth, who wilt thereby see thou hast hearkened to wrong counsellors.

And every mortal man hath but a moment in this life, either to serve, fear, and honour the Lord, and therein to receive mercy from him, or else to transgress, sin, disobey, and dishonour him, and to receive the judgment of eternal misery.

So never a one of you knows how long, or how short your day may be; therefore fear not man that can kill the body, but fear the Lord who when he hath killed the body can cast the soul into hell; yea I say unto you fear him.

From a true lover of all your souls (though a sufferer by you) and the desire of my heart is that you may take these things into consideration betime before it be too late; and set open the prison doors and let the innocent go free, and that will take part of the burden and guilt off you, lest the door of mercy be shut to you.[1]

This appeal to the King had no immediate result—for two more years she and others were left in jail.

During her imprisonment Margaret Fell also wrote four books. The first, in November 1664, was *A Call to the Universal Seed of God . . . to come up to the spiritual Worship, etc.*, and was addressed both to Jews and Gentiles.[2] In it she dwelt on the supreme importance of Jesus Christ and his appeal for a spiritual religion—an inward one. 'So come to the pure Eternal Spirit . . . and out of all dead forms,' she cried.

Two years later she wrote a book in which her pioneering mind shows her to have been long ahead of her time. It is entitled *Women's speaking justified, proved, and allowed of by the Scriptures, all such as speak by the spirit and power of the Lord Jesus.* First published in 1666, it was reprinted with an addition

[1] M.F. *Works*, pp. 325–30.
[2] M.F. *Works*, pp. 304–24.

in the next year, and translated into Dutch in 1668[1]—a comment on the importance of the spread of Quakerism in that land of toleration.

In this short book Margaret Fell makes a spirited attack on those who deny the right of women to speak in churches. She illustrates her argument by apt quotation of texts and recital of stories from the Old and New Testaments. She reminds her readers that it was to the woman of Samaria that Jesus said He was the Messiah, and to Martha that He was the Resurrection and the Life. As for the woman who poured precious ointment on His head, 'it is manifest', Margaret said, 'that this woman knew more of the secret power and wisdom of God, than His disciples did, who were filled with indignation against her'. Women from Galilee followed Him and ministered to Him, women of Jerusalem wept for Him, women boldly stood by His side at the Cross and saw where His body was laid, and above all it was women who were there in the garden first to seek Him and to meet Him after His resurrection, and to bear the message of hope to the frightened disciples. 'Mark this, you that despise and oppose the message of the Lord God that He sends by women; what had become of the redemption of the whole body of mankind, if they had not cause to believe the message that the Lord Jesus sent by these women, of and concerning His resurrection?' There was also Priscilla, the wife of Aquilla, who together were teachers of Apollos, a learned man from Alexandria—'We do not read that he despised what Priscilla said, because she was a woman, as many now do.'

Then she passed on to the words of Paul to the Corinthians, which are still, in our own time, used to keep women from contributing fully to the spiritual life of most sections of the Christian Church. She goes behind the words to the spirit and background of Paul's remark, 'Let your women keep silence in the Church'. The Corinthians, she said, both men and women, were in confusion—in which case Paul tells both men and women to be silent. But indeed Paul is speaking to women who are still under the Law, and it is they who he says must be silent, for they are not ready to speak, not having yet received the Spirit. But Paul obviously looks forward to their receiving the Holy

[1] Joseph Smith's *Catalogue of Friends' Books*.

Spirit, for he soon gives instructions that when women 'pray and prophesy' they should have their heads covered. Why should he give instructions thus, she asked, if he did not consider it right for women to pray and prophesy as men did?

And further, because Paul rebukes those women who wore costly luxurious clothes, and were obviously unsuited to give instruction to others, are all women to be penalized always for such as these? 'If the Apostle would have had women's speaking stopped, . . . why did he entreat his true yoke-fellow to help those women who laboured with him in the Gospel?' The opposition to women speaking in the Spirit has always come from the spirit of Darkness, she believed.

Then Margaret Fell turns back to famous women in the Old Testament, who taught, prophesied and led the people—Deborah, Huldah, and Sarah; and finally pleads that men should not try to limit the Power of God, by believing it exists in their own sex only.

In the reprint, after some had written to combat her thesis, she twits the priests for putting in the Book of Common Prayer the songs of two women, Elizabeth and Mary—how could they if they believed these women were incapable of receiving the Spirit of God? 'Are you not here beholden to the woman for her sermon, to use her words, to put into your Common Prayer? and yet you forbid women's speaking.'[1]

This small book of Margaret Fell's was the first one to be written by a woman since the Reformation, to plead for the recognition of the spiritual equality of man and woman.[2] It is mentioned as a pioneer work by Mr. G. W. Johnson in his book *The Evolution of Woman*.[3] It is consistent with the claim of George Fox and the early Friends that their teaching was 'Primitive Christianity Revived', for in the early days of the Christian Church there is no doubt whatever but that this spiritual equality existed. 'There can be neither Jew nor Greek, there can be neither bond nor free', wrote Paul for the Galatians,[4] 'there can be no male and female; for ye all are one in Christ Jesus.'

[1] M.F. *Works:* pp. 331–50.

[2] Two books on the same subject had been written by George Fox in 1656 and 1661.

[3] P. 256.   [4] III, 28.

Throughout the three centuries of the Society of Friends, women have been as much at liberty as men to minister to their fellows, and the whole Society is deeply indebted to the pioneer work of their forbears in this respect. The responsibility of using gifts and the liberty allowed have been one potent cause of the standing and development of Quaker women. Their position in business meetings will be discussed in a later chapter.

The other two books she wrote during her imprisonment were *The Standard of the Lord Revealed and* **'A Touch-Stone; or, a Tryal by the Scriptures of the priests, bishops and ministers'.** These two were much longer than any of her other writings, the former being 132 pages long, and the latter 115 pages in her collected *Works.* Neither of the longer books has much permanent interest. *The Standard of the Lord Revealed* is an abstract of the whole Bible, written apparently to show how God worked in and through the Jews until Christ, whose Spirit was given after His death and resurrection for the comfort of His followers. It is written for Friends, to educate and encourage them.[1]

This book was sent up to London shortly before the Great Fire in September 1666, and it was saved from destruction by Ellis Hookes who later saw to its publication.[2]

'A Touch-Stone' is, as its title suggests, an examination of the claims of the clergy, whether Papist or Protestant. It is written to explain to the bishops why six years before she had warned the King to beware of the counsel of the bishops. Under clearly defined headings, and most fully documented by long quotations from the Bible, chiefly the New Testament, Margaret accuses the clergy of not following Christ's own teaching, of relying on University education instead of the inspiration of God, of persecuting the innocent, and of gross intolerance, especially as seen in their ecclesiastical courts. She accused the Roman Catholic priests of keeping their people in ignorance, particularly of the Bible. She claims that swearing is breaking the law of Christ—that outward sacraments are unscriptural, and that many of the customs of the clergy were founded on Old Testament teaching rather than that of the New.

[1] **The Standard (1667) was not reprinted in her** *Works*
[2] A.R.B. 157-9.

There are two thoughts uppermost in one's mind after reading these two books of Margaret Fell's—the consistency with which early Friends based their beliefs and teaching on the recorded teachings of Christ and His earliest followers, and secondly, how deeply they studied the Bible, both its words and particularly the spirit which had prompted those words. One can picture Margaret Fell in her prison room poring over her beloved Bible—the large folio volume still preserved at Friends' House, London—or possibly having it read to her by one of her daughters.

Before Margaret Fell was released she wrote one more book, besides her large number of private letters to Friends. This work was *A Call unto the Seed of Israel*, and was addressed to the Jews, for whose conversion she still felt great concern.[1] This book has already been noted in Chapter 7. It was followed by an Epistle 'to go amongst those whose desires are after Truth, as it is in Jesus, wherever they are scattered throughout the Nations'—an appeal to all, both Jews and Gentiles, to come to the knowledge of Jesus Christ within.

Her release from imprisonment in Lancaster Castle came in June 1668, after many efforts by Friends in London. In May while the King and Council were being pressed to release the many hundreds of Friends still languishing in prisons throughout the country, Dr. Richard Lower, physician to Charles II, was trying to persuade some Lords who were members of the Royal Society—founded early in Charles II's reign—to plead with the King on Margaret Fell's behalf, but her correspondent Thomas Salthouse added 'Pharaoh's heart is so hard'.[2]

However the hard hearts soon afterwards softened, and in her own words is the simple record, 'I was set at liberty by an order from the King and Council in 1668'.[3]

Her old persecutor, Daniel Fleming, who had strongly disapproved of the release of George Fox two years earlier,[4] now repeated his protest to Secretary Williamson:

---

[1] M.F. *Works*, pp. 467–92.
[2] **Swm. MSS. I, 103, 19 iii [May] 1668.**
[3] M.F. *Works*, p. 8.
[4] *Extracts from State Papers*, p. 257.

Rydal, 21st Aug. 1668.

. . . Mrs. Fell having her discharge from her easy imprisonment doth not a little encourage that rabble of fanatics, and discourage all magistrates from acting against them. I observe it's now become a general policy to comply with the non-conformists; I am sure it much encourages their number, and I fear that it will much increase their confidence in designing. I wish that less than all may fully please them, which if it do, then I'll say they are not of the brood of the old Presbyterian, *Verbum Sat.* . . .

Sir, your most assured friend,
and humble servant,
Dan. Fleming.[1]

Margaret Fell's release was, as is hinted in Fleming's letter, part of a policy of greater tolerance, carried out through the influence of the King. In March 1668 the House of Commons, still very hostile to religious toleration, passed a severe bill for the continuation of the Conventicle Act of 1664, but the bill was not passed into law. Indeed the year 1668 began a short period of freedom for Friends to carry on their Meetings, as will be seen in the next chapter, although of course there was still some persecution. The spirit in which Friends were prepared to face persecution in March 1668 when there seemed every prospect of the bill becoming law, is shown by Thomas Salthouse's letter to Margaret Fell when he wrote, 'Though the Papists are named [in the Bill], yet we are like to bear the greatest part of the suffering, if it do any execution. We are resolved to meet, preach and pray, in public and private, in season and out of season, in city, town and country, as if it had never been; well knowing that the same power by which we have been preserved and delivered out of the den, is with us, and will be with us to the end, if we abide faithful.'[2]

---

[1] *Extracts from State Papers*, p. 277.
[2] Swm. MSS. I, **102. It was in fact not a bill but the proclamation issued by the king and council on 10 March 1667/8 against conventicles.**

Chapter Fifteen

TWO MARRIAGES, 1668–9

'*Love is a great thing, yea, altogether a great good; by itself it maketh light every thing that is heavy, and it beareth evenly all that is uneven. For it carrieth a burden which is no burden, and maketh everything that is bitter, sweet and tasteful.*'

From the Third Book of *The Imitation of Christ*,

by Thomas à Kempis.

WHEN Margaret Fell returned home from her long imprisonment, it was as if she came from darkness to light. Her dark damp room in the castle no longer exists to remind the visitor of a seventeenth-century prison, but Swarthmoor Hall still stands with its sun-bathed oak panelled great hall, its warmth and garden and orchards, and June is one of the loveliest of months. A great welcome met her—there was Sarah whose business capacity and spiritual strength had done so much to keep Meeting and family in good heart, and there were Mary, Susannah and Rachel. John and Margaret Rous who had been living at Swarthmoor from February 1665 until shortly before their mother's return, had now gone to London, leaving behind them their two children, Bethiah, aged a year and a half, and baby Margaret, four months old. (Margaret Rous must have made a quick recovery after the birth of her baby, as it seems from a letter written by her husband from London to Sarah, that she had travelled the long journey on horseback, borrowing Sarah's saddle and Mary's stirrup—both of which much-needed articles John Rous was trying to return quickly.)[1]

Among the first visitors to come to Swarthmoor after Margaret Fell's return were Thomas Salthouse, who had been away 'publishing Truth' in the Midlands and South-west, and Thomas Lower. The latter was engaged to be married to Mary Fell, the

[1] Swm. MSS. I, 107.

fifth daughter, at this time twenty-one years old, and fourteen years younger than her betrothed. Lower had planned to come north earlier, but a serious illness, fever and an ague, and an abscess in the thigh, had delayed him.[1] His brother, Dr. Richard Lower, was attending him. Both brothers were doctors of medicine, Thomas practising chiefly late in life, while Richard (of Christ Church, Oxford) was (as mentioned in the previous chapter) Court Physician to Charles II, 'a doctor of great repute',[2] and a Fellow of the Royal Society.

Thomas Lower had joined Friends in 1656, after visiting George Fox in his prison at Launceston, Cornwall, and in the following year he had married Elizabeth, eldest daughter of Sir John Trelawny of Trelawny and his first wife, who was a daughter of Sir Reignold Mohun. Elizabeth, older than her husband by sixteen years, had joined the Quakers about the same time as Thomas Lower. Until she died late in 1662 or early in 1663, Elizabeth Lower loyally supported her husband and other Friends during the days of the persecution and sufferings which frequently fell upon them in Cornwall.

In 1663, as we have seen, the young widower travelled in Cornwall and Devon with George Fox, Margaret Fell, Sarah and Mary, then a girl of sixteen.[3] In the following years their affection grew, and there still exist two love letters from Thomas Lower to Mary Fell, probably written about 1667, which show a surprising hostility felt by Margaret Fell to the marriage, and some hesitation also from Loveday Hambly, Thomas Lower's aunt, with whom he lived at Tregangeeves, Cornwall.

Thomas Lower to Mary Fell:
My dear M.F.
If I could have daily intercourse, my fervent love unto thee would sufficiently administer new matter unto me of writing unto thee, for though by a retrograde motion our distance outwardly each from other is like to increase, yet in that which neither distance of place nor length of days or years can separate, in that shall we mutually enjoy each other, and therein by natural attraction shall we sympathise each

---

[1] Swm. MSS. I, 103.
[2] Letter from T. Salthouse to M.F. Swm. MSS. I, 103.
[3] *A Quaker Saint of Cornwall*, by L. V. Hodgkin, and Swm. MSS. III, 182: (6.9.1662).

with other in all things that may arise to obviate or dam up the streams of our innocent and true affections one unto another. Thy desirable second love token or letter of love I received with much joy some days after I came home, and in it expected to have had the receive [=receipt] of thy first also, but the continuation and increase of thy love, health and welfare it overcame all the sad accidents that encountered me and as it were first welcomed me home. For at Looe, a town about 12 miles from my aunt's, I heard of a fire that had happened at Tregangeeves, which had burnt some part of the house, which thou may imagine was no little trouble unto me and dear T.S. [Thomas Salthouse], because we knew not certainly what part or how much, but when we arrived there we found it was not so much as report had made it. The suddenness and unexpected coming of us (for my aunt had information but the day before that we were both in prison) even transported my aunt into an ecstacy, she was so much overcome with joy at the seeing of us, but when we considered the wonderful goodness and mercy of the Lord in the miraculous preservation of all the rest of the houses, we could not but admire, bless and magnify the name of the Lord. For it seems through the negligence of a servant that was brewing (it being also the meeting time and day, the 5th day of the week) having store of fuel brought in to her, she sets a store of fuel under her pans and goes about other business, and came not again until the fire had kindled in the rest of that combustible stuff, and the whole room was in a flame, and the fire so prevalent, as it was too late to quench. But through God's mercy and the great concourse of her neighbours the fire was still confined within the walls of the brewhouse where it began and ended, though there be thatched houses within 12 feet of this house on both sides and joining unto it. The loss is small in comparison of the danger threatened unto the whole house, the sight whereof administer continual cause for us to bless and praise the name of the Lord, by whose power alone the violence of this fire was quenched, and the fury thereof abated, and farther than He permitted it could not come.

Here have of late many sad accidents happened by fire in this county, amongst which Godolphin's house[1] is most considerable, which was most of it burnt that same day that ours was; his loss is judged to be at least £1,000, all his writings burnt also. And thus it seems good unto the Lord to plead with this nation by fire as well as by plague and sword. . . .

Our meeting room was not distant above 10 feet from this that was

[1] Godolphin Hall, near Helston. G. was father of Sidney Godolphin, minister of James II, William III and Anne.

H

burnt, and yet preserved. Great, exceeding great, was the mercy and love of the Lord unto us, praised be His name for ever and ever.

I have imparted the whole progress of our love and good liking each unto other unto my Aunt Hambly, and have informed her also of G.F. approbation and commends of thee. I have also acquainted her with the better part of thy mother's animadversions unto thee upon this subject, and I have read unto her my letter and answer unto it. I have also shewed and read unto her thine and my dear Sister Yeamans last letter unto me, and unto the whole matter she hath exceeding good liking, and heartily wishes good speed unto it. It seems before I came home, there had some vilifying reports been brought into Cornwall, but after she had heard my more true and impartial account both of thy person, qualification and disposition, she did with much delight hear it and rejoice in it. My Sister Yeamans was represented (according to her deserts) as a worthy Friend and a person every way well accomplished, but thee (my dear) wert rendered less exact and with a more pale countenance, but my aunt said unto the reporters, 'thus was it with me when I was young, I was thought and looked on as the least in beauty of all my father's children, and yet (said she) God hath provided for me and blessed me as [illegible] forth as any of them, and so I hope will the Lord do Mary Fell also'. This she repeated unto me and T.S. [Thomas Salthouse] after we came home and when she understood by T.S. that thee wert the steward at home and of your frugality in general, 'Well', said she, 'I make no doubt but that God will bless them.' At Plymouth both thee and sister Yeamans were painted with naked necks and in costly array, until T.S. and I deciphered you in another dress, and quite defaced the former counterfeit, by representing you in a more amiable and more commendable posture. The authors of these unsavoury belchings I cannot fully discover, but that which brings reports will also carry; however they nor it hath gained nought but an ill repute for their ill report and you thereby are become more estimable and desirable.

When I read unto my Aunt my letter unto thy Mother she liked it very much, and when I came unto that which mentioned the estate I had in expectancy, she said, 'God forbid I should ever more alienate it from thee. I have not made (said she) the worth of a dish nor a spoon from thee. And as I have, so I still will confirm it upon thee, and therefore let them not have any doubtings of that'. Thus I thought fit to impart unto thee the state of our affairs here, and likewise how very kind [illegible] thy loving salutes unto her in the letter and desires me to return the remembrance of her very dear love [paper torn]. T.S., my very dear brother and fellow traveller, greets thee with a cordial holy kiss who is gone from home this day to Tho: Mounces. And now, my dearest, unto whom my heart is perfectly united (and in that which first begot our union each unto other) inseparably knit, in that do I most heartily embrace thee in the arms of pure affection and seal it unto thee with the lip of truth, with which I solace myself in the sorrowful days of this our distant approaches, until it shall please the Lord to make our union more entire and complete. I should be glad to receive or at least to understand what reception mine had at Swarth-moor, or whether it were received; for thy mentioning the receipt of one from thy mother, which calls for thy coming home, and speaking nought of the receipt of mine, makes me fear either its miscarriage or dislike. Wherefore I desire thee to be as candid and plain in stating the affairs of the North unto me, as I am of the West unto thee.

The match proposed for my eldest brother[1] is broken off, and my Aunt Hambly hath mentioned unto my mother for thy sister Sarah for him. T.S. says that they much resemble each other in face. If she will incline I should much rejoice in it, only I will desire her to give us leave to be married first, if the Lord permit and prosper this which he hath begun in us.

Since the writing of the aforesaid, my Aunt coming into the room where I was writing, I read these unto her, and she rejoiced in our good liking and love one unto another, and said she would confirm and make all her estate unto me in marriage with thee; and hopes thou wilt be a help and comfort unto her in this her old age, and wishes that my brother were married unto Sarah. What the Lord may bring to pass and hath ordained, I shall rejoice in, unto whom I commit this and myself also, in whose protection there is safety and peace for ever, by whom I hope to hear of thy being kept in perfect welfare, which will much contribute unto mine. And so, my dear, in that which never ends do I send and end these lines, even in that which never waxeth old, in which I sadly say farewell, my dear, farewell.

Thine,
Thomas Lower.

My dearest M.F.,

Just as I was going to seal up the precedent lines, did my Aunt Hambly bring up into my chamber thy second love token unto me since I came into Cornwall. I read them all unto her, viz., that from my dear brother Yeamans, as also thine, and part of thy mother's in it.

---

[1] Edward Lower of Tremere, Cornwall, not Dr. Richard Lower, who was the second brother. **For the Lowers of Tremere (Tremeere) see L. Violet Hodgkin,** A *Quaker saint of Cornwall* **(London 1927) p. 221.**

She very well likes of the good will and love betwixt us and rejoiced to hear my brother Yeamans call me brother, and thee to write thy dearest friend. She wishes all prosperity and good success unto it, and sends unto thee the remembrance of her very dear love whom she likes though she never saw. But truly, my dear, I cannot but take notice of thy mother's slights of me, and unfriendly deportment towards me, which I have not, nor I hope never shall merit from her. In her first unto thee at Bristol, setting all the strictness and severe enquiries therein aside, unto which I might justly have made suitable observations, but I waived it all, but in the conclusion of her letter she mentions, 'Shew the forepart unto the man'. If I had never pretended unto thee, she might as properly have styled me friend; but I smothered all these apprehensions then and hoped that I should receive more amicable treat[ment] in return to my very submissive letter unto her, wherein I am sure all the civility and respect becoming her I gave unto her and yet I am not thought worthy of an answer. Unto a more inferior affair than this I might have reasonably expected an answer, and had I been one of the baser sort I could but have been unanswered, but I am resolved to put the best construction I can upon it for the love I bear unto thee, and therefore do bespeak myself that she is desirous to conduct all her kindness unto me through thee [paper torn].[1]

This long and beautiful love-letter was addressed by Lower 'For my dearest Friend Mary Fell, these with care deliver'. At that time Mary was staying with her sister Isabel Yeamans in Bristol, and if the letter was written late in 1666 or early in 1667 (as the reference to 'fire'—the Fire of London, 1666—and 'sword'—the Dutch war which was raging from 1664 to 1667 when the Dutch sailed triumphantly up the Medway, burning the ships on the way), Mary was probably with her sister during domestic anxieties. In 1666, two years after her marriage, Isabel lost her baby, William, and in the same year (or in 1667) her elder daughter Rachel was born, a delicate child who lived only for ten years.

While the courtship was going on, Margaret Fell was in prison at Lancaster, a fact which may explain her nervousness and hostility to Thomas Lower. However all that was later changed, and on 26th August 1668, two months after her mother's release, Mary was married to Thomas Lower in the

---

[1] Framed MS. at Library, Friends' House, London.

hall of Swarthmoor Hall.[1] For the first five years of their married life, they lived first at Tregangeeves with Loveday Hambly, and then in London and later in a home of their own called Pennance, near St. Austell, Cornwall. Early in 1673 they left Cornwall for far North Lancashire, and it was at Swarthmoor Hall that in June that same year their eldest child was born, Margaret. Between 1673 and 1688 ten children were born, six daughters and four sons, of whom only four girls and one boy grew up. It is a striking fact that Margaret Fell lost in infancy only one of her nine children, while those of her daughters who had large families lost half or even more as babies, not unusual for those days.[2] The Lowers in 1676 left Swarthmoor to live at Marsh Grange, on the Duddon Estuary, Margaret Fell's birthplace, and it was there that all but the two eldest children were born. Thomas Lower travelled much, to Cornwall, to London, sometimes sharing travel and imprisonment with George Fox, and was imprisoned on several occasions for his Quakerism.

Let us return to Margaret herself. After Mary's marriage, Margaret again left home, leaving behind her Sarah and Susannah, and taking with her Rachel, now a girl of fifteen. She says in her *Relation* that she was moved of the Lord to visit Friends, and that the first she visited were Friends in prison. For them she travelled first of all in the north and west of England,[3]

[1] In the old Swarthmoor Monthly Meeting Minute Book is the entry on the 11th of August 1668: 'This day Thomas Lower of Tregangeeves in the county of Cornwall and Mary Fell of Swarthmore published an intention of marriage which is with the consent of their relations on both sides as we are informed and fully satisfied which we also approve of and consent unto that they may further proceed herein as in the wisdom of God thereto see fit, no friend here having anything to object against their aforesaid declared intentions.

'Minute signed by Thomas Salthouse, Robert Salthouse, James Lancaster, etc.'

[2] Three present-day descendants of Thomas and Mary Lower are from Mary, their third daughter, born in 1678, who married in 1701 William Arch of London. They are Dorothea and Margaret Benson of Gordon, N.S.W., Australia, and W. Noel Benson, F.R.S., etc., Professor of Geology at the University of Otago, Dunedin, New Zealand, and President of the New Zealand Royal Society. There are no children.

[3] Maria Webb, Helen G. Crosfield and Violet Hodgkin (in *A Quaker Saint of Cornwall*) all state that M.F. travelled with Thomas and Mary Lower to Cornwall after the marriage, but this does not seem consistent with M.F.'s

and then from prison to prison until she reached Bristol, where she stayed with Isabel and William Yeamans. After a fortnight she went on to visit Friends in Cornwall (no doubt staying with Loveday Hambly and the newly arrived couple, Thomas and Mary Lower), Devon and Somerset, and through the counties to London, where she met George Fox.[1] She let Rachel attend the Quaker school at Shacklewell, founded a year before on the advice of George Fox, 'for instructing girls and young maidens in whatever things were useful and civil in creation'.[2] Margaret stayed in and about London for three months, making her daughter Margaret Rous's home at Newington her centre. From there, in January, John Rous wrote to Sarah Fell at Swarthmoor to tell her of the great meetings Friends were having in London 'for the gathering of those that had gone astray'. 'Many of them were very much broken', he added, 'and gave open testimonies against that spirit which had seduced them from the unity of Friends.'[3] This spirit was the sad work of John Perrot, a man of unstable nature, who had suffered grievously in 1657 when imprisoned in Rome by the Inquisition, and had afterwards developed a form of mysticism which denied the need of any organization whatever for the growing Quaker movement. George Fox saw at once the dangers in Perrot's teaching, an exaggerated individualism such as had been the curse of the Ranters and the undoing of James Nayler. Although John Perrot had left England in 1662 and gone to Barbados, never to return (he died in Jamaica late in 1665), his influence lasted until those meetings in London early in 1669 finally restored most of those whom he had led astray, back into unity with Friends. During the years 1666 to 1668, Fox just released from his Scarborough imprisonment spent a great part of his energies in 'settling the Monthly Meetings', namely, giving a form of order and organization for a movement which was suffering seriously at that time owing to the severe persecution and death of a

own statement in her 'Relation', though in M.F.'s Testimony to George Fox she does say that after her release she 'went down into Cornwall with my son and daughter Lower'. Leeds Jnl. 1836, p. lxviii.

[1] Camb. Jnl. II, 133.

[2] G.F. Jnl. Ellwood Edn. p. 316.

[3] Swm. MSS. I, 108; partially printed in A.R.B. p. 166.

number of leaders. This organization had for its object the knitting of the movement into a self-disciplined fellowship, and aimed at a balance of the rights and duties of the individual with those of the wider community. It also acted as a counter-blow to the Perrot movement. The meetings in London in the winter of 1668 and 1669 were the culmination of this work. In them Margaret must have taken her part during her three months in London.

Then in early spring, when the orchards were full of blossom, taking Rachel with her, Margaret Fell rode through Kent, Sussex and Surrey.[1] In six weeks, from mid-April to the end of May, they covered about 330 miles (about 400 in modern mileage), a remarkable journey when we remember the difficulties and dangers of the roads of that day. Their daily rides varied up to twenty miles, and they visited Meetings in towns, villages, farms and prisons, bringing spiritual help and encouragement wherever they went.

Returning to London they stayed there until late in the summer, when they travelled west again, still visiting Friends, and reached Bristol, where they again stayed with William and Isabel Yeamans.

George Fox had just returned from Ireland and the northwest of England, and had reached Bristol also.

'And then it was eleven years after my former husband's decease', wrote Margaret years later in her *Relation*, 'and G. Fox being then returned from visiting Friends in Ireland. At Bristol he declared his intentions of marriage to me; and there was also our marriage solemnized, in a public Meeting of many Friends, who were our witnesses.'[2] This bare statement can be filled out from two or three sources, chiefly from George Fox's Journal and from contemporary manuscripts describing the Meetings. Fox himself wrote nearly as shortly as Margaret did,

[1] Young Rachel's bare record of this journey, noting merely the places visited, the daily mileage and where Meetings were held, is at the end of William Caton's MSS. book (known as Caton MSS. III) into which he and others copied many of the letters sent by Early Friends to Margaret. This record is in Rachel's handwriting, and is the only contemporary account in England. (William Penn made a very similar journey in these same counties, three years later. *Gulielma*, by L. V. Hodgkin, p. 156.)

[2] M.F. *Works*, p. 8.

'And there Margaret Fell and her daughters and son-in-laws met me, where we was married. . . . And I was moved to ask the children whether they was all satisfied and whether Margaret had answered them according to her husband's will to her children, she being a widow, and if her husband had left anything to her for the assistance of her children, which if she married they might suffer loss therein, whether she had answered them in lieu of that and all other things.

'And the children made answer and said, "she had doubled it and would not have me to speak of those things".[1]

'And so when it had been laid before several meetings both of the men and women assembled together for that purpose, and all was satisfied, there was a large meeting appointed of purpose, where there was several large testimonies.'[2]

When Thomas Ellwood edited Fox's Journal in 1694, he added considerably to this original concise account, some of the statements filling out the picture. 'I had seen from the Lord a considerable time before, that I should take Margaret Fell to be my wife. And when I first mentioned it to her, she felt the answer of life from God thereunto. But though the Lord had opened this thing unto me, yet I had not received a command from the Lord, for the accomplishing of it then. Wherefore I let the thing rest, and went on in the work and service of the Lord, as before, according as the Lord led me; travelling up and down in this nation, and through the nation of Ireland.'[3] After George and Margaret had discussed his suggestion of carrying through the marriage then, he asked her to send for her daughters. Isabel and Rachel were there with her, Mary was not far away, in Cornwall, Margaret was in London, Sarah and Susannah at Swarthmoor. Fox's scrupulous honesty in money matters is seen in his questions to the daughters. He was determined that his marriage to a well-to-do woman should not make him a wealthy man, as the English law then allowed. This attitude of Fox towards his wife's property was of course very unusual.

---

[1] This reply of the daughters seems to me to signify that their mother, now that she was re-marrying, had handed over to them that part of the Swarthmoor estate which had been left to her by Judge Fell.

[2] Camb. Jnl. II, 153–4.

[3] G.F. Jnl. Ellwood Edn. 334.

Twelve years after his marriage, during conversation with some judges, his son-in-law William Meade told them that Fox had engaged never to meddle with his wife's estate. The judges could hardly believe that any man would do so; whereupon Meade showed them Fox's promise in writing to that effect, 'at which they wondered'.[1] By her second marriage Margaret lost the ownership of the Hall and fifty acres of land, left her by her first husband, these now being added to the rest of the estate which had been left to the daughters. She did not lose her portion (one-third) of the Marsh Grange estate.

The money matters being satisfactorily settled, now everything had to be 'in right ordering' for the solemnisation of the marriage itself. Both bride and bridegroom had on many occasions given written advice on the method of Quaker marriages, for both felt that as marriage was for them a Christian rite, so it was especially incumbent on those who denied the efficacy or necessity of the priest, so to order their own ceremony that it gave dignity, security and a truly religious spirit. We are fortunate in having at least a partial record of this wedding, in a few pages of an old MSS. book, evidently written down at the time. Before the marriage itself, at three[2] separate meetings it was published, first on 18th October at a Men's Meeting, at which Margaret and her daughters and about a dozen women[3] Friends were present; the second on 21st October at a meeting of men and women Friends; the third on 22nd October when Dennis Hollister, one of the leading Friends in Bristol, published the intention of marriage at a public meeting. The marriage was solemnised at a very large public meeting on Wednesday, 27th October. All four meetings were held at Broadmead, the Meeting House for Bristol. Each meeting, both private and public, must have been very impressive. 'There was a great power of the Lord amongst Friends', wrote the chronicler. And again— 'The accomplishing of it would be to His glory.' At the first

---

[1] Leeds Jnl. II, 308.

[2] One account in this small book (at Friends' House Library, London) says there were four meetings preceding that at which the marriage was solemnised. But the marriage certificate supports the statement that there were three only.

[3] Probably these women Friends were there to support Margaret and her daughters.

meeting, after George Fox had spoken 'largely in the power of God and in the everlasting seed', Margaret Fell said, 'Friends, in that everlasting and immortal word of life and power which was in the beginning, in which God created all things, the male and the female in His own pure image, which was from everlasting, and will be to everlasting, I have my testimony sealed in my heart, unto this thing in God's everlasting covenant.' Then followed testimonies from her daughters and sons-in-law. Margaret Rous—'I am satisfied that in the life and power of God this thing hath been proposed, and I have unity with it.' Isabel Yeamans—'I must bear my testimony for the Lord, and to his Truth in this matter, and that the life and power of God in me hath perfect unity and fellowship with it—and I have long desired to see it accomplished, and now rejoices in its accomplishing, and therefore do freely assent unto it.'

Mary Lower—'Truly I am very well satisfied with the thing, and do believe the Lord requires it at your hands.'

Rachel Fell—'I am of the same mind with my sisters and give my consent.'

John Rous—'It was that which was sealed long before in my heart.'

Thomas Lower—'I have several years since seen and believed [that] would be accomplished in the Lord's due time which now I have this day heard published amongst you; at which my heart rejoices. And I do believe, that this thing is of the Lord, and that in the further accomplishment thereof, the Lord's name and Truth will be honoured and glorified; and I have in the measure of God's gift unto me perfect unity with it.'

That fine leader, George Whitehead, who had gone about among the Quaker prisoners when the plague was raging in London in 1665, added his testimony, saying that he had long foreseen and desired it, as many others he knew had done. He pleaded that Friends should marry in the power of the Lord, and not in an 'airy inconsiderate spirit'.

William Penn, not long since released from his first imprisonment, added his words of loving approval, as did Thomas Salthouse, late of Ulverston, now a member of Bristol Meeting, an old friend of Margaret, who added that even if he had been a stranger, the evidence of God's power in that Meeting would alone have convinced him of the rightness of the marriage. Then followed a number of men and women Friends of the Bristol Meeting, all approving. Finally came the testimony of Miriam Moss, about whom nothing is known beyond the curious vision here recorded: 'In the year 1657 I coming to Swarthmoor to visit M.F., I was moved of the Lord to go into her garden where I was sitting in the silence of my spirit. Then did the Lord let me see, that G.F. and M.F. were joined together in that one eternal spirit, and they should be joined together in that bond of love which could not be broken; which thing I resisted, but it sunk deep in me and I could not put it by, for in the light it rose often—then pondered I the thing in my heart, believing that the thing should be accomplished in its time. Glory to the Lord for ever over all.'[1]

At the second meeting, a joint men's and women's, on 21st October, George Fox spoke with such power that Friends were unable to take notes of what he said. Margaret also spoke, and again Isabel Yeamans expressed her great joy.

At the third meeting on 22nd October—a 'General Public Meeting'—William Penn spoke of the marriage as being 'in the Light', and as 'God's word of life to all people'. He rebuked those who criticized the marriage—a reference to those whom Fox later said were in a 'jumble' about it.

On 27th October, when the marriage was solemnised, there were great numbers of Friends and non-Friends. The writer tells us 'there was a mighty power of the Lord God among Friends, that did so overcome them, that there was many testimonies could not be taken, and there was such a mighty power that G.F. had like to have fallen down, but that he laid his hand upon another, for he could not tell whether he had a body or not a body'.

As was and is still the custom in a Quaker marriage, the bride and bridegroom, some of their relatives or friends on each side of them, sat facing the meeting. When they had stood up to make their declaration of love and faithfulness to each other, the Meeting for Worship continued, and it was then that the

---

[1] It is possible that Miriam Moss made a mistake in her date, and that her visit occurred *after* Judge Fell's death in 1658—proof of this is not possible now. Quoted in Jnl. F.H.S. XIII, 143.

testimonies and prayers of those present were given. At this marriage, Margaret herself uttered a prayer, of praise to God and thankfulness to Him for the gift of His son, who draws men to Him.[1]

The Meeting over, ninety-four Friends out of the large number present, signed the marriage certificate.[2] The first men to sign it were John Rous, William Yeamans and Thomas Lower, the first women Margaret Rous, Isabel Yeamans, Mary Lower, Sarah Fell, Susannah Fell, and Rachel. (Sarah was older than Mary, but being unmarried she gave her sister precedence, though she made up for it by writing her name on the certificate copy which is preserved in her own handwriting in London, three times as large as the others and underlined it strongly!)

Among the well-known signatories (already mentioned in this book) were Gerrard Roberts of London, George and Ann Whitehead, Thomas Salthouse, Robert Widders (from Kellet, in Lancashire), and Leonard Fell; many came from other parts of the country, the rest being Bristol Friends. It is curious that the signature of William Penn does not appear, though he was at one of the earlier meetings. He was possibly present at the marriage though he might have left for Ireland immediately after the third meeting, at which he had spoken **(see p.219).**

It is obvious that this was no ordinary marriage. Both husband and wife believed that their union was primarily, and indeed pre-eminently spiritual. It was the normal culmination of years of knowledge of each other, of close spiritual and mental co-operation in the work of the Church, which both believed was the true primitive Christianity revived. Fox knew well that their friendship had sometimes been misunderstood, and had in fact caused some scurrilous remarks from their enemies, but though some had 'long talked of' their marriage, he himself had no clear leading until about six months before it was solemnised. 'There was some jumble in some minds about it',[3] he wrote in his Journal, 'but the Lord's power came over all and laid all their spirits, and some after confessed it.' To help

---

[1] MS. in Portfolio 10, No. 53, Library, Friends' House, London.
[2] Thirnbeck MSS. 7. The certificate is reproduced in Appendix B by H. G. Crosfield, and the names in Jnl. F.H.S. IX, 100–101.
[3] Camb. Jnl. II, 154.

the Society to understand their marriage, about three weeks beforehand, on 2nd October, he sent an Epistle to be read in all the meetings everywhere, all over the World. His marriage with Margaret Fell was, he explained, of the nature of one in which God had joined together, a marriage which was a figure of Christ and his Church—a mystical spiritual union. It was a 'figure of the Church coming out of the wilderness', and as a reconciler of Heaven and Earth.[1]

The year preceding the marriage of George Fox and Margaret Fell had seen great success and triumph in the organizing of Monthly (business) Meetings, and the healing of the Perrot division, and George Fox had made a remarkable journey through Ireland where he miraculously escaped arrest time and again. On her side, it had seen fruitful travels among Meetings and prisons, after a release through the kindness and good sense of the King from a lifelong prison sentence. These successes seem to be reflected in the spiritual exaltation seen at the marriage, and were a fitting prelude to their union.

[1] See also *Second Period of Quakerism*, p. 263. This Epistle was disliked by many Friends, and seems to have been largely destroyed. A rare copy, however, exists at the end of a book entitled *Yearly Meeting Minutes, etc.*, 1668–1741, at the Lancaster Meeting House. Its language is certainly difficult to follow.

An additional note by Isabel Ross points to the fact that with the publication of Penn's *My Irish journal 1669-1670,* **edited by Isabel Grubb (London 1950), it is clear that he cannot have been at the marriage on 27 October, since he had arrived in Cork the previous day, having left Bristol (p. 19) on 23 October.**

Chapter Sixteen

MARGARET FOX'S SECOND IMPRISONMENT, 1670-1

AFTER their marriage at Bristol, George and Margaret Fox spent about ten days together, and then he continued 'the work of the Lord', travelling and preaching and visiting throughout the southern counties and later in the Midlands. Margaret returned home to Swarthmoor, 'where God had placed and sent me, and for the ordering and governing of my children and family.'[1] It was consistent with their characters and their view of their own marriage relationship, and especially of the prime duty to follow the leadings of the Spirit, that they gave liberty to each other to separate for long periods. Their frequent separations have left to posterity some of their letters to each other, proofs if they were needful of their constant love, their desire to be of help to each other in their trials of life, and their happiness when it was possible, in the intervals of work and imprisonment, to be together again. At the time of their marriage Margaret was fifty-five years old, and George Fox ten years younger.

It was not surprising that Margaret's son George Fell was not at her wedding. As we have seen, he was hostile to Quakerism, and had already grieved her bitterly during her long imprisonment at Lancaster. He and his wife Hannah and baby daughter Isabel were now living at Marsh Grange. His hostility increased when his mother married George Fox for no doubt he considered it a social humiliation. He now joined with her old enemies the Kirkbys to put her into prison again under the old Praemunire, in spite of the fact that when she had been released in 1668 it was by order of the King and Council.

George Fox was north of London, at Enfield, towards the end of December, when he heard of his step-son's intrigue against his mother and he dictated to John Rous a letter for her of comfort and advice. He assured her that, if she kept in the 'seed

[1] M.F.'s *Testimony* to G.F. in Ellwood Edn. of G.F. Jnl.

of God' (a favourite phrase of his), she might have trials, but she would also have dominion, wisdom and patience. In London, he told her, there had been a 'great noise' about her son George trying to get orders to send her to prison at Chester, and him to Jersey. He hoped for Truth's sake that news of this attempt (so far unsuccessful) would not be widely spread among Friends. The young man had been visiting Colonel Kirkby and General Monk, intending to have Swarthmoor for himself, and even trying to deprive his mother of some of her Marsh Grange estate. George Fox advised his wife to consult Matthew Richardson of Dalton-in-Furness, her sister's husband and an attorney, and to try in patience and wisdom to maintain some hold on her old home, not only for her own sake and that of the Meeting, but also to prevent her son doing evil. If her son had defamed her at Court, Fox would have her come to London to clear herself and to defeat his unworthy schemes. But, above all, she should act in peace and quietness, and 'keep over them all in the power of God that doth bind, for that must work through all things'.[1]

On the same sheet of paper is a long letter from John Rous himself to his mother-in-law telling her in detail of the efforts he was making to persuade George Fell to rid himself of his 'prejudice' against her marriage, to stop plotting to have her re-imprisoned, and to give up his efforts to turn her and his sisters out of Swarthmoor. He told her that Fox earlier had remarked that it might be well if she left that 'dark country', but considered 'that thy holding an interest in the house may be a restraint to my brother's being frequented by bad company, which may work his undoing'. John Rous had appealed also to Matthew Richardson to see if he could help to bring the young man to change his behaviour. Richardson, though by no means in favour of Quakerism, disliked to hear that his nephew was trying to send his mother to prison, and 'said that would be very unnatural'. At one time in the talk between George Fell and Rous, George offered to pay his mother an annuity of £100 if she would leave Swarthmoor, nothing if she refused, and then he would see she was sent to prison. The whole letter shows George Fell to be emotional, prejudiced, unscrupulous and very

[1] Thirnbeck MSS. 8.

difficult to deal with so as to necessitate patient diplomacy. 'I do find much may be done with him by degrees', wrote John Rous, 'if too much be not put upon him more than he can well bear, but I know the Lord hath so endowed thee with his wisdom that thou wilt know well enough how to deal with him.' Then in a short sad postscript, John Rous reported, 'Since I concluded my letter, my brother Fell was with us, and we cannot prevail anything with him about thy part of Swarthmoor'.[1]

Indeed, John Rous's efforts were in vain. Early in April 1670 Margaret Fox was in prison again. 'There came another order to cast me into prison again; and the Sheriff of Lancashire sent his bailiff, and pulled me out of my own house', she wrote, 'and had me to prison in Lancaster Castle, where I continued a whole year; and most part of that time I was sick and weakly.'[2]

A letter written by Thomas Lower in London a few days after hearing of Margaret's imprisonment, amply confirms the belief that George Fell, and behind him his wife's parents, were largely responsible for this new attack on her. Even the endorsement by Fox made many years later on the back of the letter runs 'T. Lower to M.F. of her imprisonment, 1670, by her son and his father-in-law'.[3] Lower was more grieved for his brother-in-law's 'barbarous and unnatural actions' towards her than for her own imprisonment; for, he explained, 'it will tend to thy good and preservation from and out of greater mischief, and only hasten his woe and sorrow that hath procured it'. Lower, together with his wife, Mary, and Sarah (the latter having been with them since early December) had called on George Fell's father-in-law, Mr. Edward Cook, hoping to see George. They only saw George's wife, however, to whom they spoke of the 'treacherous dealing' by her husband, whose behaviour would be considered 'abominable amongst heathens'. Her denial on behalf of her husband, of charges of intrigue against Margaret Fox, did not spare her further 'plain dealing' before they left.[4]

[1] Thirnbeck MSS. 9.
[2] M.F. *Works*, p. 9.
[3] M. Webb transcribed the name 'Cook' in this letter, as 'Luke', hence possibly both she and H. G. Crosfield (p. 144) did not notice that T.L.'s visit was to George's parents-in-law.
[4] Swm. MSS. I, 381.

Very soon, urged by George Fox, Sarah Fell and Mary Lower visited the King, and procured from him an order to the Sheriff of Lancashire for Margaret's release. This Sarah and John and Margaret Rous took in person to Lancaster, carrying with them a short letter from George Fox:

My dear heart in the Truth and Life, that changeth not.

It was upon me, that Mary Lower and Sarah should go to the King concerning thy imprisonment; and to Kirby, that the power of the Lord might appear over them all in thy deliverance. They went; and then they thought to have come down; but it was upon me to stay them a little longer; that they might follow the business, till it was effected: which it now is, and is here sent down. . . . So no more, but my love in the Holy Seed.

G.F.[1]

Even then she was not released, for in the meantime a fierce persecution of Friends and other Non-conformists had broken out, following on the re-enactment of the Conventicle Act, in April 1670, and the local justices made this new Act an excuse for keeping her in prison, especially as in her absence the meetings for Worship continued to be held at Swarthmoor. The Rouses returned to London from Swarthmoor where they had been on a visit, to continue their efforts for her release. In June, John Rous wrote to Margaret that they had seen Sir Francis Cobbe[2] (who had like Sir Jordan Crosland become a friend of Fox's during the latter's imprisonment at Scarborough) but that he could do little at Court as 'the King was so sad for the death of his sister[3] that he received no business'. In July Rous again wrote that he had seen Sir Francis Cobbe, 'who told us that they were very much offended at Whitehall because they were informed there had been several meetings at the house [Swarthmoor] since the Act came in force, and that for the present he can noways serve thee; he wished with all his heart he could. I perceive Colonel Kirkby is the informer, and that he still appears upon all occasions very opposite, but Sir Francis saith if it lie in his power hereafter to do anything he shall be very willing. He was very

[1] G.F. Jnl., Ellwood Edn. 336.
[2] Abraham MSS. 11.
[3] The Duchess of Orleans.

fair and civil towards us.'[1] In the same letter Rous relates how savagely some Friends were being persecuted—one having lost almost all that he had, so that he, his wife and children had not 'so much as a bed to lie on, or anything to eat'. But in the midst of trials and anxieties Rous found time to send by the carrier going to Preston, Lancs., 'a small box of sugar, the hasp sealed as this letter is. In it was a white mantle and a white sarsnet[2] hood for thee [Margaret Fox], and some playthings for the children [Bethiah and Margaret, three and two years old at this time]. I intend to send the Jack[3] my sister Sarah writ for and some more sugar when I can get carriage cheaper than by the carrier.' No doubt the sugar had come from the Rous plantation in Barbados.

Margaret still lay in prison in illness and weakness, and while she was there her son George died at Marsh Grange, on 14th October 1670, leaving his wife Hannah, and two children, Isabel nearly two years old and Charles, seven months old. A week before he died George Fell made his will.[4] In it, after leaving various legacies to his friends, the poor of Ulverston and Dalton, and to his servants, he left the Manor of Ulverston, which included the lordship of Swarthmoor, Osmotherley and the mills, and all the lands about Swarthmoor, to his infant son, in the first place. He had already made (in August 1670) a Deed Poll conveying Marsh Grange to his friend Sackville Greaves, for the purpose of paying his debts and providing for his daughter after his death. The arrangement was carried out when Sackville Greaves a few months after George Fell's death sold Marsh Grange to Sarah Fell for £1,250.[5]

The sad relations between George Fell and his mother have frequently been discussed[6] and his claim to the ownership of the

---

[1] Swm. MSS. I, 109.

[2] A fine soft silk material (*Concise Oxford Dictionary*).

[3] This word has a number of meanings, but probably here means a machine for turning the spit in roasting meat (*Concise Oxford Dictionary*).

[4] Crosfield, *Margaret Fox of Swarthmoor Hall*. Appendix E gives George Fell's Will.

[5] Deed now owned by Sir Wavell Wakefield, M.P. of Kendal, to whom I am indebted for permission to study it and other deeds of Marsh Grange.

[6] Jnl. F.H.S. XXX, 39 and XXXI, 27, article by Norman Penney, *George Fell and the Story of Swarthmoor Hall*.

Swarthmoor estate supported and denied. From a close study of all the available material, it appears that he had little claim to the estate of his father, who left it by will partly to his wife during her widowhood, and partly to his daughters. When she re-married her portion went to the daughters, not to the son, though the phrase 'All the lands about Swarthmoor' used by George Fell in his will might suggest that he believed he had a legal right to some of the estate at any rate, in addition to the manor. His lack of legal right to the estate, however, seems to be supported not only by many facts mentioned in the previous chapters of this book but also by a statement hidden through the centuries at the Lancaster Meeting House, in an old book dating from about 1668. It contains the 'confession of such as went from Swarthmoor Meeting in the time of persecution, and fled the suffering: whose hand owned their condemnation, upon that which led them from it, and are come to the Meeting again'. One who had left the Meeting, but returned, was James Lancaster of Walney, the man whose wife in 1652 had so fiercely attacked Fox on his first visit to those wild parts, that he had lain on top of his friend to protect him from her blows! Lancaster became a stalwart Friend, and frequently travelled with Fox. But, probably in 1670, he had 'left the Meeting' in the time of persecution 'and after it', he wrote, 'I knew by her son's own mouth, that the title was in her and not in him, and did not openly publish it, where its service was, which is condemnable in me.' This no doubt means that James Lancaster had been told by George Fell himself that he had no right to the estate, which he was now claiming when his mother was again imprisoned. Lancaster later realized that if he had made public what he knew, he would have been of service to Margaret at a time of deep trouble and anxiety. To this he confessed, and was received again into the Meeting.

Unfortunately the bad relationship did not cease with the death of George Fell. His widow carried on the attack, and even intensified it. In the next month, November, John Rous wrote from London to Sarah at Swarthmoor, expressing his surprise at 'my sister's Fell's wilfulness and foolishness, who I always feared would do as bad if not much worse than her husband, and she hath a crooked generation to be her advisers if she take counsel of her kindred, who no doubt but will do the worst they can.'[1]

One or two other Friends outside the family, tried to bring reconciliation. Old Elizabeth Hooton early in 1671 wrote a loving letter to Margaret Fox in prison, when she herself was thinking of joining the party of Friends who accompanied Fox to America a few months later. Elizabeth Hooton and a friend, Hannah Salter, had been interviewing the King on Margaret's behalf, and Hannah had indeed extracted from Charles and his Council, the paper which was to give Margaret her liberty. She would not leave the King till he had granted what was required. She saw to it that she went a day later, to have the order written and sealed, so that there could be no doubt about it. But Elizabeth had written also to Hannah Fell, and this letter she enclosed for Margaret to see and comment on, so that ' if there be anything in it that is amiss thou mayest mend it, for it were much on me to write it'. 'God is thy witness', she wrote to Margaret, 'thou hast suffered more than many have expected, yet hath the Lord delivered thee. . . . Be thou of good comfort, the Lord will deliver thee still, and they that seek to ruinate thee will the Lord ruinate and leave them neither root nor branch, if they do not speedily repent and amend.'[2]

A little later Elizabeth Hooton wrote again to Hannah Fell:

It is reported that thou hast gotten a judgment against [Margaret Fox] to sweep away all that she hath, both goods and lands. What a rebellious daughter-in-law art thou. Was there ever such a wicked thing done in England or in any age before, that thou should ruinate thy husband's mother. The same hand that cut off thy husband will do the same by thee and leave thee neither root nor branch if thou do not speedily repent and put off thy wicked invention and let thy mother alone with her estate. The Lord's terrible wrath and plagues will fall upon thee and thine. Therefore fear and dread the living God. While it is time, put by thy wicked intent, lest the same hand that took away thy husband may not take away thee in thy cruelty towards thy husband's mother, who hath not done thee any hurt nor hath not wronged thee at all.

[1] Dix MSS. **N/1E. 8 ix [Nov.] 1670. Library of the Society of Friends, London.**
[2] Swm. MSS. I, 152.

So to the light of Christ in thy conscience return, which will let thee see all thy ways.

I am a lover of thy soul,

Elizabeth Hooton.[1]

The intrigues of Hannah Fell were not successful. Indeed, the King himself prevented the 'ruination' of Margaret Fox. When in April 1671 he gave her her liberty, in the same document he granted her part of the Swarthmoor estate to her daughters Susannah and Rachel.[2] Their legal ownership of Swarthmoor was therefore restored and regularized. It is curious that Sarah's name is not in the document—she was still unmarried in 1671—but it may be that she had just then sold out her interest in the Swarthmoor estate, so as to buy the two-thirds of the Marsh Grange estate now owned by Hannah Fell. This she did in May 1671. She paid £1,250 and there was an annual rent on the estate of £4 16s. 4d. payable to the Manor of Furness.

Hannah Fell lived on at Marsh Grange until Thomas Lower bought it from Sarah Fell in 1676, and went to live there with his family. The Fell sisters now and again visited Hannah and her children at Marsh Grange and even Margaret Fox herself did so. In 1678 the Fell sisters, married and unmarried, with John Rous and Thomas Lower, conveyed the Manor of Osmotherley (near Ulverston, and part of the old Fell estate) to Charles Fell, Hannah's young son.[3]

Nine years later Hannah Fell made a new attack. With the intention of destroying the Meeting which was still being held at the Hall, she quite illegally closed the long-used footpath between the Hall and the town of Ulverston. William Meade, who was by this time married to the daughter Sarah, wrote to advise Margaret Fox to demand the re-opening of the footpath 'as thy right, which will be greatly to her shame and reproach if she refuse it'. 'If she be so perverse as to do so', he continued, 'you had better peaceably suffer it, and go further about [by the road] than begin a suit which doth but satisfy her quarrelsome mind. However, maintain your right by words and arguments as far as you can with her.' Hannah Fell had also locked the gates

[1] Quoted in Jnl. F.H.S. XXXI, 27.
[2] *Extracts from State Papers*, pp. 329–30.
[2] Abraham MSS. 23 and Jnl. F.H.S. XI, 161–2.

leading on to the footpath from the Hall. William Meade advised Margaret to demand her to open them, and if she refused, to break open the lock and get the gates open, being careful to have witnesses present. 'But before you break open the lock, read this declaration herewith sent thee; and thou mayst go to the next justice and complain that Friends are kept out of their usual meeting house contrary to the King's command herein mentioned.' The last refers to the general pardon granted in 1686 giving toleration to Friends to carry on their worship in peace. William Meade in his letter refers to a rent of £110 payable annually by Hannah Fell to her mother, but which was not being paid either regularly or in full. William Meade advised his mother-in-law to take less than her due, 'for peace sake'.[1]

All these claims and counterclaims ceased in 1691, four years later, when Swarthmoor Hall and its large estate was 'bought' by Daniel Abraham who had some years previously married Rachel Fell. By this arrangement Charles Fell, then twenty-one years old, received £3,900 out of the full purchase price of £4,500, £100 being received by each of his uncles, probably on behalf of their wives. It is probable that Daniel Abraham, a well-to-do and generous, even Quixotic man, paid this large sum of money to the young Charles, to end a long drawn-out family dispute and cause of great worry to people who must have found such a dispute both distressing and an irksome waste of time.[2] Yet above and in spite of the unkindness of George

---

[1] Abraham MSS. 42. Dated 10.2.[April] 1687.

[2] I am grateful to Mr. Alfred W. Braithwaite of New Court, Lincoln's Inn, London, for allowing me to discuss with him the complicated claims and counter-claims connected with Swarthmoor Hall and the estate. The difficulties are increased by the lack of certain documents and by the fact that in the unsettled conditions of the seventeenth century there was frequently considerable doubt as to the legal ownership of land. Mr. Braithwaite writes: 'I think the fairest conclusion to come to would really be that there was in all probability a legitimate doubt as to who was legally entitled to have possession of Swarthmoor Hall, but that, looked at from the moral aspect, George Fell and subsequently his widow were felt to be behaving ungenerously under the circumstances in trying to deprive Margaret Fox of possession, and that she was entitled to make use of her actual possession and of any legal rights she had, to resist his claims. As to what happened in 1691, I think you may well be right in suggesting that Daniel Abraham purchased the property with the idea of putting an end to the whole dispute; at any rate he was careful to get the Conveyance executed by

and Hannah Fell's behaviour, Margaret and her daughters and sons-in-law continued faithfully to nurse the Quaker movement in this second period of its history, after the first years of the scattering and spreading of the seed, when the Society's organization grew up, matured, and created a fellowship strong enough to withstand blows both from within and without.

Let us now return to the year 1670 when Margaret was still in prison at Lancaster. The passing of the Second Conventicle Act of 1670, as we have seen, not only prevented her release but caused renewed persecution of Nonconformists, and especially of the Quakers. This Act did not so much imprison as impoverish them. A person preaching at a religious meeting was to be fined £20 for the first and £40 for any further offence and a person who allowed a meeting to be held in his or her house was to be fined £20.[1] The Act also created a class of men and women— the informers—who made a living by spying on and giving information about Meetings held by Quakers and other Nonconformists and by Papists. 'Beggarly rude informers', 'these devouring informers'[2] they are described by Joseph Besse in his *Sufferings.* Their work only ceased in 1688 when liberty of conscience for Protestants was won.[3]

all the persons who had any possible claim.' Mr. Braithwaite is not responsible for the detailed opinions on this matter in this book—for these the author alone is responsible.

[1] *Second Period of Quakerism,* p. 67.

[2] Besse's *Sufferings,* I, p. xlii.

[3] The books compiled by the 'clerks' of local Meetings throw great light on the details of the suffering of Friends, and their constancy, during the long years of persecution. In *The Book of Sufferings of Lancashire Friends, from* 1654 *to* 1700 (at Lancaster Meeting House) some of the records give valuable details of the contents of shops and the furnishing of houses, for these things were commonly taken in lieu of fines. For example, the Salthouse brothers, shoemakers near Swarthmoor, had four pairs of shoes taken from them worth 11/6, for a fine of 6d. Another Friend, for a fine of 4d. had his girdle taken from him on which he should have baked his bread, 'worth eleven shillings and he a poor man and his wife able to do little and had a throng of children'.

Another had 'his pot which was on the fire boiling meat for his family' taken from him. A fourth, a shoemaker, had from his dwelling-house taken from him one table-board and brass pan, three chests, two beds furnished, two bolsters and other bedclothes, one cradle, a hand basket, three canvas bags, one firkin [=a measure equal to a fourth part of a barrel], ten pieces of leather, also

A contemporary's picture of this time of persecution following on the Second Conventicle Act is given by Bishop Gilbert Burnet in his *History of my own Time*. 'This Act was executed in the City very severely in Starling's mayoralty, and put things in such disorder that many of the trading men of the City began to talk of removing with their stock over to Holland; but the king ordered a stop to be put to further severities. Many of the sects either discontinued their meetings, or held them very secretly with small numbers and not in the hours of the public worship; yet informers were encouraged, and were everywhere at work. The behaviour of the Quakers was more particular, and had something in it that looked bold. They met at the same place and at the same hour as before, and when they were seized none of them would go out of the way; they went all together to prison; they stayed there till they were dismissed, for they would not petition to be set at liberty, nor would they pay the fines set on them, nor so much as the jail fees, calling these the wages of unrighteousness. And, as soon as they were let out, they went to their meeting houses again; and when they found these were shut up by order, they held their meetings on the streets before the doors of those houses. They said they would not disown or be ashamed of their meeting together to worship God, but, in imitation of Daniel, they would do it the more publicly because they were forbidden doing it. Some called this obstinacy, while others called it firmness. But by it they carried their point, for the Government grew weary of dealing with so much perverseness, and so began with letting them alone.'[1]

On the first Sunday after the Act came into force, George Fox attended the City Meeting at Gracechurch Street, where he

all his turves and hay 'being his winter provision', amounting to £4/1/10. Later a spinning wheel was taken from him, with hemp, more leather, salt, a turf spade and three shelves.

Sometimes, however, the persecutors did not get it all their own way. For we read that Phineas Pemberton (ancestor of a well-known family of Philadelphia) and his wife Phoebe, of Bolton, Lancs., were fined for being at a Meeting on the 20th of January 1680, and had taken from them a cow worth £4; but the account continues—'Now that cow after she was taken would neither eat hay, drink water nor give milk, whereupon, the innkeeper where she was kept turned her out and she ran home again the 27th of the same month'.

[1] Quoted in *Second Period of Quakerism*, p. 55.

expected 'the storm was most likely to begin'.[1] His arrest after he had preached, his march in a 'file of musketeers' through the crowds, his confounding of the Papist informer, his argument with the Lord Mayor, ending in his liberty, and an immediate return to Gracechurch Meeting, are characteristic of the man. He wrote in his *Journal*, 'A glorious time it was for the Lord's ever-lasting Truth, for as fast as some were taken down that was speaking, others were moved of the Lord to stand up and speak, to the admiration of people'.[2] Here was the fruit of the discipline and organization which Fox had created in the sixties. Some Friends however were not able to stand firm in this time of persecution, and a few of the Swarthmoor Friends, as in other places, left the Meeting, until they were persuaded to return either by Epistles from George or Margaret Fox or by the work-ings of their consciences. In the Minute Book at Lancaster Meet-ing already mentioned are these sad confessions: one stated that 'having departed from Swarthmoor Meeting at the time of suffering [I] was condemned in myself, and do own G.F.'s judg-ment for the same.' Another 'had no peace till I came again'. 'As for my part, when I came from Lancaster out of prison, I was fearful of persecution and therefore assented, and I own my condemnation for it.' One wrote: 'While I went I had no re-freshment nor comfort among them, and I felt my spirit refreshed when I came again to join with the church at Swarth-moor.' Most of those who temporarily fell had already stood courageously in years gone by. It was no wonder that Fox wrote to Friends everywhere, 'So the Lord hath a tender care of his sheep, his people, that the Angel of his presence should be with them in all their trials. And therefore let your minds be out of all outward things, and visibles; and fear not the fleece, for it will grow again; and if the Lord should try you now, with the spoil of outward things, after he hath blessed you with them, to see whether your minds be with them or with him.'[3]

In August (1670) the authorities (the Bishop of London and the Lord Mayor) by their violence and illegalities became the

---

[1] G.F. Jnl. Ellwood Edn.

[2] Camb. Jnl. II, 162.

[3] G. Fox's Epistles, No. 279, quoted by L. V. Hodgkin in *A Day Book of Counsel and Comfort*, p. 227.

means of a great victory for English freedom, namely the right of a jury to give its own verdict, without coercion from the judge. Gracechurch Street Meeting house had been closed and locked against the Friends for some weeks, and meetings were therefore regularly held in the street. On this Sunday in mid-August William Penn and William Meade, the latter once a captain of the City of London Trained Bands but now turned peaceable Quaker, were arrested. The story of their trial, their outspoken defence, and the courage and endurance of the twelve men of the jury has been many times told.[1] The first verdict brought in by the jury was 'Guilty of speaking in Gracechurch Street'. As street talk was and is not a crime, the Court refused this verdict. The resulting second verdict was 'not guilty'. This led to a tempestuous scene—the fury of the Recorder and of the Lord Mayor, and the bold strong voice of Penn pleading for the rights of Englishmen, and in particular the right of the subject to be judged by his equals, and the duty of the judge to act on the verdict of the jury. On this, the jury were themselves imprisoned without meat, drink, fire or tobacco, the judges hoping to terrorize them into bringing a verdict of guilty. This they refused to do, and by their courageous stand for what they felt was just, they set a precedent which established the freedom of the jury in England.

The first news of the trial to reach Swarthmoor, and so to Margaret in her prison across the sands, came in a letter from John Rous, written on the following day to Sarah Fell, who must have heard now of her future husband for the first time.

Wandsworth, 15.6. [Aug.] 1670.

Dear Sister,

. . . Meetings yesterday were pretty quiet, to what they have been sometimes. I was yesterday at Gracious-Street Meeting, which was in the street; and as near as I could judge several thousands [were] at it; but by reason of the multitude of rude people who came most of all to gaze, it was more like a tumult than a solid assembly; which was no small grief to me to see. William Penn was there, and spoke most that was spoken: there were some watchmen with halberts, and musketeers came to take him down while he was speaking; but the multitude crowded so close about him, that they could not come to him: but to

---

[1] In the various lives of Wm. Penn, *Second Period of Quakerism*, etc.

prevent further disturbance, he promised, when the meeting was done, to come to them; and so he and one Meade who is lately convinced, went to them: who carried them before the Mayor, and he committed them for a riot. I hear the Mayor was very rough with William Penn. Tho. Beedle was committed from Horsleydown Meeting for speaking. Many of the professors' [=Baptists, Independents, etc.] meetings were broken up, and some committed; but they skulk very much up and down in holes and corners, and when they are discovered, fly away. . . .

I have not much further to add, but that we are well; and remember my dear love to my mother, thyself, thy sisters, H. Hall and our little ones, and rest,

Thy dearly loving brother,
J.R.[1]

Although a verdict of not guilty was returned by the determined but exhausted jury. Penn and Meade were not released until a few days later, when Penn's dying father, Admiral Penn, unknown to his son, paid the fines for both—fines put on them for their refusal to remove their hats in court.[2]

Very soon after the Penn-Meade trial at the Old Bailey, George Fox, worn out in body by constant travels, and in mind by the brutal attacks on the Quakers, fell seriously ill. He was now unable to do anything more to get his wife out of prison. At first his illness was a violent fever and ague, but later on a great weight of the wickedness of the world lay heavily upon his spirit, and for many weeks in the autumn and winter of 1670–71, those about him despaired of his life. During this time he was tenderly nursed by several Friends, one being Margaret Rous, although she herself gave birth to her son Nathaniel on the 9th of September, and was nursing George Fox at Enfield only a month later. Throughout these anxious weeks of September and October, John and Margaret Rous constantly kept their mother informed of the illness of her husband. At one time he was reported as 'very faint and weak',[3] but later he was 'more at ease' and recovered from his fever. 'He hath all along much

---

[1] Miller MSS. 67.

[2] Penn and Meade were charged with causing a riot. If they had been charged under the Conventicle Act, the victory of the jury would have been impossible, as that pernicious Act deprived the accused of trial by jury.

[3] Abraham MSS. 14.

enquired after thee', wrote Margaret Rous, 'and always before the post day for letters I told him I was awriting to thee, he bid me remember his dear love to thee, and that he desired the Lord God Almighty to strengthen thee and that thou should be comfortable and cheerful in the life of Truth, which is over all.'[1]

That faithful friend of both George and Margaret, John Stubbs, also sent news of her husband. Stubbs was with Fox at the Widow Dry's at Enfield, and reported that he hoped he was recovering. 'Yesterday in the afternoon', he wrote to Margaret, 'I had a fine opportunity to speak my mind to him, being alone in his chamber with him. I told him I expected to have a few lines from thee that night, but it's proved otherwise—he bid me write to thee and his words were thus. "Tell her I have been ill, so I could not write, but now I am better, blessed be the Lord, praises to the Lord, and mind my love to them all." He had better rest the last night than formerly. I continue here near him for I see it is my place and I have peace in it. He enquires every post for letters but few come. . . . Also he bid me tell thee that great have been the tenderness and care of Friends to him in this condition and *nothing wanting*. Two or three women sit up every night, and sometimes I and men Friends formerly—but two good women Friends constantly. I would be glad to write to thee every week if thou would order me so to do.'[2]

Fox wrote in his Journal, that his mental and bodily illness was alleviated by the slackening of the persecution during the winter—a slackening due to the weariness of the authorities in continuing to try to defeat people who continued to worship God as they believed they should, and who bore their sufferings with an invincible courage.

Towards the spring of 1671 Fox began to recover and walk again much to the astonishment of Friends and others, some of whom had never expected him to regain his strength. And as the persecution eased off he sent Hannah Salter and Martha Fisher to beg the King for Margaret's release. Their 'faith in the Lord's power' was rewarded, and the King and Council gave Margaret a discharge under the broad seal, so that both she and her estate were cleared from the praemunire under which she

[1] Swm. MSS. I, 110. 14th Oct. 1670.
[2] Abraham MSS. 13.

had suffered for seven years, a discharge which Fox believed had never been heard of in England before.

John Rous sent the glad news to Margaret early in April, telling her how kind and generous those connected with granting the release had been—the Attorney-General had given the fee due to him to the two women Friends, his clerk had taken only twenty shillings, which was half his due, Lord Arlington, the Secretary of State and a Roman Catholic would take no fees, 'whereas his fees would have been twelve or twenty pounds, nor would Williamson's[1] man take anything, saying that if any religion were true it is ours.' Rous reported that George Fox was now in London again, and 'pretty well', and that Rous's wife and little boy Nathaniel were well.[2]

This action of Lord Arlington is in contrast to his hostility to William Penn less than three years before, when he was largely responsible for Penn's nine months' imprisonment in the Tower —a period when the young man employed his enforced rest by writing his famous book *No Cross No Crown*. Perhaps Lord Arlington had learned his lesson, for Penn's imprisonment had caused him much trouble, and he was now determined not to burn his fingers again, by keeping Margaret Fox in prison any longer.

So in April 1671 she was released, and returned home to her beloved Swarthmoor. Not for long, however, because her husband could not travel north, and was indeed now preparing to travel across the Atlantic, to visit the West Indies and America, his first visit to the many Friends in those growing Colonies.

So the brave woman, together with her daughter Susannah, travelled again to London, where they and George Fox stayed with the Rouses at their fine new home at Kingston-on-Thames, while preparations were made for the voyage to America.

From the comfort and peace of her daughter's home, Margaret Fox must have looked back to the year 1670 with deep sadness. The year which had immediately followed her second marriage had meant separation from her husband, cruelty from her only son, imprisonment in weakness and illness, troubles and defection in her own beloved Meeting, the death of her son

[1] **For** Sir Joseph Williamson **see D.N.B.**
[2] Swm. MSS. I, 83.

and the serious illness of her husband. And in a wider field she saw persecution and sufferings of Friends in many parts of the country, in a renewed attack by the State to destroy them utterly. Surely these were enough to daunt the strongest woman, but she had a never-failing faith in the power of God—a faith which gave her strength to 'keep over them all'.

Chapter Seventeen

JOURNEYS. BUILDING UP THE SOCIETY, 1671-5

'I can truly say I never thought my house so blessed as when you were in it; and it will be joy unto me if I have days on earth to see you meet here again.'

From a letter from Rebecca Travers of London to Margaret Fox at Swarthmoor, 2nd April 1672, after a visit of George and Margaret.[1]

DURING the summer of 1671 George and Margaret Fox and Susannah stayed for the greater part of the time with the Rouses at Kingston-on-Thames, and by August, Fox and his party were ready to sail to America. Ten men and two women made up that party, which included William Edmundson (who had spread Quakerism in Ireland very successfully), John Rous, John Stubbs, James Lancaster and Robert Widders. The women were the aged Elizabeth Hooton and Elizabeth Miers. Many Friends went to see them off, joining the ship as far as the Downs off the coast of Kent. Margaret herself went, William Penn, the lovely Gulielma Springett who became his wife a year later, and her mother Mary Penington, now the wife of the saintly Isaac Penington.

In a letter from Margaret to her daughters Sarah and Rachel at Swarthmoor, beginning 'My dear and blessed and beloved children', dated 19th August 1671, some vivid details are given of this journey down the Thames and to the Downs. Margaret and her friends, a party of sixteen, stayed at Deal and waited for the ship to sail; 'they have had as fair an East wind for them as ever could blow, and it is wonderful remarkable, and Friends take great notice of it that the wind should turn every way according as they had occasion, for one wind carried into the Downs one day, another wind carried out of the Downs the next day.' After seeing Fox and his party sail away Margaret and her friends returned to London by Canterbury and Gravesend.

[1] *Etting Early Quaker Papers*, p. 51, quoted in *Swm. Doc. in America:* p. 74.

As Mary Lower was seriously ill in Cornwall, and Isabel Yeamans ill in Bristol, Susannah was going to them instead of returning to Swarthmoor with her mother, who was arranging to travel north with Leonard Fell, by Warwick and Stafford.[1]

The voyage from London to Barbados (the usual Atlantic route for sailing ships in those days) took seven weeks, and had more than the usual adventures. Their ship, a yacht, leaked so badly that when the crew repaired the long hole into which a man could put his hand, there were little fishes swimming in the hold. The ship was chased by a Turkish pirate,[2] but escaped. They passed through many storms. Fox and several other Friends were very ill, and his illness continued for seven weeks after their arrival at Barbados. When he recovered he began visiting Meetings in the island, making the home of John Rous's father his centre for part of the time. This well-to-do sugar planter had been the first to become a Quaker in Barbados in 1655, since when the movement had grown considerably. On the mainland in the American colonies, Quakerism had already spread widely since those days, mentioned earlier in this book, when Mary Fisher and Ann Austin had first reached New England and been followed by a stream of men and women who had helped to start Meetings from New Hampshire in the north to Virginia in the south. For over a year and a half George Fox and his companions travelled throughout the West Indies—Barbados, Jamaica, Antigua, the Leeward Islands—and on the mainland. By boat or afoot, or on horseback, they went as far north as Rhode Island (where Ann Clayton, a former servant at Swarthmoor was now the wife of the Governor, Nicholas Easton) and as far south as the Carolinas. The story of this amazing journey among scattered whites, and the Red Indians, through forests and swamps, can be read by us in Fox's Journal

---

[1] The letter giving these facts was found in 1947 in U.S.A., and is now the property of the Quaker Library, Haverford College, Pennsylvania, to whom the author is indebted for a photostat. The letter is not in Margaret's own handwriting—probably in Leonard Fell's. She mentions that her chief secretaries in London before this had been John Stubbs, now gone to America, and Ellis Hookes, ill from a fall from his horse, on returning from Deal.

[2] Capture by a Turkish pirate meant slavery or imprisonment in North Africa, generally for years, until ransom was paid. Hundreds of voyagers suffered this fate in those days, including many Friends.

and elsewhere. Margaret Fox at Swarthmoor received letter after letter from one or other of the party giving her news of the adventures. Many of these letters, and all of hers to them, have been lost, but there are still some dozen of them to her which have been included in the Cambridge Journal or the edition published by Ellwood in 1694. Her chief correspondent was John Stubbs, who told her of the great meetings held, the long talks her husband had with Governors, justices of the peace, and other important people, the meetings at which he taught his followers why and how they, both men and women, should manage their church business, his talks to the negro slaves, and the visits from and to the Indians; in Rhode Island Stubbs reported that at a very large meeting 'all expectations and eyes were upon and for'[1] her husband. Fox's own letters to his wife on this American journey were short; little letters of love and spiritual exhortation, and to let her know of his safe arrival or impending departure to a new island or colony. Here is one, from Barbados, on the 6th of January 1672:

My dear Heart,
   To whom is my love, and to all the children, in the seed of life, that changeth not, but is over all; blessed be the Lord for ever! I have gone under great sufferings in my body and spirit, beyond words: but the God of Heaven be praised his Truth is over all. I am now well: and if the Lord permit, within a few days I pass from Barbados towards Jamaica; and I do think to stay but little there. I desire that ye may be all kept free in the seed of Life, out of all cumbrances. Friends are generally well. Remember me to Friends, that enquire after me. So no more, but my love in the seed and life, that changeth not.
                                                                             G.F.[2]

Before leaving Jamaica, where they stayed for about two months, he wrote her another short letter, telling her they were going on to Maryland.[3] While in Jamaica Elizabeth Hooton had died—she 'departed in peace, like a lamb, bearing her testimony to truth at her departure'.

Not all the letters sent from across the Atlantic to Margaret were entirely about Quaker affairs. She received one from John

[1] Camb. Jnl. II, 204.
[2] G.F. Jnl. Ellwood Edn. 361.
[3] G.F. Jnl. Ellwood Edn. 362.

I

Rous which gave family news and anxieties. When he had reached his father's home he had found that Thomas Rous had married again, and the son was nervous as to whether the money already settled on him by his father might be in part alienated to the new wife. 'She is a notable cunning woman', he wrote, 'and hath great power over my father, and a fair carriage among Friends, so that she is esteemed by them beyond her worth.' He would like Margaret to write 'a few lines' to his father 'to advise him to deal fairly and equally by me', but he wants her to write 'gently, for if he be anyways raised in his spirit, he will do the worse for it.'[1] There is no record as to whether Margaret wrote, but there seems no sign that John Rous was ever disappointed of his inheritance.

While Fox and his friends were visiting Meetings and scattered Friends in Maryland, and moving north through 'the wilderness' in the spring of 1672, Margaret set herself to visit Friends in Yorkshire. In the first period of Quakerism scattering the seed had taken many Friends, both men and women, far and wide. Now, in this second period, pastoral care, strengthening the Meetings, unifying the movement, working out the practice of the spiritual teaching, were as necessary as the seed-sowing, and Margaret's work for the Society now was largely this— faithful attendance at Meetings, both for worship and for business, and visiting other meetings, to preach, to pray and to teach. So in April 1672 she set out again, with her nineteen-year-old daughter Rachel, who kept a bare record of the journey, noting the miles covered, the places visited, the meetings held.[2]

In eighteen days they covered 268 miles (an average of fifteen miles a day), crossing England by Wharfedale to Whitby and Scarborough, and they attended fifteen meetings, at all of which almost certainly Margaret ministered. Rachel's short memorandum makes no comments on their journey—they went probably on horseback, not by coach; on their first and last days they travelled the thirty miles between Swarthmoor and a village near Settle, crossing two dangerous stretches of sands of Morecambe Bay. Their route took them to the far northern corner of Yorkshire, and along the coast as far south as Bridling-

[1] Miller MSS. 69. 7.x. [Dec.] 1671 from Barbados.
[2] Cash MSS. Jnl. F.H.S. XI, 110 *seq.*

ton Quay, and back by York, Leeds and Harrogate. Men servants must have gone with them though they are not mentioned, but a party on the roads in those days was liable to attack from highwaymen.

It is remarkable that at a time when there were so many Friends travelling, that they should have had so few encounters with highwaymen. Two were recorded, and in each case the non-resisting Quaker won the day. Once it was Leonard Fell who when travelling alone was robbed of his money and his horse. He warned the robber of his evil ways, who then threatened to murder him. 'Though I would not give my life for my money or my horse, I would give it to save thy soul', answered Leonard. The highwayman thereupon gave back all he had taken. In the other case it was Robert Barclay who when he found himself on a journey looking down a highwayman's pistol, asked how he came to be so rude. The man, trembling, dropped the pistol in great surprise, and did not so much as rifle his pockets.[1]

Margaret Fox's thought and work for the Society of Friends did not keep her from a constant loving care for her children and grandchildren. The day before she left on her journey to Yorkshire she wrote to her daughter Margaret Rous who was then expecting the birth of her fifth child. The three surviving children, Bethia, Margaret and Nathaniel, were with their mother at Kingston. (No letter mentions when the two little girls left Swarthmoor—perhaps their grandmother and Aunt Susannah took them to London when they went up in 1671—what a journey it must have been, perhaps by coach the 260 miles.)

These family letters at this time give a vivid picture, not only of the relationship of mother and daughters, but of the social and medical conditions of that century.

The letter took nine days to reach Kingston-on-Thames. Margaret Rous was facing the birth of her child without any of her near relatives being with her—her husband still in Barbados (and with no news of his coming home), and her nearest sister Isabel Yeamans unable to come to her because of her ailing husband, who died two years later. Doctors were rarely, if ever, called in for childbirth, but Margaret already had her nurse

[1] *Second Period of Quakerism*, pp. 370 and 446.

with her, and a wet-nurse ready to be called in when necessary. These women, who would be Quakers, had been secured for her by a London Friend.[1]

John Rous returned about six weeks after the baby's birth, and he wrote to his mother-in-law to tell her of his arrival, his adventurous voyage, and present political affairs.

Kingston, 22.4 [June] 1672.

Dear Mother,

This is to advise thee that Thomas Briggs and I are safely arrived in England, but some hours before we expected to see land, we fell into the hands of a Dutch privateer, who took us and carried us into Spain, where we continued about 17 days, and at last came away in a vessel I bought for our transportation. We were pretty civilly used as could be expected from such people and were very kindly entertained at the English consul's house while we stayed there.

My wife and our little ones are all very well, I bless the Lord, and the children are grown finely since I saw them.

Here is news that the French have gained a great part of Holland, and goes on very vigorously, and that the Dutch have called home their fleet.

The English fleet I hear is either out or near ready to go out again, and that the Duke of Buckingham and the Lord Arlington are gone towards Holland, but on what account I know not.[2]

We had not heard from my Father when we came from Barbados. John Stubbs intended for New England in a little time after our departure. John Hull and Elisabeth Miers do not come home till the next fleet. Friends were very well in Barbados when we came thence; and Truth in a flourishing state.

My dear love and my wife's is remembered to thyself, our sisters and friends. I rest

Thy dear son in the Truth,
J. Rous.[3]

Margaret Fox's interest in individual men and women extended to an interest in contemporary politics, and several of her correspondents, like Ellis Hookes and Alexander Parker, and

---

[1] Abraham MSS. 16.

[2] The Duke of Buckingham and Lord Arlington were two members of the Cabal, Charles II's Committee of Advisers which had been in power since the fall of Clarendon five years before.

[3] Miller MSS. 71.

particularly her son-in-law John Rous sent her news of public events. The letter just quoted shows how the travellers had been captured at the beginning of the second war against Holland, which was waged largely owing to intrigue between Charles II and Louis XIV who was making a bid for the domination of Europe. It is a little difficult to see why the Dutch privateer took their prisoners to Spain, for little friendship existed then between the two countries, except that each was threatened by Louis!

By June the war had only been going on for about two months, but already Louis had overrun the Low Countries and gone far into Holland. The Dutch saved themselves by opening the dykes and flooding large parts of their country. They dismissed John and Cornelius de Witt whom they believed were responsible for their misfortunes and called on the young William, Prince of Orange, to lead them.

Two months later Rous sent further news of Dutch affairs. London had just heard of the brutal murder of the de Witt brothers. 'Here is very strange news from Holland', he wrote, 'which thou may see at large in the *Gazette*, but lest thou should not meet with it, I may give thee a short account thereof. The 20th instant (their style), Cornelius de Witt for suspicion of having a design to murder the Prince of Orange was banished the province of Holland on pain of death, and his brother the pensionery John de Witt going to see him and being in the prison, upon some dissatisfaction among the burghers and common people they forced the prison doors open; some fired on them and some run them and being dead trampled on them, haled them to the gallows where they stripped them stark naked ... and this was done in the face of the burghers and magistrates at the Hague, and nobody asked why they did so. I hear the commonalty threaten in divers places if their magistrates will not agree to their terms, they will deal with them as with the de Witts.'[1]

All through the summer of this year (1672) two Friends in London, Ellis Hookes and George Whitehead, were busily engaged in trying to obtain the release from prison of some four hundred Quakers. This effort followed on Charles II's

[1] Thirnbeck MSS. 11.

Declaration for the suspending of the Penal Laws, made in
March that year. Ellis Hookes kept Margeret Fox informed of
his work, carried out under the strain of constant ill-health.
Her letters to him were always great 'refreshment' to him. He told
her that it was 'such a troublesome business to go through, as I
have not met with the like'. And he added, 'It [namely, the list
of Quaker prisoners] lies now in the Secretary's hands, ready
signed by the King, and wants only dating: I have engrossed[1] it
once already, and it contains six of the largest skins of parchment I could get, and I must engross it once more for the Signet
Office; and from thence it is to go to the Crown Office, or
Patent Office, and to be engrossed in Chancery hand, when I
suppose it will take at least twelve skins. If we could once get it
passed the Signet and Privy Seal, I hope it would soon be done;
in the meantime we must attend in patience.'[2]

Two months later Hookes reported to Margaret that the work
was finished, the two duplicates—eleven skins of parchment—
'under the great seal'. There were 500 names in it, for a number
of non-Quaker Dissenters had at the last moment been included,
and the lists were to be sent down to the sheriffs of the various
counties, to go on to the prisons. Among Dissenters' names was
that of John Bunyan, who by this means was released after
twelve years' imprisonment at Bedford.[3] This incident is apparently not well known among Baptist writers. George Whitehead, in his *Christian Progress*, explained that when some Dissenters found the King was being favourable to them they asked
to have the names of their prisoners added to those of the
Quakers. To this Whitehead willingly agreed, in spite of the fact
that there had been much hostility between the two bodies. 'Our
being of different judgments and societies did not abate my
compassion or charity, even towards them, who had been my
opposers in some cases.' By the end of the year all the prisoners
had been discharged, many of them having been praemunired
in the past, and some imprisoned for ten or eleven years.[4]

---

[1] Engross=to copy in a fair large hand—generally said of legal documents
(Dictionary).
[2] Swm. MSS. and A.R.B. 186. London 13.6 [Aug.] 1672.
[3] Swm. MSS. and A.R.B. 187. London, 1.8 [Oct.] 1672.
[4] Besse's *Sufferings*, p. xxix.

As for Margaret herself, she seems to have travelled again late in the year, for Ellis Hookes remarks in a letter sent in December that he was glad she was 'well returned' to her house. Perhaps she had again been visiting Meetings and individual Friends. The loving sympathy which underlay her care for people prompted Elizabeth Stubbs, wife of John Stubbs, to write to her, about this time, a letter typical of many from both men and women:

> . . . I can truly say thou hast been many times in my remembrance, and [when] I consider thy great care and unchangeable love and bountiful goodness to me and my children, it break my heart and causeth me to shed many a tear, for thou was unto me a strength in the time of weakness and supported me many a time when I was ready to fall.
>
> Oh how I have been refreshed and comforted by thee many a time. Thou hast even tended me and waited over me for my good as one of thy own. I may say in the praise of the Lord it was a good day for me when I came near thee. . . .[1]

On the 28th of June 1673 George Fox arrived at Bristol after his journeys in America, during which he had travelled over sixteen thousand miles,[2] and the same evening he wrote to tell his wife of his landing, in a letter which has a sound of triumph in it.

Dear Heart,

This day we came into Bristol near night, from the seas; glory to the Lord God over all for ever, who was our convoy and steered our course; who is the God of the whole earth, and of the seas and winds, and made the clouds his chariots, beyond all words, blessed be his name for ever! Who is over all in his great power and wisdom, Amen.

Robert Widders and James Lancaster are with me, and we are well: Glory to the Lord for ever, who hath carried us through many perils, perils by water, and in storms, perils by pirates and robbers, perils in the wilderness and amongst false professors; praises to him, whose glory is over all for ever, Amen. Therefore mind the fresh life, and live all to God in it.

---

[1] Swm. MSS. I, 151, quoted in Crosfield, *Margaret Fox of Swarthmoor Hall*, p. 39, dated 1.11.1673 [Jan. 1674].

[2] F.H.S. Jnl. IX, 192.

I do intend (if the Lord will) to stay awhile this-away; it may be till the Fair.

So no more, but my love to all Friends.

G.F.

Bristol, 28th day of 4th month [**June**], 1673.[1]

As soon as Margaret received this letter she left Swarthmoor, and reached Bristol in time for the Fair, the famous Summer Fair, which opened each year on 25th July (St. James's Day), lasting for several days. With her went Thomas Lower, and her daughters Sarah and Rachel.[2] (Thomas left behind him at Swarthmoor his wife and new-born babe, his eldest child, Margaret, born at the end of May.) From London came John Rous, William and Gulielma Penn and Gerrard Roberts, and from other parts of the country, many Friends came to welcome their leader home again. 'And the Lord's infinite power and life was over all, and glorious powerful Meetings we had there.'[3]

[1] G.F. Jnl. Ellwood Edn. 384.

[2] Camb. Jnl. II, 259.

[3] Camb. Jnl. II, 259.

Note.—The Bristol Summer Fair (there was a Winter Fair also, beginning on St. Paul's Day, 25th January) was one of the most important in the country. As early as 1292, the St. James's Fair was famous throughout the Kingdom as a cloth mart (Hutton's *Bristol and its Famous Associations*). In the seventeenth century its fame was still as great as ever. Merchants came from London and all the manufacturing centres of England, Ireland, Wales and the continent of Europe. Ships of war kept a protecting watch off the coast of Ireland and in the Severn, and convoyed ships from Bristol to the South Wales ports and elsewhere. In 1636 the Mayor of Penzance reported to his Government that twelve Turkish men-of-war, bearing English colours, were lurking in St. George's Channel to capture travellers to the Fair (John Latimer, *Annals of Bristol in Seventeenth Century*, p. 242).

Drapers, skinners, leather sellers and upholsterers rode to Bristol or brought their goods in wagons and on pack-horses to sell and buy thousands of pounds worth of goods, merchants and debtors 'met there and nowhere else' (Latimer, *Bristol in Seventeenth Century*, p. 138). In 1697 it was estimated that at least £150,000 in old silver coin would be brought to the next fair from Wales and other districts.

Added to its merchandize were entertainments of all kinds, plays, acrobatic shows, and conjurors.

It is strange to think of Fox, his wife and his Friends in the company of these crowds, gay and on business bent, and yet it was a great opportunity for Meetings, for many Friends from all over the country came to do business at the Summer Fair of Bristol.

After holding many Meetings in Bristol and district, Fox and Margaret and Rachel passed into Gloucestershire. Sarah returned to the north. Later Fox continued to travel through the southern counties holding meetings, organizing men's and women's business meetings, finally reaching Kingston-on-Thames, where his wife and Rachel met him again.[1] While they made the Rous's home theirs for two or three months, George Fox travelled back and forth, visiting in Essex, Middlesex, and London, until early in December they left London, Fox intending to see his aged mother in the Midlands, and then return south, Margaret and Rachel intending to return to Swarthmoor. They were to do the long journey north in a leisurely way, and their first visit was to William Penn and his wife at their home at Rickmansworth in Hertfordshire. Here they were joined by Thomas Lower. When they were at a Friend's house in Oxfordshire, Fox had a premonition of being taken prisoner, and on reaching Worcestershire, as the four travellers were staying with their friend John Halford at Armscott Manor—a beautiful seventeenth-century house still standing—Fox was arrested and imprisoned at Worcester. This arbitrary arrest—for he was not even at a Meeting, but talking with friends in the parlour—kept him a prisoner or in the status of a prisoner from mid-December 1673 until February 1675. Fox's visit to his mother, then over seventy and ill, had to be abandoned. When she heard of his imprisonment and knew she could see him no more in this life, the shock killed her. Though she had never become a Friend there had always been the greatest affection and understanding between her and her son.

During this period of fourteen months George Fox was tried several times at the sessions at Worcester; twice he was ordered to London on a Habeas Corpus to have his case considered by the King's Bench; he suffered much ill-health and weakness (at one time his friends hardly expected him to recover), and at intervals he was given freedom to walk about in the town, and

---

The Bristol Fairs had so far fallen from their great position by the nineteenth century, and had become such centres of corruption and demoralization, that in 1838 they were abolished.

[1] G.F. Jnl. Ellwood Edn. 390. (Margaret and Rachel were with Margaret Rous when her son Thomas was born in November.)

in London he visited Friends and attended Yearly Meeting. Throughout, Thomas Lower voluntarily shared his imprisonment, and acted as his secretary.

Margaret Fox and Rachel went on to Swarthmoor, helped on their way by some Friends who offered to accompany them —no light task riding or driving through England in midwinter. They arrived home safely, but the journey must have been one of more than physical strain. She knew well what prisons were like, she knew well how her husband's health had been shattered in his long imprisonment at Scarborough. Now, after his long and arduous travels in America, his health was likely to be broken again, and Friends would be deprived of his leadership just when they were needing it badly. It is not surprising that she showed disappointment, perhaps with a sign of rebellion in it, when he talked of imprisonment. So, soon after she had reached Swarthmoor, she received a letter from her husband.

Dear Heart (he wrote),

Thou seemedst to be a little grieved when I was speaking of prisons, and when I was taken: be content with the will of the Lord God. For when I was at John Rous's at Kingston, I had a sight of my being taken prisoner: and when I was at Bray Doily's in Oxfordshire, as I sate at supper, I saw I was taken; and I saw I had a suffering to undergo. But the Lord's Power is over all, blessed be his holy Name for ever!

G.F.[1]

On the 7th of January 1674, Thomas Lower wrote from the prison to his wife Mary at Swarthmoor, giving her news of himself and Fox.

My dearest,

Although it may be supposed that I have leisure enough to write, yet I assure thee it is as much as I can get a little spare time to acquaint thee of our welfare and how it is with us, which I praise the Lord we are both very well, and my dear Father mends upon it; and is much better in health: and hath a better stomach than he had before; and takes his rest very well by night: and many visitants we have; and by reason of many papers I want not employment: and yet could not omit to signify unto thee that we are well; and I hope that thou art well satisfied in this cross to our expected enjoyment of each other. I have

[1] G.F. Jn. Ellwood Edn. 389.

received several letters from London from my brother [Dr. Richard Lower] touching my liberty, and a letter from the King's bedchamber man, Hen. Savill to the Lord Windsor his brother:[1] but seeing it only relates to my particular enlargement I have kept it by me unsent, for I thought it might prejudice and hinder my Father's enlargement if I accepted of it. For I prize his liberty more than my own, and so have written back to my brother if he cannot obtain both our discharges not to labour any further for mine. By letter from Ellis Hookes and G.W. [George Whitehead], we hear that our case hath been debated by the King and his council, upon the solicitation of our Friend Thomas Moore, and that the King and his Council were very moderate, and seemed to be affected for our wrong imprisonment; but said they could not discharge us, until the law had passed upon us, either to our discharge or continuance at sessions, unto which the matter is left.

W.P.'s mother [Wm. Penn's mother] hath written a very affectionate letter to the Lord Windsor for both our discharges which we have sent to him, the return whereof we cannot yet have. But it is thought the matter will be left to the determination of the Justices at the Bench, where unless they be permitted to tender the oaths of allegiance and supremacy, it's thought we may be discharged. Many of the justices about the country seem to dislike the severity of Parker's proceedings against us, and to declare an averseness to ensnare us with the tender of the oaths; what the issue thereof will be, we leave unto the Lord who orders all things for good to those that fear him:

My Father's dear love and mine is unto my Mother, thyself and my sisters, and unto Friends; so rests

Thy dearly loving husband
Thomas Lower.[2]

Efforts were continued in London on Fox's behalf to have him released. The Friend at court, Thomas Moore, had an hour with the King when he read a letter to him sent up by Margaret. Charles was 'very kind' to him, but 'very timorous (it being just at the pinch of the Parliament's coming on), of doing anything to displease them, his occasions being so great for money, which might something impede the business'.[3] Charles also told him that 'he would do what he could, but not of himself, for he said the burnt child dreaded the fire'.[4] Indeed, Charles's

---

[1] Lord Windsor was Lord Lieutenant of Worcestershire.
[2] Abraham MSS. 17.
[3] Spence III, 169.
[4] A.R.B. 191–2.

extravagance and lack of money were making him more and more dependent on Parliament, and that body, through their fear of Roman Catholicism, was becoming more intolerant as the reign proceeded.

Lady Penn's efforts with the Lord Windsor were aimed to prevent Fox being ensnared by having the oath of allegiance put to him, because that would bring on a praemunire. Their efforts in that respect were however in vain. Before the month was out (Jan. 1674), at the Sessions, the oath was tendered, owing to the machinations of Justice Parker, and Fox's imprisonment was continued. Fox told his wife that the public at his trial were very critical of the justices, and said it was like the trials in the days of the persecuting Bishop Bonner of Queen Mary's reign.[1]

During this imprisonment on January (1674) the weather was so severe that the prices of all foodstuffs rose to such a height that the poor were starving and rioting in Worcester. Wheat used by the well-to-do rose to seven and sixpence a bushel, while the cereals which were used chiefly by the poor to make bread—oats, rye, barley, beans and peas—all rose in proportion, and the hungry people cut the bags in the market-place to get their food.[2]

In London prices rose even higher, so John Rous reported, wheat being sold at nine and ten shillings a bushel. The Thames was very flooded, and at Kingston 'people hath been forced to go in boats between our house and the town', the main part standing as an island, and £1,000 worth of damage had been done.[3]

So it was that when Fox's friends managed by the end of January to get him brought up to London under a Habeas Corpus, to be tried before the King's Bench, his journey was made very difficult by flooded rivers and roads.

Fox travelled with Thomas Lower, whom the Under-sheriff had actually appointed his deputy for the journey! In London he appeared at the Court of the King's Bench, where he was

---

[1] *Etting Early Quaker Papers*, Philadelphia. Jnl. F.H.S. XI, 98 and *Swarthmoor Documents in America*, p. 78.

[2] In a letter from G. Fox to Margaret, written on 21st Jan. 1674. *Etting Early Quaker Papers*, Philadelphia.

[3] Spence III, 172

treated with moderation though not given a formal release.
Rebecca Travers was again his hostess, and after about three
weeks he went to the Rous's home at Kingston. Lower then
travelled to Swarthmoor for a short visit to his wife and baby
Margaret. Fox had so much freedom in London that he was
able to write a book to explain the refusal, on Christian grounds,
of Friends to take the oath. This book was given away widely
to the King, his Council, the Parliament, the Lord Mayor of
London and his Council. It was sent overseas, to Barbados, the
American colonies, Scotland and Ireland. He asked Margaret
to have it distributed to business meetings of the Society, for
them to send to the Judges and to those who wielded power,
for these books 'do give a great light to dark people'.[1]

At the end of March (1674) Fox was back again in Worcester
and early in April wrote again to his wife telling her the story
of his new appearance in court—this time before Judge Turner,
his old persecutor of Lancaster days, ten years before. Obviously
the judge and other justices wanted to finish with this obstinate
man, and give him his liberty, but that was prevented by the
vindictiveness of Justice Parker; back and forth did the argument go, and in the end the justices promised the prisoner that
he should have his liberty in the town and stay at a friend's house
till the next sessions.[2] It was during this tedious Worcester imprisonment that George Fox and his wife sent each other presents. At one time Margaret sent him a salmon while he was in
London in March—the Duddon River which runs by Marsh
Grange is famed for its salmon. And Fox had bought her 'as much
Spanish black cloth as will make thee a gown and it did cost us
a pretty deal of money'[3]—this because she had sent him three
pounds to help to lessen the rigours of his imprisonment. But
Fox was always most scrupulous never to use his wife's money,
and he even went to the length of changing her wifely gift to
him into a present for her! The black cloth was now being sent
by a Wolverhampton carrier to John Higgins in Lancaster 'for
him to send to Sarah Fell at Swarthmoor', Higgins being the
family postman and carrier across the sands.

[1] A.R.B. 195–6.
[2] Jnl. F.H.S. XI, 99–102.
[3] Jnl. F.H.S. XI, 157 in letter 18 of Abraham MSS.

Early in May the authorities again sent Fox up to London—three times was he 'tossed to and fro'[1] between Worcester and London.

Fox stayed in London until July, technically a prisoner, but in reality free to go about as he wished. He attended Yearly Meeting in London in May, to which Friends came from all over England, and a General Meeting in June to which a number of Friends from overseas came, two from Norway, some from Holland, Scotland and Ireland, and 'three men came from Danzic, pretty sober men', as he explained in a letter to his wife.[2]

In July he returned to Worcester, to be tried again at the Sessions. This time he found several errors in the indictment, but in spite of that the judge determined to get the better of his prisoner, and passed the dread sentence of praemunire on him. By this he was 'fixed in prison'.[3] When she heard this news Margaret left home in August on horseback accompanied by Thomas Lower and her daughter Susannah, and came to Worcester to share her husband's imprisonment.[4] She and Thomas did all they could to get freedom for him, first at Worcester and then in

[1] Camb. Jnl. II, 285.

[2] Port. 36.35, dated 9.4. [June] 1674, at Library, Friends' House, London.

[3] G.F. Jnl. Ellwood Edn. 402.

[4] Abraham MSS. 19. This letter from Thomas Lower to Sarah Fell is one of the few which tell us exactly how Margaret Fox and her friends travelled about the country. The letter was written at the White Bull, near Garstang, a village about half-way between Lancaster and Preston. It was written on 'the first night after our setting forth', which means that they travelled that day a full thirty miles, including some twelve over the sands of Morecambe Bay. As they passed through Lancaster, they had time to inquire the selling price of malt, so that Lower wrote 'My Mother would have thee send to Lancaster as much as Sumpter [a name of a horse mentioned in *S.F. Act Bk.* p. 135] can traice [=draw] in the cart of her malt; thou must send Jamy of the Marsh [=James Cooper, servant at Marsh Grange, and agent for Joseph Sharpe (see *S.F. Act Bk.* 517.)] with it to sell it, and if the sugar be come he may carry that home with him: and if it be not come to send another load again: for it sells well at Lancaster 16/- per bushel there.' Then he adds news of their journey—'We are well thus far. Joseph Sharpe fears the bay mare will tire, we think we must put my boy to ride her: and Joseph before my mother or myself.' Evidently there were four horses for the party of four adults and one boy—Margaret, Susannah, and Thomas Lower each had their own horse, and the bay mare carried Joseph Sharpe and the boy. But Lower now thinks the bay mare will have to carry the boy only, and Joseph Sharpe would then have to ride in front of either Margaret Fox or Lower himself. Joseph Sharpe was a trusted servant at Marsh Grange. He is frequently mentioned in Sarah Fell's

London. Fox himself, before severe illness laid him low, sent a long letter to the King to put before him what the Quakers taught. 'The principle of the Quakers is the spirit of Christ', he began, 'by which we know we are his, and he dwelleth in us by his spirit; and by the spirit of Christ we are led out of un-righteousness and ungodliness'. This Spirit, he explained, led them out of all plottings against the King, and away from vice, and into goodness and right living, and if the King would give the Quakers liberty to teach the people, he would find he would not need to employ so many judges and magistrates. (This might be looked upon as a very politic suggestion to the im-pecunious King!) Finally, to swear an oath, Fox argued, was contrary to Christ's teaching, but the King would find that their yea was yea and their nay, nay.[1]

In London the appeals for release made by Ellis Hookes, William Penn,[2] Thomas Moore, George Whitehead, Martha Fisher and others, caused the King again to offer Fox a pardon, but this he refused, as he claimed he was an innocent man. His severe illness however softened the heart of Justice Parker suffi-ciently to allow him during October now and again to leave the noisome gaol and take the air in the city.

Account Book, various sums of money passing between them on loan. He was also in partnership with her in the coal business, and with her and Susannah in the grain trade. Judge Fell left fifty shillings to him in 1658, describing him as 'my faithful and careful servant at the Marsh Granges'.

It is only from an entry in Sarah Fell's *Account Book* that we discover that Susannah went with her mother to Worcester (though several letters written later mention her at Worcester and in London), and also that the date of their setting out was 13th August—'By money to Mother and Sister Susannah when they went to father to Worcester, £10.'

'By money to Brother Lower then   £2.6.0.'

And Susannah on her departure gave a present of 1/-, and Margaret 'gave the servants at Swarthmoor' 3/6 (pp. 118 and 119 of *S.F. Act. Bk.*).

Thomas Lower ends his letter with dear love to 'my dear wife, thyself and sister Rachel and my little maid' Margaret.

The *Account Book* (p. 132) notes that Joseph Sharpe returned from Worcester late in September.

[1] G.F. Jnl. Ellwood Edn. 402. The original letter now in the possession of Isabel Ross, Ambleside. It is in the handwriting of Thomas Lower, to whom it was dictated.

[2] The affectionate and grateful letters from G.F. and M.F. to Wm. Penn are in Jnl. F.H.S. VII, 73-5.

Margaret then went to London, prompted thereto by Ellis Hookes who wrote to Fox soon after his wife's arrival at Worcester, 'I thought if Margaret had freedom to come up and speak with him [the King] it might have some good effect, he having a respect to her; she may come up in the coach [the stage coach] and Thomas Moore will be willing to help'.[1] She was, as in days gone by, received by the King, who 'spake kindly to her and referred her to the Lord-Keeper'.[2] But here there was still further delay. In spite of the friendliness of the King, he was powerless against the rigidity of his ministers. So on 25th December 1674 after a still further visit to the King, Margaret wrote direct to the Lord-Keeper, Sir Heneage Finch:

For the Lord Keeper,
Whom I desire to consider the long and sad imprisonment of my dear husband who hath wanted his health a long time, and hath not gone forth of his prison chamber about 23 weeks but about 3 times, and it is 20 weeks since I and my son [Thomas Lower] and daughter left my family, not knowing that I should find him alive, and we have stayed ever since waiting and expecting the King and his governors would have some pity and some compassion upon him for to set him at liberty, he being an innocent man, and was never found in anything that was evil or against the King or his government.

Then she recounted how he and his son-in-law had been arrested at Armscot while travelling, not even at a meeting but in a private house, and how the oath of allegiance had been put to him, and how he had 'been tossed to and fro without any just ground'.

Now I beseech thee, she continued, consider of our condition, for I am now 200 miles from my own house and hath been from it ever since I came to Worcester; and I was yesterday with the King and he desired me to come to thee. I am informed that the King had signed a warrant a pretty while since. We heard before I came from Worcester that it was stopped by thee. So I beseech thee and entreat thee let pity and tenderness enter into thy heart and consider that it is a sad thing both to be sick and in prison, and let him have his liberty, that we may return home to our own country; for it is for the Lord's sake and his

[1] Camb. Jnl. II, 301.
[2] G.F. Jnl. Ellwood Edn. 404.

Truth's sake that we suffer and have suffered these many years and not for any evil, and so if thou do good in thy place and office, the Lord will reward thee.

Margaret Fox.[1]

Fox continued to refuse the pardon which was offered him, 'for I had rather have lain in prison all my days than have come out in anyway dishonourable to Truth'.[2] However, early in February 1675, he was brought up again to London, by the stage coach, together with the under-sheriff, the clerk of the peace, and some others. He appeared again in the Court of the King's Bench, and the errors of his indictment were proved to be so gross that he was discharged by proclamation, a free man.

Thomas Lower did not accompany his father-in-law to London,[3] but had already returned to his wife and baby daughter at Swarthmoor.

When the joyful news of George Fox's release reached Swarthmoor, Lower at once wrote to Margaret expressing the deep thankfulness of all at Swarthmoor, adding, 'And he could not have been more nobly released, and his adversaries and malicious persecutors less gratified than by this way and manner of discharge, which was always unto me the most probable way to be effected in. And I think my father's mind mostly inclined that way also, though by some it was obstructed, but in that it is at last effected, we do rejoice and bless and praise the name of the Lord who is the author of all our good things.'

A little later, on the 4th of March, Lower and Sarah wrote again to George and Margaret Fox, Lower rejoicing in the news of their coming return to Swarthmoor, and adding, 'I have been to Holker [the home of the Prestons, former persecutors] and Conishead [the home of their near neighbours, the Myles Doddings] and have mentioned thy honourable discharge over the heads of thy persecutors and it doth damp and discourage the envious spirit very much; and I think they will be afraid to meddle any more'.[4] Lower reported that his wife was better

---

[1] Spence MSS. III, 129.
[2] G. F. Jnl. Ellwood Edn. 405.
[3] Spence MSS. III, 167.
[4] Spence MSS. III, 174

since taking some of his pills, and his 'little Margaret a lovely thriving child'. This reference to his daughter, and an earlier one in which he calls her 'the thrivingest well-liking child that ever I beheld and very apprehensive of her age', are particularly touching, as within a few days of the writing of this letter the little girl died. There are no letters extant which tell us the manner of her death—the very suddenness suggests that she met with an accident.

Sarah's letter shows the preparations being made for the welcome home.

Dear Mother,

We received thine with our dear father's yesterday, with great joy and gladness upon several accounts. And as for what thou mentions about sister Susan staying with sister Rous, as for our parts we freely leave it to you to do as you see fit and convenient, and give our consent, and shall, as we have done, do our utmost according to our capacity to supply her place in her absence; but I look it will lie more upon sister Rachel than I, and she is willing to leave it to you, and will, I doubt not, perform to the full, having manifested her abundant care, diligence and frugality, now in your absence, being very able to go through her business, having a large and copious capacity. So we can say no more in it only shall be very glad to see sister Susan when the Lord order it, and also we do believe her company to sister Rous will be very acceptable and needful in brother's absence, so what you do will be to our content.

We desire to know as soon as thou can, when we may expect you with our dear father, for several reasons, as thou may well know. And thou should buy us a cask of wine, of what sort thou judgest father likes best, for we have none only some cider and March beer,[1] bottled up; also you should buy us some anchovies, some olives and two larding needles[2], and some oranges and lemons, and what else you think fit; and pray let us know some certainty of your coming as soon as you can.

We are all well, and our endeared love and duty is to thee, and our dear father, and our dear love to our sisters and cousins, and cannot

---

[1] March beer is strong ale or beer brewed in March (*Oxford English Dict.*).

[2] Larding needle = a sharp-pointed instrument with which meat was larded, i.e. prepared for cooking by having pieces of fat bacon inserted in it (*Oxford English Dictionary*).

but admire Bethiah's writing[1] and that she is so active and ingenious. This is all at present from

Thy dear daughter

Sarah Fell.[2]

In spite of the eager expectation at Swarthmoor of the speedy return of George and Margaret Fox, they remained in the south for three months more. Their centre was the Rous home at Kingston, where another baby, Bridget, had been born in February, whose tragic death from small-pox occurred eight years later.[3] (Her brother Nathaniel had the dread disease two years afterwards, when he was about sixteen, but he recovered.)

When Fox had regained his strength in the clean air of Kingston, he went to London again. His time was much occupied with Meetings, consultations, and writing books. In May they attended the Yearly Meeting, filled with Friends from all over the nation and some from overseas. Then they were ready to return home.

They came by coach, as to ride on horseback was too great a strain for George. Susannah came with them. They made almost a triumphal journey—Friends accompanying them to Highgate and Dunstable, Friends coming to visit them as they stopped at towns on their leisurely way, and in time they reached Lancaster, where he had last been as a prisoner about to be taken to Scarborough. Here they were met by Thomas and Mary Lower, Sarah Fell and others, and the next day, joined by several other Friends, the large party—some in the coach, others on horseback—crossed the two wide strips of the sands of the Bay. So they reached Swarthmoor on 25th June 1675[4] the first time since their marriage six years earlier, that husband and wife had been together in their own home.

---

[1] It was very natural for Sarah, who wrote and spelt so excellently, to take special note of her niece Bethiah's writing. The little girl was then eight, and had been born at Swarthmoor and lived there for the first four years of her life.

[2] Spence MSS. III, 174. (**Postscript to letter 4; [March] 1674/5**).

[3] She died in Jan. 1683.

[4] Camb. Jnl. II, 311.

Chapter Eighteen

LIFE AT SWARTHMOOR HALL, 1673-8

I. The Household and Estate

IN this chapter an attempt is made to give a picture of the home background of Margaret Fox and her family. It is possible to see this in considerable detail, as there exists the household account book kept with scrupulous care by Sarah Fell who acted as bailiff and accountant for many years. The account book, as it is now, covers only five years, from September 1673 to August 1678, but that is due to its loss in the eighteenth century. It seems to have been taken by John Abraham to Lancaster when he left Swarthmoor Hall in 1759, and was found about 1800 in its present condition by a Quakeress, Bridget Whalley, in a grocer's shop in that town, being used for wrapping up the groceries.

However, the accounts of those five years include transactions of income and expenditure made in the two years (June 1675 to March 1677) when Margaret was at home again and with her husband. For him this was the longest stay he made during his life of wandering and imprisonments.

Most of the food used by the household was grown on the estate. Even the wheat for the bread was largely grown, as Swarthmoor lies in low Furness where wheat can grow, and oats were used extensively for 'clap-bread', the local kind of oatcake, freshly cooked each day. This clap-bread is flattened by clapping the hand on it on a girdle or griddle and cooked over the open fire. It has been eaten from time immemorial till the present day. Visitors to Swarthmoor enjoyed the clap-bread, and we find that Margaret Fox sent presents of it to her friend Ellis Hookes in London and Gulielma Penn at Rickmansworth in Hertfordshire.

Beef and mutton were supplied from their own beasts, and many animals were bought in the local markets for draught.

Sometimes however meat was bought, a 'barrel of Irish beef', dried mutton, chickens (2d. each), geese, woodcock, tufted duck (called 'douker'), teal, pigeons, partridges, and snipe. Salmon too were bought, large quantities of preserved herrings, and the char, a fish found in Windermere Lake, famous for its good flavour and used extensively in the seventeenth and eighteenth centuries as potted or made into pies, and sent all over the country. Margaret once sent a present of potted char to Gulielma Penn. An old recipe states it was preserved by being seasoned with mace, cloves, nutmegs, cinnamon and black pepper.[1]

When William Penn visited the Swarthmoor family in April 1676 the account book tells us that Sarah tried to get some char, but failed; however they killed a fat sheep which cost them seven shillings and sixpence.

Other fish used were crabs and cockles, for which Morecambe Bay is still famous.

Both for food and for medicines, herbs were grown. Thomas Lawson the botanist, and one of the earliest Furness Quakers, taught the Fell sisters the properties of the herbs, for which tuition he was paid ten shillings.

On the back of one of Margaret Rous's letters, Sarah wrote down a list of vegetable seeds she needed—2 oz. of parsnips, ½ oz. of carrots, 1 oz. of onions, 2d. of turnip, 2d. of sweet marjoram, 2d. of radish, and some 'winter savery'.[2] Cabbages were grown and also sold—they went to the Ulverston market, 10 for 1/3½. The large orchard provided an abundance of fruits such as apples and pears, plums and damsons, but cherries and strawberries, currants, raisins and prunes appear in the accounts. Plenty of the Lancashire cheese was made, both at Swarthmoor and at Marsh Grange (accounts were kept for both estates), and a good deal sold, but now and again carriage was paid for the transport of Dutch cheeses, via Newcastle and Kendal, and 'a great cheese sent out of Cheshire to father', which cost eight-pence to be brought by Higgins across the sands from Lancaster.

Some food came from even further afield. Sugar was sent from Barbados, shipped to Lancaster, no doubt from the Rous

[1] From *Home Life in N. Lonsdale*, by John Fell, in *Transactions of Cumb. and West. Ant. and Arch. Soc.*, 1891, p. 387. Also see Armitt, *Rydal*, 296 seq.
[2] Spence MSS. III, 179.

plantation. And once a box came as a present to Margaret from the Quaker Ralph Fretwell, formerly one of the chief Judges in the Court of Common Pleas in Barbados, who sent oranges, a sage cheese (a soft cheese flavoured with sage) and a 'runlet of socketts', which means a cask of candied peel.[1]

In the brew-house, the chimney of which can still be seen against the wall of a farm-worker's cottage next the great barn, were brewed cider and ale; white wine, brandy, and claret were bought, and home-made wines were made from fruits like the gooseberry and currants.

As with food and drink, so with clothes and furnishings—some were home-produced and some were bought. Flax and hemp were grown in the fields; women were employed to do much of the spinning (though probably all the Fell daughters used a spinning wheel also), and men did the weaving.[2]

Wool came from their own sheep, and woollen and cotton stockings were knitted locally and also re-footed. Dress materials were usually bought in London or Lancaster. Lancashire plush was bought through Henry Coward, a Quaker merchant of Lancaster, some of which was re-sold. Scottish cloth (a linen cloth, not as fine as holland) was bought from a Quaker in Aberdeen, and Cumberland cloth, tweed woven from the wool of the hardy Herdwick sheep, was bought from Friends in

---

[1] **Footnote deleted 1984.**

[2] One entry, 18th Dec. 1673 (p. 25), gives a valuable comment on the craft of spinning as done in the Lake District. Twopence is paid for 'spinells or whorles', which means 'spindles and whorls'; this was the primitive method of spinning, before the spinning wheel was invented. According to Mr. H. S. Cowper, in his book, *Hawkshead*, the primitive method was carried on in many parts of the Lake District until late in the eighteenth century, and even later occasionally. He adds, 'Though there is absolutely no evidence to tell us when the spinning wheel began to displace from general use the spindle and whorl, it is difficult to imagine that it was not fairly well introduced by the beginning of the seventeenth century', p. 268. At Swarthmoor probably the purchase of spindles and whorls was for the servants. We know from a letter written about 1660 by William Caton to Margaret Fell that she used the spinning wheel for flax spinning, and in the *Account Book*, a Dutch spinning wheel is bought for Rachel, in 1678. It is interesting to see that the Women's Institutes of to-day are reviving the old spinning by spindle and whorl—see *Women's Institutes*, by Cicely McCall.

Cumberland. This cloth probably was made into coats and riding-coats, one of which Sarah had made up for her for five shillings and sixpence.

Matthew Fell was the family tailor, making clothes for both men and women. In 1677 he was paid three shillings and sevenpence 'for work and other things for mother when her black loose gown and petticoat was made'.

Margaret Fox was no believer in what came in the next century to be called 'Quaker grey'. In a later chapter her letter written in her old age is quoted, beseeching Friends not to think a uniform dress and colour bespoke the pure life within. Her daughter's accounts give a colourful picture of their clothes, though avoiding luxury. Black was a fashionable colour, so we have a black allamode[1] whiske[2] for Rachel, costing 2/–, while Susannah, not to be outdone by her younger sister, had two. Sarah had blue aprons and strings, and 'sky coloured' worsted (woollen thread for stockings), and later on red worsted, while Susannah preferred white. Rachel liked blue and green for her colours—she bought two blue calico aprons and later she had a pair of stockings dyed sea-green. Susannah also chose green for her 'say' (serge) apron—an expensive one at 2/9—and sky colour for two pairs of her stockings. Many yards of ribbon were bought; 18 yards of black and sky-coloured for Susannah for 4/9, black and green ribbons for Mary, and 4 yards of green gallowne,[3] while Sarah bought 9 yards of black ribbon. White kersey (woollen cloth) was bought by Sarah for a petticoat for a servant, and Susannah bought three black handkerchiefs 'to give away'. Petticoats varied too in colour, one was of white flannel, others ash-coloured, black, red and dove-colour. They were worn as the skirt of the wide open gown. Garters and many pairs of gloves were bought, and shoes were sent to the Hall from Kendal, though sometimes William Salthouse of Dragley Beck supplied them. Clogs[4] were given to the servants.

[1] A thin black glossy silk. Armitt, *Rydal*, p. 592.

[2] A neckerchief worn by women in the latter half of the seventeenth century. *Ox. Eng. Dict.*

[3] Gallowne = narrow ribbon or braid of gold, silver or silk thread, used for trimming articles of apparel. *Ox. Eng. Dict.*

[4] The clogs of Lancashire are derived from the sabots of Dutch refugees.

Perhaps shoes were sometimes mended at home, as 'tapps', soles of boots or shoes, come into the accounts. White fustian (a thick strong cotton cloth) came from Manchester and 'a pair of boddis' (corsets) from London. Sarah paid 'John Woes' 4d. to mend her muff.

Materials for house-furnishings were more often home-produced than the clothes. The home-grown flax was spun and woven into huckaback for towelling, and other household linen, the wool was spun and woven into blankets, rugs and curtains, the hemp was made into sacks, and into coarse materials used in house and farm, for ropes for horses and carts, and for ticking for the feather beds and chaff beds.

After being woven, blankets were milled and dressed by James Walker, the 'Walkster' or fuller, one who worked a walk-mill. The material was stretched and dried on hooks of frames called tenters (hence 'on tenterhooks' means to be on the stretch) and was widely done in North Lancashire and Westmorland where there was abundance of barren rocky land, useless for agriculture, but suitable for sheep farming and the woollen industry.

By the time the Account Book opens, the Hall must of course have been already well furnished, but a few pieces of furniture were added during these years. Some tables and chairs were bought at sales, some bedsteads were made of timber from their own woods by the carpenter hired with his men. Fifteen days' work of several men was needed to make one bedstead at the cost of 5/11.[1] Later the same man and his assistants took five days to make 'a great firrdale[2] chair, Mother's account', for which they were paid 2/4.[3] (No doubt they would have their food and drink in addition.)

Red leather and nails were bought to make up some stools for the Hall. Dishes and spoons were of pewter, though the best spoons were silver. There were drinking glasses, earthenware jugs, porringers for the good oat porridge, a flagon, and knives. In the kitchen and dairy were wooden trenchers, a 'little seive', milk pots, pans, kettles (small and large), wooden bowls for

[1] *S.F. Act. Bk.*, p. 11.
[2] *Firrdale* means deals or planks of fir. *Ox. Eng. Dict.*
[3] *S.F. Act. Bk.* 209.

setting the milk before churning, skimming dishes and ladles. Pans and plates were bought in Kendal. For the laundry, a washing tub was bought, and many times 'bucking ashes' are mentioned, which are an alkaline 'soap' for a large wash of clothes.

Accounts for repairs tell us that there was a clothes stool box (the predecessor to a chest of drawers), a looking-glass, a clock, and the 'high balcony' overlooking the garden from the first story, from which George Fox preached.

In the wide open fireplaces, peat was burnt, cut from Margaret Fox's own moss, or from that of Myles Dodding of Conishead Priory. Firewood also was used from their own timber.

The wages of the servants, both indoor and out, were very low, as was the case throughout the country then. In addition to the cash wage, food and clothing were given, and small presents and even legacies from time to time. The usual wage for a woman servant was one pound a year, but if they undertook responsibility the wage would be two pounds. That Sarah was a disciplinarian is shown by the following entry made in November 1676—'By mo pd. Ann Standish in full yrs wages £1.17.6. of which we received back of her for a silver spoon she lost 8/– and for a pot she broke 6d, so paid her £1.9.0.' Perhaps it was natural that a fortnight later, Ann 'went away', taking with her one shilling given as a present by young Rachel Fell who seems to have felt some pity for her. The men servants had up to four pounds a year, but many of the crafts like spinning, weaving, walling and carpentry were done by local craftsmen and paid for as the work was finished.

In the fields, from which much of the produce was sold in the local markets, outdoor servants were paid from 1d. a day to 6d., with about 8d. worth of food. Local husbandmen—men owning a cottage and barn and three to four acres of land—were employed in the extra work of harvest and sheep-shearing.

Women worked in the fields alongside the men. One woman servant, Peggy Dodgson, is frequently mentioned in the Account Book, and her work was as varied as her strength and endurance were great. Her occupations included washing and 'swingling' (beating the flax or hemp so as to separate it from the stalk or pith), filling manure into the carts and scaling it (spreading it over the fields), rubbing, scouring, spinning and knitting, har-

rowing and dressing meadows, spreading and dressing and setting peats, weeding garden and corn, hay-making, picking and
pulling hemp, raking bracken, reeing (riddling beans, pulse,
etc.) and scaling mole hills. Her wage was between one penny
and twopence a day.

Ploughing was done by oxen. Sarah had to see to the purchase of seed, of manure, the hiring of fields beyond the estate,
and repairs to ploughs, farm-carts, the barns and stables. She saw
to the sales of cheese, butter, beans, pease, wheat, malt, oats,
cabbages, onions, apples, rabbit skins, turkeys, the skins of cows
and sheep, linseed, bulls, oxen, heifers, sheep, geese, and lamb's
wool. The wool was sold to merchants in Lancaster and as far as
Leeds.

The purchase of books is never mentioned among the accounts, except a primer bought for Isabel Yeamans's little son
William after he came to live at the Hall (August 1674), and
The Young Clerk's Tutor bought by Thomas Lawson for one
shilling and sixpence for the use of Sarah in her accountancy.
The rebinding of an old history book, and of the 'Great Bible'
are mentioned, the latter probably being the Treacle Bible later
given by George Fox to the Swarthmoor Meeting, and now on
loan at Friends' House, London. Margaret Fox had a Library of
books, now scattered, many of which were the booklets so
plentifully supplied by early Friends for the convincement of
others.[1]

Material for writing was needed in the household, so Sarah
bought quills, inkhorns and ink, sealing-wax, paste board, a
skin of parchment (for George Fox), mastic (gum-resin),
scissors and knives.

From entries in the Account Book it is possible to learn something of the horses ridden by the Fell family. Margaret had a
white horse, Sarah had a filly and a mare, and also 'Grey Robin',
Susannah had a Galloway (a small strong riding horse originally
from Galloway in Scotland), Isabel Yeamans had a mare, Thomas
Lower had a bay mare and a gelding called Dick, and other

---

[1] One of these bound volumes of tracts is now at the Library of Congress,
Washington, D.C., and is marked 'Ex Libris Margaret Fox'. A second has
recently (1948) been found in London, and given to the Library, Friends'
House, London.

horses were named Bonny, Peggy, Sumpter—the last a name given to a pack-horse.

Many medicines were bought and operations recorded, for horses and other animals. Verdigris was used for sore feet; quick-silver, black soap, alum and vinegar, brimstone and treacle, sugar-candy, ale, beer, 'bolalmanacke' (which presumably is meant to be bolbanac, an obsolete herbal name for the plant Honesty), were all used as animal medicines. Linseed oil was bought for horses' backs, tobacco was used as a horse-wash for the itch, horses were blooded with leaches or with a 'fleame' or lancet, the smith being the surgeon. The scab is frequently mentioned as a disease of both sheep and horses.

The Account Book shows how Sarah was entrusted with the money of others. In addition to the money subscribed by Friends to their Meetings, and the disbursement of these, she also had loans up to £200. Small sums were given her by her boy servant, Tom Harrison, whose savings she kept for him until he needed to buy something for himself. She had the newly minted coin, the guinea, sent her from Bristol and Scotland, to exchange, its value being £1.1.6 in 1677.

She did business for her attorney uncle, Matthew Richardson of Dalton, steward for the manor of Pennington, and on his death in August 1677 she was responsible for arranging his affairs, his wife being incapable owing to mental illness. At his funeral the nine gallons of wine cost £1.16.6, the 30¾ lb. of cheese cost 5/-, and 4/6 was paid 'a messenger for going to Lancaster for biscuits for said funeral and for bringing them to Higgins, etc'.

The Account Book also has entries of the payment of the unpopular hearth tax. Legalized after the Reformation it was finally abolished soon after the accession of William and Mary. The tax was two shillings on each hearth or chimney every year. At Swarthmoor twelve shillings, rising to thirteen owing to some new building added by its mistress, were paid each six months. This shows that Swarthmoor with its twelve or thirteen hearths was the largest house in the neighbourhood, except Conishead Priory, the home of Myles Dodding, which had the same number. In Ulverston no other house had more than five hearths. Marsh Grange paid for six hearths. A rent rather similar to ground rent in a modern leasehold, was also paid on Marsh Grange. It came to £2.8.0 every half-year and was paid at Dalton to the Duke of Albemarle, son of General Monk, who had been rewarded by Charles II with the lordship of the Manor of Furness, representing the old estate of the Abbot of Furness.

II. Commercial Concerns and Charities

In one of Thomas Lower's letters to Margaret Fox, he mentions the 'concerns' (meaning commercial dealings) which her daughters carried on at Swarthmoor. The Account Book tells us what they were in addition to the daily supervision of household and estate and the sale of produce already described. One was the smelting of iron ore at Force Forge, some ten miles from the Hall, and others were the sending of cargoes by ship to Liverpool, Bristol and Cornwall. The mining and smelting of iron ore in Furness is believed to have been a very old craft, possibly going back to Roman times. Certainly it was one of the sources of revenue of the Abbots of Furness and to the great benefit of their tenants, and at the dissolution of the monastery in 1537, the rights to smelt iron ore by means of charcoal were granted to two local landowners, William Sandys and John Sawrey. This right was withdrawn nearly thirty years later, because of the serious destruction of the trees for the making of the charcoal, and nearly a century had to pass before the bloomeries, as the charcoal smelting furnaces were called, were re-opened. Some time before 1658 Force Forge was built. Placed on the bank of a swiftly flowing stream (Grisedale Beck, in the Rusland Valley), with a force or cataract a little above it, and coppice woods around to supply it with charcoal, the Forge was reached by pack-horse way over the fells. The ore was mined in the district around Dalton in Furness at the southern tip of the peninsula ('Plain Furness' as it was called in contrast to 'High Furness' where the fells lay), and the old wide road along which the ore was carried can be followed to this day—from Stainton and Adgarley, Elliscales and Roanhead, to Martin, whence the pack-horses climbed higher over the wide fell by Horrace and Osmotherley Moor down to Lowick Bridge. Then up the valley a mile to Nibthwaite lying at the foot of Coniston Water,

and again the way climbed over the fell and down into the Rusland Valley, and straight to Force Forge. There were in the
seventeenth century two other forges established in Furness, at
Cunsey, close to the western shore of Windermere, and at
Coniston. There was also a Bloom Smithy, about half a mile
up the Beck above Force Forge, near the Corn Mill, and this
Smithy was owned by the Rawlinsons of Graythwaite.

By the time the Account Book opens, Force Forge had been
the property of the Fells for fifteen years. An old deed dated
1681 gives us the only existing record of the ownership and
history of the Forge from 1658 to 1684, other than the frequent
references to it in the Account Book (1673–8), in one or two
letters among the Abraham and other MSS. and in an old
Quaker Minute Book. From these we learn that early in 1659,
a few months after Judge Fell died, Force Forge was bought by
his son George. Whether or not young George Fell worked the
Forge is not known, but the probability is that he did not, as
from 1658 he was usually in London. In June 1666, George Fell,
now living with his wife and growing family at Marsh Grange,
sold the Forge to his four unmarried sisters, Sarah, Mary,
Susannah and Rachel. They seem to have arranged with Thomas
Rawlinson to act as their steward, to manage the Forge or at
any rate the accounts. He was the eldest son of Captain William
Rawlinson of Graythwaite and Rusland Hall, who had been a
prominent Parliamentarian leader in the Civil War but had
been granted an indemnity on the Restoration. Thomas Rawlinson, in the days of George Fox's visits to Furness, became a
Quaker, much to his father's displeasure. He remained a Friend
all his life, and some of his children and grandchildren also.
(One of his daughters was Lydia Lancaster, a famous Quaker
preacher and traveller in the early eighteenth century.) But his
stewardship of the Forge on behalf of the Fell sisters was called
in question in 1668, and the matter was brought before arbitrators for settlement. Rawlinson refused to follow the decision of
the arbitrators, and the subject then came before the local
Quaker Monthly Meeting. This process accorded with the
general advice given by George Fox to Friends who had disputes with each other, namely, before going to law, to bring
the matter before the local business Meeting of the Society,

where it was believed that when the Meeting was held in the spirit of Christ, a just solution might be found. The first Minute relating to the dispute occurs in July 1668 at the Monthly Meeting held at Newton in Cartmel—'It was ordered that James Taylor, and William Wilson and Reginald Holme should speak with Thomas Rawlinson concerning the difference betwixt M. Fell's children and him about the accounts of his stewardship at Forge which is brought before us at this Month's Meeting whereby his guilt of wronging M.F. and her children is more manifest and seen by Friends than herebefore. And that they give an account of the effect of their discourse with him at the next Monthly Meeting.'[1] The dispute appears in the minutes of other Monthly Meetings in that year, and was sent on to the Quarterly Meeting held at Lancaster, at which Rawlinson was asked to be present. In a letter to Margaret Fell, who was then in London, Thomas Salthouse, who was one of the signatories of the minute quoted above in January 1669 reported that Rawlinson did not attend the Quarterly Meeting. The reason he gave for non-attendance was that he could not get his horse to cross the channel in Morecambe Bay, but Salthouse believed this was a mere excuse and that he was but playing 'peep and hide' with Friends.[2]

A month later the Monthly Meeting at Swarthmoor decided to 'read a paper' at the three local Meetings, evidently condemning Rawlinson's action. One result of the dispute must have been that the management of the Forge was now taken over by Sarah Fell herself, for that is what we find in a letter to her in 1671 and also in the Account Book which opens in October 1673.

The Fell daughters seem to have been the only women to own any of these Furness Forges, in the haematite iron industry. Sarah herself has the distinction of having been the only woman to manage one.[3] She employed a forge clerk, who probably

---

[1] Minute Book of the Swarthmoor Men's Monthly Meeting. 1668–74. At Friends' House, London.

[2] Spriggs MSS.

[3] It is curious that Mr. Alfred Fell, the author of *The Early Iron Industry of Furness*, published in 1908, made the mistake of writing that Force Forge was owned by the Rawlinsons in the 1660's. Mr. Fell knew of the deed which con-

lived in the house next to the forge.

Iron ore was bought partly from Matthew Richardson, husband of Margaret Fox's only sister, who owned freehold property at Roanhead and Elliscales, both close to Dalton, where ore had been found for many centuries. Sarah herself and Thomas Lower went (for example in May 1674) to buy the ore at Dalton. Other sources of supply were the mines on the east side of Dalton, at Stainton and Adgarley, part of the 'Manor', the old Abbey demesne, later in the ownership of Sir Thomas Preston. Shortly before Sarah's purchase of ore from the Manor, Sir Thomas had entered a Jesuit house, so his estate was confiscated by the Crown. However Sarah was able to buy the ore from Sir Thomas's relative, of Holker Hall, 'old Preston of Holker', as he was called by Fox in his *Journal*—a great persecutor of Friends. So excellent was this haematite iron ore that when Fox was visiting Holland in 1677 he arranged with Sarah Fell to send him ore from Adgarley. On 9th August 1677 is the entry, 'In expense at Adgarley when we went to choose ore to send Father, 4d.'[1] and a week later, 'Paid Higgins for carrying some iron ore to Lancaster, that is to be sent to Father into Holland, 1d.'[2] According to West's *Guide to the Lakes* the Stainton and Adgarley iron ore mines were the richest in Furness.

Both the ore from the mines to the forge, and the iron from the forge to various buyers were carried by Galloway packhorses. There are numerous entries of payment for the purchase of these ponies, their saddles, their halters, the cruppers (the old

clusively proves that the Force Forge was Fell property from 1659 until 1681. He seems to confuse it sometimes in his book with Force Smithy, a bloom smithy built and owned by the Rawlinsons but higher up the stream. Remains of both the forge and the bloom smithy can be seen to this day.

Mr. Cowper, in his book *Hawkshead*, made a similar mistake. Perhaps both historians could not believe that an Iron Forge was owned and managed in the seventeenth century by women! Certainly these two writers had no knowledge of Sarah Fell's *Account Book* (not published until 1920) nor the old minute book of the local Furness and Cartmel Meetings. (I am indebted to Arthur Raistrick, an authority on the Iron Industry, for his confirmation of my conclusions on this matter.)

[1] *S.F. Act. Bk.* p. 411.
[2] *Ibid.*, p. 413.

word 'crippin' is used), for the weaving, making and repairing
of the hemp bags in which the ore was carried, the saddle trees,
oats and grass, the wages of the men who led the ponies, the
blooding of a sick horse, 'garthweb, tags and buckles for ore-
leading saddles, 2/2'.[1] The shoeing of the packhorses was another
item, and one entry tells us that a smith was established at
Adgarley, close to one of the mines, and he shod the ore-leading
horses. Horse shoes made from the haematite iron ore were
particularly hard and lasting. When Celia Fiennes was riding
'through England on a side Saddle' about 1700, she remarked
on the steep and stony tracks she found in the Lake District, and
had to have her horses re-shod almost as soon as she arrived, but
between Windermere and Ullswater she found a smith who
shod her horses so well and with such excellent iron that the
shoes held for six weeks,[2] an unusual comment on the local iron
and craftsmanship.

Substantial sums of money appear in the Forge Accounts.
Henry Coward, Quaker ironmonger at Lancaster, in August
1678, bought twenty-five pounds' worth of iron. Seven years
earlier, William Callow, a much persecuted and frequently
exiled Quaker of the Isle of Man, had ordered from Force Forge
a griddle (the popular round iron plate to bake bread, oatcake
and cakes on), and 'a 100 or half a 100 of iron', as on his return
home from a term of exile, he had found 'things decayed and
out of order'.[3] In 1674 iron to the extent of twenty-six pounds
ten shillings was sold to William Bickerstaffe of the Fylde, near
Preston, Lancs., possibly for the repairs of a bridge over the
River Wyre.[4] In June 1677 iron from the forge was taken to
Pennybridge, where a small boat took it down the Bay to
Barrow, where it joined the coasting ship which Sarah was load-
ing for Cornwall. Sarah records receipts of twenty pounds and
other sums from the forge clerk, Reginald Walker, an educated
'statesman'[5] whose home was in Little Langdale. He remained

[1] *Ibid.*, p. 469.
[2] *Celia Fiennes*, p. 164.
[3] Swm. MSS. I, 325.
[4] *S.F. Act. Bk.* pp. 154 and 555.
[5] The word 'statesman' in N.W. England is from 'estatesman', a yeoman
owning and working his own land, frequently a small acreage. They were a
very independent people. (See *Hawkshead*, by H. S. Cowper, etc.)

clerk until about the middle of 1676, when William Wilson took his place.

The Forge itself would not employ many men. There is mention of 'our hammerman', and a picture of the working of this rather simple form of forge is given by the entries for purchase of bellows from Grayrigg, near Sedbergh for 2/1,[1] and tongs for 7d.[2] The charcoal and iron ore were placed together, and the bellows were worked by water power from the nearby stream, and the iron when reduced to solid pieces was taken out by the tongs.

It is fitting here to look ahead to the few years outside the period covered by the Account Book. The Forge continued to be worked by Sarah Fell probably until 1680 when it was let to Thomas Rawlinson. In 1681 Thomas Lower, who had become part owner through his marriage to Mary Fell, sold his and his wife's share to Rawlinson. The deed of this sale has already been referred to. The sale not only included the forge and its machinery and tools, but also the house adjoining, with its furniture. However, letters written after Sarah had married and left Swarthmoor seem to indicate that she and her sisters Susannah and Rachel still either were part-owners or had money invested in the enterprise. George Fox's income is a perennial source of interest to Quaker historians, so it is of value to find that he too had money, apparently £144, invested in the forge in 1683. When Sarah left home the business of the estate was carried on by her sister Rachel. She and her mother however missed the business care of Sarah, who had to be appealed to for information from time to time. Thus in December 1683 Sarah (who had Susannah at that time staying with her in London) wrote to her mother giving details of the account between her and Susannah, and added: 'And this is as full and plain an account as I can give, and which I hope will be to thy understanding and satisfaction. This much I writ you formerly, which you were satisfied with at that time; but then it goes out of your minds again, and it seems strange to you afterwards, having not thought of it a pretty time; wherefore to prevent future mistakes and trouble I would advise sister Abram to put it down in a book by way of

[1] S.F. Act. Bk., p. 55.
[2] Ibid., p. 93.

account what was owing to sister Susan, and how paid her; as also the £122 owing to my father. Then, on looking into the book, you would see how the account stands without the trouble of examining former letters.'[1]

Certainly Sarah had profited from her study of the *Young Clerk's Tutor* and her long accountancy experience.

A few months later (July 1684) Sarah wrote to her sister Rachel: 'I take thy care in getting in the forge money, very kindly, which would be hard to get, if not looked after carefully by some in the country, and since you have got 30/- of that ill smith, do not use any severe course for the remainder, but if you cannot get it, by fair means, it must be lost; and I shall abate it, out of that which is due to me of it. I do entreat thee to pursue the getting of £10.10.0 from John Marshall [agent to the Prestons of Holker Hall] which is time it were paid, and must be called hard for, for when some begins to linger in paying they are mighty loath to do it at all.'[2]

As in no extant letter later than 1684 is there any further mention of Force Forge, probably Sarah and her sisters sold out their interest in it soon after this letter was written. The forge as it was in the seventeenth century ceased to work about 1713.

The only other connection of the family with the early iron industry of Furness was through Thomas Lower who in 1717, three years before his death, got a licence to "dig delve search for and get" in certain customary lands in Martin [near Dalton] "all such quantities of iron ore or mine as he shall there find, carry away . . . at his will and pleasure".[3] There is however no trace of any mining having been done under this lease, and at his death it was granted elsewhere.

Another commercial concern of Sarah Fell's was the sending of cargoes of produce to Liverpool, to Bristol, and to Cornwall. Sarah had made contacts with merchants at Bristol in July 1673 when she had gone there with her mother to meet George Fox on his return from America. Several Bristol merchants were Friends. Between January 1674 and January 1675 trading by ship was done both with Liverpool and Bristol. Considerable sums of

[1] Abraham MSS. 26.
[2] Dix MSS. z/3 10 v [July] 1684.
[3] Alfred Fell, *The Early Iron Industry of Furness*, p. 33.

money were invested by neighbours in these ventures; Margaret Petty of Urswick lent £25, William Postlethwaite of Little Urswick lent £15, and other sums were £12, £10, £6, all for 'our voyage with corn to Bristol', while Matthew Fell the tailor whose work clothed the Fell family lent £4 for the Liverpool voyage. Sarah herself managed the business arrangements, in Ulverston, but chiefly in Dalton, where at one stage expense was caused by the delay when the vessel was stopped by the customs officer. It was however soon discharged after Sarah's visit in person. The cargo included bigg (barley), groats, wheat and oats. Forty pounds and twenty pounds were spent on buying wheat at Lancaster, though some must have been grown in the neighbourhood of Ulverston. There were several partners in the venture, Margaret Fox, Thomas Lower, the three unmarried Fell sisters, James Lancaster of Walney and Joseph Sharp of Marsh Grange. Advantage was taken of the voyage to send food to Isabel Yeamans then at Bristol—two hogsheads of meal, and several pots of salt butter.

On the return voyage glass bottles were brought for sale to Myles Dodding of Conishead and William Kirkby of Ashlack Hall.[1]

In 1677 another ship-load of goods was sent, this time to Cornwall where Thomas Lower had an estate, including an interest in tin mines. Sarah visited the ship and gave 1/2 to the 'shipmen when I went aboard'. George Fox had money in this venture. The cargo included oats and corn largely from the Swarthmoor fields and iron from Force Forge, and on its return journey it carried brandy, a quart of which was sold to Isabel Yeamans for 1/–, and two gallons for 8/– to John Fell, shopkeeper of Ulverston, and a cartful of wine was sold in Lancaster. Henry Coward travelled on this ship to arrange in Cornwall for the sale of the corn and iron.

A little light is thrown by the entries in the Account Book on the social relations of the Fell family with their neighbours. In addition to the presents from William Kirkby of venison and a hare, the Fells on one occasion had a loan of £20 from 'old John Kirkby' of Coniston Hall, through the good offices of one of his servants, a Quaker. Once they lent Myles Dodding of

[1] *S.F. Act. Bk.* p. 533.

Conishead £30, no interest being charged. Thomas Lower was on visiting terms with the Andertons of Bardsea Hall. He also received presents from time to time—one wonders if they came from patients grateful for his medical care (in 1675 he told Margaret he was so thronged with patients that he hardly had time to write)[1]—one such being from Captain Hudleston, a member of an ancient family living at Millom Castle, South Cumberland, who sent him two turkeys, two capons and a piece of venison. Why these facts creep into the Account Book is because the servants bringing the presents or the servants of the house visited received gratuities in return. No reason is given for a visit to the Puritan, Roger Sawrey of Broughton Tower, made by Sarah and Rachel, when one shilling was given to the servants.

Beggars, sometimes feeble-minded (called 'Bedlemers' from the Bethlehem Hospital) called at the Hall, and were given small sums of money. There was a wider charity to Quaker work and individuals. Presents of 1/- or 2/- were given to girls going to London to apprenticeship or service, a Swarthmoor Friend returning from London to visit her relatives was given 1/- by Margaret Fox, and 6d. from each of the three sisters; larger sums were given to Joseph Nicholson and his wife when they went on Quaker ministry to New England, and Sarah carefully looked after his land for him during his absence. A poor man who had lost his vessel, another who had lost a cow, and another who had lost money out of his pocket, all were helped, though none too lavishly! In the days before there was fire insurance, the Fells responded to appeals to help victims of fires in Cheshire, Northampton and as far away as Southampton. Larger sums were given to the 'Stock', as the fund was called which Friends subscribed for the expenses of their Meeting and for the poor among their members.

Sarah had charge of all the money collected at the three local meetings, Swarthmoor, Hawkshead, Cartmel, and it was she who disbursed the gifts on the order of the Meetings to those who needed help, in clothes, food or rent. The conscientious and regular attendance at these Meetings by the Fells, mother and daughters, is seen in the careful entries of expenses, charged of course to their personal accounts. Once Margaret Fox and

[1] Camb. Jnl. II, 309.

Sarah rode as far as Portinscale, on Derwentwater, to attend a Meeting at Hugh Tickell's, the cost being 5/6. In April 1676 Margaret and Sarah went with Thomas Lower and William Penn to an important meeting at the home of John Blaykling, near Sedbergh. It was here that the question of women's meetings, described in the next chapter, was discussed. To attend a General Meeting at Lancaster cost 4/6, and in June 1677 the three sisters and their mother rode to a Women's Meeting held at Coppull, in South Lancashire, the expenses of which came to £1.9.3. When Lawrence Newton, a Friend of Height on Cartmell Fell, died and left money for the building of one of the earliest Meeting houses in England, Sarah attended to much of the business. The first Meeting House at Lancaster was built about the same time, and both Swarthmoor and Hawkshead Meetings contributed well to the fund.

Most typical of Margaret Fox's generosity was her payment of £20 to Roger Haydock of Coppull, to be sent to Cheshire Friends. When she and her daughters were at Coppull in June 1677, they went on into Cheshire, where at a large Meeting, informers were present. Because she had preached she had been fined £20. But the Cheshire Friends for allowing the meeting had also been fined £20. Margaret therefore on her return home sent £20 to repay them. Two months later however the £20 was returned to Margaret, for the Cheshire Friends 'would not take it'.[1] These fines were meant of course to ruin Friends— £20 in those days would be worth about £200 nowadays.

III. The Family

George Fox lived at Swarthmoor, on his first visit after his marriage, for twenty-one months, from June 1675 until March 1677. Much of his time was occupied by his completing the dictation of his *Journal*, and the writing of a number of Epistles to Friends, and by receiving many visitors, Friends from far and near, and neighbouring non-Friends and even some of his former persecutors such as Colonel Kirkby. Entries in the Account Book record the carriage of presents to him—three salmon sent from Lancaster, and a runlet of wine from Newcastle; a number of

[1] *S.F. Act. Bk.* p. 484.

things were bought for him by Sarah, silk laces, writing paper, ink, paste-board, parchment, juniper berries (used then for dropsical illnesses), almanacks, red herrings, stockings, tobacco pipes (two entries!—perhaps for presents as well as his own use), and at the end of 1676 Sarah paid £6.13.4. 'for a white horse for Father', ready for his journey in March.

We have seen that the Lowers were living at Swarthmoor until mid-1676 when they bought and moved to Marsh Grange. Shortly before Margaret Fox left London to return home (1675) Thomas Lower had sent her money with which to buy various garments. Instead of a coat for him (as he was going to convert his cloak into a riding coat for the summer), he wanted a gown of hair for his wife, and two barrateen[1] hoods such as Rachel already had, a pair of shoes for himself, a hat and a coat for his little daughter, and a French hat 'large enough in the head' for George Fox.[2] These items did not appear in the Account Book, where however Sarah noted a number of household needs for them at the time of their removal and later—one dozen trenchers, a side of mutton, a bed mat, a bedstead from Lancaster, dishes of various kinds, candles and candlesticks, a child's bed, ribbons, a leather purse, lace, garters, and 'a little rattle that I bought for Margery Lower' (then two months old). The third Lower child Humphrey was born a few months after they had made their home at Marsh Grange, in November 1676, and the entries record presents from the Fells to the midwife, and the baby's wet-nurse, and the father bought for 1½d. a pair of cradle strings for his son and heir.

Before the Lowers left Swarthmoor the widowed Isabel Yeamans and her nine-year-old daughter Rachel had come, some time before November 1675. Isabel's son, 'little Will Yeamans', had already been living there for more than a year. His uncle described Will, at six, as a 'dainty fine, good-natured child; learns finely, fine and orderly',[3] and that he and the baby Margaret Lower were very dear to each other.[4] The healthy climate

---

[1] *Barrateen* probably means *barragon*, a Lonsdale dialectal word meaning *fustian*.
[2] Spence MSS. III, 174.
[3] Camb. Jnl. II, 308.
[4] Spence MSS. III, 165.

of Furness had much improved Will's health, since he had left Bristol. Sometimes Isabel went visiting Friends. When she rode into Cumberland Sarah's boy servant, Tom Harrison, went with her. Sarah gave her 5/– for the journey, and lent Tom 1/–.

Three months later, in June, Isabel lost her little daughter Rachel. Nothing in the Account Book tells us how this ten-year-old girl died. There is simply the entry, 'By mo given Ann Daniell for her pains about Rachel Yeamans when she died and some burnes water given her, 5/–'.[1] At her funeral at Sunbreck, £2.7.3. was given to the poor.[2] She was the third child Isabel had lost. Her only remaining son Will lived to adult life but died of consumption when he was twenty-eight. Isabel stayed on at Swarthmoor, and in September she 'went towards York'. Again Tom Harrison accompanied her, and for the first part of her journey, the crossing of the first arm of Morecambe Bay, she had also with her Susannah and Rachel, as all three attended a Meeting at Cartmel. Just before, her mare had been shod, in readiness for the long journey over rough moorland roads, and she was given £1.5.0 and her boy 2/–.

Back at Swarthmoor next month, Isabel stayed the winter there, several items such as garters, ash-coloured ribbon, and black silk lace being bought for her. During this time she wrote a fine letter to women Friends throughout the country, appealing to them to take their proper and right share in the women's Meetings (see next chapter). Her only visit that winter seems to have been to Kendal, with Thomas Lower, but that must have been no easy task, as riding over the fells in January means meeting snow and storm.

In March 1677 the Account Book tells us that Isabel went to Bristol, Thomas Lower going with her most of the way as he was visiting Cornwall on business, and Sarah accompanying them to Lancaster. For her journey Isabel had £2.3.0 and Thomas Lower £5.5.0.

During these years 1673–8 there were four grandchildren living at Swarthmoor, Margaret and Margery Lower, both born

---

[1] S.F. Act. Bk. p. 285.

[2] Ibid. p. 309. An old copy-book of little Rachel's still exists, and in it has been written, 'R.Y. deceased about the 5th hour in the morning upon the 21st day of the 4th month being the 4th day of the week: 1676.'

there, and Rachel and Willie Yeamans. Of these four two died
in that period, Margaret when only twenty months old, before
her sister was born, in addition to Rachel who died at ten years.
The only other mention of grandchildren is the present of ginger-
bread to 'little Charles Fell' from Sarah,[1] and the present of 100
quills sent by Susannah Fell for her niece Bethiah Rous in
London, when at ten and a half years she was learning to write.
She may have been on a visit to the Hall the following year, as
Matthew Fell the tailor was paid 1/11 for 'firritt thred and work'
for her,[2] and it is hardly possible that the country tailor was
employed to make garments to be sent to London.

When James Pennington's wife ceased to be nurse to Margaret Lower at a year old, a pewter suckling bottle costing
2/4 was bought, and Sarah gave the baby a hat, and the nurse
received presents from the sisters. Later a porringer and a pan
were bought for the child, and leading strings when at a year
and three-quarters she was beginning to toddle. 'Treacle and
comfits for little Margaret', and a few days later 'treacle and
saffron', and again 'treacle and sugar candy for little Margaret',
all before she is eight months old, were given her.

Besides the Primer given to Will Yeamans there is frequent
mention of clothes for him; garters, white fustian for sleeves and
drawers, a hat costing as much as 5/-, buttons, silk and the
making of a vest, gloves, a little comb, and stockings, and the
tailor is paid for making his clothes. At the age of six he was
given a knife costing one penny.

Family illnesses are only known through the herbs or herbal
medicines bought for their cure. Cinnamon water, juniper
berries, aniseed, hiera picra (compound of aloes and carrella) are
used, and treacle with turmeric, and saffron and ale make a
drink for the cure of jaundice (called janesse in the Lancashire
speech) on several occasions, specially for 'us three maid sisters'.[3]
'Eelets and fennigreeke seeds for Pegg Gowth's knee',[4] 'Bur-
gandy pitch and frensh flyes for Edmond Adlington when he
was here not well',[5] 'diascordium, liquorice and anneseeds for
little Marjery Lower, Bro. Lower's Acct'.[6] '40 leetches to blood
with for sister Rachel',[7] mithridate for Willy Yeamans 'when

---

[1] *Ibid.* p. 423.   [2] *Ibid.* p. 505.   [3] *Ibid.* p. 383.   [4] *Ibid.* p. 249.
[5] *Ibid.* p. 253.   [6] *Ibid.* p. 253.   [7] *Ibid.* p. 493.

he had a cold',[1] white wine 'for physic',[2] brandy, and 'ale for sisters Susannah and Rachel for a diet drink',[3] are among the entries.

Perhaps the most curious items are 'by mo pd John Fell smith, for making a collar for sister Susannah and setting her issue 3/6' and four months later 'by mo pd John Fell smith for mending sister Susannah's collar 6d.' Norman Penney gives the following explanation, 'This seems to refer to a metal collar which was connected with an issue or running sore, set up often in those days on the neck or elsewhere as a derivative. It had a barbarous appearance'.[4]

A few more items, some rather unexpected, fill out the picture of life in the 'seventies at Swarthmoor. Tobacco and pipes are in 'Mother's Account', probably to be given as presents to the men servants. Susannah buys a 'little pocket looking-glass' for 4d., and Rachel a pair of scissors for 2d.; twice (in June 1674 and May 1677) the 'three maid sisters', Thomas Lower accompanying them the first time, rode to Cartmell Well, a medicinal well on the shore of Morecambe Bay. Why the expense of the first visit was so high, 9/– compared with 1/2 for the later one is not explained. In October 1674 Sarah bought for 1/4 a vizard mask for herself, and a year and a half later she bought two for 2/6, for herself again and Rachel. One wonders how they can have been used, specially as in letters to Friends generally George Fox deprecates in words of scorn the wearing of anything so frivolous and deceiving.

'By mo pd Leo: Fells wife, yt shee paid Rich. Petty wife of ye Nooke in pt of 4/6 for a sheep, that a mastiff dog of ours worried long since, upon sistr. Susannah's account because shee was some cause of preventing ye dogg from hanging before, 2/6.'[5] Behind that entry must lie much family discussion.

Towards the end of the book is the note of 1/– expense when 'mother was summoned to appear before the Commissioners, about the money given by my Father to the poor and school of Ulverston',[6] a legacy twenty years old of Judge Fell's, when the school, now grown to Ulverston Grammar School, was founded.

[1] *Ibid.* p. 189. [2] *Ibid.* p. 1. [3] *Ibid.* p. 353.
[4] *Ibid.* p. 520. [5] *Ibid.* p. 371. [6] *Ibid.* p. 479.

In 1676 and 1677 there are some entries which tell us that Sarah was imprisoned at Dalton. On 5th May 1676 she gives 'little Margerie's nurse when I went to prison to Dalton',[1] 2/–, and ten days later Margaret Fox gives the nurse 2/– more while Sarah adds 'by mo left with Sister Rachel to lie out at home, £1.17.2',[2] which we can presume is petty cash for Rachel with which to housekeep while Sarah was in prison. But Sarah was in no mood to submit quietly[3]—she wrote to a sugar merchant, David Poole, of Preston, about her imprisonment (why a sugar merchant and not a lawyer we cannot tell), and in the following March she paid Ellis Hookes 1/– 'for searching the office at London about my imprisonment'. But she was out of prison long before this; in fact, it seems only to have lasted for a month, as on 9th June 1676 she 'received of sister Rachel of the money she had of me to lie out, 1/9'.[4] The food in Dalton jail, or the close confinement to one so active as Sarah, necessitated the purchase of '1 pint of stomach water, 8d.', which having paid as part of a family account, she carefully repaid a day or two later from her own account.[5] Finally, in December a little belatedly (unless the entry itself is late), Sarah records that George Fox gave 2/6 to Thomas Benson, 'bayliff of the Liberties for his civility to me being a prisoner'.

Nothing in the Account Book gives any idea why Sarah was imprisoned, nor is there any mention in Besse's *Sufferings* or contemporary letters. Possibly a testimony, written by Sarah in 1675, against the payment of tithes may show that her imprisonment was due to this refusal, which was for many generations a most fruitful source of persecution. 'I never paid tithes of any sort', wrote Sarah in the Lancashire Women's Quarterly Meeting Book, 1675 to 1777, 'nor anything of that kind, nor none for me, though it hath been several times demanded of me, at which time, a testimony arises fresh in my heart against them. to deny it. And I believe as I keep to that testimony, I shall never pay any, which is the desire of my heart, never to depart from whatever may be met with, upon that account.'

As Sarah Fell's accounts were accurate and careful, so was her

---

[1] *Ibid.* p. 271. [2] *Ibid.* p. 275. [3] *Ibid.* p. 275. [4] *Ibid.* p. 278.
[5] *Ibid.* pp. 299 and 300.

rule firm. It is characteristic of her method that any member of the family who journeyed should keep careful account of money spent. So we find that when Margaret Fox and Rachel returned in December 1673 from their five-months' visit and travels in the south, they had to return to the family stock £1.6.9, left over from the journey—the original sum they had set out with is unknown owing to the loss of the earlier pages of the book. When Joseph Sharpe, their trusted servant at Marsh Grange returned in September 1674 from his journey with Margaret and others to see Fox during his imprisonment, he gave back 6½d.! Sarah had given her mother £10, and Thomas Lower £2.6.0 for the journey and visit.

Before the Account Book closes George Fox had left Swarthmoor; his health having improved by his stay there, in March 1677 he started off again to preach and visit Friends. Sarah gave him £5, and to his wife and Rachel who were to accompany him into Yorkshire she gave £1, though on their return a month later she found she had to increase the sum by 7/7 to her mother and 6/11 to her sister.

Sarah's care and diligence and conscientiousness in recording income and expenditure is consistent with the belief in the wholeness of life, characteristic of Quaker teaching. In the case of Margaret Fox and her daughters it was one of the things which grew out of belief in the immanence of God. It is perhaps not surprising that for nearly a century and a half throughout the Society of Friends in Great Britain, among the advices read from time to time in Meetings for Worship, there should be one entitled *Keeping Clear Accounts*. It runs: 'Whilst engaged in business, let Friends be very careful to make themselves well acquainted with their annual income and expenditure. This will be facilitated by adopting, and conscientiously keeping up, a clear and methodical system of accounts, in regard not only to trade, but also to domestic and personal expenses. These accounts should be so kept that they will be easily understood if at any time it is necessary for others to see them. Whilst the foregoing advice is specially intended for those who are engaged in trade, the principles embodied are applicable in almost every sphere of life. It is the duty of all to arrange their expenditure with due regard to their income; and clear and correct account-keeping is a means of avoiding reckless expenditure on the one hand or unjustifiable accumulation of wealth on the other.'

This 'Advice' was drawn up in 1826, but Sarah Fell put it into practice earlier by a century and a half.

Chapter Nineteen

WOMEN'S MEETINGS, AND THE WORK OF MARGARET FOX AND HER DAUGHTERS FOR THEM

'*What he [Fox] was concerned with was to give them [women] their place, their right place, and to stir them up to take it. His prime motive, as in the case of the Men's Meetings, was to liberate for the service of the Church the gifts of government which lay dormant and barren both in men and women, though the need of their time called for their use. The venture, in the case of the Women's Meetings, was a daring one, and taxed seventeenth-century feminine capacity to the utmost, but this only adds to its significance as a landmark in the movement for giving woman her true place of equal partnership with man.*'

The Second Period of Quakerism, pp. 273–4.

THE spiritual equality of men and women had been taken for granted from the very beginning of Quakerism. We have already seen how, for example, Elizabeth Hooton was the first woman preacher among George Fox's followers as early as 1647, and how Margaret Fell (as she was then) in 1666 had written a book on the right and indeed the necessity for women to speak in the church and to exercise their spiritual gifts. This was written not for the conversion of Friends, but of those outside. The Quakers believed that Paul meant what he said when he told the Galatians 'there can be no male and female; for ye all are one man in Christ Jesus.' And they therefore acted on it. It is significant that on the spiritual side there has never been any occasion for a struggle by Quaker women to wrest a 'right' from their menfolk. This has obviously had much influence on both the men and women of the Society, and on their relationship to each other.

There has not been quite the same serene development however where the work of organization and discipline has been concerned.

George Fox's spiritual gifts were supplemented by his gift for

organization. The savage persecution of Friends (with consequent death of many of the leaders) in the first fifteen years convinced him that for the very life of the Society an organization
must be created which would not only cover the British Isles
but other countries to which Quakerism had already spread.
'The movement was suffering from arrested organization and
poverty of leadership.'[1] In 1666, as soon as he was released from
his imprisonment at Scarborough, he travelled throughout the
country, in great bodily discomfort and considerable ill-health,
and everywhere gathered those already convinced of the truths
they had received, into corporate bodies who could and would
look after and help each other. In this work, he already had to
build upon the experience of some of the Meetings in the north
which had as early as 1654 created 'Meetings for Discipline', for
the oversight of the members, the help of the persecuted, and
the regularization of marriages. And so were formed the
Monthly, Quarterly and eventually the Yearly Meetings, which
are still the basis of the Society's organization. Fox, however,
with his views on the spiritual place of women, and with his
knowledge and experience of the work both spiritual and
practical of women such as Margaret Fell and many others, took
the bold step of calling on women to form themselves also into
groups for the work of the church. The settling of the Women's
Meetings was seriously taken in hand in the summer of 1671,[2]
after Fox had recovered from his illness and while Margaret was
with him during her fourth visit to London. But before describing this more widespread organization, we must notice the much
earlier establishment of two Meetings of women in London as
early as 1660. It is characteristic that both these meetings grew
out of the urgent needs of the time during a year of great persecution and suffering. The Box Meeting (which still exists in London, and has an unbroken record of minutes from 1671) was
composed entirely of women, and got its peculiar name from
the fact that it gathered money into a box, and disbursed it for
the relief of the poor and needy.[3] Its formation was due directly
to George Fox. It met once a week, and was not accountable

[1] *Second Period of Qism.*, p. 251.
[2] *Ibid.*, p. 273.
[3] Camb. Jnl. II, 342.

to any other body. The other meeting of women, possibly formed a little later, worked in association with the Two Weeks' Men's Meeting, and its first work was the visiting of the sick and the prisoners, and in looking after the poor, the widows and the fatherless.[1] Its work developed very soon to include the moral care of women Friends, the stopping of false reports or difficulties tending to disunity among Friends. It found places for Quaker maid-servants, and dealt with women who married non-Friends or who went to a 'priest' to be married. It was this Two Weeks' Women's Meeting which set the stage for the later organization which Fox set on foot in 1671. This was the formation of Women's Monthly and Quarterly Meetings, to come together at the same time and place as the Men's, but to have definite pieces of work to do, distinct from but complementary to the men's. Over and over again in the many Epistles which he felt obliged to send forth over many years, concerning these meetings, he used the expression, that women were and should be 'helpsmeet for men'. He wanted to use and to develop their special gifts. Their particular work was (as in the case of the Two Weeks' Women's Meeting, which was only a London and not a nation-wide meeting) to visit and relieve the poor and needy, and the imprisoned sufferers from persecution, to see to the education of children, the employment and apprenticeship of young women Friends, the proper care of marriages, and the consistent refusal to pay tithes.

When we remember the subordinate position of women in the Protestant Church generally (though women in some of the Puritan sects sat alongside the men in their business meetings) it is perhaps not surprising to find that George and Margaret Fox met with considerable opposition to their formation of Women's Meetings. Opposition also came because there were some Quakers who seemed to have still much of the spirit of the Ranters (John Perrot, as mentioned elsewhere, had) and who repudiated any form of outward organization whatever. Some of the men separatists strongly objected to appearing before the Women's Meetings in addition to the Men's Meetings, before marriage. Some, alas, of their opposers were hostile through jealousy and envy—of this there is abundant evidence in the

[1] *Second Period of Qism.*, 272.

letters of the time. The opposition centred in two Westmorland
Friends, who had done fine work previously, John Story and
John Wilkinson. It spread through many counties, to Wiltshire
(in 1673, just after Fox's return from America), to Buckinghamshire, Bristol and Gloucestershire (in 1678) to Hertford (in
1680), and lasted well into the '80's, though Story died in 1681
and Wilkinson a little later, and both had lost standing and
influence by 1681.

Throughout these sad years however, Fox, supported by
practically all the best of the Society, kept a fine dignity, and
faith that he was in his work of organization guided by God—
working in the light of Christ—and the end of the struggle
proved him right, for it was his work which prevailed, and not
that of his opposers. Before he died (in 1691) he felt that unity
was to a large extent restored though in some parts disaffection
still continued for another decade. Throughout he had never
acted the dictator, but had striven to persuade by the spoken and
written word.

With this as background, let us see what part in the development of women's meetings was played by Margaret Fox and
her daughters. Margaret's work for and influence on the Quaker
movement and its members all through the first period of 'seed-
sowing' had been of such great importance that it would indeed
be surprising if we did not find that her influence extended into
the period of growth, settlement and first-fruiting. The evidence
for this lies partly in letters to her or about her, and partly in the
minutes of the Meetings themselves. As early as 1672—a year
after the first Women's Monthly and Quarterly Meetings were
begun—we find a north-country Friend, Jean Simcock, writing
to Margaret that she is making arrangements to have Margaret's
letter to the Women's Quarterly Meeting distributed. She adds
that there were many Friends who objected to collecting money
(namely, for relief and the upkeep of the movement, the 'Stock'
mentioned in Sarah Fell's Account Book), and also who had
'heard of thy letter and was troubled that the dispute should go
so much abroad'.[1] This most probably refers to the beginning of
the Story-Wilkinson objection to the women's meetings. It was
in this year that Margaret went into Yorkshire visiting Friends.

[1] Swm. MSS. I, 365.

Most significant to the appraisement of Margaret's influence is in a letter written to her in 1684 by Gulielma Penn from her home at Worminghurst, Sussex. After a most loving salutation she continued:

In the unity of the Spirit of Truth . . . I see thee over all those bad spirits, that may touch thy heel but no further; and it rises in my mind as I am writing, something that I saw concerning thee in my sleep long ago, at the beginning of these bad spirits. I saw thee, and dear George and many Friends in a Meeting, and the power of the Lord was greatly manifested and methoughts there came dark wicked spirits into the meeting and they strove exceedingly against the Life that was in the meeting, and their chief aim was first at thee and George, but mostly at thee, and they strove to hurt thee, but methought thou gottest so over them they could not touch thee, but only went to tear some little part of thy clothes, but thou escaped unhurt or touched, and a sweet rejoicing and triumph was over them through the meeting.

It was long ago [this letter was written twelve years after the trouble began], but it rose now I was writing to thee fresh in my mind, and the Lord has so brought it to pass, but thy life reigns over them all, for it was thee they began with, but the Lord has, and will give thee victory over them all, to the joy and comfort of his people.[1]

Margaret Fox was often deeply hurt by the opposition that she encountered from some Friends. John Burnyeat, one of the Cumberland 'First Publishers of Truth', traveller in Scotland and Ireland and America, founder of Baltimore Yearly Meeting, pointed out to her that one reason for the trouble with Story and Wilkinson and their followers was their desire to shun persecution in the tragic days following the passing of the Second Conventicle Act.[2] Fox had pressed Friends to continue to hold their Meetings in their accustomed places and to go on refusing to pay tithes and other Church taxes, and those who fell were to be persuaded if possible to come back into the fellowship of the Meeting, and confess to their weakness. Hence, in the old minute books, we find 'Condemnations', written as confessions by those who had 'gone out' and 'come in again'. Story and Wilkinson and their friends strongly objected to this discipline.

---

[1] Caton MSS. III, 460–2. Copied into this book long after Caton's death (1668), probably by Rachel (Fell) Abraham.

[2] Portfolio 31. 127, dated 1676–7, Library, Friends' House, London.

William Penn in March 1676 wrote to Fox when the latter was at Swarthmoor, describing the separatists as 'foolish, short-sighted and puffed up spirits', as people who 'have inwardly departed from the living God'. But he added, 'my soul is in full confidence of its downfall'. He begged Fox to attend the Meeting in the north to be held at John Blaykling's, Draw-well, near Sedbergh, where the whole matter was to be discussed in the near future, adding, 'and because poor Margaret is so much smit at, and run upon (as I believe never woman was, for which God the righteous judge will judge, and plead with them) as if she was the cause, and of an implacable temper, without bowels, or the spirit of reconciliation, to show them that she can pass by all that passed between them that concerns herself; and so make the most of the good or the tender things, if it arise never so little in either of them, this would be a deadly stroke upon that back-biting spirit, and so confound them that smite, yea so stop their mouths, that there would be no place for them to hide in; and then would this dark serpent's head lie so fair for the blow.'[1]

The Meeting was held early in April 1676, but George Fox was not present. We know from Sarah's Account Book that Margaret Fox went, with her daughter Sarah, Thomas Lower and William Penn, who was then staying with them at Swarth-moor largely for the purpose of this meeting.

A year and a half later Margaret had to report to William Penn how the 'separate' meeting refused to read the epistles sent to them by both Penn and Fox from Holland, very 'precious' Epistles, meant to bring peace. 'Some of them grows more hard and obstinate than ever', she told him, 'others that is more simple is troubled and tormented. We wait in hope, for the return of such. Friends Meetings [are] more precious, powerful, fresh and lively since they went from them, than they have been many years before.'[2]

Next year, the sad controversy still continuing, Mary Woolley of London wrote to Margaret for her comfort. Calling her 'mother of the faithful', she told of her love and loyalty to her and her husband, being thankful that 'no temptation ever takes place with me to dishonour what the Lord honours in this day

[1] Luke Howard MSS., Library, Friends' House, London.
[2] Portfolio 36, Library, Friends' House, London. Dated Oct. 1677.

of deep exercise and trial which is great amongst us'. She longs for a return of their former unity and assures Margaret of her 'faithful love' to her.

In spite of the 'separation' however, the Women's Monthly and Quarterly Meetings were generally established, though not throughout the country.

They were also set up in the American colonies, and in 1682 a letter to Margaret Fox from three Friends (two men and a woman) in Maryland gives strong confirmation of her influence not only in the Society as a whole but particularly on this organization of women's meetings. After calling her a 'dear and tender nursing mother' they tell her how much her travail of soul has strengthened and comforted them. Then, addressing George Fox as well as Margaret, they write of their fellowship with them 'who are as epistles written in our hearts, and your good instructions and holy precepts given forth from the spirit of God . . . we all know, and in readiness of mind do practise, . . . that all we are concerned with may come under the government of good order prescribed to us by you, whom the Lord put it into your hearts to first set up and establish men and women's meetings; and this we know as friends come to live in that blessed power that moved in your hearts to establish these meetings we shall labour together for the prosperity of the Truth. . . .' They beg George and Margaret to send Friends across the seas who really know how men's and women's meetings should be carried out, and only let those go there on the public service of Truth who are well approved by them as wise and spiritually minded. Finally they ask Margaret for her advice how to deal with Friends who slacken in their loyalty, for she and George Fox had met similar trouble.[1]

The date of the establishment of the Women's Meetings is of interest when it is set in its chronological frame. In 1670 the Second Conventicle Act had begun an orgy of persecution. In April 1671 Margaret was released from Lancaster, and in May went up to London, there to be with her husband at the Rous's home, he having recently recovered in health as the persecution eased off. Later in the same month they attended Yearly Meeting in London. In June Fox wrote a circular letter advocating the

[1] Spence MSS. III, 182–3.

establishment of women's Meetings.[1] In August he left for America, his wife returning to Swarthmoor. Two months later the Swarthmoor Women's Monthly Meeting met for the first time, it being the very first of its kind. The Women's Monthly Meeting at Kendal began in the next year, 1672, and at Lancaster in 1676, and other places at various later dates.

Their success much depended on the capacity of the leading members, particularly the 'clerk', as the chairman-secretary was, and still is, called. In that respect, Lancashire and Swarthmoor were fortunate, as Sarah Fell was the first clerk of the Swarthmoor Women's Monthly Meeting, and also of the Lancashire Women's Quarterly Meeting. Her sister Rachel took her place when Sarah married and went south. As for Margaret herself, she regularly attended the Monthly Meeting, and also the Quarterly, and to reach the latter meant crossing the sands over to Lancaster or beyond. This she continued to do until July 1698, when she was eighty-four years old, and within four years of her death. Her last Monthly Meeting signature is in 1700. Mary Lower, Susannah and Rachel were also most regular attenders. Isabel Yeamans attended these Meetings when she was staying at Swarthmoor, and her signature appears at other Women's Quarterly Meetings also. For instance, in July 1675 she is the last signatory out of twenty-seven (and therefore probably the clerk) of an Epistle sent from the Women's Monthly Meeting of Somerset, to the Box Meeting in London. The Epistle expresses the longing of these women that they may be used for the service of God.

A year later, when Isabel was at Swarthmoor, she boldly advocated Women's Meetings. Writing in October 1676, to Women Friends generally, soon after her return from Yorkshire, she told them how she had for long been 'pressed in spirit' to lay before them 'the weight and service of that great work which the Lord has called us unto in our Women's Meeting and the great necessity of our diligence and faithfulness therein . . . to be constant and frequent in coming together'. The necessities of the poor, the relief of the widows and fatherless, the visiting of the sick and afflicted—these are the 'true practice of the pure religion'. In addition it is the duty of women to admonish and

[1] *Second Period of Qism.,* p. 273.

reprove those who are 'drawn aside', and to teach the younger women, and each to follow in the 'footsteps of the holy women that have gone before us'. Women must also train their children with care, and 'not give way to a foolish pity or fond affection to indulge or bear with children'. Especially is sternness recommended when children or servants 'that profess the Truth' fail to attend Meeting or look out for wives or husbands 'in the world'. Reproof, advice and admonishment are suggested, but if ineffective, then two or three 'faithful women' should be asked to give their help; if these should fail, the matter should come before the Women's Meeting. 'Here will be work and business enough for us all that none need to be idle in God's service.' Isabel then gives many examples from the Bible for the position and work of women, emphasizing also that women were to be 'meethelps' to men. She denies the right of men to claim that they only shall be allowed to collect money![1]

The minutes of the early Swarthmoor and Lancashire Women's Meetings throw a vivid light on the work and spirit of this organization. The Swarthmoor Minute Book, bought for one shilling and sixpence by Sarah Fell from the shopkeeper of Ulverston, Richard Fell, who had bound and repaired the big Bible, covers the years from 1671 to 1700. The first sixteen pages are in Sarah's handwriting. At the first Meeting, in October 1671, a collection was taken for the support of the poor and for any future need, and at the next meeting in December at Hawkshead, it was decided to meet each month on the first Tuesday, in succession at Swarthmoor, Hawkshead and Cartmel. These earliest meetings are only briefly described; the first one at which detailed minutes were kept was held at Swarthmoor Hall in February 1674, when Margaret Fox, Mary Lower and Sarah were among those who signed as being present.

The business is varied, but the aim is consistent—relief, material help, spiritual discipline. Centuries before nursing, midwifery, social welfare and widow's pensions were thought of as national services, we find these women discussing and arranging for help of this sort among their own members. In February 1675 at Swarthmoor the following Minute, beauti-

[1] The only extant copy **located by IR before 1949 was (then) in Nottingham FMH. She later noted that Amy E. Wallis had found another copy among the records of Staindrop M.M.**

fully expressed by Sarah, was passed—'Whereas we have been informed that Mabel Brittaine hath exercised the place of a midwife, and that certain women have been long in travail, and have been delivered of dead children, under her hands; and some doth suppose that it was for want of judgment and skill in her. Therefore in tenderness and love to the Lord, who is the author and giver of Life, and to his Truth that we are made partakers of; and in love and tenderness to women and children (having had many things under examination, and thereupon to find her defective, in some cases), it is our judgment and testimony (and we do warn her) that she do not meddle in that employment hereafter (where there is any difficulty) without the help and assistance of another midwife; And if any do suffer thereon making use of her, for the future, they must take it upon themselves. For we have given this forth, for the clearing of the Truth, and ourselves; having a godly care upon us, and desires, for the good of all. And as for all words and discourses that hath been past, touching this concern, let them not be mentioned any more.'

Help to the poor and needy members of the Meeting is often given. Jane Strickland, widow, receives help (evidently help in kind) from the 'houses of Swarthmoor and Marsh Grange and Baycliffe' (the village where Leonard and Mary Fell lived), but if later on she needs more the rest of the Friends of Swarthmoor 'are to send her something'.

Jane Woodell is another pensioner of the Meeting, and she is mentioned frequently both in the Meeting Minutes and in Sarah Fell's Account Book. 'Also this day 6.9.1677 Sarah Fell of Swarthmoor gives account, that she hath bought three yards of cloth for a petticoat for old Jane Woodell, Swarthmoor Meeting, as was ordered formerly by the Meeting, which cost two shillings, tenpence halfpenny, which cloth is sent to her, and it's the order of this meeting that if she do not live to wear it out, then the petticoat is to be returned to the Woman's Meeting, to dispose of, as they see cause.'

Old Jane Woodell died a year and a quarter later, so the petticoat and an underwaistcoat given previously to her, find a home with Jane Fisher ('a poor woman of Swarthmoor Meeting', Sarah calls her in her Account Book), together with enough cloth to make two shifts. All these are to be returned to the Meeting if Jane does not live to wear them out. Perhaps these conditions are as much a comment on Sarah's care, and its influence on the members, as on the good wearing quality of homespun cloth.

Sometimes a member shows lack of gratitude for what is done for her. Ann Birkett of Cartmel 'let up a cross peevish spirit of prejudice in her against Friends without a cause', in spite of her 'distress and necessity'. But the Meeting 'cannot see her in such great want, as to suffer for want of food, but to assist her with some little, to sustain her outward body', so they gave two and sixpence to two competent Women Friends for the recalcitrant Ann's need. They were asked also to 'exhort her to cast out that cross wicked spirit (which hurts herself) and come to that, in which we can distribute to her necessity in love, and that she may receive it in the same, which will be for her own good, both inward and outward, which we much desire'. Next month one of the women visitors reported that Ann Birkett was 'rather more tender and sensible of Friends' love'.

While help in the form of money, food or rent was given to the old or sick, the younger were helped by gifts of material for them to work on for sale; there is for example the entry of £1.17.6 paid for some wool towards putting a Friend 'into a way of getting a livelihood'.

The Meeting also helped to find employment for the young people. There is the case of the twelve-year-old Isabel Colton who had recently lost her place, her mother Jane being very poor, and a pensioner of the meeting. The Meeting would prefer her 'to be kept among Friends, than to go to live with people of the world, which would do her hurt, and be apt to bring her up in wildness and vanity, which we hope living with a Friend may prevent'. After some search a mistress was found to take her and train her, but not to put her to 'anything more than she is able to perform, being she is but young', for twelve shillings a year. But Isabel was a problem, for she soon returned to her mother 'in a stubborn unservantlike state. . . notwithstanding Friends' trouble and care touching her at our last meeting'. What happened to Isabel we are not told. Her mother too showed an ungrateful spirit, but at a later Meeting it is recorded that she had confessed that she had done wrong and had 'vexed the good spirit of the Lord'.

One of the most important pieces of work of the Women's Monthly Meetings was the care for the marriages of their members. In the first place they aimed to see that each partner of the marriage was free, and had the consent of their near relatives; secondly, they aimed to have their members marry in the Society and not out of it, and thirdly, they disciplined any member who went to be married at a church by a priest. The legality of Quaker marriages without the offices of a clergyman had been settled in 1661 by the ruling of a Judge of Assize at Nottingham,[1] but the leaders of early Quakerism emphasized the need for great care in both the preparation for marriage and in conducting it in the true spirit of Christ. Friends who went to a clergyman or who married a non-Friend were appealed to, and if possible persuaded to write a paper condemning their action. To help the young people to be certain of their own minds, and to enter matrimony after due consideration, the consent of near relatives had to be reported to the Meeting, and the couple had to appear three times before the Monthly Meetings. All things being proved 'clear', a Meeting for Worhip was appointed at which the marriage could take place.

Sarah's Minutes sometimes remind us of the tempestuousness of the weather of Furness, so much so that the resulting paucity of numbers prevented business being done. In March 1673, she recorded that 'at this time, the weather was so extreme, and the highways blown up with snow, that none could travel, but with the hazard of their lives, which was the cause, that none of Swarthmoor Meeting was at Hawkshead'.

The last minutes in Sarah's handwriting appear in December 1680. Next year she married William Meade, and moved to London, where she became clerk to the Box Meeting, which she considerably reformed. She remained its clerk for twenty-seven years until within six years of her death in 1714. At Swarthmoor, Rachel Fell took her place, and though her writing and spelling are poor, her power of expression is not very inferior to her sister's. Sarah maintained a lively interest in her old Monthly Meeting, and from time to time sent generous contributions to

[1] Jnl. F.H.S. V, 139.

the Stock. Her gifts as much as three pounds in 1690 (representing thirty pounds in modern money) 'showing her tender and charitable sympathizing with us', were minuted. So the Swarthmoor Women's Monthly Meetings continued, faithfully attended by Margaret Fox, and also by her daughters. After 1697 Margaret does not seem to have attended, unless the meeting was at her own home.

The other Women's Meeting of which Sarah and later Rachel were clerks was the Quarterly Meeting for the whole county of Lancashire. Begun in 1675, the first sixteen pages of the Minute Book were written by Sarah, until 1680. She carefully described first of all the geographical make-up of the Quarterly Meeting. It consisted of four Monthly Meetings, Swarthmoor, 'being behind the sands' with its three Particular Meetings; Lancaster with its six meetings (Yealand, Chippin, Wyresdale, Wrea, and Fylde, in addition to Lancaster); a third including Bickerstaffe, Penketh, Knowsley, Coppull (near Wigan), and Manchester; and the fourth, Rossendale, Marsdon, Sawley and Oldham; eighteen in all. The meetings, though called 'Quarterly', met only twice a year, always between April and September. The first was held at Lancaster, the second at 'Widow Haydock's at Coppull'; later Lancaster was the usual meeting-place as being more convenient. The chief business, other than the spiritual fellowship, was (in the early days) to bring in testimonies, where women were concerned, against the payment of tithes or any other church rates. In those cases where Friends had succumbed to pressure, and paid tithes, then the Meeting was to attempt to persuade them to write a paper condemning their action. These papers were each individually expressed, and copied into the Minute Book. Any other matter affecting good order in the church could be brought up also; the field was as wide as necessity or circumstances made it. Perhaps nowadays it is difficult to understand the energy with which Friends from the earliest time down to 1873 (when legal relief came) waged a constant battle against the payment of tithes. It was based on the belief that Christ's teaching had been freely given to man, and no man ought therefore to be paid for passing on that teaching. Also a State Church, they held, was contrary to the liberty which the Gospel conferred. The suffering that Friends put up with in the bearing of this testimony was prodigious—a number died, lingering for years in loathsome prisons at the dictate of a clergyman or tithe-farmer, hundreds were imprisoned for varying periods, and still more hundreds suffered loss of property which even in the century from 1730 to 1830 amounted to over £767,000.[1] It is perhaps not surprising that some Friends could not stay the course, even in the seventeenth century when enthusiasm was at its highest. In the Minutes of the Lancashire Women's Quarterly Meetings we have a vivid picture of the two-fold struggle, one against the State-Church exactions, the other against those in the Society who would compromise the standing of their fellows. It was a right instinct to get the women as well as the men to make their written 'testimonies', and so offer not only an individual stand, but one in which family unity, or at least unity of husband and wife, was certain and sure.

It must have been a joy to Sarah to be able to record at the last Meeting where she was clerk (in 1680), that great satisfaction was felt with the staunchness of women against the payment of tithes.

It was expected that every one of the Meetings in the county should send representatives to the Quarterly Meeting; when they failed to do so a message would be sent asking them the reason, or if they disapproved of Women's Meetings. Manchester women sometimes failed to come, and Oldham women, but at a subsequent meeting it would be reported that there was no disapproval, but that 'some occasions hindered'. Once the old record says that the menfolk were so imprisoned that their wives could not be spared to come. This was in 1684.

Another subject discussed by the Women's Quarterly Meeting in addition to being dealt with by the Monthly Meetings, was the discipline of members who had already been married by a priest. There again persuasion and admonition were used, and every effort made to bring the defaulter back to Quakerism. In 1677 a paper of condemnation is read from a member of Swarthmoor Meeting, 'touching her sorrow and repentance for her being married with a priest, and of her great desire to be restored into the unity with the Lord's people; with which we are refreshed, and our hearts truly gladed.' Exhortation follows that

[1] *Later Periods of Qism.*, R. M. Jones.

Friends should have 'an holy eye' to prevent such things, specially as they had been occurring at Lancaster, Fylde and Manchester. These strictures against intermarriage with a non-Friend were due to the use of the services of a paid clergyman as much as or even more than the fact of union with one who did not see 'Truth'. In modern times this 'testimony' has been dropped—perhaps it is hoped that the non-Friend partner will become a Friend—but it continued until at least the end of the nineteenth century.

After 1690 other subjects are minuted. In 1692 Lancashire women Friends advocated the appointment of schoolmasters and mistresses in every Meeting, a recommendation which was not followed everywhere, though in 1696 Leonard Fell was being helped by Gilbert Thompson (a notable schoolmaster of the Friends' School at Penketh, near Warrington) to find a schoolmaster for Swarthmoor.[1] They found James Goad, of Baycliffe, near Swarthmoor, a former pupil at Sedbergh, who went late in 1696 to Penketh school to study the methods of a Friends' school. This school at Swarthmoor continued under a number of schoolmasters for eighty years, one of its early pupils, under James Goad, being Margaret Fox's grandson, John Abraham.[2]

In 1695 the first warning was given by the Lancashire women Friends to keep their children from mixing more than was necessary with the 'world'. Later, appeals were made against luxury, 'superfluities' at marriages, births and burials. But there must have been happiness at Swarthmoor when Rachel brought back the news from Lancaster, three weeks before her aged mother's death, that a minute had been passed saying all was 'in good order', and that the Meeting had been very conscious of the presence of God among them.

Rachel, who took over the clerkship after Sarah's marriage, seems to have remained clerk until 1708, when she was fifty-five years old. Six years before, we have the first request made that Friends should avoid 'superfluity' in their dress, a subject which was, throughout the eighteenth century, to occupy the attention

[1] Dix MSS., Library, Friends' House, London.
[2] *Swarthmoor Meeting House, Ulverston,* by Harper Gaythorpe, p. 32 *seq.* (Kendal, 1910).

of Friends to a somewhat exaggerated extent. Margaret Fox had already seen the danger of that emphasis on outward things, and her advice we shall read in a later chapter.

That the Lancashire Women's Meeting believed in the fundamental importance of their work is shown, not only by the minutes which Sarah specially and her successors drew up, but also by a long Epistle which they sent out probably between 1675 and 1680 to all Women's Meetings 'everywhere'. Using many Biblical phrases as letters of early Friends so often did, the writers gave many examples from the Old and New Testaments of women prophets and religious workers. After reciting the story of the woman of Samaria, they add 'see what love and plainness be manifested unto this woman not despising her nor undervaluing her in the least, but he spake the plain everlasting truth unto her, and set up that worship of his own spirit unto her, there which remains and will remain for ever'. They remind their comrades of the brave women who were the first bringers of the news of Christ's resurrection, and the women in the early Church. Therefore, they add, let Quaker women take up their work and responsibility. Then follows, under ten heads, a recital of the work which needed to be done by both the Monthly and Quarterly Meetings of women, practical work which we have already seen was being done by the writers. The last two heads advise the purchase of a book for recording the business, one for each type of Meeting, and in them the collections are to be set down, and also testimonies against the payment of tithes.[1]

Both from the language of the Epistle, and the detail of the practical advice, one can clearly see the influence of Sarah Fell in its composition.

The story of the Fell influence on Women's Meetings would not be complete, however, without mention of Sarah's instructions 'how you may order the business in the Quarterly Women's Meeting Book',[2] written for the help of her sisters, Mary, Susannah and Rachel, a few days before she was married, and after ten years' experience of clerkship. Too long to be quoted here in full—they occupy one and a half pages of her

[1] **The only copy located by IR before 1949 was (then) in Nottingham FMH. She later noted that Amy E. Wallis had found another copy.**

[2] Thirnbeck MSS. 15.

small handwriting—they give detailed advice. On a sheet of paper the business should be written at the time, 'for then things are the freshest upon the mind, and words will rise most suitably to answer the matter in hand; and at leisure it may be written fair in the book, observing my way and method, that I have used formerly.' The names of each Meeting should be called out, and if no women have come from any, that Meeting should be written to, to find out the cause of neglect, and if necessary, reproved. At every September Meeting, inquiry has to be made as to 'clearness of their testimonies against tithes' and other Church dues. 'About the middle of the book, look, and there you will find the women's testimonies in order recorded, as the meetings are in the book.' Also papers of condemnation are to be fixed in the book, in an orderly way. 'What good papers or Epistles, of my Father's or other Friends, as comes to you, may be read in the Meetings, from time to time, as there is occasion: There are some loose in the book, that have been read formerly; which you may get Thomas Dockray to record some of the best and suitablest in the book, near the latter end of the book. I have often had it in my mind to record some of them in the book, but had so much business, etc., that I could not get it done; but would desire you, that it may not be neglected much longer. This in short is what is in my mind at present; and its my belief and confidence that the Lord God, who supplies all his people with what is needful, will fit and furnish you, in his holy wisdom, to perform and manage, this his work and service, as there shall be a necessity; unto whom I commit you, for strength, wisdom and counsel; to whom be praises for evermore.'[1]

Sarah Fell's work for the Lancashire Meetings closing in 1681, her mental and spiritual gifts were transferred, as has been mentioned, to the Box Meeting in London, of which she was clerk from July 1681 until August 1708. In 1692 she became clerk also and a little later keeper of the accounts of her local Women's Meeting, that for Plaistow and Barking, for her home was near by at Gooseyes, near Romford, Essex. Of this meeting she remained clerk until 1701, and for another five years her handwriting occurs occasionally in the minutes, and her gifts of money continue until her death in 1714.

[1] Published in full in Jnl. F.H.S. IX, 135–7.

Sarah's care and conscientiousness were equalled by her gift of expression. Her minutes still bring to the modern reader a vivid and living picture, whereas many of these old records in Minute Books are dull and lifeless. Hers are comparable to those of Thomas Ellwood, the friend and secretary of John Milton. Ellwood was 'considered one of the best Quaker writers by his contemporaries'.[1] Both he and Sarah had fathers who had been Justices of the Peace, and they had been reared in cultured and legal homes. It was not flattery which her friend Thomas Salthouse used when he told her that her recent letter to him was 'a very great rarity of a high price, having not had a letter so excellently penned and so eloquently expressed for many months'.[2]

In this chapter one Epistle has been described as having been sent out by the Lancashire Women's Quarterly Meeting. In London the women sent out Epistles rather more frequently, and in this work the four Fell sisters who lived there took a leading part. Usually in the Epistle, women elsewhere were urged to group themselves together to carry out the practical work of the Society, and to maintain the purity of their beliefs.

These Epistles were signed by upwards of thirty prominent women Friends, and frequently one or more of the Fell sisters is included. Among the manuscripts of the Box Meeting is an Epistle signed by twenty-nine leading women of London, including Margaret Rous. Opening with the statement 'Truth is that which is pure', it goes on to say that those who rise against Truth are for condemnation. 'And when anything is once condemned and judged let it not be raised up again, and keep it in the grave. . . . All are to live in the love of God, which gives dominion over all, and unites and edifies all that abide in it.' All backbiting and whisperings must be stopped and searched out, and for that purpose older women should be chosen out to make investigation, and so stop rumours and reports. Then follows a very interesting and unexpected piece of work for these women to do who sign this paper—to 'take notice of all such as goes to

[1] *The Minute Book of the Monthly Meeting of The Society of Friends for the Upperside of Bucks* (1669–1690). B. S. Snell. (Records Branch, Bucks Archæological Society, 1937.)
[2] Swm. MSS. I, 104.

sea, seamen, merchants, masters of ships, and passengers out and home, that profess the Truth, that if they have anyways dishonoured the Lord God and brought an evil report, either in their trading or lives or conversations, upon the Truth', they were to be sent for, and if found worthy of condemnation, 'let it be passed upon them without respect of persons', but if the report was found to be false, their innocency was to be shown and the report removed.[1]

Another Epistle sent out by a group of women Friends, probably in 1697, bore the signatures of five Fell sisters—Margaret Rous, Isabel Morrice, Sarah Meade, Mary Lower and Susannah Ingram, together with eighteen other leading women. These women were called 'Ministers', that is, they were known and recognized as preachers, and were recorded in the Society's documents as ministers, but they were of course unpaid, and their presence in a Meeting by no means precluded other Friends from preaching or praying. This group had just been holding a joint Yearly Meeting in London with 'ancient Friends and brethren', namely, leading men Friends and ministers—the first time this had happened in the Society, and the women express gratitude for 'the condescending love of God in our brethren', in that they were allowed to share in their 'testimonies, wholesome advice and counsel, living exhortations and admonitions'. The long letter deals almost exclusively with the ministry of women—the great responsibility it entailed, the need for young women to control their gift of ministry and never to use it for 'popularity or to be seen or heard of men'. (This of course does not mean that if men were present, women were to keep silent, but that young women were not to speak so as to attract attention to themselves!) Older and more experienced women should train the younger ones in the use of their spiritual gifts; young women should be warned not to use too many words when speaking in Meeting—'A few words fitly spoken, from the sav-

[1] Box Meeting MSS. No. 16. Library, Friends' House, London. (See also *Quaker Women*, M. R. Brailsford, p. 286.) This epistle is similar to one in a collection of papers belonging to Southwark Monthly Meeting. (Jnl. F.H.S. XXVII, p. 59). Almost certainly drawn up by Fox himself, it is dated 1668 and signed by twenty-nine men and twenty-five women. It is perhaps curious that it should appear in the Box Meeting Minutes also, where it is of course signed by women only.

our of life, would be as apples of gold in pictures of silver, and would be more refreshing, and answer the life in others, as face answers face in a glass.' If young women feel drawn to visit other Meetings, they should go to those which are not far from their own homes, and should not take with them 'too much superfluous company' which would be a burden on their hosts, nor should women who are with child do such travelling. Parents should be careful not to overpress their children in the use of their spiritual gifts, but should keep them diligent, 'in the outward creation', and not to go beyond their true gifts, which might lead to vanity.

All this was valuable advice at a time when there was a tendency to lose the spirit in a multitude of words and prohibitions.

For well over thirty years Margaret Fox and her daughters had been among the chief creators of Women's Meetings, which were not only of vital importance for the education and development of Quaker women, but of very great value to the Society of Friends in general. The world still awaits the full partnership of men and women in the service of the Christian Church.

Note.—The later history of Women's Meetings and the general position of women in the Society does not concern us here—it can be read in the *Later Periods of Quakerism*, by Rufus M. Jones. It is perhaps enough to say here that in 1896, Yearly Meeting recognized women Friends as 'a constituent part' of all meetings for church affairs; in 1907 the Women's Yearly Meeting became an integral and undivided part of London Yearly Meeting, and in 1943 the first woman clerk of the united Yearly Meeting was appointed.

Chapter Twenty

JOURNEYS, MARRIAGES, AND PERSECUTION, 1677–89

WHILE George Fox was at his home at Swarthmoor with Margaret, from June 1675 to March 1677, he worked hard for the consolidation of Quakerism. In addition to the tasks mentioned in Chapter 18, he made collections of letters he had formerly written to Oliver Cromwell and the King, to magistrates, Members of Parliament and the Council; he put together the certificates he had received from many governors and people in authority, for these reflected primarily on the good standing of the truths he taught. He collected Epistles and letters sent to and from him and numerous other Friends, received and stored at Swarthmoor during the preceding twenty-three years, letters which he carefully endorsed and dated, in his strong sprawling handwriting. He wrote one or two books, made records of Friends who had first gone out of the North to preach, and those who had gone abroad; he wrote several Epistles including one in 1676 to strengthen the movement to establish women's meetings. By March 1677, though still but weakly, and unable to travel far each day, he set out for the south. With him at first went his wife and her daughter Rachel, other Friends joining him later. Riding by easy stages, they crossed the fells to John Blaykling's house, near Sedbergh, where meetings were held. From here, Margaret wrote to her two daughters left behind at Swarthmoor, Sarah and Susannah. Their stepfather was 'not so weary as he was', she told them, 'but he cannot endure to ride but very little journeys, and lights often; but he is pretty well and hearty.' Then she tells them how that morning she had visited Sir John Otway, Vice-Chancellor of the Duchy of Lancaster (whose high office her first husband had held twenty years before), at his home nearby. 'He was very loving and kind to us,' she wrote, 'and I acknowledged his favour that he had done for us at the last Assizes.' This refers to some trouble still continuing after Sarah's imprisonment in May 1676, mentioned in her Account Book. In her talk with Sir John Otway, she told him how the Court had even threatened the Bailiff—the man to whom Fox had given two shillings and six-pence for his 'civility' to Sarah—but Otway comforted her by saying he 'would see to that'. When Sarah had been released ten months before, it was by means of an 'order', but if there was another order come since then, the imprisonment would of necessity be continued, he told her. Sir John asked his secretary to look out the pleas in the case, and he said that he had them in his 'poke-mantle' (a word which is the northern form of port-manteau) at Kendal, and that he would look at them at Lan-caster. 'Thy father', Margaret told her daughter, 'gave me a guinea to give him, and he was mighty well pleased, and said, he loved Sarah dearly, he would do whatever laid in his power for her; I gave Thomas Heblethwaite [Otway's secretary and cousin] 5/- and desired him to be careful to look about it . . . and I gave him [Sir John] the warrant and he called for Tho: Heblethwaite to take a copy of it; and after he had written it, another young man and he examined it, and gave me it, and I saw he looked for something more and I had a shilling in my pocket, and I gave him it; and so they were mighty well pleased, and I believe they will do what they can: and we had a fine opportunity with them.'

Margaret's visit—and then tact—were evidently a great help to her daughter, who did not return to prison.

Margaret and Rachel returned home a week later, George Fox and his friends riding on through Yorkshire. From York her husband wrote to her that 'the way was many times deep and bad with snow, our horses sometimes were down, and we were not able to ride; and sometimes we had great storms and rain; but by the power of the Lord I went through all.' These storms were not unusual when crossing the Pennines—the 'backbone' of England—in early April; but his joyous letter containing a long list of meetings held, attended by men and women from many districts, ends 'so I am in my holy element, and holy work in the Lord, glory to his name for ever!'[1]

Five weeks later, after attending Meetings all through the

[1] G.F. Jnl. Ellwood Edn.

Midlands, Fox and his party reached London in time for the Yearly Meeting, which included Friends from as far afield as Holland.

Staying for the next few weeks with William and Gulielma Penn at their new home, Worminghurst, Sussex, and with the Rouses at Kingston, and elsewhere, George Fox, towards the end of July (1677) left England for Holland. With him went a party of influential Friends, William Penn, Robert Barclay, George Keith and his wife, Isabel Yeamans and others. This visit was in natural sequence to the work twenty years before, of William Caton, John Stubbs, William Ames and Samuel Fisher. There were in Holland and Germany at this time some groups of Protestants who had broken away from their Church and who held somewhat similar views to those of the Quakers, particularly in their reliance on the Inner Light.[1] There were also individuals who, while not actually forming sects or groups, were looked upon as seekers of a purer form of Protestantism than that of the State. Such an individual was the Princess Elizabeth of the Palatinate, who as early as 1659 had met some travelling Quakers. Born in the Castle of Heidelberg in 1618, she was the daughter of Elizabeth of England (daughter of James I), and Frederic the Fifth, Elector Palatine of the Rhine. In the year of her birth, the Thirty Years' War broke out, which devastated Germany, and within a few months of its beginning her parents became the King and Queen of Bohemia and the leaders of the Protestants against the Roman Catholics. Princess Elizabeth and her sisters and brothers (one was the Electress Sophia, mother of George I of England, and another was Prince Rupert who fought for his uncle, Charles I, and was so kind to Mary Fell when she pleaded with Charles II) were brought up in Holland in poverty and exile. The Princess as a young woman was the pupil and friend of the philosopher Descartes, and became known as one of the most learned women of Europe. At thirty-five she began to take an active interest in the affairs of the Protestant Abbey at Herford in Westphalia, and in 1667 became its Abbess.

---

[1] Most interesting accounts of these earlier mystical and spiritual reform movements, are given in *Studies in Mystical Religion* and *Spiritual Reformers in the Sixteenth and Seventeenth Centuries*, by Rufus M. Jones.

Four years later, the Princess was visited by the young William Penn, and letters passed between them for some years. It was thought that the Princess might be won over to Quakerism. Certainly there were two Quaker tenets, which were a logical fruiting of their belief in the indwelling Spirit in man, religious toleration and a hatred of war. These must have appealed strongly to the Princess, for she had suffered cruelly all her life from religious intolerance,[1] and from war, not only the Thirty Years' War of her childhood and young womanhood, but the more recent wars of Louis XIV against Holland, when in 1672 that small country voluntarily flooded itself to defeat the enemy. The menace of Louis XIV to the whole of Europe continued for some years, but wars and rumours of wars did not prevent the British Friends from organizing the visit to Holland and Germany in 1677. The personnel of this visit was well chosen. Fox, the leader, now fifty-three years old, spent most of his time among the Quakers and others of Holland and North Germany; the younger men, Penn, Robert Barclay (himself a distant cousin of the Princess Elizabeth), Benjamin Furly and George Keith (all scholars) travelled more widely, getting into touch with educated thinkers. Penn and Barclay visited the Princess, while Fox contented himself with sending her a letter by the hand of his step-daughter Isabel Yeamans. George Keith's wife and a Dutch Quakeress (sister-in-law of William Caton) who acted as interpreter went with her. Isabel Yeamans was chosen no doubt as much for her personal qualities as for her spiritual. Some of the Continental reforming Protestants believed that women should be allowed to preach, and Isabel was well known as an effective preacher. Gerard Croese recorded that the Princess was 'especially pleased with' Isabel's discourse for she indeed had 'a curious voice and a freer way of delivering herself'.

From Herford, Isabel Yeamans returned to Amsterdam, while Penn was travelling in Germany, and Fox was in North Germany and in the country then belonging to the Danish King. Everywhere these men exhorted their hearers 'to the Light and

---

[1] It is perhaps not surprising to find Penn writing of the Rhineland in 1677 that 'fear' was its 'common disease'—apropos of the effects of religious persecution (p. 155 in *Wm. Penn and the Dutch Quaker Migration*, etc., W. I. Hull).

Spirit of God',[1] and to those in high positions in the Church Fox proclaimed that they would never know God's Law and Gospel by 'studying, nor by philosophy, but by revelation and stillness in their minds by the Spirit of God'.[2]

On returning midst great adventures by land and water, to Friesland, Fox was there met by Isabel, who crossed the Zuyder Zee from Amsterdam, and they had another short spell together. She finally left Holland in September 1677, some weeks before her stepfather and others of the party. She returned to Swarthmoor for the winter and spring. She did not go empty-handed, for some time after her return to England parcels arrived at her old home—bread-baskets, 'Holland-ware' and brushes, a Dutch spinning-wheel for Rachel, cheeses and maps, Holland being famed for its map-making.

During the summer of 1678 Isabel Yeamans went to Scotland, there to visit Robert Barclay and his wife, and later to travel with him among Friends in Scotland. Robert Barclay had a deep friendship with all the Fell family. He shared with them, especially with Isabel, Sarah, Susannah and Rachel, the letters he received from the Princess Elizabeth and her friend, the Countess of Hoorn,[3] knowing that they would both appreciate the deep humility and searchings of heart of the writers, and at the same time would respect their privacy. The correspondence and visits of Robert Barclay and William Penn with these outstanding women on the Continent resulted at least in winning them over to an understanding of Quakerism, and deep sympathy with it, and also in successful efforts through the Princess's brother, Prince Rupert, to free the Quaker prisoners (including Robert Barclay's father) in Aberdeen, near Barclay's home.[4]

For Isabel Yeamans to have been one of this picked group of Friends on their expedition to the Continent must indeed have

[1] *Short Jnl.*, p. 246.

[2] *Short Jnl.*, p. 251.

[3] Thirnbeck MSS. 12.

[4] Another important result of the journey of 1677 was the encouragement of Quakerism in certain towns of Germany from which emigrants soon after went to people the new Pennsylvania. Some of these founded Germantown, near Philadelphia, and became leading colonists. One, Francis Daniel Pastorius in 1688 was the first man to protest against slavery, and blazed the trail for the great Abolitionist movement.

been one of the great experiences of her life. And for her and her sisters and mother the friendship between them and Robert Barclay was a great happiness to both sides. Robert Barclay was the son of Colonel David Barclay of Ury, near Aberdeen, who after a varied career and much searching of heart had joined the Quakers in 1667. His mother was Katherine, daughter of Sir Robert Gordon, youngest son of the 9th Earl of Sutherland. Robert, the eldest of their three sons, was born in 1648 at Gordonstoun, near Elgin.[1] After an education at the Roman Catholic Scots College in Paris, where his uncle was Rector, the boy of sixteen was recalled to Scotland, at the request of his mother on her deathbed (1664), and soon after his father's convincement, Robert joined Friends also. His description of the effect on him of the Quaker meeting for worship has often been quoted—'When I came into the silent assemblies of God's people, I felt a secret power among them which touched my heart; and, as I gave way unto it, I found the evil weakening in me and the good raised up.'[2] There were not many Friends who came from a Roman Catholic background (even though Barclay's was only partially so)—most came out of Puritanism. Both he and his father suffered several imprisonments in Aberdeen from 1676 onwards, and the first letter in existence from Robert to the four Fell sisters was in that year during one of these imprisonments. Evidently the sisters (Rachel was then twenty-three and Isabel about forty) had written to the young man to encourage him and comfort him in his sufferings. In his reply he wrote of 'that love and regard for you which I will not adventure to express, lest I should seem to sway from the sim-

---

[1] Sir Robert Gordon was one of the founders of Nova Scotia, and in recognition was made the first baronet of that colony. (It is interesting to find that his grandson, Robert Barclay, was later one of the proprietors of New Jersey, and was appointed the first Governor of East Jersey.) Sir Robert Gordon built Gordonstoun on land which originally belonged to the Roman Catholic Bishop Hepburn, uncle of Bothwell, whose first wife was Lady Jean Gordon, discarded later for Mary Queen of Scots.

Gordonstoun is now (1948) used for a Public School where H.R.H. the Duke of Edinburgh was a pupil.

(For the historical information concerning Gordonstoun I am indebted to Mrs. Alec G. Fraser and Mr. Brereton, Vice-Principal.)

[2] *Apology*, R. Barclay, prop. XI, sect. VII.

plicity of the Truth, but only put it in that which is beyond
words, in the flowing whereof I do at present dearly salute you.
Blessed be the Lord', Barclay added, 'that hath brought us to
the knowledge of this kind of love and friendship, which stand-
eth in that which is more excellent than all the world . . . as the
precious Truth alone brought us to that outward acquaintance
as well as inward friendship.'[1]

In this same year Robert Barclay published his famous book,
Apology for the True Christian Divinity. As he was a scholar and
a theologian, he used his gifts to systematize the Quaker principles, and to open them to the world of learning. For that
purpose, the book was written and first published in Latin, but
two years later he published an English translation, which has
gone through several editions.[2]

Letters still extant between Robert Barclay and Sarah Fell
refer to later imprisonments in Aberdeen, to family affairs at
Swarthmoor and Marsh Grange, to further letters from Princess
Elizabeth and the Countess of Hoorn, and in the year following
Isabel's travels with Barclay in Scotland, to the sending of a
copy of the *Apology* in its English translation for the use of the
four sisters.[3] Barclay visited Swarthmoor in the early summer of
1685, on his way from London to Scotland.[4]

Another valuable friendship which was increased by the visit
to Holland and Germany, was that between Margaret Fox and
William Penn. He had sent her 'a sweet and blessed letter', which
she had read to the Meeting at Swarthmoor, and which had
given them 'comfort and joy and gladness'. 'My heart and soul's
love is dearly remembered unto thee', she wrote in reply, 'and
my spirit doth rejoice in thy faithfulness and diligence in the
Lord's work and service, who art a noble and faithful instrument in the hand of the Almighty, for the spreading abroad of
his Truth . . . and thy name will be had in everlasting remembrance, with all the faithful, as they come into that same spirit
of grace and life and power by which thou art clothed and

[1] Thirnbeck MSS. 12.
[2] **D. Elton Trueblood,** *Robert Barclay* **(New York 1968).**
[3] Crosfield MSS. 10, and *Rel. Bar.*, pp. 44, 45, 51.
[4] Dix MSS. Z, 4, Library, Friends' House, London.

carried; and for the good service that thou dost for the Lord, and for his Truth and the gathering of his elect seed, he will reward it a hundredfold into thy bosom.'[1]

She asked him to send her a copy of the journal that he had kept of the memorable travels on the Continent, for she wanted to add it to the records kept at Swarthmoor. This journal was written primarily for the use of his friends, and was not published till seventeen years later.

Let us briefly follow Isabel's further fortunes. After her visit to Scotland, she again spent the winter at Swarthmoor, George Fox being there also, and in 1679 she wrote her only booklet or tract. Addressed specially to men and women in the North, she pleads with them to be guided by the spirit, the voice within, and to be convinced that until they come to know the power of God they are not come 'to the substance'.

Between 1680 and 1690 Isabel lived in various parts of the country. For a time she was in London, at Yearly Meeting with Fox, or as one of the ministers regularly attending various Meetings, or as a 'sufferer or testimony bearer'[2] (in 1686), probably on account of her preaching; then she lived at Stockton-on-Tees for a time, where she took a prominent part in the women's Meetings. She returned to Swarthmoor from time to time, where her young son William was still living. She had an *affaire de coeur* with a Bristol Friend,[3] out of which she came with more credit than he, and finally in January 1690 she married Abraham Morrice, a silk merchant and prominent citizen of Lincoln, who had given the land for the Quaker burial ground and later the Meeting House. Both Abraham Morrice and Isabel died in 1704, she being then about sixty-seven years of age.

Let us return to Swarthmoor in 1677. Margaret Fox's life was now primarily in her own home and Meeting. She was sixty-three, and though her travels and her trials from persecutors were by no means over, her work was also as a mother and grandmother, wise in her dealings with individuals, faithful in her service for the Church, and constant in her insistence on the working within of the Light of Christ.

[1] Portfolio 36. Library, Friends' House, London.
[2] Besse's *Sufferings*.   [3] Jnl. F.H.S. XII, 56.

The separation from her husband was a sore trial to her, though she usually took it with serenity, in her belief that it was God's will. 'And though the Lord had provided an outward habitation for him' she wrote after her husband's death, 'yet he was not willing to stay at it, because it was so remote and far from London, where his service most lay. And my concern for God, and his holy eternal truth, was then in the North, where God had placed and sent me, and likewise for the ordering and governing of my children and family: so that we were very willing both of us, to live apart for some years upon God's account, and his truth's service, and to deny ourselves of that comfort which we might have had in being together, for the sake and service of the Lord and his truth. And if any took occasion, or judged hard of us because of that, the Lord will judge them; for we were innocent.'[1]

On his return from Holland towards the end of 1677 Fox spent nearly a year in Southern England and London, constantly occupied in writing, in visiting Meetings and individual Friends, in trying to stop the Story-Wilkinson trouble, and in attempts to mitigate the sufferings of imprisoned Quakers. He was able to report to his wife comforting news of Friends abroad, news given at the Yearly Meeting held in May 1678. And yet, in spite of all her efforts to be patient and submissive, she could not but express her longing for his return.[2]

Dear Love, [she wrote from Swarthmoor on the 18th July 1678,] Glad I am to hear the Lord preserves thee in health and capacity to travel in His work and service. . . . We hope and expect He will draw thee homewards in his blessed time. Thou art much expected and longed for here, but we must all submit to the Lord's will and time.

I received thy kind token by Leonard [Fell], which I did not expect, but I know it is thy true love to remember us [thus]. I thought to have sent something by Mary Fell to thee, but I [considered] thou would only buy something with it for me, as thou used to do, which caused me to omit it. I perceive thou hast sent things to the children by Leonard, he hath not yet delivered them; but thy company would be more and better to us than all the world or than all the earth can afford; but only for the Lord's truth and service [are we willing to resign it], we would not exchange it for all beside.

¹ Testimony of Mt. Fox, in Leeds Jnl. LXX.
² G.F. Jnl. Ellwood Edn., p. 458.

This day Isabel set forward on her way to Scotland. Thomas and Mary Lower, Sarah, Susannah and Rachel with little Bethiah [Rous], their love and duty are dearly remembered unto thee and gladly would they see thee here. I am glad to find thou hath writ to my daughter Rous. Poor woman! I am afraid she will have a heartless being there.[1] The Lord uphold her over all her trials.

We desire much to hear from thee and what way thou passest. All things are well here with us, praised and honoured be the Lord.

From thy endeared and loving wife,

M. F.[2]

Two months after this letter was written George Fox returned to Swarthmoor, where he stayed for a year and a half. Again much of his time was spent in writing books and epistles —an increasing effort to make the world understand the beliefs and acts of Quakers.

At the beginning of March 1680, George Fox left his home for the last time. Until his death eleven years later, he lived in and near London. When in these latter years his health would only let him stay in London for a few weeks at a time, it was to the hospitable homes of the Rouses and Meades that he usually went for refreshment of body and spirit. Margaret Rous had many anxieties as a mother. She lost five of her children in their infancy, and in January 1683 her eight-year-old Bridget lay dying of smallpox. We have Fox's own words of the help he was able to give—'I hearing that Margaret Rous's child was sick, I went to see it and as I stood by it considering its condition I felt the Lord's power to go through it, and the word was "The Lord's power was come to raise it up or to fetch it away". And so I came away fresh in the Lord's power and was satisfied in myself. And the next day her mother came to the town and desired me to go with her to see it, and through her tenderness I went, though I was satisfied in myself. And so I saw the child was full of the power of the Lord and it rested upon it and rested in it. And at night it died. And after the spirit of the child appeared to me, and there was a mighty substance of a glorious

[1] Margaret Rous had recently gone to Barbados with her husband and some of their children. Her mother is probably referring here to Colonel Rous's second wife, who was not approved of by John Rous.

[2] From the Thwaite Collection, quoted by H. G. Crosfield, p. 170–1, and Webb, *Fells*, p. 293.

life in that child, and I bid her mother be content, for it was well, and it was well that she had such an innocent offering for the Lord. And she was finely settled and contented through the Will of the Lord.'[1]

Later in the year, and again two years afterwards, Margaret Rous's second surviving daughter, Margaret, was very ill, and both times Fox was sent for, and stayed until the young girl recovered.[2] In 1685 the only surviving son, Nathaniel, had small-pox, and again Fox went to be with the boy and his family, and stayed until he had recovered.[3]

From 1681 to 1688 Fox laboured to persuade both the City of London authorities as well as Members of Parliament of the iniquity of persecuting the 'harmless' Quakers. He himself attended Meetings regularly, even when they were held outside the Meeting-houses, and in the presence of soldiers and constables. His courage never flagged. His example was contagious. His Epistles to the sufferers lying in prison helped them to hold out to the bitter end. By 1686 the struggle was almost over, and between fifteen and sixteen hundred Friends were allowed out of prison (except for non-payment of tithes). In 1689 the Toleration Act made religious toleration the law of the land, though in a limited form.

Much happened at Swarthmoor while Fox was in the South. Not long after he left, Sarah, the eldest daughter still unmarried, became the wife of William Meade of London and Essex, in 1681. Sarah was then about forty, and her husband, who had been a widower for two years, was thirteen years her senior. In addition to our knowledge of Sarah described in previous chapters, we have a short account of her given by Gerard Croese, the Dutch seventeenth-century writer. She was a great preacher, he said, 'whom these people do so much extol, that they say she was not only beautiful and lovely to a high degree, but wonderfully happy in ingeny and memory; so stupendously eloquent in discoursing and preaching and so effectual and fervent in her addresses and supplications to God, that she ravished

---

[1] *George Fox's 'Book of miracles'*, **edited by Henry J. Cadbury (Cambridge 1948) pp. 141-142.**

[2] *Short Jnl.*, pp. 89 and 126.

[2] *Short Jnl.*, p. 134.

all her beholders and hearers with admiration and wonder.' He
added that she taught herself Hebrew, so as to be able better to
understand the Bible and answer her critics.[1]

William Meade, whose stand alongside the young William
Penn in the Old Bailey case in 1670 has already been described,
was a wealthy linen-draper of Fenchurch Street, London, and
a member of the Company of Merchant Tailors, and descended
from an old family of Buckinghamshire. He already had a leading position in the Society of Friends, and was a writer of some
Quaker books, and on several occasions visited the King.

Soon after his marriage to Sarah, which was solemnized, not
at Swarthmoor as were those of most of the other daughters, but
in London, he bought an estate, Goosehays or Gooses, near
Barking, Essex; it was 'a quiet still place, which best suits old
age',[2] she wrote towards the end of her life. Fox too found it a
gracious, restful place to be in.

Margaret Fox had accompanied her daughter Sarah to London in May 1681, so that husband and wife and three daughters,
Isabel, Sarah and Margaret Rous, were together for Yearly
Meeting, and the wedding which almost immediately followed
at the Devonshire House Meeting House, Bishopsgate. Margaret's visit, her seventh to London, was a short one, for in July
she was writing to her husband from Swarthmoor, telling him
of the severe persecutions Friends there were suffering from, of
the death of John Abraham of Manchester, and making the
suggestion that John Abraham's son, Daniel, might come to
Marsh Grange on a visit to the Lowers, for the young man was
'so much dejected and cast down with his father's death'. She
added, 'I should be glad if thou would incline to come home,
that thou might get a little rest; methinks it's the most comfortable when one has a home to be there, but the Lord give us
patience to bear all things,' and she ended with her 'dear everlasting unalterable love which thinks no evil'.[3]

[1] Exaggerated or not, Croese's statement was thought reliable enough to be
adopted without alteration by the local historian Lucas, who between 1710
and 1740 wrote the history of a village across the sands from Swarthmoor,
Warton near Carnforth, Lancs., a district which included Yealand Conyers,
then a village almost entirely Quaker.

[2] Spence MSS. III, 200.

[3] Thirnbeck MSS. 16.

Two years after Sarah's marriage came Rachel's (1683). Her bridegroom, eight years younger than herself, was Daniel Abraham. His father had been the first to become a Quaker in Manchester.[1] John Abraham, a merchant, was an old friend of Margaret Fox, and there are letters still extant between them, but for some reason Margaret was at first against the marriage to Daniel, as she was once against Mary's to Thomas Lower. Daniel was only twenty-two at his marriage, but if her objection was on the score of the bridegroom being so much younger than the bride, she was being very inconsistent! The Abrahams were later connected by marriage with the famous Chetham family of Manchester, as Daniel's sister Mary became the wife of Edward Chetham, nephew of George Chetham, Sheriff of Lancashire, and great-nephew of Sir Humphrey Chetham, founder of the Blue-coat School (Chetham's Hospital) in Manchester and the first free Library in England.[2]

Perhaps the young people first met when Daniel Abraham came to stay at Marsh Grange, though there is a hint in a letter from Margaret written in London just before John Abraham died that the old father had already expressed a wish for the marriage.

On his return to Manchester from Marsh Grange there was no doubt whatever in Daniel's mind, as the following love-letter shows:

Entirely affected R.F.,

Can any love be so firm and constant as that which originally is excited by, and derived from something which in itself is of an immutable being, and therefore in its progress doth not allow of any mutability or wavering, which those are liable to, whose basis in this so weighty concern is only . . . laid upon some outward preferment; or otherwise the fire of their affection kindled from something that is merely superficial. So that these foregoing objects they being removed

[1] It is interesting that three of the Fell daughters married sons of the first men to become Quakers in their districts: Margaret whose father-in-law was the first Quaker of Barbados, Bridget whose father-in-law was the first Quaker of Headlam, Durham, and Rachel. The Abraham family were originally from the village of Abram (still pronounced with the first A short, Abram), between Wigan and Warrington. Its name derives from the Anglo-Saxon, Adburgham.

[2] The Chetham Library is just a century older than the British Museum, and contains many valuable books and MSS. (Baines *Lancashire*).

from, or in any measure disappointed of, consequently a coolness and a flatness must needs be the sequel of their attempts, which in no sort can betide the former state and condition; the tranquility of which state being not wholly drawn from a superficial centre.

Dear Rachel, for to declare the nature and full extent of that centrinal, fixed and abiding love, the course and motion whereof is in no wise to be stopped, neither the warmness of its stream refrigerated by the interposition of length of time or distance of place, its nature and course to theeward for me to demonstrate were for to render myself extremely prolix. . . . Although the enjoyment of the company one of another may possibly communicate more heat to the already quickened affection, yet methinks I find a daily increase of true and ardent affection, tending to and pressing much for the more full enjoyment and accomplishment of that which at present may be but seen as at a distance. . . .

Dear Rachel, . . . I got well home and lodged at Preston the first night after my departure from Swarthmoor Hall; and for thy satisfaction only I was willing that Joseph [Sharp] should have accompanied me behind Lancaster, but was prevented, thy horse casting a shoe. I cannot tell but I may see thee at Quarter Meeting.

So in that love which is firm and abiding with thee, dear Rachel, I take my leave until another opportunity.

Thy truly affected Friend,
D.A.

Manchester, the 26 of 10br [December], 1681.[1]

When Margaret Fox was finally persuaded of the suitability of the match, Daniel Abraham and Rachel were married at Swarthmoor on 17th March 1683. But they had to wait for a year and a quarter after this love-letter was written. The marriage certificate was signed by seventy-six witnesses, the phrase 'with several others then present' following the list of names. Friends came from Manchester and Coppull, as well as a wide local circle, to the wedding of Margaret's youngest daughter, her constant companion. Daniel Abraham gave up living in Manchester, and made Swarthmoor Hall his home. His father had made him a rich man, and as was explained in an earlier chapter, a few years after his marriage he 'purchased' the Hall and estate from his nephew, Charles Fell. This generous action, which the writer believes was due to his desire to end an old family dis-

---

[1] Thirnbeck MSS. 17.

agreement, is consistent with the faithfulness to the Quaker testimonies for which Daniel Abraham repeatedly suffered both imprisonment and fines. The pages of the old record books and elsewhere show him to have been in prison twice in the year after his marriage, for 'absence from the national worship',[1] again in 1685 (through the enmity of William and Roger Kirkby, Margaret Fox's old persecutors) and towards the end of the century he was in prison at Dalton in Furness for three years for refusal to pay tithes.[2] For several months of that time he was kept 'in a cold open room, where at times it rained on his bed', Besse tells us. He was there when his mother-in-law died (1702). He continued prisoner at Dalton until he was removed to London by Habeas Corpus in 1704, and soon after discharged. All this was for a demand of one shilling and eightpence for 'small tithes'. So persistent was this refusal to pay tithes that Daniel Abraham lost (taken in cattle and sheep) about £130 (possibly £1,300 in modern value) in the fifteen years from 1701, for demands of about £92.[3][4] Of his Lancaster imprisonment in 1684 he wrote cheerfully to his wife, left at their home after only a year of marriage—'I am through mercy come very well to Lancaster, both in health of body and contentedness of mind. We rode fast lest had tide enough over sands. The constable appeared kind to me, and when we came to Lancaster, he went to his usual inn and I went to Judah Yates.' He met other Friends there, also committed to prison. 'The gaoler was very high and rough and said we were a stubborn rebellious people or such like words, and that we put the country to great charge and trouble in carrying us to and fro.' The Friends were taken to the Castle, but before nightfall they were all allowed to go and lodge in the town. 'I desire thou would not take too much thought for me', the young man added, 'but rest satisfied in that which is able to preserve us together and asunder.'[5]

[1] Besse's *Sufferings*, I, p. 327.
[2] *Book of Yearly Meeting Minutes*, etc., at Lancaster Meeting House.
[3] *Lancashire Quarterly Meeting Book of Sufferings*.
[4] It is difficult to assess comparative values of money, as between the centuries. Dr. G. M. Trevelyan in his *English Social History* states that in the fifteenth century 'a country parson who had £10 a year from all sources was considered to have a tolerable income' (p. 85).
[5] Miller MSS. p. 75.

Of Daniel and Rachel Abraham's four children—three sons and a daughter—only one survived their childhood, John, born in 1687.[1] Between this child and his grandmother there was great affection. While Margaret Fox was in London in 1698, the eleven-year-old boy sent her a letter the first draft of which has survived on the back of another letter received some years before. Here is John's letter, in the original spelling:

D.H.G. [=dear and honoured grandmother],
   The R[emembrance] of thee is very much upon my mind and thy kindness to mee every way, boeth when I had hapnes to bee with and since I am sencabel of to be greatt and I desier I may allwayes rightly vallue it, and wall [walk] worth in som degree of it and I hope as I groe in yeares shall more and more sttudy to performe my duty and due respects to thee I r[eceived] by L.F. [Leonard Fell] thy very kind [and lardge][2] token and all so yesterday my sadell and brydell came safe which I was very glad of and returns my thangfull acknowlidments. I hope to lener [learn] now consta[n]tly if I have my helth; for I know it is thy minde I should bee a good scoller and I often thinks of thy good advice to mee consarning it.
   Dear Grandmot thou art oftener in my mind then I can menshon and my love and respects for thee is great. I hope to see thee next Springe att Swath wh I shall be exceed glad this being moest at present but my dearest duty to thee and my respects to all my unkell, antts and cosen, from

duthfall granch

John Abn.

I must bedge thy excuse for bad
writing for I am moestly kep to my Laten.[3]

When Margaret Fox lay dying in 1702, she exhorted her grandson, then fifteen years old, to 'stand for God'; when Rachel told her that they intended to educate their son according to her mind and desire, she said: 'All that I desire for him is that he may be faithful.' And later: 'John, the Lord loves thee, and will love thee for my sake, and my prayers and tears that I have put up to him for thee many times.'[4]
   Daniel Abraham was not the only member of the Swarthmoor

[1] Abraham MSS. 34.
[2] Crossed out by John!
[3] Gibson MSS. II, 7.
[4] M.F. *Works.*

family in the 'eighties who suffered for his religious views. Margaret Fox for five years, from 1680 to 1685, was constantly being attacked. In October 1680 Thomas Lower reported to George Fox that his mother-in-law was expecting shortly to be taken to prison, and that the magistrates were anxious to arrest Fox also if they could tell where to find him. The 'envy' of the Flemings of Rydal was another cause of the persecution of Furness Friends in these years, for non-attendance at church.[1] In fact this was the time of the second Stuart despotism, the closing years of Charles II, when intolerance had full sway, and the Quakers were the bulwark of Dissent. At the end of the reign there were nearly 1,400 Friends in prison, including about 200 women, enormous fines had been collected from them[2] and 100 had died in prison in the five years. In Lancaster Prison alone there were 65 Quakers in June 1685. The chief causes of conviction were the holding of their own meetings, the refusal to attend church, to swear any oath, or to pay tithes and other church dues. Fear and bigotry ruled the day, and both were increased by the discovery of the Rye House Plot in the spring of 1683. It availed little at the moment that Friends again published the declaration against all plots and the use of carnal weapons for any cause, which they had written twenty years before.

The full force of persecution this time however did not fall on Margaret Fox until 1683. In September two informers—a man who had already been imprisoned for sheep-stealing, and a woman accomplice who was later hanged at Lancaster—were the cause of the summoning of Margaret, her newly married daughter Rachel and Daniel Abraham, before Justices Roger and William Kirkby. Leonard Fell and his wife Mary also appeared. Margaret was heavily fined, and then with her daughter and son-in-law, was imprisoned at Lancaster for sixteen days, Leonard Fell for two months.[3] This was for absenting themselves from attendance at church. The Justices added insult to injury by

---

[1] Portfolio 36, 55. Library, Friends' House, London.
[2] In Bristol alone, in 1683, fines imposed on the Quakers amounted to £16,440 (*Annals of Bristol*, by John Latimer).
[3] Swm. MSS. IV, 215. *An Account of the Sufferings of Friends at Swarthmoor Meeting*, 1683.

indicting Margaret Fox as 'Margaret Fell, widow', as they wanted to make out that her marriage to Fox was illegal.

In January 1684 Margaret Fox sent a spirited protest to the Justices for the 'abuse and wrong' they did her by their calling her 'Margaret Fell, widow'. She reminded them that she had been married to George Fox for fourteen years, and that the King himself and his Council had used that surname when they had given her their pardon under the Broad Seal in 1671. The wrong they did her was in the amount of the fine. She told them that by calling her a widow they used the law to fine her twenty pounds, whereas a married woman could only be fined ten shillings. 'I do not believe it is the King's mind', she concluded, 'to have his subjects ruined.'[1]

Two months later the High Constable, petty constables, churchwardens 'with divers others' came to Swarthmoor Hall and 'opened the doors where the beasts laid, and took four kine, and heifers with calf, and two kine that had calves sucking on them, with two steers and a fat ox, nine in all worth above £30'. These were all sold the same day, in spite of the owner's appeal.[2] A little later she had forty pounds worth of cattle taken.

Indeed the persecution of the Quakers in these years was general throughout the country. It was the more easily carried out because they never held their meetings for worship in secret or behind locked doors. From London in September 1683 Sarah Meade wrote to her sister Rachel Abraham. 'It's a trying time with many, sufferings being great. . . . Many has their goods taken by informers; some quite ruined as to the outward, and shut up shop, several run in upon for £20 amounts, and knew nothing of the prosecution till it's run up to 5 or £600, and so all they have is seized.' In some cases the constables, having taken what they pleased from the Quaker's shop, would break into his house, and take away 'beds, bedding and all, and was very mad and rude'. Even friends of the victim who as witnesses of the aggression begged for moderation of behaviour, were haled off before the mayor and bound over to keep the

---

[1] Letter from M.F. to 'the Justices of the Sessions at Lancaster'. The original is in the County Record Office at Preston; **printed** in Nightingale, *Quaker Movement in Lancashire*, pp. 155–6.

[2] Besse's *Sufferings*, I, p. 326.

peace.[1] Sarah warned her sister that letters being carried up privately by a Swarthmoor servant were liable to bring him into custody, as searchers at Highgate and other entrances to London were out to catch these private carriers, in the effort to enhance the revenue of the post office.

At the same time, Thomas Lower, who had left his home of Marsh Grange to visit Cornwall to settle the business of an estate[2] which had recently become his, was arrested, praemunired and imprisoned with a number of other Friends in the loathsome dungeon of Launceston jail. His mother-in-law wrote loving encouragement to him and his fellow-sufferers, 'Therefore with hearts and courage may his servants and children suffer for him, without fear or fainting, under those that have but power over the outward man. The Lord preserve you in the dominion over them all; and I am glad to hear in every letter that comes from thee, that ye are well satisfied and content.'[3]

In November 1683, after some months of imprisonment, William Meade was using his influence in Court circles and his friendship with Thomas Lower's brother, Dr. Richard Lower, to obtain freedom for Thomas, but unsuccessfully.[4] Conditions in the winter were very bad, and the prisoners were 'much nipped with the asperity of the weather and cold situation of the place, and though fuel be pretty plenty, yet dear, and the smokiness of the chimneys make our fires less serviceable unto, us,' but they were 'well content' for 'the Lord supports and bears us up above it all, and refreshes us with his living power and presence which sweetens all our exercises . . . and makes the time to pass with delight . . . and the prison to seem as a palace or place of pleasure unto us.'[5]

When spring (1684) was approaching Lower reported to Fox that he had sent an account of their sufferings to the Chief Justice Jeffreys. It was not until the next year, after the rebellion of Monmouth that Jeffreys earned by his 'Bloody Assize' his reputation for terrible cruelty, but in 1684 he plainly told Lower

---

[1] Spence MSS. III, 186.
[2] Probably Loveday Hambly's estate.
[3] M.F. *Works*, p. 530. 28 vii [Sept.] 1683.
[4] Spence MSS. III, 184.
[5] Letter. Lower to Fox 12 xi [Jan.] 1683/4 in MS 'Original Records of Sufferings, 362' in LSF.

that he did not make the laws, and could do nothing to help those who had already been praemunired, though he would help those not yet committed, and he would approach the King on behalf of Friends. Lower gave several details of affairs in Cornwall, which add to the picture of these times of fear and unrest—Jeffreys insisting on the oath of allegiance, a Presbyterian priest offering to conform rather than suffer persecution, many Nonconformists paying money so as to escape, 'except poor Friends who have none to fly unto but the Lord . . . in whose will we rest content to wait his blessed pleasure'. Lower could see no quick release for himself, so he asked Fox for his advice as to his wife and children leaving their Northern home to come to a house near his prison. There the children would be able to attend a school run by Friends, where they could learn 'to read, write and cypher excellent well', which they could not do at Marsh Grange. Even if he were freed here, he believed he would soon be arrested again if he returned to the North, 'for the Kirkbys have an inveterate enmity to Truth and Friends, and to me in particular, and as the present humour of men in authority stands I see little other but imprisonment and afflictions attending Friends.'[1]

Mary Lower and her children did not leave their Northern home for Launceston, as in May of that year (1684), two months after Thomas had written to Fox, he was released, and Sarah Meade was writing to Swarthmoor that she supposed he was there already or would be shortly.[2]

This holiday from imprisonment is confirmed by a reference to it in a letter from Gulielma Penn to Margaret Fox.[3] It was however for a short time only, and Lower returned to prison at Launceston.

It was during these years of persecution and suffering at Swarthmoor that Gulielma Penn wrote three letters to Margaret Fox, the friend thirty years her senior whom she had loved for many years.

The first letter was written on the 21st of August 1683, a year after William Penn had left to found Pennsylvania. Before leav-

---

[1] *Original Records of Sufferings*, p. 370. 15.1.1683-4.
[2] Spence MSS. III, 184.
[3] Thirnbeck MSS. 18.

ing England he had confided in Margaret the story of his trials
and perplexities connected with the founding of this colony
which he intended to be for the spread of Truth and the ideals
of universal religious freedom for which he and all Friends
strove.[1] On the eve of his sailing he had written her a tender
loving farewell—'Dear Margaret, I am agoing. Remember me
in the Father's love and may God be with thee and bless thee
and thine with his eternal and temporal blessings. . . . Dear
George I left yesterday at Enfield much better. My soul loves
him beyond the love of women. His dear love and care and
council are in my heart and a sweet parting I had. . . . I have not
else to add, but my wife's dear love, who is sweetly consenting
and satisfied.'[2]

A year later, Gulielma, left with her little children, only three
living out of six, at Warminghurst in Sussex, wrote a letter to
Margaret which in addition to portraying a beautiful friendship
gives such a remarkable picture of the courage and sufferings of
these women, both of whom were then bearing separation from
their husbands in days of danger and insecurity, that it must be
quoted in full.[3]

21.6 [August] 1683.

Dear M.F.

My dear and truly honoured friend in the sense of that which hath
made thee so among the Lord's faithful chosen people, I most dearly
salute thee, and I can truly say it is often brought before me how
aimable [spelt thus, meaning in French 'lovable'] thou hast been and
art in the eyes of those that truly have kept their first love, and the
Lord has and will crown thee with blessings for thy faithful service
all along to him and his truth, even when there was very few that
stood for his name, and though it is forgotten by many that are wandering abroad from their habitations [this refers to the remnants of the
Story-Wilkinson separation], yet it may be brought to their remembrance to their confusion, and they that abide therein sees and knows
thee.

---

[1] Cash MSS. undated, but probably late 1681, or early 1682.
[2] Caton MSS. III, 494–5. Copy in Rachel Abraham's handwriting, dated
14th August 1682.
[3] L. V. Hodgkin in *Gulielma* points out that the letters from Gulielma to
Margaret are the only surviving documents of hers written after her marriage.
That we still have them is due to the care taken of records and letters at Swarthmoor Hall by three generations there.

Dear M.F., I received thy dear and tender lines long since when I lay in; several things prevented me from writing to thee again, which I hope thou wilt pass by; I was very weak a long time after my lying in and it pleased the Lord to take away my little one, when it was about three weeks old. It was a mighty great child and it was near dead when it was born, which I think it never got over. Dear George Fox came a-purpose to see me, which I took very kindly and was truly refreshed in his company. I have since had a sore fit of illness, that they call St. Anthony's fire, in my face [=Erysipelas] and a fever. I could not see very little several days and nights, my face and eyes were so swelled, but it pleased the Lord to raise me up again. I am not wholly come to my strength yet, my eyes are very weak. Thy son and daughter Rous has been here since to see me. Bethia [their eldest daughter] has been here a pretty while; I think she will write.

I have had several letters from my husband; he was then very well, and Friends they have large meetings at Philadelphia which is the city, 300 at a meeting. I lately received this Epistle from him and Friends, which I was desirous thou should see it. I know not whether thou hast had it from any other. I expect to hear shortly what my husband will have me to do, whether I shall go this year or no, but fear if he does send I shall scarce be well enough yet to go.

I am truly glad when I hear of you or from you. . . .

Then with messages of love to the Lowers, the Abrahams, to Isabel, and to Margaret herself 'again beyond expression', she ends:

Thy truly affectionate friend that truly loves and honours thee in the Lord.

Gulielma Maria Penn.[1]

A year later Margaret and Gulielma were again writing to each other, Gulielma sending her sympathy and encouragement during the time of threatenings and persecutions at Swarthmoor (August 1684). She gently suggested that if Margaret 'found a clearness and freedom in the Lord' it would be happy if she were nearer her husband and children in the South, but 'that I leave to the Lord's ordering and thy freedom'.[2]

[1] Portfolio 36, No. 21. From a copy made by Friends' House Library in 1915, from the original in possession of Henry Whitwell of Winchmore Hill, London, N., now in possession of A. C. Myers, U.S.A.
[2] Thirnbeck MSS. 18, with copy in Rachel's handwriting in Caton MSS. III, 496–7, dated 24th August 1684.

Margaret however continued on at her home for another three months, taking upon herself the heaviest part of the persecution aimed to destroy her Meeting.

Rumours reached her husband in London, in October, that one of the Justices Kirkby had taken a fat ox at the Hall and killed it for his own table, an illegal proceeding disapproved of by the Chief Justice and his colleagues in London. Fox wrote to his wife for full information, with the statements of witnesses of these attacks on her and his property, for he wished to appeal to authorities in London.[1] He had heard that not even a cow to give her milk had been left.

In the account of her troubles in reply to Fox's advice Margaret said that she had been fined £100 under the Conventicle Act, namely £40 for holding the meeting in her house, and £60 for speaking and praying in her own home, that the Justices had taken twenty-four head of cattle which belonged to her husband 'under the colour that I am a widow, although I showed them the King's warrant and pardon which owneth me to be Margaret Fox.' She also was able to confirm the rumour that Kirkby had taken the fat ox for his own use.[2] 'Their intentions were to ruin us, and to weary us out', she wrote years later, 'and to enrich themselves; but the Lord prevented them.'[3]

As she had done earlier in her life, so she did now when she was seventy years old—she travelled to London to appeal to the King on behalf not only of herself and her family, but of suffering Friends throughout the country. She travelled up in November 1684, with Mary Lower and Leonard Fell, and stayed until March or April 1685, her eighth visit. With the help of her husband and son-in-law, William Meade, she drew up two papers, describing the persecutions.[4] The short paper she intended to present to James, Duke of York, who had in former days befriended her. 'I went with this paper', she wrote in her *Relation*, 'to James's house; and after long waiting, I got to speak to him.

---

[1] Cash MSS. (This letter is largely quoted by Webb (*Fells*) and H. G. Crosfield, p. 180, but the date is not 1681, but 1684.)
[2] Spence MSS. III, 1.
[3] M.F. *Works*, p. 10.
[4] Spence MSS. III, 1.

But some who were with him, let him know that it was I that had been with him and his brother, soon after they came into England. So I gave him my little paper, and asked him, if he did remember me. He said, "I do remember you". So then I desired him to speak to the King for us, for we were under great sufferings, and our persecutors were so severe upon us, that it looked as if they intended to make a prey upon us; and he said, he could not help us, but he would speak to the King.'

Next day Margaret managed to reach the King, her 'great paper' in her hand. The King, ill, weary, full of anxiety, and nearing his end, was 'rough and angry' to the woman to whom twenty years before he had shown kindliness. He refused to take her paper,[1] but she managed to give several copies of it to the nobles about him. Afterwards she saw Judge Jeffreys who had lately 'been in the North country with us', and he promised to speak for her to the King, but with a short paper, not the long. So she wrote a short note, still confessing that however severe their sufferings were they refused, even to death, to deny God.

Margaret also wrote to Lord Ancram, one of the courtiers who had promised George Fox to help his wife, telling him shortly of her parents and relations, and how all she wanted was to be allowed to worship God freely in her own home.[2]

It was now February, and she and her friends called at White-hall to reinforce her letter to Lord Ancram. She arrived just as the King was dying. 'So we waited and walked up and down, and several came down from the King, and said, "He could not stand"; others said, "He could not speak". Then after some hours' waiting, we got through Scotland Yard and came away; and the King continued sick and ill until the sixth day after, and then he died. So this confirmed my word, which God put into my heart, that I was sent to bear my last testimony to the King.'[2]

The day after the King's death Margaret wrote to her daughter at Swarthmoor. (It will be seen from the letter that in spite of its being mid-winter Leonard Fell had returned North: Mary **had gone to Launceston, where her husband was in prison: see page 329.)**

[1] Thirnbeck MSS. 20, in Jnl. F.H.S. IX, 143–5.
[2] See Appendix 11.
[2] M.F. *Works*, pp. 11, 12.

London **7 xii** [**Feb.**] **1684/5**
Dear Son and Daughter Abraham,
  I received your letter and I praise the Lord for your preservation in
the Truth and in your health as we are here all at this time, glory to
the Lord for ever. Our business at the [Law Courts?] [paper torn] is
not yet ended, but we hope in the Lord to get it ended this next week.
Here hath been a great and **a** sudden change. King Charles was taken ill
on 2nd day morning, and departed this life yesterday about mid-day,
and in the afternoon King James the 2nd, late Duke of York, was
proclaimed, so that this day the judges have received commission to
sit again (as we hear). We expect your sister Lower to be here the next
week, for I writ to her to return as shortly as she could because ye writ
the smallpox was so near hand, which I confess I was afraid of. We
do not know how things will be as yet, but we will wait upon the
Lord to manifest his will and pleasure, and for your suffering you must
be content and in the strength of the Lord give up to do his will; and
I hope in the Lord it will not be very long till we shall end[eavour]
[torn] to return to you. My dear love and constant prayer is to the
Lord for you, that in his powerful arm and strength you may be preserved. My dear love is to Leonard Fell and his wife and to all the
servants and friends. We can give no account of what will [become]
[torn] of Mary Woodburn's business till our motion comes on. Your
brother and sister Mead and sister Susannah have their dear loves
remembered unto you, which is all at present.
                    From your dear Mother in the Lord
                                    M. F.
Your cousin Bethiah hath her
dear love remembered unto you.[1]

  Soon after James, Duke of York became King, Margaret
had another interview with him, begging him for his word to
check their persecutors. He told her she could return home,
which she did in March, accompanied by Mary Lower. They
travelled by public coach as far as Newcastle-under-Lyme,
where no doubt they were met by horses and servants from
Swarthmoor.[2]
  But even then she was not left in peace. Soon after her return
Justice William Kirkby, 'one of our greatest persecutors', as she

---

[1] Portfolio 41, 83, Library, Friends' House, London, and Jnl. F.H.S. VI,
79–81.
[2] *Short Jnl.* 104.

described him, told Daniel Abraham, when he met him on the road, that if she continued to hold Meetings in her house, she would have 'to expect the same again'. When Daniel replied that they would have to keep their Meetings, unless they took their lives, Kirkby said, 'We will not take your lives, but whilst you have anything, we will take it'. On this, the mistress of Swarthmoor again wrote to the King, reporting the threats made by Kirkby. As her persecutors troubled them no more, she supposed that the Privy Council had given them a private caution.[1] The King's action however was wider in scope than that. Within a month of the new King's accession, he had been petitioned by Friends to release their sufferers in prison. Two months later he told a Quaker deputation that he intended to release Friends and stop the ravages of Informers. All through the year Friends continued to press for release, and in March 1686 the King's General Pardon preluded the issue of a Royal Warrant releasing Friend prisoners and discharging all the fines laid on them for non-attendance at church.[2] Informers soon afterwards were suppressed.

This movement to toleration by James II, so persistently backed by his friend William Penn, became unfortunately a source of suspicion among many Englishmen owing to the fact of the King's Roman Catholicism and his favouritism of Catholics against the will of Parliament.

In the spring of 1687 James issued his Declaration of Indulgence for all Nonconformists. It is a sad commentary on the bigotry of the times and on the fear felt towards Roman Catholics and the King's loyalty to that Church, that this Declaration which ended the persecution of Quakers and others should have been received generally without enthusiasm and in some quarters with hostility. The Declaration was indeed one of the factors which drove the King off the throne and created the Revolution of 1689, the accession of William and Mary, and the establishment finally of a Protestant and constitutional monarchy in England.

One of the first acts of the new reign was the passing of the Toleration Act of May 1689, which gave a great though in-

[1] M.F. *Works.*
[2] Abraham MSS. 29.

complete victory for religious liberty.[1] It was incomplete because Roman Catholics and anti-Trinitarians were excluded,
but at last the Quakers were able to worship as they felt right,
without suffering loss of their freedom or property.

[1] For a full account of the political struggle up to the Toleration Act, and
the part played by Friends and particularly William Penn, see *Second Period of
Qism.*, Chapters V and VI.

**Isabel Ross had amended her note at the foot of page 326 after the
1949 edition, adding that Thomas and Mary Lower were in London in
February or March 1685, he then returning to Launceston and she to
Swarthmoor or Marsh Grange.**

Chapter Twenty-one

MARGARET FOX AND HER FAMILY RELATIONSHIPS

I. Toleration, Death of Fox, 1691, Susannah Fell, The Rouses

GEORGE Fox in London in 1687 saw that toleration was about to come, after these long forty years of persecution. Neither he nor his wife could expect many more years of life. Swarthmoor Hall might pass out of the ownership of a Friend. It would be well therefore if the beloved Meeting there should not be dependent for a home at the Hall, but should now have its own Meeting House. So early in 1687 when he was staying with the Rouses at Kingston-on-Thames, and the Meades at Gooses, Essex, Fox wrote to Thomas Lower at Marsh Grange to tell him that he offered and gave up 'freely to the Lord for the service of His sons and daughters and servants called Quakers', the house, barn and kiln, stable and all the land, the garden and orchard of a three-acre 'tenement' called Petty's, five minutes' walk from the Hall. This was a husbandman's home which had some years before been bought by Fox from Susannah and Rachel Fell for the sum of seventy-two pounds. The cottage and barn were to be made into a Meeting House. 'Slate it and pave the way to it and about it, that Friends may go dry to the Meeting', wrote Fox. To maintain the house, the land (which was free from all tithes) and malt house were to be used or let out, and a 'poor honest Friend' could live in the cottage. His four stepsons-in-law, John Rous, Thomas Lower, William Meade and Daniel Abraham, were to be trustees to draw up the 'safe and firm writings' concerning the gift, together with some members of the Swarthmoor Monthly Meeting and of the Lancashire Quarterly Meeting, so that Friends might for ever have a free Meeting house, and one which would maintain itself. He wished a porch, with seats, to be built at the entrance, and fir trees and an orchard to be planted. He gave twenty pounds over and above the property as he did not want any other

Friends to give anything, unless it were their services to cart some stones and provide lime. For the furnishing of the attached cottage, Fox gave his ebony bedstead (a bed unusual for the seventeenth century, in that its four posts are slender instead of thick), with its 'Pintado'[1] curtains, a large elbow chair which had been given him by his old friend Robert Widders,[2] a great sea chest 'with bottles in it', all to be heirlooms, 'so that Friends may have a bed to lie on, a chair to sit in, and a bottle to hold a little water to drink'.[3]

The bottles have now disappeared, as have the curtains, but added to the original gift there is a similar Cromwellian oak arm-chair, given by Margaret Fox, and a fine Coverdale 'Treacle' Bible (the gift of George Fox) with its ancient chain and its engraving of Henry VIII presenting the English Bible to

[1] Pintado or pantado was printed cotton material imported from the East Indies (*A History of Everyday Things in England*, 1500–1799, by M. and C. H. B. Quennell, p. 100). It was used to hang on walls of rooms, etc. It was sometimes 'full of figures great and small, prettily representing sundry trades and occupations of the Indians with their habits'—quoted by Quennell from Evelyn's *Diary* of 1665.

[2] Margaret Fox, soon after Robert Widders's death in 1686, wrote a beautiful testimony to him.

'He never did shrink nor start aside in no service nor sufferings, the Lord suffered him to be exercised in. I have known him and been conversant with him 34 years, and we were made partakers of the eternal Truth near together, in the beginning of the infancy of Truth among us, now in our age, when the morning Stars sang together. He went forth in the power and demonstration of the Spirit and turned many to God early in his day. He was of a quick understanding, and the gift of the spirit of discerning was plentifully bestowed upon him. . . . His very presence and countenance and eye was refreshment and comfort, the power of the Lord was so quick and lively in him. . . . He was a dear and faithful brother to me, and to my children, in all our trials and sufferings. It is too much for me to write here, what comfort, strength and assistance he hath been to me and mine, both when we were in prison or out of prison. He would not have failed to come to see us night or day over two dangerous sands, if it had been in the deep of winter, many a time hath he done so of his own accord; and for the most part I have been sensible of his coming before he came, so near and dear he was unto me.

'But what shall I say? His life, and all that ever he had, was given up freely to the Lord and his service; I believe he never neglected any service of the Lord if it was made known unto him, either in England or Scotland or America beyond the Seas'. (*Life and Death of Robert Widders*)

[3] *Book for Pious Uses*, at Cartmel Meeting House, and Camb. Jnl. II, 361.

his subjects. And there stands the old Meeting House still, with its paved way and stone-seated porch and stone panel 'Ex dono G.F. 1688' above the entrance. It is used Sunday by Sunday, for worship by Friends and 'friends of the Friends'.

As is usual with country Meeting houses of the seventeenth century, there is a small stable attached to the cottage, where Friends could leave their horses, and a mounting block close by. On the other side of the house is the burial ground which has been in use since about 1710. In springtime it is filled with wild daffodils, which grow profusely in Furness and the Lake District.

In April 1690, when Margaret Fox was seventy-six years old, she made her ninth visit to London, to be with her husband who was now too infirm to ride or drive the long journey North although he was ten years her junior.[1] She rode on horseback across the sands and at Lancaster hired a coach to London.[2] It was to be their last time together. She had the beautiful homes of her daughters at Kingston and Gooses to stay in, and many friends to meet. 'I was very well satisfied, refreshed and comforted in my journey, and found Friends in much love.'[3] And again she wrote: 'Of all the times that I was at London, this last time was most comfortable, that the Lord was pleased to give me strength and ability to travel that great journey . . . to see my dear husband, who was better in his health and strength than many times I had seen him before. I look upon it, that the Lord's special hand was in it, that I should go then, for he lived but

---

[1] *Short Jnl.* 206. Margaret Fox and her family were singularly spared the attentions of highwaymen in their many journeys to and from the South. Two months after Margaret's journey on this occasion, Lady Rodes wrote to her son, Sir John Rodes, that her brother had been robbed only twenty miles from London. 'They took twenty guineas from him and what silver he had and his sword. He was in a hackney coach, and there was three men besides him and one woman, and they took her watch from her and robbed them all, and there came a gentleman and his man by whilst they were searching of them, and they fell upon them and robbed them also. They would have persuaded them to have left them something to have borne their charges, but the thieves answered and said: such gentleman as they, had credit upon the road.' (*Quaker Postbag*, 16–17.)

[2] Spence MSS. III, 192 (H. G. Crosfield, pp. 213–14).

[3] M.F. *Works*, p. 13.

about half a year after I left him; which makes me admire the wisdom and goodness of God in ordering my journey at that time.'[1]

Soon after her return home in July, by coach, accompanied by Thomas and Mary Lower and their children, she wrote a loving letter to the Women's Meeting in London,[2] acknowledging their 'dear, tender and kind love' when she was with them, and their love and tenderness to her husband, and exhorting them to unity and faithfulness to God.[3]

On 13th January 1691 George Fox died, two days after he had attended Gracechurch Street Meeting, where he had spoken and prayed with great power. William Penn at once sent the news to Margaret at Swarthmoor. 'O he is gone and has left us', he wrote, 'in the storm[4] that is over our heads, surely in great mercy to him, but as an evidence to us of sorrow to come. . . . A Prince indeed is fallen in Israel to-day.' And in a postscript: '. . . He died as he lived, a lamb, minding the things of God and His church to the last in an universal Spirit.'[5] In a long testimony[6] to her second husband, Margaret wrote how he had been made even in his youth an instrument to preach the everlasting gospel which had been hidden for many generations. In this she was referring to his consistent emphasis on the Spirit, the Light Within, the supreme importance of understanding the heart of Christ's teaching, and of endeavouring constantly to make the mind sensitive and the life consistent. Among much that was written by his friends about this great man and rugged saint, we are told of his tender care of his people, his gift for understanding the spiritual condition of those who came for his help, because he was 'deep in the divine mysteries of the Kingdom of God',[7] his unselfish leadership of the Church, the sacrifice of

---

[1] Leeds Jnl. *M.F.'s Testimony.*
[2] *Short Jnl.*
[3] M F. *Works*, p. 14.
[4] The storm referred to by Penn was the charge of treason brought against him at that time by the Government of William III. For nearly three years Penn lived in retirement, till in November 1693 he was honourably acquitted 'of all the false charges'.
[5] Thirnbeck MSS. 21.
[6] Leeds Jnl.
[7] Testimony by his stepsons-in-law and stepdaughters. Leeds Jnl. I, lxxii.

worldly ease and comfort. 'So meek, contented, modest, steady, tender, easy,' wrote William Penn, 'it was a pleasure to be in his company. He exercised no authority but over evil, and that every where and in all: but with love, compassion and long-suffering. A most merciful man, as ready to forgive, as unapt to take or give an offence. . . . The most excellent spirits loved him with an unfeigned and unfading love. . . . I never saw him out of his place, or not a match for every service or occasion. For in all things he acquitted himself like a man, yea a strong man, a new and heavenly-minded man; a divine and a naturalist, and all of God Almighty's making. . . . Civil, beyond all forms of breeding, in his behaviour; very temperate, eating little, and sleeping less, though a bulky person.'[1]

At her husband's death Margaret Fox was seventy-seven. Freed from persecution, the last eleven years of her life were spent, except for one more visit to London, at her beloved home. The Sunday Meeting for worship was now, after 1690, held, not in her large hall but in the near-by Meeting house.

The letters still preserved of the last twenty years of her life are chiefly, though not entirely, family letters. No longer did she receive letters as in the early days from the Friends carrying their message to all parts of the world, for indeed by this time the Society had spread far and wide, most of the pioneers were already dead, worn out with their labours and imprisonments, and this was the time of consolidation. The records of that do not come usually into letters, but into the Minute Books of Meetings. From these there is constant evidence of the faithful attendance of Margaret and her family at the Monthly and Quarterly Meetings, to and from most of which a journey on horseback over fell roads or across the sands of Morecambe Bay was essential.

In the rest of this chapter we shall follow the fortunes of five of Margaret Fox's daughters and their relationship with her.

After Rachel's marriage in 1683 only one of the Fell daughters still remained unmarried, Susannah, then about thirty-three years old. When Sarah in 1681 went to London to be married, Susannah stayed at home with her younger sister, but

[1] Preface to Leeds Jnl.

soon after her mother's return from London (July 1681), Susannah left to go to Gooses to live for some years with Sarah and William Meade. It is from there in February 1682 that Susannah wrote to Rachel one of the very few letters of hers which still remain. Indeed she was no writer—her letter sprawls on a slant across the paper, her spelling worse than phonetic. (However she was writing in a hurry, she explained.) But it is a 'short salutashon of onfened love' to her younger sister and 'my duty to my deare mother, for youer rememberanc is very plesent to mee and I can truely saye its neder lenth of time nor distance of miles make uide [=void] or elenette [=alienate] my love to youe.' Her health in Essex was much better than at Swarthmoor (one remembers her iron collar, mentioned for repair in Sarah's account book) and the air was agreeing with her.[1]

When Sarah's only child, Nathaniel, was born early in May 1684, Susannah was with her sister, who wrote to her mother, when the baby was three weeks old—'She hath been and is mighty careful and tender of me and my little boy (as I know she hath been of others of my sisters in the like condition), but I hope not to hurt herself; my husband and myself looks upon ourselves much engaged to her, for her good company, love and care; and to thee, that thou art pleased to spare her; and I hope it will not be to her hurt, being much to our comfort.'[2]

As to Susannah's health, Sarah reported that she was 'much as she used to be, but at spring and fall, finds herself a little worse.'

It says much for Sarah's good sense, as well as her mother's wise advice, that at the age of forty-two when her only child was born, she nursed the baby herself, instead of employing a wet-nurse, as was so usual for the educated women to do in those days. In nearly every letter she was able to report that the baby was 'fine and well' or 'thriving'.

For ten years Susannah lived at Gooses with the Meades, returning, so far as we know, only once during that time to her old home, in May 1687, to be there at the birth of little John Abraham.

[1] Abraham MSS. 28.
[2] Spence MSS. III, 188. 31 iii [May] 1684.

M

On 2 v [July] 1691 when she was forty-one she married William
Ingram, a widower, some ten years older. He was a merchant, a
citizen of London, a tallow-chandler of Fenchurch Street, a
friend of William Meade, and doubtless he had met Susannah
at the Meades' home. He was a man of education and good
sense—his letters are both well written and well expressed—
and a Friend of long standing. He knew George Fox for forty
years, and was one of three—the other two being Sarah Meade
and George Whitehead—who proved the handwriting of Fox's
will. By his first wife, also Susannah, he had had eleven children,
so though Susannah Fell never had her own child, she had step-
children to mother. Four or six of the eleven children survived
their childhood, the youngest being five years of age when their
father married Susannah Fell. One of William Ingram's children, Joseph[1] (born 1686), married Mary, the elder daughter of
John Bellers, the Quaker pioneer of social reform and education
and the inspirer of Robert Owen in the nineteenth century and
of other pioneers.[2]

One of William Ingram's daughters, Elizabeth, who died in
1699, at the age of nineteen, left a legacy to the Box Meeting.

Susannah herself for many years was a member of the Box
Meeting, and her signature to the minutes appears with that of
the other members almost continuously from 1692 to 1708, in
which year her sister Sarah ceased to be clerk.

Although William Ingram was a Friend of such long standing—he had suffered imprisonment in 1686 and was a member
of Meeting for Sufferings (the Executive of the Society of
Friends)—he had never met Margaret Fox before his marriage
to her daughter. So some months after that event he wrote to his
mother-in-law to tell her of the 'health and welfare' of himself
and Susannah, and of their happiness. 'The goodness and love of
God is preciously enjoyed by us both', he told her, 'as being
that which we earnestly desire and hoped for, and had a true

---

[1] The high rate of infant mortality, even among the well-to-do, is remarkable not only among Joseph's brothers and sisters, but among his own children.
His wife Mary bore thirteen children between 1711 and 1731, and of these only
four lived to grow up. The tragedy to the parents is emphasized in this case
by the ages of the children at their deaths—at five years, at one and a half years,
at ten, at four, at two, at one, at three, at eighteen hours, and at sixteen years.

[2] *Second Period of Qism.* p. 572, note.

prospect of when the Lord by his power first wrought to bring us into a nearness of affection. . . . And indeed as to myself I do in spirit often return thanks unto the Lord, who has cast my lot into such a family, where for many years I have been sensible, the glory of his name and truth has been sought and exalted over all, and the remembrance of it does always create in me a joy.' His joy would be more full, he added, if he could live to see her face, but if this is denied him, 'I shall acquiese in full assurance of hope hereafter to meet thee, with the Lord's sanctified ones in the Kingdom of eternal rest and quiet.'[1]

Margaret Fox and William Ingram did not meet each other until she came on her tenth and last visit to London in 1697. In the meantime, however, others of the sisters reported news of the Ingrams. During 1693 some disquieting news or criticism of Susannah must have been sent to Margaret at Swarthmoor, and Sarah and Susannah had evidently written conciliatory explanations, for we find Margaret in December (1693) writing to Sarah Meade that she was heartily glad to hear from her about Susannah. 'If she demeans[2] and behaves herself according to truth and righteousness in that place where God has set her, my heart and soul praises the Lord for it, and it is his doings and goodness that frames and fashions and moves into his own image and nature, for we are in his hands as the clay is in the hands of the potter. And what is good in everyone, He makes it, it's of him, and our eye must be upon him, to receive and ask counsel and wisdom of him, and then we shall be furnished with grace and wisdom to serve him and obey him in our several places, . . . that therein . . . his precious truth . . . may be verified. And so for my daughter Ingram's letter I am very well satisfied in the relation she gives . . . and let no more troubles nor rehearsings be about it. . . . And so the Lord God Almighty keep us all in love and unity with God and with one another, and then all will be well.' She sent her dear love to the Ingrams and their children, 'they are as dear to me as ever, and my heart's desire and prayer to Eternal God is and shall be for them as it is for my own soul and for all my dear children and offspring'.[3]

---

[1] Abraham MSS. 44.
[2] Demeans = conducts herself (in seventeenth century).
[3] Spence MSS. III, 194. 11 x [Dec.] 1693.

In this letter was Margaret Fox's whole philosophy of religion
and life—the God within, shown forth in love, one with another. Her heart rejoiced, when a few months later, Sarah told
her mother—'Sister Ingram is now here, and hath been here
some days, to be in the country air, her husband thinks to come
down to-morrow; they are both well; and truly they live in
much love and tenderness to each other, which much rejoices
my heart. He is a tender-spirited man, and tender of the Lord
his truth and honour; and it grieves him to see any Friend appear
in anything that is out of the spirit of Truth.'[1]

A couple of years later the Ingrams sent Margaret a present,
and in reply to her letter of thanks, William Ingram wrote
(March 1696) an affectionate letter to his mother-in-law, now
eighty-one. (His handwriting was as neat and careful as his wife's
was untidy.) He was thankful that she was 'still preserved, not
only in bodily health, but in lively sense and unity of the eternal
Spirit'. They are 'much refreshed to hear the winter season has
had no greater influence on thy tender and aged disposition; it
is the Lord's mercy and goodness unto us, in affording comfort
to us, in such thy preservation; we pray for the continuance of
it till he please to make an alteration'. He gives her the good
news of the passing of the Act, through the House of Commons,
to relieve Friends of the necessity to take the oath—they now
could affirm instead—a right for which they had struggled and
suffered continuously for half a century. William Meade had
been spending several days lobbying in the House, on behalf
of Friends. Ingram tells also of the lately discovered French-
Jacobite plot for the invasion of England—'but the Lord in his
great mercy has prevented it, and yet continues his wonted
favour and goodness towards this poor nation. . . . blessing it
with peculiar preservation.'[2]

A year and a half later William and Susannah were able to
welcome Margaret Fox in London, where she stayed several
months. Towards the end of her visit she wrote a letter to King
William III, and it was Susannah whom she chose to present it
to the King.

William Ingram's staunch character impressed Margaret Fox,

[1] Thirnbeck MSS. 25.
[2] Abraham MSS. 33.

and the last three letters still preserved from and to this son-in-law show him as the business and legal adviser to Daniel and Rachel Abraham. Daniel, at Swarthmoor, asked William to arrange money bills for their mother-in-law[1] while she was staying with the Ingrams in London in January 1698, and to do business for him with his nephew, Charles Fell. In the following year he (William) with the other brothers-in-law wrestled in spirit with Daniel Abraham, when the latter was mistakenly refusing to pay certain rents (fee-farm rent charge) on his Swarthmoor estate, believing that they would go to pay the priest's salary. Daniel's over-conscientiousness was quite unnecessary, as the charge was a local form of rent, and not connected with the church, but it caused great mental suffering to his family, as he was threatened with dispossession if he refused to pay. At length, on a visit to London in 1699, Daniel was persuaded to give up his stand, and Ingram wrote a full letter explaining the position to those at Swarthmoor.[2] At the same time, knowing the anxiety it had caused Rachel, he wrote her a letter of loving sympathy—'we greatly pity thy exercised condition, but know as the Lord is eyed and had regard unto, he is able and in due time will give ease to the afflicted.'[3]

William Ingram gave much praise to Thomas Lower for his share in persuading Daniel Abraham to pay the fee-farm rent. Another Friend who helped was George Whitehead, who after studying the law of Charles II relating to fee-farm rents in Lancashire wrote to Margaret Fox: 'I do not understand that they are tithes or tenths . . . but distinct from them, and referred as payable to the Crown or as a Crown rent.' He added that there was no reason for conscience to refuse this payment: 'Friends had need', he wrote, 'to have good reason for conscience and see the same be consistent with our Christian profession in every case, when they profess a conscientiousness, and not to strain that to dubious cases.'[4] Wise advice indeed, which finally Daniel Abraham was persuaded to follow, as were some other Swarthmoor Friends who had taken the same line.

[1] Abraham MSS. 37.
[2] Abraham MSS. 39, and printed in full in Jnl. F.H.S. XI, 177-9.
[3] Abraham MSS. 40.
[4] Portfolio 42, 35. Library, Friends' House, London.

Our last touch with Susannah's husband shows his kindness and wisdom. He was concerned when he heard that Margaret Fox feared for the spiritual welfare of young Nathaniel Meade, who at the age of sixteen was being allowed by his parents to leave their country home, and live as a law student in London, at the Middle Temple. No doubt she thought sadly of her own son, many years ago, living in Gray's Inn, and learning ways of extravagance and worldliness, leading to tragic estrangement from her.

'I was somewhat concerned', he wrote to her in 1700 about young Nathaniel, 'to desire thee not to let in any trouble to thy mind about that matter; for I hope all will come out well at last, for I know in part the great care and diligence they have used to have him preserved in a sense of truth, and out of the pollution of this world, which I and many more that know him are satisfied he is clear and clean from; but so it has happened that he, being of an active mind, could not content himself without some business and diversion, more than the country life with his father and mother did afford. So their care and great concern was to fit him with what might be most suitable to his condition and inclination, which they were endeavouring about for a considerable time.' So these elderly parents of this clever only son first sent him, no doubt with his tutor, on a visit to Holland, and on his return, as he still would not accept a country life, they left the choice of a profession to him, and the young man chose the law. Ingram explained that probably he would not practise later, as there was no financial need of that, but that it was for his education and to remove him from someone whom to know would not have been to his advantage. His parents, 'to whom I know', (Ingram wrote), 'he is as dear to as the apple of their eye', had placed him in chambers in the Temple next to a 'kinsman and counsellor, who hath the character of a very sober and honest man'. 'So the issue must be left to the Lord, in whose power it only is, to make our children such as He would have them be. I write this that thou mayst be satisfied in my brother and sister's care in this business, and that according to my sense they have not done anything on their parts that may be occasion of trouble either to thee, who I know art greatly concerned for cousin Nathaniel, nor any other that have respect for him.'[1]

[1] Abraham MSS. 41.

A few months later Mary Lower, from London, told her mother that the Meades came once a fortnight to see their son at the Temple, 'but the hazard of his continuing there I think they apprehend not so well as people think they might, but there is no room for advice'.[1] Nathaniel Meade however seems to have withstood his youthful temptations successfully, for he remained a Friend all his life, and rose as a barrister to be Serjeant-at-law, received a knighthood, and died in 1760, 'a gentleman universally respected'.[2]

William Ingram's wise letter to Margaret, supporting the Meades' plans for their son, was justified in its results.

Susannah's happy married life ended in 1706 when her husband died. Her death is not recorded, but it must have been after 1710 when she left London, where her health was not good, to go to live again with Sarah and William Meade at Gooses, who at the same time gave up their London house. 'We are now all together at Gooses', wrote Sarah to Rachel Abraham at Swarthmoor at the end of 1710, 'and are comforted in the Lord and one another; we are at a quiet still place, which best suits old age, and my husband has put off most of his business, and let his ground to farmers. Sister Ingram and I are also better in our health than sometime formerly, having fallen to eating mostly oatbread of late, which is some advantage to our health, but can eat little of meat.'[3]

Let us turn now to Margaret Fox's eldest daughter, Margaret Rous. For most of her married life, as we have seen, she and her husband John had lived at Kingston-on-Thames. Here in his later years George Fox frequently had found rest, and himself had given comfort. Margaret Fox also on her visits to London often stayed at Kingston. She was there when Thomas was born in 1673, and when Bridget was born two years later both she and Susannah were there to help.

Margaret Rous made at least two voyages to Barbados, to meet her husband's family, once as a bride, and again in the summer of 1678. On the latter occasion some of the children

[1] Thirnbeck MSS. 28.
[2] H. G. Crosfield, p. 220.
[3] Spence MSS. III, 200.

went with their parents, though the twelve-year-old Bethiah, who was the eldest, was sent to stay at Swarthmoor. It is difficult for us now to imagine the risks, and indeed misery of the long voyage across the Atlantic in the seventeenth century, specially for a delicate woman and her family of little children.

Of the eight (or nine) children the Rouses had, only four grew up, two dying in infancy, and one Bridget, the youngest, dying of smallpox when she was eight years old. Smallpox and consumption were two of the worst and most common diseases of the seventeenth century. Even the wealthy and well housed did not escape. When Nathaniel Rous was a schoolboy of sixteen he also had smallpox, though he recovered, and grew up to marry. But four of his children died as babies, the longest to live only reaching three years. He himself died of consumption at the age of forty-seven.

Very few letters from John and Margaret Rous to their mother at Swarthmoor, written in the last fifteen years of her life, have survived. The following from John Rous, dated March 1686 from Kingston, gives a picture of the family in some of its troubles:

Kingston, 20: [**March**] 1685/6

Dear Mother,

We received thy acceptable letter and were very glad to hear of all your welfare. Our daughter Nanny [Ann, born in May 1672] hath lately had a sore throat and a fever, but through the Lord's mercy is well again; and we intend after a little while, if she continue so, to send her to Ann Travers's school at Chiswick. [Possibly the Ann Travers who had for so many years looked after Ellis Hookes.]

Nathaniel we sent to Richard Scorier's writing school[1] near William Shewen's, where he was between seven and eight weeks, but it being a nasty place, the air did not agree with him, but from his first going he fell away of his flesh very much and the latter end of last week was taken with a shivering and not well, which they gave my brother Meade notice of on 7th day, and he ordered his man John Kemble to bring us word on 1st day; but Nathaniel growing rather worse, the schoolmaster hired a coach and sent him home and John Kemble came

---

[1] This 'celebrated college' was at Southwark until Scorier moved in 1693 to Wandsworth. R.S. taught his pupils writing and arithmetic, and apparently had a special method. Later than 1686 he offered to give free training to young men Friends who wished to learn his methods. Jnl. F.H.S. VII, 46.

on horseback with him. We presently sent for a doctor, who gave him a vomit that afternoon . . . and cleared his body very finely; the next day after that he was pretty well and came downstairs, but towards evening the smallpox began to break out, but he was very well, neither feverish nor lightheaded nor pain in his head nor back, but hath continued as well as can be expected, though it is that sort they call the fluxing pox, and there doth not appear any sign of danger, which I desire the Lord if it be his will to continue.

My father Fox came hither this day, who not resting well last night is asleep, that I cannot ask him about Willm. Penn's journey into the north, but I heard Willm. say that he intended to go through Lincolnshire and Yorkshire and to see his sister in Cleveland, and then to go to Swarthmore, which I believe he will do. As to news I shall leave it to my sister Meade who can better inform thee, and with our dear love to thee, my brother and sisters and little cousins, I rest,

Thy dear son in the Lord,

John Rous.[1]

On the back of this beautifully written letter, Sarah Meade, to whom John Rous evidently sent it while she was in London, to be forwarded to the north, told her mother that the King's pardon to Friend prisoners was now signed and about to be sent to all the country jails.

Nathaniel Rous, as has been mentioned, recovered from his smallpox, but possibly it left him delicate and susceptible to consumption, which attacked him later.

The eldest daughter, Bethiah Rous, at twenty-six married David English, a 'grocer' [=dealer in gross, a merchant] of Pontefract, Yorks. They were a delicate couple, and lost three out of their four children in infancy.

In 1699 after Margaret Fox had returned from her last visit to London, she wrote to Bethiah and David English, when a friend visiting her was about to go to Pontefract. (The cross-country post was non-existent—letters into Yorkshire had usually to go via London, so they were not very often sent.) Bethiah's mother had recently written telling how very ill David English had been for a long time, adding: 'She meets mostly with many exercises, poor child.' So Margaret passes on to them the wisdom won from a long life, in which happiness and sorrow had

[1] Abraham MSS. 29.

mingled. 'I write . . . desiring you to keep close to the Lord's pure love and life and there you will grow and abide near the Lord, and he will bide near to you as you abide inwardly to him. Dear Bethiah, keep up to the Lord, be content with his will whatever it be, for it is the best and the safest for thee; wait upon him in obedience, and it is the way for the Lord to give thee thy heart's desire.'[1]

Of the three surviving daughters of John and Margaret Rous, the second one, Margaret, gave her parents much anxiety. The cause of this is now unknown, though it was probably due to her marriage to a man called Manwaring. But when she was twenty her father wrote to Margaret Fox to ask for her advice. 'Thou desireth to hear from me', came the reply, '. . . I desire the Lord to guide you and direct you how to do, so as to preserve your child to God, that she be not utterly cast away from the Lord and his truth. Outward things are of little value in comparison with that, for her preservation to the Lord and his truth is altogether in my eye, and if you be too severe and hard with her, I am afraid lest she, despairing of your favour, it may cause her to lean more upon them and so be further from recovering. There must needs be some tenderness and mercy shewed towards her eternal good or how can she be preserved.

' I have writ and enclosed a few lines which I would have her to have; if you think it convenient. . . .

' I desire you to use your endeavour to gain and recover what is lost, and remember Him that left the ninety-and-nine and went to seek that which was lost and brought it home and rejoiced more over it than over all the rest, and consider though she hath done evil she might have done worse.

' So no more, but the Lord's powerful arm guide you, and direct you and lead you the way He would have you to go.'[2]

We do not know if Margaret Fox's wise advice was followed or not, but there was no reconciliation. Young Margaret went her own way, the girl who as a baby had been left with grandmother and aunts at Swarthmoor ('pretty little babe', Thomas Salthouse had called her), and who later had twice been so

---

[1] Portfolio 31, 108. Library, Friends' House, London. 17.9.1699.
[2] Crosfield MSS. 17. 3.2 [April] 1687.

seriously ill (when she was sixteen and seventeen) that George Fox had been fetched to their home to give all the spiritual help he could. Her father in his will, drawn up five years after this letter, wrote of his daughter as one who 'hath several ways disobliged me', and he left her only ten pounds, but added 'if after my decease she shall by her obedient and dutiful carriage oblige my now wife' then she was to be given £500.

Some years later (1699) her mother wrote to Margaret Fox that she had told her daughter (now thirty-two years old) that if she would be 'governed' by her she might come and live with her, and she would 'want for nothing that was convenient and necessary for her'. Possibly the girl was now a widow, for her mother added, 'I had a fear before how she would prove if I should meddle with her, and since I knew her mind, wrote to her, being she was so wickedly bent and resolved in her mind, I would not meddle of her, but leave her to her husband's relations, and her salt concerns, since which I have heard nothing from her. But I understand by others she is still in the salt business. I know not what it will benefit her, but she spends her time about it. I have left her at present.'[1]

So Margaret Manwaring passes out of the life of the family. She had one child, who in 1699 was at the Friends' School at Penketh, near Warrington, and doing well, and being 'very orderly'.[2] Her grandmother left her in her will one guinea, half what she left to her other grandchildren, but the same bequest as to the children of her undutiful son.

In 1696 tragedy came to Margaret Rous, not for the first time. At the end of 1693 John Rous had sailed to Barbados again. His father, Colonel Rous, of that island, was now dead. John was his eldest son and heir. Rous's son, Nathaniel, and daughter, Ann, had gone with him as far as Gravesend.[3] His safe arrival at Barbados was reported by Sarah Meade from Gooses in April the next year (1694).[4] In March 1696, however, bad news came. The ship he was sailing home in was lost at sea in a storm, and Rous was drowned. His widow wrote to her mother:

[1] Spence MSS. III, 197.
[2] Ibid.
[3] From letter from Thomas Lower to M.F., Dec. 1693. Thirnbeck MSS. 23.
[4] Letter from S.M. to M.F., in Thirnbeck MSS. 25.

London, 1st of 1st Mo. 1695.
[=March 1696.]

Dear and honoured Mother,

We do not hear anything yet of the ship my dear husband was in, eleven more being wanted. One master that is come tells me he was aboard his ship some days before the storm and he was very weakly and much out of health, but saw him several days after, before the storm, walk upon the deck, but when they were parted did not see one another afterwards; so how it have pleased the Lord to deal with him, poor heart, I am in great doubt. The consideration of the thing is very hard, but I have no way but to look unto the Lord and submit to his divine hand of Providence, who is able and all sufficient to preserve through all perils and dangers as He hath been pleased to do my poor husband several times, and He is the same God still and His power is the same and to His blessed providence I must leave it, but my exercise is great.

I received thy letter which is of great worth to me. My poor children are sadly troubled. If you please to write to Bethiah and send it hither, I shall send it to her. Nathaniel and Ann are pretty well considering our great trial, as I am myself. All our duties and dearest loves is to thee, and all our dear love to Brother and Sister Abraham and cousins. Desiring thy blessing and prayers for me and mine and desiring to hear from thee, I am,

Thy truly loving daughter,
M. Rous.[1]

John Rous was a wealthy man, and he left his family well provided for, from estates and property both in England and Barbados.[2]

Three years after her father's death, the youngest daughter, Anne, married a Friend of Colchester, Benjamin Dykes, as his second wife. Her husband seems to have been rather a mischief-maker in the family. In 1701 Mary Lower wrote to her mother that Anne Dykes and her husband were criticizing without cause, both among London Friends and to the relatives at Swarthmoor, Mary's daughter Loveday who had in 1699 married William Swan of Halstead, Essex. 'We cannot imagine, wrote Mary, 'what should make them be so envious as they are against us, but most against Loveday who behaves herself very inoffensively to them and all people, and hath the report of

[1] Abraham MSS. 32.
[2] His will is in Jnl. F.H.S. IV.

Friends and others of her obliging, humble behaviour. And I must say I know nothing that makes them so much against both my son and daughter Swan, but that they have the better report of all people; for my son Swan is a very exact man to his word, dealings and payments, and the other is far otherwise. Loveday doth not keep her parlour, but is a good country wife and minds her husband's business in his absence, and makes a careful[?] nurse, and the child is a strong, lusty, forward child.'[1] Loveday had been provided by her parents with a £500 dowry, but Benjamin Dykes had been spreading abroad that she only had £150.

This jealousy among the grandchildren did not harm the good relations of the two sisters, for Mary at the same time had the widowed Margaret Rous living with her, adding, 'I think she is pleased with her lodgings'.[2]

Benjamin Dykes had not only made trouble about Loveday, but also had accused Nathaniel Rous, who was executor under his father's will, of not carrying out the provisions properly where Anne's portion was concerned. Margaret Fox was appealed to, and sent Nathaniel a supporting letter which he described as a 'testimony for the justness of mine intentions towards them'. 'I hope', the young man added in his reply to his grandmother, 'the Lord will close the coveting eye in them, and open the eye which sees things as they are, and judges righteously. Mine heart rejoiced at the reading of it, and the Truth contained in it was so clear, that I expected all further disputings would have been at an end.' Not so with brother Dykes, however, who continued with his 'stories'. 'It is much more exercising', commented Nathaniel, 'to find these dealings from so near relations than from others.'[3]

Margaret Rous, who suffered in her old age from rheumatism which made her lame, lived in London until her death in 1706 aged seventy-three, surviving her mother by only four years.

II. The Meades

Of all the family letters written in the last two decades of Margaret Fox's life, the most varied in interest are Sarah's.

[1] Thirnbeck MSS. 28.
[2] Thirnbeck MSS. 28. 2.3.1701.
[3] Thirnbeck MSS. 27.

Margaret Rous and Mary Lower wrote of many family events, and now and again referred to Quaker affairs, but Sarah gave not only family news, but wrote of public events affecting Friends, news of people in London known and loved by her mother, and for long after she had left her old home, she continued to send them business and financial advice. She was her mother's most frequent correspondent. Between 1683 and 1689 there are some thirteen of Sarah's letters still preserved; in the 'nineties there is but one (1694). Possibly many others of that decade were given away after 1759 by John Abraham, and have since been destroyed or lost. The last letter written by Sarah still extant is dated 1710, eight years after her mother's death.

The first letter of these years, though long, is so vivid and gives such a picture, both of Sarah's generosity and affection, as well as of the fashions of the time, that it must be quoted in full. It was written two years after Sarah had left home to be married, a few months after Rachel's marriage to Daniel Abraham, and while the new persecution of 1681 to 1686 was on the Swarthmoor family; Thomas Lower was in Launceston jail, and the Meades were trying to get release for him.

London, 19th of 10th m. [Dec.] 1683.
Dear Sister Abram,

I have endeavoured to fit my dear Mother with black cloth for a gown, which is very good and fine, and as much as Jno. Richards saith is enough to the full (five yards and a half) and what materials as he thought was needful to send down; viz., silk both sewing and stitching, gallowne[1] ribbon and laces, and I was very glad to know what she wanted, for it has been in my mind a pretty while to send her and you something, and I could not tell what she might need or might be most serviceable to her was the reason of my thus long forbearance; and so I desire her acceptance of it and yours of these small things underwritten:

3 pairs of doeskin gloves, such as are worn in winter, for Mother, Sister Lower and thyself; the thickest pair for Mother if they fit her, but that I leave to you to agree on as you please.

1 pair same sort of gloves for Brother Abraham;
4 ells of holland for Sister Lower and thyself, each 2 ells;

---

[1] Gallowne in the seventeenth century was a narrow close-woven braid of gold, silver, silk or cotton, used for binding dresses, the modern galloon (*Concise Oxford Dictionary*).

2 pots of balsam, one for my mother, the other for Sister Yeamans;
3 pocket almanacs for Sister Yeamans, Sister Lower and thyself;
1 muslin nightrail [dressing-gown] for Sister Yeamans;
100 needles, of which half for Sister Yeamans, which she sent for,
the other half hundred for Sister Lower and thyself.

Sister Susanna, understanding from Sister Yeamans that Hen:
Coward expected something from her for the care he had took about
her money (though she did not reckon herself behind, if things of all
hands were considered), yet, as a small acknowledgment of his care
and respect in it, she hath sent him and his wife each a pair of doeskin
gloves, which she desires thee to send them, with the remembrance of
her kind love to them.

Here is for Sister Lower, which she sent to Sister Susanna to buy
her, a coloured stuff manteo [a loose upper garment worn by women],
cost 14s and 11 yards and half of black worsted stuff at 2s. per yard,
cost 22s. Sister Sus. exchanged the old 20s. piece of gold, as she desired,
which yielded 23/6, so she is out of purse for her 12/6. Black stuff was
worse to get than coloured, which is now mostly worn, of such coarse
things; but she hath done as well as she can, and hopes it will do well
and please her; its a strong serviceable stuff. Also Sister Lower sent for
a Bible for Cousin Margery, which Sister Susanna sends to the child
for a token, and hopes it may suit her well; I feared it was too small a
print, but several tell us its fittest for a child having young eyes, and
should learn all prints, both small and great.

Sister Yeamans sent to me for Will Yeamans' old clothes that he had
left off wearing, for Ja: Geldart and Dan Cooper. I have sent for them,
but its such a crossway to where he is, they are not yet come, nor I
fear will not before Ja. Geldart goes out of town, so I must send them
by the carrier, and if they be not worth carriage, I cannot help it, it
was her own request to have them. She mentioned Ja: Geldart going
that way for them, but it is too much out of his way, and not worth
his while. Tell her she did not lose her needle case here, nor at Bridget's
room, that we can hear of; also tell her Mary Frith presents her service
to her and takes it kindly that she should send her her fillet.

Nought else, but mine, my husband's and sisters' duty to our dear
Mother; and dear and kind love to thee, to brother and to Sister
Yeamans and Sister Lower.

I am thy affectionate sister

S.M.

We advise you to make my mother's cloth gown without a skirt,
which is very civil and usually so worn both by young and old in stiffened suits.

I send my mother's books and papers that were in my father's chest as she desired, but my husband desired to have the King's grant kept a while longer, being there will be some occasion for it, about Brother Lower's business, and I hope it will be no prejudice to you. Also I send my Sister Fell's bond, which belongs to the last articles she made to my mother; it was left here through some mistake among other papers; be careful of it and put it to the articles of the bargain; you do not know but you may have occasion for it hereafter. I have put it in the paper among your gloves, where thou may find it.[1]

The King's grant refers to the document sent by Charles II in 1671 to pardon Margaret Fox after her year's imprisonment and praemunire, and to grant the Swarthmoor estate to Susannah and Rachel. Perhaps it was being kept in London a while to help in the release of Thomas Lower who had also been praemunired. The grant was returned to Margaret five months later, direct to Lancaster, in time for the Assizes where her case was to come up again.[2]

Shortly afterwards Sarah made one of the rare comments on an illness her mother had had ('griping and colic'), and wrote of the very severe frost and snow, making it hard for Friends who owing to persecution had to hold their Meetings standing in the street. 'You had need to keep warm and put on good store of clothes; and I hope to the Lord, he will preserve thee in health, and lengthen thy days, for he is the only support and strength of all his children.'

She asked her mother to send up to London a full account of Swarthmoor Friends' sufferings, and what losses they had had— these facts were to be sent to the 'Meeting for Sufferings', and when added to others from all over the country, to be presented to the King.

There was an interesting postscript to this letter. Susannah (now living with the Meades) entreated her sister Rachel to get in three money loans of hers, one of £50 from a shopkeeper of Lancaster, one (£40) on a piece of land, and the third (£10) lent elsewhere, together with interest on them, as well as the overdue interest on the first.[3] This £100 total, probably repre-

[1] Abraham MSS. 25.

[2] Miller MSS. 79. Letter from S.M. to M.F. **25 v [July] 1684.**

[3] Abraham MSS. 26. This letter is reproduced in Webb, *Fells*, p. 329, but with inaccuracies and omissions.

senting about £1,000 of present money, gives some impression of the finances and business dealings of these Fell sisters.

In the following May Sarah sent a joyful letter to her mother, on the birth of her son Nathaniel.

London, 17th 3rd m. [May] 1684.

My dear and honoured Mother,

My dear husband gave thee an account last week how mercifully the Lord hath been pleased to deal with us, and being indifferent well at that time, I now write a few lines myself that thou might know how it is with us. I was about six hours in travail, and though it was sharp the Lord was good to me in giving me strength to go through it and endure it and gave me deliverance in his own good time of a sweet babe.

My sweet babe has been very likely thus far, and is thriving as much as could be expected in the time. He has been a little **froward** this day and last night, but I hope it is but wind, and that he will soon be better again. I am fine and well, and endeavouring to make a nurse if the Lord give me milk and strength to do it. The weather is hot at present, and so may be some hindrance to my milk coming so freely yet, as I hope it may be hereafter. He is a fine child, and we desire never to forget the Lord's mercy in giving him, and that we may resign him to the Lord, committing him to His arms, who is able as He pleases to give life and death, and unto whom we are to be subject in all things.

Sister Rous and all her children are in town and indifferent well, as is Father. We have yours by H. Coward. I cannot enlarge only to add my husband's and sister's [Susannah] affectionate duty and respect to thee, with our kind love to brother and sisters.

I am thy dutiful daughter,

S.M.

Frances Kent [the midwife] stayed with me a week after I was laid. She is a fine woman; it was the Lord sent her to me. It was the Lord's mercy that I had her, who is a very skilful and tender woman for that employment.[1]

A fortnight later Sarah is writing again to her mother, thanking her for her letters and for 'thy kind motherly advice about suckling my child'. She is able to feed the child well, now that she is up and about, and reports that he is 'now fine and well, and thrives, his sore mouth being over'.[2] They were very soon

---

[1] Miller MSS. 77, **as printed in Jnl. F.H.S. vol 30 (1933) p.42.**
[2] Spence MSS. III, 188.

going out into the country with Susannah to Gooses, and away from the bad London air.

Susannah's health at Gooses was usually better than when she lived in the North. But she was often ill in the spring—'when she is ill, I am fearful for her', wrote Sarah.

At Lancaster this year, Margaret and Daniel and Rachel Abraham were imprisoned for three weeks, and heavily fined. When the news of this reached Sarah in July her comment is characteristic—'We perceive the spoil that wicked men makes. I question not but the Lord will fit his people for these things, and reward them for what is suffered upon his account, unto whom we must fly and call upon him, in every time of trial, and blessed be his name, who affords his living power and presence to his people, which is more than outward things: and he sees and beholds all, and will reward his enemies in his own due time.'[1]

Sarah was the daughter who not only shopped in London for the family at Swarthmoor, but also dispatched parcels of goods by ship or carrier on behalf of others. At one time mops and chairs and a box from Thomas Lower to his wife were sent by ship to Liverpool. And in another box, by carrier, there were Barbados China Oranges sent by John Rous to Margaret Fox, Rachel, Mary Lower and her children. And Sarah had bought pins for Rachel, in paper, as loose ones could not be bought. The looking-glasses which Mary had wanted could not be sent as they were not procurable.[2] At another time Sarah sent her mother and Rachel two pounds of chocolate and two books of the Testimony to the life and work of that pioneer Friend, Anne Whitehead, who had for long been clerk of the Box Meeting in London. Anne had died the previous year, and the book sent by Sarah was entitled *Piety Promoted by Faithfulness*. Anne, the daughter of an Oxford clergyman, became one of the earliest Quaker preachers in London. When Fox was in the dungeon in Launceston, Anne 'came afoot about 200 miles to me . . . and she laid in the town of Launceston . . . and carried herself very wisely',[3] ministering to their needs in prison. Her second husband was George Whitehead whom she married in Newgate jail. He was a loved colleague of George and Margaret Fox, out-

---

[1] Dix MSS. Z. 3. Library, Friends' House, London.
[2] Abraham MSS. 27.   [3] Camb. Jnl. I, 441.

living both of them. Like Margaret he frequently visited royalty on behalf of Friends—four kings and a Prince of Wales received him.

The child Nathaniel flourished, though Sarah shared her anxiety with her mother when there were teething troubles— 'pretty weak and low . . . and I am a little fearful of him about it, though he is pretty cheerful, we give him strengthening things, but he drinks spring water yet, which we have thought has done well with him'. She begs her mother's prayers for his preservation 'that he may be an instrument in his hand to his glory, and may fear and serve him all his days'.[1]

When Nathaniel was a boy of seven, William Meade arranged for Thomas Lawson to live with his family and be the tutor to his son and his nephew, Richard Lower, a boy of ten. Richard was the only surviving son of Thomas and Mary Lower, who very wisely sent him—a boy with four sisters—to grow up with his cousin. Lawson, now a man of sixty-one, had been vicar of Rampside in Furness, when George Fox's preaching in his church brought him into Quakerism. His scholarship in Hebrew, Greek and Latin, and his fame as a botanist, had led him into school-mastering as well as authorship, and now in 1691 he offered himself as tutor to the young grandsons of his old friend Margaret Fox.[2] William Meade's letter gives a picture

---

[1] Abraham MSS. 30. 1686.

[2] He was also one of the Quaker pioneer social reformers, worthy predecessor of John Bellers. He suggested the establishment of labour offices in every parish, and in 1660 addressed *An Appeal to Parliament, concerning the Poor, that there may not be a beggar in England* (*Quakers in Commerce*, by P. H. Emden). A few months before Meade's offer, Lawson had written from his school in Great Strickland, Westmorland, to Sir John Rodes, Bart., of Barlborough Hall, near Chesterfield, a Friend, asking, as he (Lawson) had made a great study of plants all over the country, and was acquainted with most of the botanists of the Royal Society, if Rodes would be willing to employ him to grow both plants and trees on his estate. He could also teach him Latin, Greek and Hebrew. He relates an interesting suggestion made by George Fox and others, which is best described in his own words. 'Some years ago, George Fox, William Penn and others were concerned to purchase a piece of land near London for the use of a Garden School-house and a dwelling-house for the master, in which garden, one or two or more of each sort of our English plants were to be planted, as also many outlandish [=foreign] plants. My purpose was to write a book on these in Latin, so as a boy had the description

of the terms and conditions of such employment in the seventeenth century. 'I am now without one to instruct my son and his cousin Richard Lower', he wrote, 'Thou art to live at our country house, with us, and have all things necessary for thee, viz. meat, drink, washing and lodging; and I would have thee propose, what sum of money yearly thou dost expect, that thou mayst be at a certainty as well as myself; I would that my son might not change his schoolmaster any more, until he be perfected in his learning; for I hope thou may stay with me many years. The young lads can make a piece of Latin, and piece it and construe it, in some measure, and are apt lads to learn, such as I hope, thou will take great delight in.'[1]

Unfortunately Thomas Lawson died soon afterwards, before he could tutor the two boys. However Nathaniel continued to learn well, for Margaret Fox sent him the following letter in December 1693, when he was nine.

Dear Nathaniel Meade,

I received thy dear letter gladly, by which I perceive thou learns very well both to read and to write, for which I am very glad of.

But, dear child, I would desire also that thou would learn to know God thy maker, and Jesus Christ thy Redeemer, whom to know is eternal life: and this thou must know by the calling in of thy mind to within thee and there thou wilt remember thy Creator, and then he will bless thee and preserve thee out of sin and evil and all lightness and vanity, and so thou wilt learn to fear the Lord and to be low in thy mind and there thou wilt know thy duty to God and thy parents. And this lesson I desire Almighty God to learn thee. And this is from thy grandmother, and I desire thee to write this out with thy own hand and to keep it; and remember my dear love to thy cousin Richard and let him write another copy for himself, which thou hast procured by thy diligence in writing to me.[2]

of these in book-lessons, and their virtues, he might see these growing in the garden, or plantation, to gain the knowledge of them; but persecutions and troubles obstructed the prosecution hereof, which the Master of Christ's College in Cambridge hearing of, told me was a noble and honourable undertaking, and would fill the nation with philosophers.' (*Quaker Post-bag*, pp. 20–2. 18.11.1690. [Jan. 1691]) But a seventeenth-century 'Kew Gardens' never materialized, nor did John Rodes take up Lawson's suggestion, and soon afterwards Lawson wrote to William Meade concerning tutoring his son.

[1] Jnl. F. H. S. Vol. 30, p. 40.
[2] Spence MSS. III. 194.

A little later William Meade arranged for a French Quaker, Peter Johan, to come to their home, to teach the two cousins French. He had been recommended to them some years before by George Fox.

William Meade took a fatherly interest in and care of young Will Yeamans, who in 1694 was doing well in trade, having been apprenticed to a merchant in Holland. It was at the Meades' home that this promising young man died of consumption in 1698.

With the exception of Sarah's minutes and accounts in the records of the Box Meeting of which she was clerk until 1708, the last picture of her which we have is in the letter, already referred to in connection with Susannah, sent to Rachel Abraham in 1710. Her husband, then eighty-three, was well and still a good walker; they had given up their London house, and together with Susannah were now living at Gooses. Nathaniel was a practising barrister and was in London in term time. He was then twenty-six.

The Meades had been busy arranging the publication of the life and works of Margaret Fox, indeed a labour of love. They were about to send a few copies to Rachel, but 'at the spring when the roads will be better and safer for carriage' they would send a large parcel for distribution among 'honest, faithful Friends that might know something of her singular service, and so will have a better sense and value of them'.

Sarah reminded Rachel that she had written to her nine months before, but had had no reply. Susannah too had not had a letter for long. 'I write the freer that we may not be such great strangers one to another in our old age, and do hereby give the remembrance of dear and entire love, from my husband and sister and self to thee and my brother and to cousin John whose welfare and happiness we much desire every way.'[1]

Shortly before he died William Meade wrote a book, in collaboration with George Whitehead, entitled *The People called Quakers, truly represented, and vindicated from some mistakes, wherein they are misrepresented in the representation of the Lower House of Convocation.* As in the early years of Quakerism their

[1] Spence MSS. III, 20.

enemies sometimes called them Jesuits, so now, in a different age, they were being accused by the highest body in the Established Church, as those who denied the divinity of Christ. Meade and Whitehead wrote this theological treatise to deny that charge, and to uphold their belief in the unity of the three-fold Godhead. Also they were believers in the immortality of of the soul and held 'true notions and distinctions of good and evil'. Their beliefs were consistent with the Bible, they held that Christ was the true Light, and they believed in the inspiration and guidance of the Holy Spirt—the very foundations of goodness of life. They regretted that so many priests allowed sports and pastimes on Sundays, and led bad lives—a reproach frequently justified in those days. Their comment on the wickedness in the country was, 'People's fruits must show, whose plants and what trees they are.' They begged the House of Convocation to be more charitable in their judgments to Quakers, and 'to do as you would be done by'.[1]

William Meade died in 1713, and Sarah survived him one year, being sixty-seven at her death. In his will he left some £500 to charity—to the poor, both Quaker and non-Quaker, and to hospitals—and the bulk of his fortune to his widow and son.[2]

III. The Lowers. The Abrahams

Let us now turn to the Lowers, and their relations with Margaret Fox in her later years. Mary, who as a girl of seventeen had been 'lovingly' treated by Charles II when she pleaded on behalf of her praemunired mother, was by 1686 a woman of forty-two. In this year her husband had been released from his imprisonment and praemunire at Launceston, and had returned to their home at Marsh Grange. Their last child, Bridget, was

---

[1] From *York Collection*, Vol. 6, at Woodbrooke, Birmingham. 'In 1697 a bill against blasphemy was before the House of Lords. Under this specious title was hidden an attempt to punish all who denied the doctrine of the three Persons of the Trinity. Penn wrote a cautionary letter which he circulated among the Peers, and the bill was dropped'. (*Wm. Penn* by J. W. Graham, p. 240)

[2] Jnl. F.H.S. III, 42.

born there in 1688.[1] They had had ten children, but only five lived to grow up. Of their four sons only one survived infancy, Richard, who as a schoolboy lived with the Meades, and of the six daughters only four survived. The first two had been born at Swarthmoor, all the others at Marsh Grange. The five dead babies lay in Sunbreck Burial Ground.

George Fox in his will appointed his friend Thomas Lower, together with William and Sarah Meade, his literary executor, and to Lower he left his saddle and bridle, spurs and boots, his 'inward leathers', the New England Indian Bible, 'my great book of the signifying of names', and his book of the New Testament of eight languages and all his medical things which came from across the Atlantic, with the 'outlandish' cup and 'that thing that people do give glisters[2] with'. Also he bequeathed him his two dials, one being an equinoctial dial. He left a great part of his library to his four stepsons-in-law. Lower was also to have his hammock, one of his prospect glasses, a pair of gloves and his Spanish leather hood.[3]

The work necessitated by being Fox's literary executor must have occupied a great deal of the time, from 1691 on, of the Meades and Thomas Lower. Many writings had to be collected from Meetings all over the country. Finally three volumes were published, the Journal in 1694, the Epistles, 1698, and the Doctrinals, 1706. Much care was taken in these productions, and they are remarkable source books not only of the personality and life of the founder of Quakerism, but of far greater importance, of the great spiritual truths of which he had such a clarity of view.

No doubt it was this work of editing which drew Lower and

[1] Mary seems to have recovered from this confinement, in October 1688, very quickly, for in May following she and her eldest daughter Margaret, aged fourteen, were in London, visiting the Rouses at Kingston (*Short Jnl.*, p.196). As the whole Lower family was in London while Margaret Fox was there from April to June 1690 (the last time she was with George Fox), and returned with her, in a coach, it may be that the Lowers left Marsh Grange early in 1689 and stayed South for more than a year. Otherwise, it is almost painful to think of Mary Lower travelling between London and Marsh Grange so frequently, specially with children, all under fourteen!
[2] Glisters = an injection or enema (sixteenth and seventeenth century).
[3] Camb. Jnl. II, 355.

his family to leave Marsh Grange, probably in 1693, to go and live in London. They still however kept the ownership of Marsh; the difficulties of having an estate over 200 miles away are reflected in Lower's remark to his mother-in-law at the end of 1693—'As to disorders at Marsh Grange my wife when she comes down will take care to mend what she can: and what cannot be cured must be endured.' Apparently Mary Lower was about to travel in mid-winter—on horseback—to North Lancashire from London![1]

A year later Margaret Fox is able to report that their concerns at Marsh Grange are in good order and doing well.[2]

It was in this year that Sarah Meade reported to her mother that Thomas Lower had a considerable and successful medical practice in London.[3] His reputation was such that Daniel Phillips, a doctor of physic at Leyden in 1696 dedicated to Lower and others his treatise on smallpox. Now he was more able also to join in with other prominent Friends in public affairs, than while he lived at Marsh Grange. In 1695 we find Thomas Lower being one of twenty signatories to a Petition of Quakers to Parliament to ease the sufferings of Friends who were in prison for their refusal to swear. William Meade also signed it, and spent much time lobbying at the House,[4] and relief came next year to allow Friends to make an affirmation in place of the oath.

A more unusual piece of publicity was the signing of a letter, in which Lower shared with four other Friends, addressed to the Czar of Russia, Peter the Great, when he visited England in 1698. William Penn was one of the signatories also. The letter admonished the Czar to practise mercy and truth. The writers tried to visit him at Deptford where he was, among other things, studying the building of ships, but the Czar was not well. 'We understood the meaning whereof', later wrote George Whitehead, 'as what such great persons (and too many) are incident to, who do not keep within bounds of temperance and moderation, in their manner and course of living.'[5] So they left their

---

1 Thirnbeck MSS. 23. 2.10 [Dec.] 1693. Printed in Jnl. F.H.S. IX, 175.
2 Miller MSS. 85. 24 x [Dec.] 1694
3 Thirnbeck MSS. 25. 18.2.1694.
4 Abraham MSS. 33.
5 *The Christian Progress*, by George Whitehead.

paper with a prince, and 'returned in peace'. On a later occasion, however, the Czar did receive some Friends and maintained an interest in Quakerism for many years.[1]

Thomas Lower was also chosen with George Whitehead, and Daniel Quare (the famous clock-maker for the King, and inventor of a remarkable barometer), to appear before William III to present to him an account of the sufferings of Friends still in prison for refusing to pay tithes, and to take oaths.[2]

In a long newsy letter to her mother in May 1701 Mary Lower gives many details of her family. She is grateful for her mother's concern for the 'preservation in the Truth' of young Richard Lower, for that was their anxiety too, and indeed their desire more than great riches or outward treasures, for him. The young man was now in Holland, apprenticed for two years to a merchant, working well, and lately she had been comforted to learn from his letters that he was inclining more to the religious teaching of his youth. When he returned to London he would still be apprenticed to a merchant, for he would not be of age for another year and a half. Then he could enter into partnership. He could speak French, Dutch and Spanish, and understood the Dutch way of book-keeping. (Alas, this promising young man, their only surviving son, died about three years later, unmarried.)

Their eldest daughter Margery had been married in March this year, to Benjamin Robinson of London. The wedding at the Bull and Mouth Meeting house was described by George Whitehead as 'a great solemnity and meeting', at which 'many great persons (some members of Parliament) were present, . . . and generally civil and sober'.[3]

The young bride's mother described the bridegroom as 'a very honest good man, and one that is very sharp[4] in business. I am well satisfied that she may have more true comfort in her station now than she might have had in a higher, so that I believe it was in love to her that other things was disappointed.'

---

[1] *A Journal of the Life of Thomas Story.* (**Newcastle upon Tyne, 1747**).
[2] *Short Jnl.*, p. 339.
[3] In a letter to M. Fox from G.W. Mar. 15th 1701. Port. 42. 35. Library, Friends' House, London.
[4] Sharp=bright, intelligent (Wright's *English Dialect Dictionary*).

This remark perhaps proves the truth of the statement made by that old gossip John Tomkins who two years previously had told his friend Sir John Rodes that when Edmund Waller, son of the poet, had joined Friends (1698), he had 'happened to fall into the hands' of the Lowers, 'and there did appear too great forwardness in the old folks to promote their daughter', but the young eligible had retired into Buckinghamshire where he had stayed twelve months, and 'has remained ever since'.[1]

Thomas Lower was endowing his daughter generously with £100 for pewter and linen, and a £500 dowry. Benjamin Robinson had settled £200 a year on his wife, in houses, ground rents and free land.

In 1699 their second daughter Loveday had married William Swan of Halstead, Essex. She also had a £500 dowry. She now had one child—'a strong, lusty, forward child'.

The third daughter Mary was also about to be married, to William Arch of London. She too would have a £500 dowry. 'Our children goeth pretty fast one after another, which puts us a little to it, but we do as well as we can, and if our tin works [in Cornwall] be not hindered by the discourse of the war [the war of the Spanish succession between Louis XIV and England] which makes tin fall, we might soon be in a way to help our son.'

Mary Lower who had, when a young woman at Swarthmoor, suffered frequently from jaundice, had it again now, and she had suffered much in anxiety when her daughter Loveday had had her baby with great risk and suffering.

Daniel Abraham was at present staying with them, much to their delight—'he is no trouble in any family', and 'very good company for my husband in the evening'. Mary ends her letter with expressions of love from every member of the family, and begs for Margaret's prayers, specially for her son Richard, to whom she asks his grandmother to write, for it 'might do him good'.[2]

The youngest child Bridget married in her early twenties Evan Ward of London, 'little of a Friend', Sarah wrote about him 'servant to a banker in Lombard Street, and a rich man'.[3]

---

[1] *Quaker Post-bag*, p. 161.   [2] Thirnbeck MSS. 28.
[3] Spence MSS. III, 200.

Both Thomas and Mary Lower died in 1720, he aged eighty-eight, she seventy-three.

The story of Daniel and Rachel Abraham as already told needs some amplification. Daniel not only suffered much, both by imprisonment and loss of money, by his refusal for many years to pay tithes, but he took part in his local Meeting by being clerk and cashier, and travelled frequently to represent his Meeting on the larger bodies, Quarterly Meeting and the Meeting for Sufferings which dealt with the persecuted of Lancashire.[1]

In December 1694 Daniel Abraham left his wife and mother-in-law at Swarthmoor, to travel to London. Margaret Fox wrote to Thomas Lower, with whom Daniel was going to stay—'He hath had a concern upon his mind concerning the city of London this twelve month: how it will please the Lord to discharge him of it, we must commit it to him, for the exercise is very weighty, and hard upon us all. It hath been much in my mind since he went if he could find liberty and freedom in himself to write what is upon him, and upon Friends' consideration and approbation it might be printed and dispersed in the City. I desire much your tenderness with respect to his present state and condition, and also your advice and council as in the wisdom of God you see meet. For thou knows he is young and so easily hurt.'[2] (Daniel was then thirty-two years old.)

What this concern was is not now known, and no pamphlet by him was printed, which seems to suggest that Daniel was not supported on this occasion either by his brothers-in-law or by the Morning Meeting of Ministers and Elders which examined all Quaker publications before being printed.

The following affectionate and business-like letter from Rachel shows that other matters also were being discussed by the brothers-in-law now that they were all together in London —the question of tithes, the recent 'purchase' of the Swarthmoor estate, and the difficulties they were having with their nephew, Charles Fell.

[1] Old book of *Minutes of Meeting for Sufferings*, at Lancaster Meeting House. Swarthmoor Monthly Meeting Minute Book.
[2] Miller MSS. 85.

Swarthmore. 7.11.1694. [=7th Jan. 1695.]

My dear,

Thy second letter from London I received which I was exceeding glad of, and I cannot but take it very kindly and tenderly from thee that thou should so often visit me with thy dear affectioned lines which are so comfortable, and joyful to me.

I thought not to have writ this post, fearing thou may think I writ too often, but that I know it will be welcome to thee to know how our dear little ones are, which the Lord in his sweet mercy hath blessed us with and spared unto us hitherto. Thomas is something better through the Lord's great love and mercy to him and us; but John was worse since my last letter to thee than before. But my confidence is in the Lord that he is again on the mending hand. He hath been feverish and much out of order, but I am sensible of the Lord's love and mercy towards him, for which I desire we may with true reverence and thankfulness return him the praise whose regard is known to be over us, and his care towards us as we continue in faithfulness and sincerity before him.

I writ to thee last post and enclosed some things which made my letter very bulky, but I hope thou will excuse it. If anything can be done in the business about tithes it might be well to hinder a sequestration, being many Friends as well as thee are concerned. Betericks Curan [=Beatrix Curwen?] was also served with one of them which I sent up. She seems much concerned about it: the Lord strengthen the faith and patience of his people, if it stand good in his sight that no drawing back or fainting may be in the camp of Israel or an evil heart of unbelief. That so the Lord may never withdraw his presence from us nor the lifting up of his covenant upon us, whatever [exercises] outwardly may attend us.

I could be glad thou [got something] done about them abatements[?] with Cousin Fell which he cannot reasonably deny. There was also upon his contract with thee when thou made the purchase of his estate £400 and £20 which he articled to allow thee for the payment of his mother's annuity. The £20 he hath never yet allowed. Thou may very justly insist upon it all, so that business about Henry Leatham which is still undecided, it's a good making an end of such matters when people are together and when the Lord affords an opportunity. And remember to get a full receipt from him of what Brother Ingram paid him upon thy account, with an endorsement also on the bond, both which are necessary and reasonable for him to do. I desire thee not to be short in all the things above mentioned and get Brother Lower and Brother Ingram's assistance and do not hearken to his aversions [spelt aueshons], which thou hast cause to know in many things hath been unjust.

I am in haste, must conclude with endeared love from Mother, self and children, dearly unto thee.

Many Friends of our Meeting doth exceeding kindly and tenderly enquire of thee very often. With true gladness I do believe to hear of thy well-being. Robert Salthouse with many more desire dearly to be remembered to thee when I wrote which in answer to their desire I do here mention. Many people enquire when I expect thee home which would be joy to me to hear of, but I am resigned unto the will of the Lord, yet do earnestly desire thee not to be slack or backward therein, when the Lord is pleased to give thee liberty.

I conclude thy truly loving wife,
Rachell Abraham.

Our dear loves is dearly to all our relations, in particular to Bro. and Sister Lower and cousins. My Mother bid me write thee [she] would be glad to hear from Bro. Lower, being he is so intelligible. Remember us dearly to dear James Dickinson. I desire thou will continue letting me hear from thee as often as thou canst.[1]

Three years later Daniel sold Hawkswell, the part of his property which had originally belonged to Judge Fell and his father before him. His refusal to pay tithes was the chief reason for his gradual impoverishment, and he was now willing to sell even more of his estate, that near Ulverston. He wanted to sell to relatives if that was possible, even at pecuniary loss to himself, if by that means the land would not pass into non-Quaker hands.[2]

Daniel Abraham's unnecessary and indeed dangerous refusal to pay fee-farm rent in 1699–1700 has already been described, as also his imprisonment from 1701 to 1704 for refusal to pay tithes. When Margaret Fox died in April 1702 Rachel was therefore the only member of the family left at Swarthmoor, together with her young son John. The following letter from Rachel to Mary Lower, written in August 1702 gives a picture of those sad and troubled days.

Swarthmore. the 7 of 6 [1702].

Dear Sister Lower,

It hath been long my desire to give thee a few lines, but having so

---

[1] Miller MSS. 87.

[2] Abraham MSS. 37. 22.11.1697-8. [Jan. 1698], and printed by H. G. Crosfield, pp. 226-7.

frequent occasion to give our dear brother the trouble and care of our many concerns which attends us to our exercises, I forebore; but it would be no small refreshment to me to have the privilege of a letter from thyself. Sister Meade is pleased sometime to afford me a few lines which is very acceptable; I am one separated but I hope not altogether forgot; and although it hath been my lot to have many sorts of troubles and perplexities, which often is as much as I can bear, since we was concerned with Swarthmore; (yet upon a search [spelt sherch] and a true consideration we did not desire to compass or seat ourselves here further than what providence appointed and brought to pass unexpectedly) I am somewhat stencked [=strengthened] with Faith that the Lord the righteous judge will help us and sustain us through our many difficulties and troubles and recompense the cruelty and envy of our enemies upon themselves; and as it was our dear Mother's desire that this place should be preserved and continued for the service of Truth and the Lord's people which was all that was in her eye.[1]

(The letter is unfinished.)[2]

The portraits of Daniel and Rachel Abraham would not be complete unless mention were made of their relationship to one or two outside the family, and to their son John, as seen in letters to and from them.

Phineas Pemberton (these Christian names from the Bible were very popular in Lancashire in the seventeenth and eighteenth centuries) had been apprenticed to John Abraham in Manchester about 1670. He later emigrated to Pennsylvania, acted for some years as William Penn's steward, and rose to a high position in the government of the colony. In 1695 Daniel sends Phineas, by the hand of a Friend travelling to America, a letter full of both affection and news. '. . . Though our bodies [are] far separated, and though the time of my acquaintance with

---

[1] Miller MSS. 83.

[2] This letter originally was with a packet of letters, endorsed by Rachel's son John many years later, 'Some copies of letters of my very dear and most affectionate mother to my aunts Meade and Lower relating to our great loss in parting with my honoured and worthy Grandmother Margaret Fox. The letters are badly spelled but contain excellent matter. For my son Tomy to read and consider.' The other letters have long ago disappeared. This one with most of the Miller MSS. was destroyed in the Second World War when the train caught fire while carrying the MSS. from their owner's house for safe keeping at Friends' House, London.

thee was in my minority when thou was in my father's family, yet thy truthlike behaviour and fidelity hath an evidence in my heart.' Daniel writes of his home of Swarthmoor, and that 'the Lord hath been pleased . . . to provide for me a very loving wife, and one I believe truly fearing the Lord and seeking the honour of his name and truth, and in a few words a meet help for me (blessed be the Lord)'. He tells of his three sons and a daughter, only one of whom, his son John, is living, aged about eight. (It is curious that though only two days before the father wrote this letter he had buried his little son Thomas, there is no mention of this loss.) He writes of the marriage of his sister Mary to the well-known lawyer Edward Chetham of Manchester.[1]

'My dear mother's wise deportment was such that she was much respected', wrote her son John on a letter (1706) written in a handwriting considerably better than that of her late mistress Rachel, by an old servant, Abigail Trindel. Abigail was very apologetic for not having written before; 'But I trust your wonted goodness will put another construction upon my actions, since my heart will ever bear a most dutiful remembrance of your many favours.' She had not written oftener because she thought she had displeased her mistress by marrying 'out of the Meeting'—a non-Friend—'and though I have had the misfortune to marry so, yet I have got a very honest man who never debars me of going to the Meetings of Friends as oft as I please; so that I want for nothing but the conversation of a husband of my own principles which yet I must own is a great loss.' Abigail hopes still for 'thy favourable opinion towards me' and sends a dozen and a half of lemons as a present, which would have been more only she was afraid they would 'corrupt' before reaching Swarthmoor, for she was sending them from Dublin. She begs Rachel for news of them all, and ends 'thy most thankful obliged humble servant'.[2]

John Abraham, as a young man of twenty, was in love with Jennie Rawlinson, the seventeen-year-old daughter of their Quaker neighbour, William Rawlinson of Graythwaite Hall. His anxious letter to her father was until recently among the Miller MSS. 'I must say', he wrote, 'it is not in the power of

[1] Abraham MSS. 34.
[2] Abraham MSS. 45.

language to express the surprise, the near exercising account I just now receive in thy affectionate lines of my dear Jennie's being seized with the smallpox. I am in the greatest distress, in the greatest agony, for my Jenny, for her who is the dearest of women. We have none to rely on, none to confide in, save the sure providence of God, who is infinitely merciful to us all.'[1]

Jennie recovered, but the youthful love affair ended, and she later married elsewhere.[2]

When John Abraham was twenty-two his friend John Green, travelling in Holland, tried to entice the young man to come over and see the curiosities of a foreign land for himself. 'It would be the finest divertisement in the world for such a gentleman as you, and I assure you if I had your estate I would not be kept so under confinement to my pen, for there's nothing in the world that so accomplishes young men as travelling.' The letter gave an account of Holland in 1709. 'The inhabitants are the cunningest people in the world for money, and indeed I must say it's far pleasanter for the traveller than the inhabitant, it being a very unhealthful place.' Then he told of the sluices, capable of flooding the country in time of invasion, of the country lying below the level of the sea, of the great banks of earth 'rampired with strong planks', of the mills for pumping the water out, of the cities 'built as in the sea, having water run through their streets, so that they can bring the ships each to his door', of the travels by water and the rarity of travel on horseback, and 'many other excellent conveniences'.[3] But young John Abraham was not to be tempted to leave Swarthmoor for Holland.

The young man, however, three years later, went to London, to stay with the Lowers, and to meet his many relatives in and near the City. During this visit he fell seriously ill, and was lovingly nursed by his Aunt Mary Lower, and cared for by his doctor uncle and young cousin Evan Ward, the husband of

[1] Jnl. F.H.S. XXX, 43. 1707.
[2] Jennie's brother Thomas, who is mentioned in the letter, later owned and managed some iron forges in the Western Highlands of Scotland (Glengarry), and it was he who introduced the modern Highland kilt (Foster's *Lancs. Families*, and Fell's *The Early Iron Industry in Furness*, and *English Dialect Dictionary*, by Dr. Joseph Wright, *s.v.* fillibeg).
[3] Abraham MSS. 46. 1709.

Bridget Lower. His mother's letter to him combines love, anxiety for his health and strength, and longing to have him home again. 'As to thy improvement in speaking I would not have us too much to think of that, I am not doubtful but in that respect it will be well, to all our satisfaction and be not in the least careful of any charge, or expense, any way that may tend to thy occasions, or advantage, upon any account. If it were never so much, it will not be thought too much, if it were all that we have; for I desire nothing in this world more, if the Lord be so gracious to us as to give thee health and strength again.'[1] And there is a little postscript—'Dear son, be not sparing of charge in any respect, I desire thee.'

John's marriage to Sarah, the third daughter of Thomas and Sarah Foster of Hawthorn, Co. Durham, took place some years before his parents died (Daniel in 1731, Rachel in 1732). Sarah Foster's grandfather was one of the early Friends, and a member of an old family of small landowners. All the children of John and Sarah Abraham, four sons and seven daughters, were born at Swarthmoor Hall, and lived there until 1759, when the business failure (in the importing of tobacco) of the eldest son Thomas, a merchant at Whitehaven, forced the sale of the old home and estate, following on the sale of the manor to Lord Montagu, ancestor of the Duke of Buccleugh, the present lord of the manor.

The sale was a tragic blow to John Abraham, then aged seventy-two. He and his wife and family removed to Skerton, near Lancaster, and were so poor that money was from time to time sent them from the charitable funds of their old Meeting. He lived on until 1771, when his body was brought back across the sands to be buried at Swarthmoor.

When they left the Hall they left behind some of the old seventeenth-century furniture—the great four-poster carved bedstead, and a 'remarkable cupboard . . . carved curiously; the top hath two dragons curiously executed', as described by the eleven-year-old Quaker schoolboy of Ulverston, William Fell, nearly twenty years after the sale. The new owner, Captain Lindow, cared little for the place, and let it to tenants who cared less. A great deal of the building was pulled down in those

[1] Abraham MSS. 47, and in Webb, *Fells*, pp. 411-12.

N

years, and the beauty of the woods was spoiled by 'hagging down the trees'; 'as I went by the wood', the boy wrote, 'it grieved me to see the trees destroyed in their utmost verdure, for it was spring.' 'The gardens belonging to Swarthmoor Hall are overgrown with thistles, briars, thorns, etc., but there are some of the garden flowers growing wild. It would almost melt the hearts of Lord Abraham's daughters, as, I believe, there is only one or two living afar off; I believe one is, poor creature! gone to be an actress on the foolish stage. But, to return again, it would melt their hearts with grief to see the place, where once they lived, tumbling down in ruins.'[1]

Until 1912 the old Hall was neglected, and sometimes indiscreetly restored; much of the oak panelling was destroyed, most even of the fruit trees in the large orchard allowed to die and not replaced, the garden neglected. In 1912 a descendant of John and Sarah Abraham, Emma Clarke Abraham of Liverpool, bought the Hall and about 100 acres of the former estate, restored the buildings, replaced much of the panelling, added fine carvings done by herself, and began the re-creation of a garden gay with flowers and herbs.[2]

And so Swarthmoor Hall of the present is able to give us visions of that in the seventeenth century when it was the home of Judge and Margaret Fell, their son and daughters, and of George Fox, of the little grandchildren, the servants, and the visiting Quakers coming and going.[3]

---

[1] *The History of Antiquities of Furness*, 1777, by Wm. Fell, S.B., aged eleven years. Ed. L. R. Ayre, 1887. ('S.B.' means 'Schoolboy'.)

[2] When Miss Abraham bought Swarthmoor Hall she made an agreement with trustees of the Society of Friends. They provided a mortgage on half the property, and agreed that after the death of her heir, Edward Mitford Abraham, the Society of Friends **had** the option to purchase the Hall and estate. **The option was exercised in 1954, after an agreed interim period of temporary occupation. For a short account of the Hall, see Elfrida Vipont Foulds,** *Swarthmoor Hall* **(London 1979).**

[2] Before John Abraham left Swarthmoor he endorsed the numerous letters of early Friends still there and gave away a number. He also gave away Margaret Fox's Library. Abraham MSS. 48.

Chapter Twenty-Two

MARGARET FOX'S PUBLIC QUAKER WORK, 1691 TO 1702

'He who neglects the Inner Light is lost in body's darkness,
He who follows the Light of Heaven ever reflects its radiance.
This is called the Eternal Heritage.'
From *The Simple Way of Lao Tsze,* born 604 B.C., p. 24.

'It's the Spirit that gives Life.'
Margaret Fox

IN the last chapter we have been seeing Margaret Fox in the lives of her married daughters and their children. Now let us see what her work was for Quakerism in her last eleven years, during her second widowhood.

Not only did she guide and serve the local Meetings, both for worship and for business, but from time to time she felt called to address epistles, sometimes to the Women's Meetings in London, at others to Friends generally. These were lengthy Epistles and the replies to them were as long as her own, but this was the custom of the times.

The first of these latter-day Epistles was sent to London women Friends a few months after her husband's death, and in reply to a letter of sympathy from them. As she had a year previously expressed her gratitude to them for their loving friendship to her on her visit in 1690, so now she wrote 'acknowledging your tender love and care to me, and my dear husband, when he was with you, in his service and travels for the Lord; and for your tender care and love unto him, you will have an everlasting reward'. Then she pleaded with them to keep to the eternal testimony which Fox had preached, to keep in this same spirit, life and power, and to live with mutual love among them, 'that not any of us ever wax cold'. She knew their great care and service for God, 'therefore I counsel you', she added, 'in the power of the Lord, to continue in it and to give up freely

to it, in the strength and wisdom of God. and you are sure to
have comfort and satisfaction at the present, and in the end, an
everlasting and eternal reward.'[1]

Four years later (1695) Margaret Fox again addressed the
Women's Yearly Meeting in London, asking that copies of her
letter should be sent throughout the country. As the 'blessed
Truth lives for ever and waxes not old', so she longs for them
all to live in that Truth and grow daily in grace. She reminds
them that the 'seed is one in male and female', and that they
should learn of Christ, and take his yoke upon them. 'The
humble and lowly are Christ's scholars, and so keeping chaste
and constant to his teachings there is the daily comfort, and
there we receive the daily bread, and the daily strength in the
Lord is renewed, and here is the chiefest portion and inheritance
that can never be taken from us.'[2]

To this letter the Women's Quarterly Meeting in London
replied. Their style was far more wordy and prolix than Margaret's, but their matter expressed great love for her, and
appreciation of her letter, 'received in the sense of that savory
life and virtue which the Lord hath made many partakers of.'[3]
Of the thirty-eight women who signed this Epistle, four were
Margaret's married daughters living in and near London.

In the late summer of 1697 Margaret Fox, undefeated by her
eighty-three years, left her home again to travel, on horseback
and by coach, to London. She stayed chiefly at Gooses, Sarah
and William Meade's home in Essex, travelling in her son-in-
law's chariot to London from time to time. In October 1697 we
find her name heading the list of women Friends attending the
Box Meeting, her daughters, Mary Lower, Susannah Ingram
and Sarah Meade, also being there. There were several difficulties which were creating some disunity among Friends in these
years, and Margaret, as one of the few leaders still alive who had
known the spirit of the early days, tried to influence Friends in
the way she believed Fox would have wanted. One of the diffi-

---

[1] Box Meeting MSS. 1671–1753, No. 43. Copy in Sarah Meade's handwriting, she being clerk of the Box Meeting.
[2] The only copy of this letter I have found is at Nottingham Meeting
House.
[3] Spence MSS. III, 195.

culties was due to the Act recently passed by Parliament (1696) to relieve Friends and others of the need to swear oaths. To win this freedom countless Friends had suffered for half a century, including herself and her husband. But now with victory assured, some with an over-sensitiveness of conscience, believed that the words of the affirmation, which the Act allowed as an alternative to the oath, were as objectionable as the oath itself. The affirmation allowed by this Act (which was for seven years and renewable, and was only made permanent in 1715 by George I) were: 'I, A.B., do declare in the presence of Almighty God, the witness of the truth of what I say.'[1] It was the mention of God to which a minority of Friends objected. Discussions, which had a sadly divisive influence in the Society on this matter, continued both at the Yearly Meetings and the smaller Meetings in the country for a quarter of a century. Appeals were frequently made to Government for a change of words. Finally, in 1721, a 'more easy form' was granted to them by the then Government—safely removed from the revolutionary years following 1688. The new form ran: 'I, A.B., do solemnly, sincerely and truly declare and affirm, etc.'[2] and it is this form nowadays which all, whether Quakers or not, who object to swearing an oath are legally allowed to use, and which finally won for Quakers the battle they had so strenuously fought since the beginning of their movement.

To return to Margaret Fox early in 1698. In her thankfulness for the religious toleration of 1688-9, and now for the easement in the matter of oaths, she longed to persuade the minority to see that their objections were unscriptural and were causing unnecessary division in the Society. So while she was staying with William and Sarah Meade in January 1698 she wrote an Epistle to all Friends. This Epistle, written in a clear good hand, with a few corrections made by Sarah, was formerly in the Miller MSS. but seems not to have been published in recent times, nor was it included in her *Works* in 1710. It is too long to be here quoted in full, but its importance justifies extracts. She reminded Friends of the great desire of George Fox for relief from oath-taking, and of the long and severe suffering of Friends—'This is

---

[1] Sewel, *History of the Quakers,* II, p. 571.
[2] Sewel, II, p. 669, note.

forgotten, now there is not such severity and hardship. The afflictions of Joseph they know not. Now it hath pleased the Lord to remove those governors that were so cruel, and has placed those in their room that are more merciful, who are inclining to give more liberty to tender consciences, and have granted such a liberty as Friends desired instead of an oath. Now here's some amongst Friends', she continued, 'of a contrary mind, against ancient Friends' testimonies and also the Scripture, and hath brought in another thing, that we must not use the sacred name of God about outward things, and speaks of pawning our souls. I know no Scripture that saith this.' Then with a wealth of apt references to both sayings and incidents in the Bible to emphasize that we are to acknowledge the presence of God in the earth and in ourselves and our lives—'Can his will be done on earth, as it is in heaven if he must not be called upon, nor named?'—she adds: 'I am sorry that Friends should be so weak, and so childish in the Truth. When Jesus spoke to his disciples, that they should not swear at all, he saith, let your communication be yea, yea, nay, nay, that is, be true and righteous in your communication. . . . So he would have Truth to rule them in all their communication. That was that, which he knew was beyond swearing. He did not say as some say now, that they might not mention the name of God about outward things. He put no such difficulty upon his words. Truth in all things was what he aimed at. These that speak as before, it is to darken and muddle people's minds. Whatsoever words are spoke in Truth and Verity, answers Christ's words in place of an oath.' She refers to the trouble-makers and perverters of the gospel in the early days of the Christian Church, and adds, 'So there is now, many troublers as well as witnesses for the Eternal Truth.' She pleads with Friends to accept what the King and Parliament have granted to them, and reminds them of the deceit that some Friends in the past have practised in paying a clerk to swear an oath on their behalf, in proving a will, for instance. 'Are not these false foul things? Whereas now they may go plainly before the face of all to speak their solemn declaration. So I desire Friends generally, let not this false blind doctrine prevail upon you, but make use of the mercy that God hath granted you for your ease and benefit.' Then, with approval, she asks Friends to remember that William Penn nine years before, early in 1689, when writing to the Earl of Shrewsbury to deny that King James II had ever tempted him to be a Papist, had affirmed in the words now incorporated in the new Act: 'In the presence of Almighty God, I do declare, etc.' And in her final appeal she wrote: 'Methinks that faithful sensible Friends may easily see through these things. The rise and beginning of all this contest and difference was that Friends might not seek [=look] to this power and Government for anything, which God hath now placed over the powers of darkness, praises be to his Holy Name.'[1]

In this last sentence Margaret put her finger on one of the sources of division in the Society in the nineties; a political division. Some Friends were Whig and enthusiastic for William III and the Revolution of 1688, among whom were William Meade and Thomas Lower, while a minority leaned still to a loyalty to James and the Stuarts. But loyalties were not clear-cut and simple, and here we see that though William Penn had been always a friend of James II and lay under suspicion (which careful historical research has entirely cleared away) during the years 1691 to 1693, and though there was by 1698 considerable hostility felt by William Meade against Penn, Margaret Fox herself writes of him with approval. The sad alienation of Penn and Meade, whose loyal and courageous stand together in the Old Bailey Trial in 1670 led directly to the freedom of the jury, has caused some of the biographers of William Penn to take it for granted that Margaret Fox was as hostile to and critical of her old friend as was her son-in-law. But there seems little evidence of this in the original documents. It certainly does not appear in this 1698 Epistle. Margaret still preserved for her family and for Quaker records the beautiful and affectionate letters written to her by both William Penn and his wife (some of which have already been quoted in this book) down to the death of George Fox in 1691. If there had been complete alienation, no doubt these letters would have been destroyed. The reputed hostility

[1] Miller MSS. 89. 19.11.1687–8. Penn seems to have changed his mind later in life, and sided with those Friends who objected to the mention of God in the affirmation (Janney's *Life of Penn,* p. 476). He had written in 1675 a most remarkable and scholarly book on oaths, *A Treatise on Oaths.*

of Margaret Fox towards Penn seems to be based on the remark, which was intended by the writer to be private, made by John Tomkins to his friend Sir John Rodes, in February 1698, a month after Margaret had expressed approval of Penn in her Epistle about the Affirmation. He wrote, 'our ancient Friend M. Fox is here about town. I wish she had stayed in Lancashire, or returned back soon after she came—I fear, by reason of her age, that she will be led by her son William [Meade] into something or other, which may not be of the best consequence to Truth, nor the quiet of the Church, nor her own honour. This by the bye to thee.'[1]

During the spring and summer of this year, William Penn, accompanied by Thomas Story and others, travelled in Ireland, holding very large Meetings and preaching to great crowds. While he was away, at Yearly Meeting in May, an attack was made on him by the Meade party, who criticized the 'honour and dignity' with which he was surrounded, and the possible temptations to worldliness.

John Tomkins, Tory and great admirer of Penn, was very grieved at these attacks, and blamed Margaret Fox, 'whose extreme age some few did impose upon to her dishonour, and the grief of many faithful brethren'.[2]

There is more criticism of Penn made early in the following year when Margaret Rous in a   newsy letter to her mother tells her that William Penn was in London and 'great crowding after him', and added, 'I believe there is little alteration in him or others, but much as they were when thou was here'.[3] Three months later Margaret Rous wrote to her mother, 'We hope if W[illiam] P[enn] be brought to condemn that which he hath been so far wrong in (to the hurt of many), though but in part, that things will grow better among Friends and Truth come up in its ancient purity over the false wrong spirit which hath so much prevailed to its dishonour and hurt, which the truly honest will be right glad of'.[4]

---

[1] In *Quaker Post-bag*, p. 134. Quoted by Prof. Dobrée in his *Life of Penn*, but omitting the last short sentence.
[2] *Quaker Post-bag*, p. 140.
[3] Dix MSS. z/5 23.1 [March] 1699.
[4] Spence MSS. III, 197. 13.4 [June] 1699.

This is flimsy evidence to support the strictures on Margaret Fox, made by Professor Dobrée, who has written that 'she seems never to have lost an opportunity of girding at Penn',[1] and that she was an 'old troubler of the waters'.[2] Her letters and epistles to the end of her life show her rather to be loyal to old friends and specially to the truths she had learnt in her youth, and also to be entirely capable of acting independently of others, even of her sons-in-law.

Of the hostility of Meade and Lower to William Penn in these post-Revolution days there is no doubt. It was Meade who prevented the inclusion of Penn's beautiful Preface to *George Fox's Journal*, so that many copies were bound without it. It was Lower who was very critical of Penn in December 1693 when his retirement from public life had ended with a complete acquittal from the King, and had written to his mother-in-law that Friends were hurt that he had not come to them to be 'reconciled' before preaching publicly. This behaviour was to him and others 'too triumphant and high, and is not well resented amongst some Friends here'.[3] Lower indeed shortly after wrote to Margaret Fox that he had drawn up a letter for William Penn to sign and present to Friends, asking for their pardon for having caused them, by his sympathy with James II, much distress, and begging their reconciling forgiveness.[4] This letter Penn, however, refused to sign. But the incident shows how political divisions were creating divisions in the Society in these insecure and troubled years after 1688. Two of the older leaders, Stephen Crisp and George Whitehead, in 1693 added to the Yearly Meeting Epistle, an appeal that Friends should not side with either James or William, or interfere in what was too high for them, but should live peaceably, and avoid strife and schism. 'Meadites' and 'Pennites' were terms already bandied about in the Society. In the Epistles of several subsequent Yearly Meetings there were warnings against disunity and strife, and appeals for the increase of love.

Lower and Meade were so well known as critics of Penn that

[1] *W. Penn*, by B. Dobrée, p. 326.
[2] *W. Penn*, by B. Dobrée, p. 339.
[3] Thirnbeck MSS. 23.
[4] *Second Period of Quakerism*, p. 173.

in 1706 and 1709, Penn's enemies in Pennsylvania wrote their complaints of him to Lower and Meade. But this was several years after Margaret Fox's death, so she cannot be blamed for that. Perhaps at this distance we tend to magnify these differences. Frequently these men are found working together in amity during these years, when political differences and difficulties (acute as they were) seemed to divide them. Penn and Meade and Lower all co-operated in 1695 and 1696 in their work with Parliament to win freedom to affirm, and Meade was indefatigable in lobbying. Again in 1698—the very year when the attack was made on Penn at Yearly Meeting—all three together visited Peter the Great of Russia at Deptford, and won his interest in and even sympathy with Quakerism. It is good to know that when Penn, after years of delay, left for America in September 1699, he took with him supporting minutes from the Committee of London Ministers (the '2nd Day's Meeting'), the Bristol Monthly Meeting, and Horsham Monthly Meeting in whose district his earlier home of Worminghurst, Sussex, lay.[1]

There can be no doubt that Margaret Fox attended the Meetings of the Women's Yearly Meeting in May 1698, but in those days it was only the men assembled for Yearly Meeting who had the legislative and executive power in the Society. Leading women had been invited the preceding year to join with the men, but that does not seem to have been repeated in 1698. The minutes, if any were kept, of the women's Yearly Meeting are now lost, so we have no record of any definite action taken by or under the influence of Margaret Fox. From the records of the Men's Yearly Meeting we find that of her sons-in-law Abraham Morrice (Isabel's husband) represented Lincolnshire, and Daniel Abraham, Lancashire. Thomas Lower was among those appointed to write the Epistle, and William Meade was also present.

Before leaving London for her long and arduous journey home, at the end of June 1698, Margaret wrote two letters which her relatives felt were of sufficient interest to include in her *Works*, published eight years after her death. One was to young Edmund Waller, son of the poet of Stuart and Cromwellian days, and the other was to William III. To Edmund Waller she gave a warm welcome into the Society of Friends, which he had

[1] Janney, *Life of Penn*, p. 416.

recently joined. She reminds him of the simplicity of Christ's teaching, and how it can be hurt by the 'subtilty of the serpent' which brings disunity. 'Where Christ is the leader and guider, there will he bless and prosper.'[1] When writing this letter she must have had in mind the knowledge of the very worldly background of the young man's life.

To King William, Margaret Fox related how at the age of eighty-four she had travelled two hundred miles[2] to bear her testimony to the Eternal Truth. She looked back in her own life to the time when she travelled up to plead with Charles II and to explain to him their principles and to the long years in which they had suffered, even to the death, for those principles, and not for evil or wrong done to either man or government; 'for our principle', she wrote, 'is the Light of Jesus Christ, and his eternal Spirit, which leads into all truth and righteousness, but not into any untruth or evil actions.' They were against all plots and rebellions and deceit. 'Now God has placed thee over us, in this Government, who hast been very moderate and merciful to us, and we live very comfortably under thee and it, and do enjoy our Meetings quietly.' She was indeed thankful for the King's 'gentle government and clemency and gracious acts', and she hoped that Friends would be a blessing rather than a grievance to the nation, 'for so it will be, as we continue in the blessed Truth'.[3]

This grateful letter was presented to the King by Susannah Ingram. William III received several deputations of Friends, expressing their loyalty and gratitude, but they always consisted of men only, and were official ones from Yearly Meeting. This letter of Margaret's was different, informal and personal.

Between the time of her homecoming (late in June 1698) and 1701, the year before she died, Margaret wrote two remarkable Epistles to Friends, both men and women, and made a statement of her Quaker beliefs. Her visit to London had shown her that something was happening to the Society of Friends, which was contrary to the great and simple teaching given them fifty years

---

[1] M.F. *Works*, p. 533.

[2] The seventeenth-century mile was longer than the present-day one; the distance from Ulverston to London is about 250 modern miles.

[3] M.F. *Works*, pp. 531–2.

before. Not only was disunity showing itself, but an over-emphasis was being given on unessentials, on outward things. These defects are not visible in the minutes drawn up by the Meetings, on the contrary the Minutes of Yearly Meetings in the last decade of the seventeenth century continually report progress, the building of new Meeting houses, increase of numbers and faithfulness in the refusal to pay tithes. But she saw beneath and through these things to a spirit which was sowing the seeds of deterioration. These seeds grew in the next century into a quietism, a separation from the world which did much to weaken the service of the Society and to bring about strife within its borders, and divisions. One of the new 'outward ceremonies' which had been creeping in was the grey costume of women Friends. For many years protests had been made in the meetings for discipline against Friends dressing in the extravagant fashions of the time of Charles II and his successors—and these protests were not unnatural when we remember the outbreak of vulgar luxury and extravagance of the Restoration years—but a simplicity of dress did not mean a uniform, and Margaret was outspoken against this new fashion of separating oneself from the rest of mankind by wearing a set costume. She and her family never gave up colours in their dress, as Sarah's household account book shows.[1]

---

[1] After Margaret's death, we find Yearly Meeting (1704) passing a minute asking Friends to 'keep clear from the world's vain fashions and apparel, unnecessary extravagant wigs, from making, selling or wearing any striped cloth, silk stuff or any flowered or figured thing of different colours'. (*Y.M. Epistles* in Lancs. Q.M. Min. Bk.) In the same year the Lancashire Women's Quarterly Meeting minuted thus: 'Farther we tenderly request and desire that whereas advice in the Love and Council of God hath gone forth in the Meeting against superfluity in tying and broadening of their handkerchiefs upon their breast and let a decent tying be come into, and that Friends of every monthly Meeting take care that Friends keep clear of having their hoods made with superfluity and long tabs, and so that all the youth dress their heads decent as becomes Truth.' Later still 'cutting and powdering the hair and needless pinches in the forehead manties, with short skirts or any other dress that are not consistant with Truth', are discussed, and alas, *some* women Friends were found 'wearing something in their petticoats in imitation of a hoop'. As the century goes on, so do the protests, but as was only natural, it was found that many young women paid more and more attention to the intricacies of the grey dress and of their shawls and cloaks and bonnets.

The first of these two Epistles was written at Swarthmoor late in June 1698. After referring to the work of George Fox for forty years in directing men and women to the 'Spirit of the Eternal God',[1] she pleaded that Friends should 'continue hand in hand in the unity and fellowship of this Eternal Spirit in humility and lowliness of mind, each affirming others better then ourselves'. She tells Friends how Jesus had rebuked the Jews for their outward ceremonies and how ill he liked them— 'So let us keep to the rule and leading of the Eternal Spirit that God has given us to be our teacher. . . . Let us beware of being guilty or having a hand in ordering or contriving that which is contrary to Gospel freedom. . . . It's a dangerous thing to lead young Friends much into observation of outward things, for that will be easily done, for they can soon get into an outward garb, to be all alike outwardly. But this will not make them true Christians: it's the Spirit that gives life. I would be loath to have a hand in these things. . . . We have lived quietly and peaceably thus far, and it's not for God's service to make breaches.'

Two years later, in April 1700, she again begged Friends to let the Holy Spirit be their leader and guide and teacher. Again she deplored the spirit appearing recently among Friends, which was leading some into 'things outwardly', and into a separation from others, who were not Friends. 'Jesus would have all to be saved', she wrote, 'and to come to the knowledge of his blessed Truth. And he testified against the Pharisee that said I am more holy than thee. Let us beware of this, of separating or looking upon ourselves to be more holy, than in deed and in truth we are.' Evidently some Friends were refusing to share in the joys and sorrows of non-Friends at the time of funerals, or feasts after a birth. 'Away with these whimsical, narrow imaginations, and let the spirit of God which he hath given us, lead us and guide us; and let us stand fast in that liberty wherewith Christ hath made us free, and not be entangled again into bondage, in observing proscriptions in outward things, which will not profit nor cleanse the inward man. . . . This narrowness and strictness is entering in, that many cannot tell what to do, or not do. . . .

[1] Printed *in toto* in M.F. *Works*, pp. 534–5. Partly reproduced in Webb, *Fells*, p. 398.

Poor Friends is mangled in their minds, that they know not what
to do; for one Friend says one way, and another, another.

'But Christ Jesus saith, that we must take no thought what
we shall eat, or what we shall drink, or what we shall put on;
but bids us consider the lilies how they grow in more royalty
than Solomon. But contrary to this, they say we must look at
no colours, nor make anything that is changeable colours as the
hills are, nor sell them nor wear them. But we must be all in one
dress, and one colour. This is a silly poor Gospel. It is more fit
for us to be covered with God's eternal Spirit, and clothed with
his eternal Light, which leads us and guides us into righteousness
and to live righteously and justly and holily in this present evil
world. . . .

'This is not delightful to me, that I have this occasion to write
to you, for wherever I saw it appear, I have stood against it
several years. And now I dare neglect no longer. For I see, that
our blessed precious holy Truth, that hath visited us from the
beginning is kept under, and these silly outside imaginary practices is coming up, and practised with great zeal, which hath
often grieved my heart.

'Now I have set before you Life and Death, and desires you
to choose Life and God and his truth.'[1]

Perhaps her appeals for an inward spiritual religion and a
broad freedom did not fall entirely on deaf ears. Certainly during the eighteenth century more and more the Meetings for
Discipline—if one can judge from the minute books—went into
great detail as to the various minutiae of dress, both men's and
women's, but many a Meeting for Worship had the true spirit
of an inward waiting on God.

One more paper for her friends Margaret wrote, in November 1701, five months before her death. 'Now in my old age I
am forced to renew my testimony again, through a false lying
spirit gotten up amongst us to oppose and withstand our gracious, blessed Truth, in the which we were begotten. . . . But
an imagining, false and untrue spirit hath gotten into some, by
which they are deluded, and will not see or apprehend, by any
means used to give them satisfaction. Yet for the satisfaction of

[1] Portfolio 25. 66. Friends' House Library. The copy of this Epistle was
discovered in Australia and brought to England.

Friends and others I give this my testimony, while I breathe upon the earth, that I shall stand for God and Truth. He hath taught me to render to all men what is their due, and not to owe anything to any but love. In that which is righteous and just, God hath taught us and manifested his will. And he commands that we should render to Caesar the things that are Caesar's, and to God the things that are God's; which I shall by his holy assistance and power endeavour to fulfil both to God and man. This I am moved of the Lord to acquaint all with, whilst I have breath and being upon the earth.'[1]

In these last three writings by Margaret Fox the mental vigour and spiritual wisdom which lasted to the end of her long life are clearly seen. Her emphasis on a spiritual and inward religion, with its fruit in goodness of life, her faithfulness to the belief in the Inner Light of Christ working in men and women, her balanced judgment in days of difficult decisions, her capacity to give clear and outspoken criticism in no uncertain terms—all these gifts and qualities made her indeed the Nursing Mother of Quakerism.

On 23rd April 1702 the bodily weakness which had been growing on her for some months ended in death, shortly before her eighty-eighth birthday. Peaceful she lay, forgiving any who had done her wrong, as she desired to be forgiven, glad to be leaving 'this troublesome painful world'. She blessed her young grandson, John, and 'a little before she departed, she called Rachel saying, "Take me in thy arms", and saying "I am in peace" ', she died.[2]

She was buried at the burial ground of Sunbreck, a small walled field on the side of Birkrigg Common, overlooking the wide sands of Morecambe Bay, and two or three miles from Swarthmoor Hall, her home for seventy years. Friends and others from many counties came to her burial, but, as was customary with Friends in the early days, no stone marks her grave. Later on when her daughters and sons-in-law wrote about her they spoke of her wisdom, her 'pious conversation',

---

[1] Webb, *Fells:* p. 404. Hannah Thorp who owned the original of this statement in 1865, was a direct descendant of Judge and Margaret Fell. Unfortunately the original of this testimony is now lost.

[2] M.F. *Works.*

her care for the church, her preaching and her Epistles sent to many parts of the world, her great and long sufferings, which she endured with much patience. 'The Lord kept her easy', they wrote, 'and so cheerful under them, that her enemies were amazed to see it.' They remembered her faithful attendance at Meetings, both for worship and for business, almost till her death, and also how she spared no pains to visit and encourage those who suffered imprisonment and the spoiling of their goods.

When Thomas Camm of Cammsgill, near Kendal, wrote about her, he remembered especially her wonderful hospitality from which he and countless others had great benefit. She became a 'tender nursing mother unto many, condescending in great humility unto those of low degree; her heart and house being open to receive the Lord's servants.' She 'shined as a morning star, being filled with real wisdom and understanding'.[1]

And for us, in addition to the estimate of her contemporaries throughout her long life, we see the love she inspired, her inexhaustible energy, her pioneering mind and her kindness tempered with a strength and courage to say the stern word when necessary. She possessed a sanity and a sense of fitness and proportion only marred in the earlier years by one or two instances of 'enthusiasm' quickly controlled. She saw life whole, and she never forgot that God has compounded us of material and spirit, and that if we lose the balance we lose the richness of life.

At Sunbreck

I

When Friends came to Sunbreck
    To bury their dead,
They crossed the wild moor
    To a grey farmstead.

To a bare walled garth,
    Where the rock juts through,
With green springing grass
    And a wind-swept yew.

[1] M.F. *Works.*

The sea was before them
    The tossing waves,
On the spaceful hillside
    They dug their graves.

Hard their wayfaring
    Even to dying;
Bare is the ground
    Where their bones are lying.

Sunshine and cloud
    Sweep up from the sea—
This is the graveyard
    Of souls set free.

II

There is *room* on this hillside by the sea,
    It is a place where wings may be outspread,
Where the great winds blow jubilant and free—
Free as the faithful daring of the dead.

III

This is a harsh place for a burying,
    Grey rock, grey wall, the wind-swept trees around,
This is a cold place for a burying
    No garden ground.

Yea, harsh, yea, cold, yea, walled about with grey,
    Wind-swept—there is scant shelter from the sea,
But here will be God's spacious silences,
    His liberty.

MARGARET CROPPER.

APPENDICES

Appendix One
(Chapter One)

MORE DETAILS OF SWARTHMOOR HALL

The oak staircase is a remarkable feature of the house. There is only one other like it in the country. It consists of a hollow square of four oak posts going from the bottom to the top of the house, round which runs the staircase in groups of four treads and little landings. Upstairs one of the two large panelled bedrooms is known as Judge Fell's room. It is entered through an unusual porch or waiting-room, with carved panels round the top. The original latch is still there, made by hand and ornamented. All round the room, at the top of the panelling, is carving, showing the lozenge which was part of the Fell coat of arms.

The fireplace has some remarkable carving, very deep and bold in design. As the pattern is almost identical with that of the famous carving in the choir of Cartmel Priory Church, which is known to have been done by a Belgian or German craftsman in 1620 (at the expense of George Preston of Holker Hall, near Cartmel), it is probable that the same craftsman came to Swarthmoor to decorate the fireplace of the chief bedroom. The Cartmel Priory carved screens have been described as 'some of the finest made since the Reformation',[1] and again 'the best carving in the seventeenth century'. Both at Cartmel and at Swarthmoor the carver has used the vine to decorate his panels and pillars. Some panels, in honour of James I, display the fleur-de-lis, the Tudor rose, the thistle of Scotland, and again the vine.

In 1800 a visitor to the Hall recorded that there were scriptural subjects in this carved fireplace. Possibly these panels were in the large spaces where now plain modern ones stand as a sad reminder of the depredations of the past.

In this room stands a large double bed of early seventeenth-century workmanship. Tradition says it was originally at the Hall. The bed-head is well carved, and until 1914 the foot had two heavy moulded posts, which however were then cut off and placed in the new carved fireplace in the parlour.

[1] Baddeley, *Guide to the Lake District*, p. 99.

In the south-east corner of the room is a second doorway leading to a little lobby which has on one side a clothes cupboard, on the door of which is a pair of 'cock's head hinges', and opposite is a doorway opening on to a balcony. The door with its ancient iron bolt of extremely simple design (for it merely runs into a hole in the wall) is original, but the old balcony long ago gave way and was replaced at the restoration in 1914. Possibly originally an outside staircase gave from the Judge's room into the garden direct. It was from this upper doorway that later in the seventeenth century George Fox preached to those gathered in the garden.

The lobby leads on into the other bedroom which still has the original panelling. It is traditionally known as 'Margaret Fell's room', perhaps where she died in 1702.

The bay window, so beautifully shaped, looks over the little brook and the Swarthmoor fields and trees to the shining water and sands of the bay, and on again to the Bigland Fells and to Ingleborough, thirty miles to the east in Yorkshire.

At the top of the house are the high lofts, showing oak beams in as good condition now as when they were put in in the early seventeenth century. Tradition has it that after a skirmish in 1643 on Lindal Moor, two miles away, between Royalists under Colonel Huddleston of Millom Castle, and Parliamentarians, some sixty of the latter who were victorious were billeted in the large loft, at the invitation of George Fell's son, Thomas.

Appendix Two
(Chapter One)

BULSTRODE WHITELOCK

In Penn's *Works*, Vol. I, p. 431 (1726), Whitlock was stated to be author of 'Memorials of English Affairs', one of the Commissioners appointed by the Lords and Commons to treat with Charles I for a peace, Commissioner of the Great Seal, Ambassador to Sweden, and some time President of the Council. A scholar, lawyer, statesman, he was 'one of the most accomplished men of the Age'.

Towards the end of his life, when he lived in Berkshire, Penn visited him, and he said to Penn, 'I ever have thought there has been one true religion in the world, and that is, the work of the Spirit of God in the hearts and souls of men. There has been indeed divers forms and shapes of things, through the many dispensations of God to men, answerable to his own wise ends, in reference to the low and uncertain state of man in the world; but the old world had the Spirit of God, for it strove with them; and a new world has had the Spirit of God, both Jew and Gentile, and it strives with all; and they that have been led by it, have been the good people in every dispensation of God to the world. And I myself must say, I have felt it from a child to convince me of my evil and vanity, and it has often given me a true measure of this poor world, and some taste of divine things; and it is my grief I did not more early apply my soul to it. For I can say, since my retirement from the greatness and hurries of the world, I have felt something of the work and comfort of it, and that it is both ready and able to instruct, and lead, and preserve those that will humbly and sincerely hearken to it. So that my religion is the good Spirit of God in my heart; I mean, what that has wrought in me and for me.'

He held a Meeting in his house, open to all, after which he was so pleased that he said, 'This is the everlasting Gospel I have heard this day.'

Appendix Three
(Chapter One)

THE ASKEWS

A good deal of research has been carried out on the Askew (or Ayscough) family, scattered as they were in various counties. One genealogical table compiled by Joseph Foster stretches from eleven generations before Anne Askew, down to their descendants in the nineteenth century. These Askews were chiefly in Lincolnshire and South Yorkshire. Anne Askew's father and eldest brother were both knighted by Henry VIII, and a younger brother was cupbearer to Henry VIII.

Also there were Askews in Cumberland and Furness in North Lancashire dating from the time of King John. One of these was Sir Hugh Askew of Bootle, Cumberland, knighted by Henry VIII on the battlefield of Musselburgh in 1547. He had been yeoman of the cellar to Queen Catherine, and later to Henry VIII, and in succeeding reigns was sheriff of Cumberland. He bore the same coat of arms as the Askews of Lincolnshire and Yorkshire, and (according to Joseph Foster in his *Pedigrees of Lancashire Families*) was descended from the same ancestor, who had held land in the lordship of Millom, Cumberland, in the time of King John.

Anne Askew, one of the first Protestant martyrs in England, was tortured on the rack, and burnt at the stake in 1546, during the reaction in favour of Catholicism at the end of Henry VIII's reign. She had been married as a girl and against her will to Thomas Kyme, but after she had been turned out of her home by her husband for her religious beliefs, she resumed her maiden name for herself and her two children. The story of her trial and sufferings was related by Foxe in his *Book of Martyrs* and by Bishop Bale.

Extensive research has not so far discovered what happened to Anne Askew's two children. But it is at least curious that two families unrelated have a strong tradition of descent from her. Among the Irish Shackletons (descendants of Margaret Fell) that tradition is held to the present day, and can be traced back to their ancestor Margaret Abraham, who was born within twenty-four years of the death of Margaret Fox, her great-grandmother. In a letter written in 1865 by John Abraham of Liverpool (another descendant of Margaret Fell through a brother of Margaret Abraham, both grandchildren of Rachel, Margaret Fell's youngest daughter and constant companion) we are told that the Shackletons at that time 'have a sure tradition of it, and that their grandmother knew it. There is nothing strange in their knowing the facts better than I did for various reasons.' One of these reasons was the fact that John Abraham's father was only seven years old when his own father died, and so the tradition failed to be passed on.

The other family which has a tradition, but no proof, of descent from Anne Askew is now represented by Woodalls and Davies, to whom I am indebted for information. They can trace their ancestry to the seventeenth century when they were living near Bootle in Cumberland, and since then in every generation the names 'Anne Askew' have been given to at least one girl.

It is to be noted that in both these families the old tradition cannot be proved.

It is suggested that possibly Anne Askew's little children, with the unpopular background of their mother's history, were sent away from Lincolnshire to their distant relative living in Cumberland, Sir Hugh Askew. As he was in favour with the King, possibly the children would be safe. But their relationship to their mother would probably be hidden in the neighbourhood, though known in the family.

It is significant that Sir Hugh Askew's property went partly to his widow and partly to a son 'or nephew, according to some authorities' (Joseph Foster). This very uncertainty lends colour to the suggestion that this 'nephew' might have been Anne Askew's son.

Margaret Fell herself gives us very little help as regards her ancestry.

She merely says that her father was John Askew, a charitable and honourable gentleman whose family for some generations had owned that estate, Marsh Grange, her birthplace. Through the kindness of the present owner of Marsh Grange, Sir Wavel Wakefield, M.P., and his solicitors, Messrs. Arnold, Greenwood and Son, Kendal, I have been able to examine the deeds of Marsh Grange, but none of them goes back earlier than 1670, so they give us no information about John Askew's forbears. In 1912 search was made in vain for his will. I have examined the Dalton Registers, again in vain, except for the entry of the marriage in 1613 of John Askew, probably Margaret Fell's father. It looks as if the old tradition that Margaret Fell was a great granddaughter of Anne Askew must remain a tradition, and be 'unproven' by any written records.

Appendix Four
(Chapter Two)

HOW GEORGE FOX TRAVELLED

George Fox travelled on foot in his early years. This we know from his Journal (Cambridge Journal, I, p. 33) where he says early in 1652 he 'was very sore with travelling afoot so far'. And again (Cambridge Journal, I, p. 38), also early in 1652, he tells of a clergyman who spread false reports of wizardry about him, that he carried bottles and made people drink of them, which made them follow him, and that he rode on a great black horse which carried him from one part of the country to another sixty miles away 'in one hour', but these 'hellish lies' could easily be refuted 'for I was and went on foot, and had no horse at that time'. When he was travelling among the villages near Swarthmoor he was still afoot (Cambridge Journal, I, p. 61), but when Margaret Fell heard of the cruel treatment he had received on his second visit to Walney Island, she sent a horse for him. In 1653, when he went further north to Cumberland, he was on horseback, for he tells how some people offered to put his horse to graze in the churchyard while he was preaching, but he refused to take what he considered was the property of the minister, and told the men to take his horse to the inn.

In 1657, on his first journey to Scotland, he records how he saw sparks of fire springing from his horse's hoofs, as he was nearing the border, and he took it that it was a sign of the seed of God (Cambridge Journal, I, p. 310).

That he had a love of his horses is shown at his indignation when a dishonest innkeeper in Wales stole the oats meant for the horse.

Late in life, when his ill-treatment in prisons had stiffened his joints with rheumatism, he usually rode in a coach, private or public, and in London he frequently went by boat on the Thames, a water-way more popular then than now.

Appendix Five
(Chapter Two)

SOURCES FOR STORY OF FOX'S FIRST COMING TO SWARTHMOOR

We are fortunate in having five separate accounts of these days at Swarthmoor in June and July 1652, and each one gives little details which added together allow us to have a vivid picture. George Fox described his first visit in his Journal (Camb. Jnl. I, p. 47 *seq.*); Margaret Fell left three accounts, one in her *Relation* (her *Works*, p. 2), one in her testimony to George Fox and after his death (Leeds Jnl.), and a most touching story which seems to be a fragment of a larger account, and which is preserved among the Spence MSS., Vol. III (No. 135). There is also the history of the coming, in the Lancashire Quarterly Meeting Minute Book preserved at Lancaster Meeting House.[1] The writer of this is unknown, and the story is part of the replies to the queries sent out to all the Meetings by the Yearly Meeting of 1676, in the attempt to record, on George Fox's initiative, the sufferings and testimonies of the early Friends—the 'First Publishers of Truth'. The Lancashire replies were lost for two and a half centuries, but found by Professor Henry J. Cadbury in 1933 on a visit to Lancaster. It is to this Lancaster record that we are indebted for the exact date of George Fox's coming—late in June 1652. Some writers have put it in the winter of 1652 (M. Webb, *Fells of Swarthmoor Hall*, p. 39). It is good to know that his first visit was when the Furness Fells were most colourful. William Caton in his Journal said that Fox's first visit occurred 'about the middle of the fourth month' (i.e. June), 1652, but it is impossible to believe that Fox would have taken less than a week to come on foot from Sedbergh where we know he was during the Whit-week (6th to 12th June), preaching and working at four import-

[1] Jnl. F.H.S. XXXI, 6, but 'Eesture' should read 'Lecture', and there are some other mis-transcriptions.

Appendices 391

ant centres, and at several other less important places on the way. So most probably the writer in the 'First Publishers of Truth' record, mentioned above, is correct when he says that 'upon 5th day of the week in the 5th month, 1652, he went to Ulverston steeple house, it being their lecture day'.[1] This '5th day' or Thursday was probably 1st July, in which case his arrival at Swarthmoor was on the preceding Monday, 28th June. However, there is some disagreement here with Thomas Camm's account of the Sedbergh Meetings and the following fortnight, as described by him in the 'First Publishers of Truth', where his story would bring the arrival at Swarthmoor to the preceding Monday, namely, 21st June. But Thomas Camm was at the time a boy of twelve, and he wrote his story of these stirring times in 1709 or 1710,[2] when an old man of about seventy, and his memory may not be exact. The account in the Lancaster Minute book was written probably about 1681 or 1682.

Appendix Six
(Chapter Three)

THE FREE GRAMMAR SCHOOL OF HAWKSHEAD

This Elizabethan Grammar School, founded by Archbishop Sandes (or Sandys) who was born at Esthwaite Hall, near Hawkshead, has had a very varied career of usefulness. It still possesses a very beautiful sheet of vellum, of the Royal Letters Patent, dated 10th April 1585, written in Latin in a beautiful hand of the period, the initial letter containing a portrait of Queen Elizabeth, dressed in a wide flowing robe, and wearing a crown and an orb, an ermine cloak around her. The first line ('Elizabeth Dei gracie Anglie Francie et Hibernie') is very ornate, with a border depicting the lion, crowned rose, dragon, fleur-de-lis and harp.

The statutes and rules of the school, in English, and drawn up by the Archbishop in 1588, are also still preserved at the school; in great detail they ordain that the school shall give free education for ever, shall have one schoolmaster who 'shall be well seen and have good understanding in the Greek and Latin tongues, and shall teach and inform the same to such scholars of the same school as shall be most meet and apt for the same', and there was one usher for the smaller children.

[1] The first month each year until 1752 was March, and the year began on 12th March.
[2] F.P.T. 241 and note.

In the summer months the master had to begin his teaching at six in the morning, or at half-past six at the latest, and continue until eleven o'clock, and then from one until five in the afternoon. In the winter months the hours were from seven or seven-thirty until eleven, and again one-thirty until four.

The master and usher were to teach 'all such good authors, which do contain honest precepts of virtue, and good Literature, for the better education of youth', and once a week 'the principles of true religion' were to be taught. The master and usher were not to absent themselves, save for 'honest, necessary and reasonable causes', and only for six weeks' holiday each year.

The Archbishop drew up three prayers for the daily use of the scholars, one for the morning, one for Queen Elizabeth, and one to express gratitude to God for his gifts, including the gift of a free education, and 'breeding in good literature and learning'.

The teachers and scholars were to attend the Church services and sermons and were 'at all times to behave themselves soberly and reverendly in the Church'.

The schoolmaster shall lose his office if he is drunken or guilty of a crime, and he is to be paid £20 a year in salary, while the usher will have £3/6/8.

There will be two holidays each year, one at Christmas and one at Easter.

Governors, including the Bishop of Chester, are the final authority.

The scholars are not to frequent taverns or alehouses, nor are they to bring into the school, such as swords, daggers, wasters [perhaps =fish spears, used in salmon fishing], nor 'unlawful games, as cards, dice, tables and suchlike'.

The founder left for the maintenance of the school a variety of property in Lancashire, Westmorland, and Yorkshire, and the difficulty of collecting the rents of these scattered properties was the ruin of the school. Sometimes one or other of the governors spent time and money in visiting and collecting rents, and sometimes the master himself did. By the beginning of the nineteenth century so much of the property had been neglected or lost entirely, and so carelessly had the deeds been kept, that most of the founder's money had gone for ever. Some however was saved, and the school existed until 1908.

There is a library of over a thousand volumes, going back to the founder's own Bible dated 1572.

Among the old archives are some money records of the year 1631 and 1647 to 1651. It was in 1651 that George Fell and William Caton were there as scholars. (They were not 'free' scholars, as their homes were not in Hawkshead parish; their parents, probably Judge Fell for both boys, paid fees.) Mr. William Bordley was master then, from 1647–69, but he complained much, and grew 'weary of Hawkshead', and contemplated if he could not 'live elsewhere'. He paid £1 for new gutters, 1/6 to Giles Walker 'for wrighting ye barne', 6d. for walling the same barn, 14/– 'spent in going about the seasing before Candlemas[1] 1651', 3/8 for 'mossing [=thatching with moss?] and glassing the schools', 6d. for 'a new key to the school door, the old broke at the last barring out'. He lost £3 on a mare, which he had had to buy for the journey he had made to collect the rents. He notes how he had had to travel eight times to Yorkshire on school business, and then had had to bear 'daily exclamations that have been and are against me for neglecting the school when I was busied merely concerning it', and 'for any negligence or absence about mine own occasions, my worst foes cannot say that in four years I have spent six weeks, albeit the school statutes (say) every year six weeks'.

Reading these old entries of 1651 it is not surprising to find that William Caton, the thoughtful scholar of fifteen, recorded that there 'I met with many temptations, and seldom good company, but such as were given to folly and wantonness', and again 'we were often wild, vain and wanton, and sported ourselves in folly, to the extinguishing of the good oftentimes in ourselves'.

It is interesting to note that the Hawkshead Grammar School was rebuilt in 1675 by Daniel Rawlinson, a merchant of London, who was the founder of the firm of tea importers who were the first to import tea into England in 1650. It was this same firm who sold the tea which was thrown into Boston Harbour and precipitated the American War of Independence in 1773. Daniel Rawlinson was a cousin of Thomas Rawlinson of Graythwaite who became a Friend, much to the disgust of his family.[2]

Appendix Seven
(Chapter Six)

LETTER FROM HENRY FELL

The following letter is from Henry Fell to Gerard Roberts, wine cooper of London, and a man who did many a valuable service for

[1] =Collecting the fees before Candlemas (2nd Feb.).

[2] Facts taken from *Hawkshead*, by H. S. Cowper.

Friends. It describes the voyage which Fell and John Stubbs took,
intending to go to the Far East.

Alicant Roads. 18.4 [June] 1661.
[off S.E. Spain.]

Dear Brother,

Much I might write concerning the largeness of the love of God
unto us whom He hath called forth in this His service, making us
willing to forsake our native country and whatsoever was dear to us
there. But we have a reward; for His presence is with us and His Love
doth daily refresh our hearts, and we want for nothing. . . . We are all
well thus far on our way, and the master of the ship hath been exceedingly kind and loving to us beyond expectation, and all the ship's
company. We were in Malaga Roads [off S.E. Spain] but did not
come to an anchor there where some Spanish merchants came on
board, and we delivered them that book wherein those papers are to
the King of Spain, to the Pope, to the King of France, and the governor
of Malta; and they received it, and carried it ashore with them, and
likewise here we got some delivered, but we saw little of going ashore
ourselves. We have been here for two days and more, and now are
under sail to pass away for Leghorn, if the Lord will.

I have this further to certify concerning the two women Friends,
Catherine Evans and the other,—that they are prisoners in the Inquisition in Malta: for this morning we spoke with one Captain Harris (he
may be the bearer of this), who was there, and endeavoured very much
to have them released, but could not. He said they took shipping at
Leghorn in a Dutch ship for Alexandria, and were put into Malta by
contrary winds, where going ashore they dispersed some papers, and
thereupon the officers of the Inquisition laid hold on them, and confined
them, first to the Consul's house till they sent to Rome, for order
what to do with them, which when it came, was that they should be
put into the prison of the Inquisition, and there lie till they die. At first
they were put in together, but after some time they were separated.
He saith when he was there they had been eight or nine months separated, but now he thinks they are together, and did not know whether
one another was alive or no. He saith they have been there about
twenty months. Likewise he saith there was a letter came to the Grand
Master (so called) of Malta. It was in Latin, and in it was enclosed to
the two Friends which it's like they had. This man got the Consul to
go with him to the Grand Master, and he had the letter translated into
Italian, for there is none could speak English on the Island. It is like
it was G.F.'s [George Fox] letter. Captain Harris saith he himself did

proffer to be bound in a £500 bond that the two Friends should not set foot upon the island again, if they would release them and send them aboard his ship; but they would not, except he would engage that they should never come within the Catholic dominions again. He made that offer unknown to the women—he was not given the liberty of seeing them, but the Consul (since dead) went in and saw them. They were knitting and he saw them have bread and water allowed them. He saith he did believe they were in much want, though they said they were pretty well and contented, and wished him not to trouble himself for them. At present there is little likelihood of their releasement. This man saith he doth believe that John Parrott doth write to them sometimes, but whether it comes to their hands or not is uncertain.

Dear Gerrard, I would desire thee to write to Thomas Salthouse, to let him know concerning these two Friends, for he and Thomas Murford did write to me and John Stubbs about them. If we hear any further of them when we get to Leghorn, it is likely we may write. I rest thine in true and unfeigned love,

Henry Fell.[1]

These two courageous women, Katherine Evans and Sarah Chevers, were prisoners of the Inquisition for four years, and only released through the influence of George Fox with Lord d'Aubigny, Lord Almoner to the Queen Mother.[2] Their sufferings and the bravery with which they bore them are described by Sewel in his history, and can be read in their own little book, *This is a Short Relation of some of the cruel sufferings of Katharine Evans and Sarah Chevers in the Inquisition in the Isle of Malta*, etc., 1662.

John Perrot, who is mentioned by Henry Fell as having written to these two women, was himself a prisoner of the Inquisition in Rome where his sufferings drove him into madness.

[1] Swm. MSS. IV, 184.
[2] Camb. Jnl. II, 3-4.

Appendix Eight
(Chapter Six)

MEMBERS OF SWARTHMOOR MEETING AS QUAKER MISSIONARIES

Members of Swarthmoor Meeting who went out as Quaker missionaries:
William Caton (England, Scotland, Holland, Germany).
Ann Clayton (England, Barbados, New England, Rhode Island).
Richard Clayton (England, N. Ireland).
Henry Fell (Barbados, Egypt, Turkey, Germany, tried for Far East).
Leonard Fell (England, Scotland).
James Lancaster (Cumberland, Ireland and N. America).
Thomas Salthouse (S.W. England mostly).
John Stubbs (S.E. England, Holland, Germany, Italy, Turkey).
Margaret Fell and her daughters Margaret, Bridget, Isabel, and later Sarah.
Robert Salthouse (Scotland).
Thomas Lawson.
Thomas Curwen of Baycliffe, nr. Swarthmoor.
Walter Miers of Baycliffe, nr. Swarthmoor.
Alice Curwen of Baycliffe (New England, Barbados).

(Note: Seven deletions have been made from the original text.)

Appendix Nine
(Chapter Eight)

MARGARET FELL'S LETTER TO JAMES NAYLER, 15 OCT. 1656

Swarthmoor, 15th of the 8th month (56).
Dear Brother,
I have received thy letter and it was gladness to me when I received

it and I could receive and bear what thou had written in it, if thou had kept in subjection love and unity as thou did express in thy letter. But since, I have heard that thou would not be subject to him to whom all nations shall bow; it hath grieved my spirit; thou hath confessed him to be thy Father and thy Life bound up in him and when he sent for thee and thou would not come to him where was thy life then; was thou not then banished from the Father's house; as thou knows thou hath writ to me, and that which showed thee this which was to come I own; but that which banished thee I must deny, and when he bended his knees to the most High God for the seed's sake, and thou would not bend nor bow nor join with him, how wilt thou answer this to him who hath given him a name, better than every name to which every knee must bow. This is contrary to what thou wrote to me, where thou saith George is burying thy name that he may raise his own, but it was thy name that stood against him then. And thou wrote to me that Truth should never suffer by thee for where the seed suffers the Truth suffers; doth not the seed and all the body suffer by that Spirit that holds not the head but rebels against him. Oh consider what thou art doing; I am sure, the lamb in his suffering is in subjection not resisting nor exalting, but in the time of his suffering he is servant to all the seed and if thou stood in the suffering for the seed thou had not resisted him who is the promise of the Father to the seed who hath said blessed are ye that are not offended in me. Oh dear heart, mind while it is called to-day what thou art doing, lest thou walk naked and be a stumbling block to the simple. And be tender of the Truth which thou hath [known] before and suffered for, which draweth thine ear from unclean spirits which is like frogs which cometh out of the mouth of the dragon, the beast and the false prophet. These was seen when the sixth Angel poured out his vial upon the great river Euphrates; read and understand and return to thy first husband.

My dear brother, I can bear all that hath been passed if thou wilt be subject to the will of the Father and he who doeth the will hath learned obedience and is subject.

And I could lie down at thy feet that thou might trample upon me for thy good or so I know would he whom thou hath resisted, though to that spirit that rebels it cannot be, for that is not one with your Father. So in dearness and tenderness have I written to thee, my Father shall bear me witness, and I warn thee from the Lord God that thou beware of siding with unclean spirits lest thou be cut off for ever. Let me hear from thee as shortly as thou can after the receipt of this.

Thy dear sister in the Eternal Love.

M.F.

I wrote to thee after I had received thy letter which may be may come to thee after this, but then I did not know of this.

My husband took some letters from the foot post which was to me which mentioned the difference between G. and thee and he read them.[1]

Appendix Ten
(Chapter Nine)

JUDGE FELL'S WILL

'The will of THOMAS FELL, of Swarthmore Hall, in the parish of Ulverston, in the county of Lancaster, esquire, proved 4th December 1658.'

'The twenty-third day of September, in the year of our Lord God one thousand six hundred fifty and eight. Be it remembered that the day and year before written Thomas Fell, of Swarthmore in the county of Lancaster, esquire, being sick and weak in body, but of a perfect memory and understanding, blessed be the Lord for the same, doth hereby declare and publish his last Will and Testament in manner and form following, That is to say, I do hereby appoint nominate and ordain Richard Radcliffe, yeoman, and Thomas Coulton, yeoman, both my menial[2] servants, to be my Executors, jointly and severally; nevertheless upon this trust and confidence and to the end and purpose following; That is to say, that after my debts legacies and funeral expences be discharged, then they shall dispose and give the residue and overplus of all my real and personal estate, **unto** my seven daughters, Margrett, Bridget, Issabell, Sarah, Mary, Susana, and Ratchell, equally to be divided amongst them. To whom I do hereby give and bequeath the residue and remainder of my real and personal estate, equally amongst them, my debts, legacies, and funeral expences being first discharged as aforesaid. First, I give and bequeath unto the most aged impotent and necessitous persons within the parish of Ulverstone, the sum of Ten pounds, to be distributed by my executors, taking the information and assistance of the overseers of the poor within the said parish. Secondly, I give and bequeath unto the said overseers of the said parish for the time being, Thirty pounds, with the interest whereof they are to put forth one or more yearly of the poorest children born

[1] Spence MSS. III, 38.

[2] Menial in seventeenth century = a trusted domestic servant.

within the town of Ulverstone, excluding such as are born within the hamlet or elsewhere, save only those that are born within the precincts of the said town, and the overseers of the poor for the time being shall have the consent and allowance of such person and persons as shall be heir or owner of my estate at Swarthmore, for the putting forth of such impotent persons yearly. I likewise give and bequeath Thirty pounds, the interest whereof yearly is to go towards the maintenance of a school-master, to be kept at Ulverstone, for the teaching of poor children, which sum of Thirty pounds my executors are to pay within one year after my decease, to such person or persons as will give unto them good security for answering yearly the interest thereof, to the end and purpose aforesaid. Item, I give and bequeath Five pounds, unto the most aged impotent and necessitous persons within the parish of Dalton, to be distributed by my executors, taking the information and assistance of the overseers of the poor within the said parish. I like-wise give and bequeath unto my very honorable and noble friend the Lord Bradshaw, Ten pounds to buy a ring therewith, whom I humbly beseech to accept thereof, as all the acknowledgment I can make, and thankfulness, for his ancient and continued favors and kindness un-deservedly vouchsafed unto me since our first acquaintance. I likewise give and bequeath unto Mary Askewe Twenty pounds, for her faithful and careful service performed unto my wife and children in all their extremities. I further give and bequeath unto Joseph Sharpe, my faith-ful and careful servant at the Marsh Graynges, Fifty shillings and the like sum unto Ann Jaykes, who hath approved herself a very honest and careful servant ever since she came to the Marsh. I do hereby likewise give and bequeath unto my dear careful and entirely beloved Margrett Fell, my wife, Fifty pounds, as a token and testimony of my dearest **love and** affection unto her. I likewise give unto James Fell, my servant, Twenty shillings, to buy him a ring therewith as a token of my love unto him. I likewise give unto Thomas Knype of the Manor, gentleman, my old true friend Twenty shillings, to buy him a ring therewith, as a small token of the remembrance of my love unto him. As for my executors, who are to have no other benefit nor advantage by this my Will and Testament than is hereafter expressed; That is to say, I give to each of them Five pounds apiece. for the pains and care they are to undergo in the discharge and trust hereby imposed on them; and as concerning the charges they or either of them shall be put to, in proving this my Will and other necessaries incident thereunto, or in recovering or suing for any debts, or defending any suits commenced against them as my executors, the same is to be deducted and taken forth out of the residue and

o

remainder of my personal **estates**, my debts and legacies being first discharged. I desire my very true friends Anthony Pearson of Ramp-shaw in the county of Durham, gentleman and Jarvise Benson of Heay-Garth in the county of York, gentleman, to endeavour what in them lies to see this my last Will and Testament truly performed by my executors, to whom, (scilicet), to the said Anthony and Jarvise, I do give Forty shillings apiece, desiring them to accept of it to buy each of them a ring therewith. I do hereby revoke and make void all former Wills and Testaments by me made, and I do hereby give unto my beloved son, George Fell, **as** many of my Lawbooks as will make those which he hath the complete body of the law, and wherein they shall prove defective, my executors shall sell so many of the rest of my law-books as will buy those that are wanting. I do hereby in further token of my love and affection unto my dear wife, give and bequeath unto her, my Dwelling-house, onsett, with all the buildings, stables, barns, orchards, gardens, therewith all used and occupied, with Fifty acres of ground, lying most conveniently unto the said house, and to be set out and divided by my executors; all which **hereby** I give and bequeath unto my said loving wife, so long as she shall continue and remain in my name, and as my widow, and unmarried to any other, and no longer, in hopes that she will be careful and loving unto my poor fatherless children. And lastly I do publish and declare this to be my last Will and Testament. In witness whereof I have hereunto set my hand and seal, the day and year first above written.

THO: FELL.

'Witness hereof, GEO: FELL.   THOMAS KNYPE.
THOS: GREAVES.   WILLIAM BENSON.

'This Will was proved at London, before the Judges for Probate of Wills and granting Administrations, the fourth day of December 1658, by the oath of Richard Radcliffe, and Thomas Coulton, executors, to whom was committed administration, they being first legally sworn truly to administer.'

(Endorsed) 'December the 1st, 1658.

'Thomas Coulton, one of the executors within named was sworn before me,

'JA: MASTER.'

(From *The Fells of Swarthmoor Hall*, by Maria Webb, pp. 141–44, and extracted from the Registry of the Prerogative Court of Canterbury. **Corrections included in 1983 reprint were made by Isabel Ross from a copy of the will which had been compared with 'an original copy' by John Abraham in 1851.)**

Appendix Eleven
(Chapter Twenty)

LETTER FROM MARGARET FOX TO LORD ANCRAM

31.11 [Jan.] 1684/5.

Lord Ancram,

I am very much engaged to thee for thy Christian kindness to me who am a sufferer for the Lord of Heaven's sake, and for worshipping of him in his own spirit and truth (as he hath left it upon record in John 4 to the woman of Samaria), not for any evil or wrong that I have done to any man but for the Lord's sake do I suffer; I write this to thee for thy own satisfaction which thou desired me concerning my relations and parents, for my own self I have very few, my father was a gentleman living in Furness behind the sands, his name was Askew, and had a good estate as it was counted in his time, and he had children only me and another daughter, and he left us as good as six thousand pounds, when I was married to my first husband, who was a barrister-at-law of Gray's Inn, and practised the law many years, and was the Vice-Chancellor of the County Palatine of Lancaster, and in his own country a Justice of Peace and coroner, and in the latter end of his days he was a judge of Chester and Wales, he died above 26 years since, and left me eight children unpreferred, seven daughters and one son, but through the goodness of the Lord they are all except one preferred very well; and I am left to the stroke of persecutors. See if thou canst make me any help that I may live peaceably at my own habitation serving the Lord the rest of the time that he hath allotted me, I shall acknowledge thy kindness very much, and I believe that the Lord will reward thee many fold into thy own bosom in such a Christian act of charity, etc

From her that desires thy happiness in this world and that which is to come.

Margret Fox.[1]

[1] A.R.B. MSS. 105.

Appendix Twelve
(Chapter Twenty-One)

LETTER FROM MARGARET FOX TO DANIEL AND RACHEL
ABRAHAM

Kingston, 25th of 3rd mo. [May] 1690.
Dear Son and Daughter,
   We have received your dear and acceptable letters and I am very
glad and praise the Lord for your children's good health, and by this
you may know that I and we all here at Kingston, through the Lord's
goodness, are all very well and in good health, and your Brother and
Sister Meade was here the last week to see us and I trust in the Lord
they are all well there, and your Father is now at London and I intend,
if the Lord will, about a week hence, to be there ready to see Friends as
they come to town.
   I received a letter from your brother Lower by which I perceive he
intends to be at the Yearly Meeting and so for the North with his
family, but I perceive he will be a little stayed by the way by some
business for Widow Rawlinson so that he cannot reach Kingston till
the very latter end of the week so that I cannot [wait?] but I must be
at London before that, for I shall have a better time and opportunity
to see Friends before the Meeting than I can have afterward. Your
Brother and Sister Morrice will be there the next week. Your Brother
Lower desired me in his letter not to conclude of my going unto the
North till he be there, for he saith he has some business which he must
do after the Meeting in Sussex, which he hopes will be done in a
week's time but that's uncertain. He desires that we may return
together so that I cannot give you no certain notice of our return.
I ever had and yet have an intention to be at the Quarterly Meeting
at Lancaster, if his business do not hinder me; however, when we
know more I shall let you know.
   The letter which I am afraid you did not receive was the first letter
I writ from Gooseyes, in which I mentioned that you should get
John Bell to make us a place in the Meeting-house, the length of it
should be the half breadth of it and so broad as it will hold a seat
round about that one may sit of both sides; plank it and board it
under foot and also a seat of the outside of it (this was writ in that
letter and some other things).
   Thy sister very kindly received thy letter and she was very glad of

it. Her husband's and her dear love is dearly remembered to you, and Bethiah and Ann present their love and respects to their Uncle and Aunt; they are all very dear and tender to me. I hear of your Sister Lower and the children and hope they are well. My dear little John Abrahams is often in my remembrance, so is dear little Thomas. Even the Lord God Almighty preserve them and bless them.

Remember me to all the family, and my dear and entire love is dearly remembered to you,

So I remain

Your dear mother in the Lord,

M.F.

P.S.—I would ye to enquire after the maid at William Satterthwaite's whether we can have her or no.[1]

LETTER FROM SARAH MEADE TO MARGARET FOX

Gooses ye 18th of ye 2d moth 1694: [April]

Deare & Honoured Mother,

Haueinge the Conveniency, to send this, by the bearer, doe hereby giue thee my duty and deare Respects, being greatly Refreshed and comforted in the particular Acct shee gaue us, of thee & thy welbeing and of thy continueinge soe chearfull & hearty consideringe thy years, wch giues us occasion to blesse the Lord, for his great goodness, and Continued preservation to thee; wch is to the Joy and comfort of all thy Children; also the account wee had, of Brother & sistr Abraham & their Children, did much glad our hearts;—And sister's time being pretty neare, wee are not wantinge in earnest supplications to the great God in her behalfe, who is ye deliuerer & helpe of all his Children, in euery needfull time and neuer failes those who putts their trust & confidence in him;—and will J doubt not, be gratiously pleased, to afford her, his helping hand, who is all sufficient:—wee shall bee glad to heare how it is with her.—And Dr. Mother wee are all well here euery way, praised bee ye Lord, (as this ffriende cann informe thee, who came downe to Gooses to see us, and was at our Meetinge) and truely wee haue cause to say, the Lord is uery good & gratious to us, & affords us his blessed & sweett presence, in our little Country Meettinges, to the comforting & Refreshinge of our soules;—And our gratious God is very universall & large in his mercies, in Generall,

[1] Abraham MSS. 43.

o*

for it is & hath been a sweett & fruitfull springe, as hath been knowne this seuerall years, in these parts:—wch is A Confirmation that his mercifull hand is still Extended in Loue & goodwill, to the Creation, the workes of his hands;—Notwithstandinge the forward speeches, of some froward brittle spiritted men, who doth not rightly know their owne spiritts;—But God is the same as euer hee was & changes not, his wayes are not as mans ways, nor his thoughts as mans thoughts, but is abundant in mercy and Loueingkindness;—ffor ye Lord will not forsake his people, for his great names sake, neither will hee forsake his Jnheritance;—But will giue strength unto his people, & will blesse them with peace (Psal: 29: 11):—Therefore, it behooues us, and a cry runns thorrow the hearts of the ffaithfull, that all ye Lords people may bee kept Low & humble before him, and kept neare him, in a true sence of his goodness and mercies to us euery way, with thankefull hearts to him;—Soe may wee Expect the Continuance of his goodness to us,—and that none may bee Num or unsencible, or like ye barren heath that knows not when good comes; But that wee may bee a thankefull, sencible people, with which the Lord is well pleased. This [day reaches us] the good Newes of Bro: Rous his safe arrivall in Barbados; for which my heart & soule returnes hearty thanks to the Lord;—Who is the Preseruer of his people, at sea & at Land, & thorrow many dangers and difficulties;—wch will be Joyfull newes to his poore wife, who was in much Concerne for him.—all our Relations in these parts are well (for any thinge J know) Bro: Lower is fallen into Considerable practice & is like to doe good service to many, (ye Lord giueing him success,) and wch will also bee of service to his owne family. Cousin William Yeamans is like to have a good Trade;—And my Dr Husband failes not to continue a ffather to him, in his constant care & assistance, of wch the younge man is uery sencible; & J hope will grow in sobriety, wch will bee a comfort to all his Relations.— Sistr Jngram is now here, & hath been here some dayes, to bee in ye Country aire, her Husband thinks to come downe tomorrow;—they are both well;—and truely they liue in much loue & tenderness to each other; wch much rejoyces my heart;—Hee is a tender spirited man;—and tender of the Lord his Truth & honour;—and it greiues him, to see any ffriend, appeare in any thinge, yt is out of ye spiritt of Truth, hee writt to his wife, (wch shee Receiued this day) yt hee had Recd a lettr last post from Bro: Abraham, giueing an Acct of all your welfare at Swarthmore,—wch wee are uery glad to heare.—and soe Dr. Mother haueing beene more large than J intended, J shall conclude; —with ye Remembrance of my Dr Husbands duty, & mine to thee, with Sistr Jngrams, & Nathanaells and Richards, with all our deare &

tendr Loue, to Bro: & Sistr Abraham & their Children.—J Remaine, who am
> Thy truely Loueinge and
> dutifull daughter
> > S.M.

My Husband hath contracted with a friend to come into the House, to teach our sonn Nathanaell & his Cousin Richard the frensh tongue, his name is Peter Johan, & is ye same man yt our Dr. ffather advised us to, in his life time; hee comes this weeke or next.

[Addressed]
> To My Honoured Mother
> > Margarett Fox   These deliuer
> > at Swarthmore in
> > > Lancashire[1]

Appendix Thirteen
(Chapter Twenty-Two)

THE WILL OF MARGARET FOX

I, Margarett Fox, of Swarthmore, in the County of Lancaster, Widdow, being in the eighty fourth yeare if my age, yett, blessed bee God, in a good measure of health, and of a sound and perfect memory, Doe make this my last will and testament in the manner and forme following:

First Item. I doe give unto my son in law, Daniel Abraham, of Swarthmore aforesaide, and Joseph Goade, of Beakeliffe in the aforesaid County of Lancaster, yeoman, Tenn pounds for the Poore of the people called Quakers, belonging to Swarthmore Meettinge, to bee kept by the said Meettinge as A Stocke, and the Intrest of it yearly to help to mentaine Such poore of the people called Quakers as shall bee in want, belongeing to Swarthmore Meettinge Aforesaide.

Item. I doe give to my grand children, Nathanaell Rous, Bethiah English, Ann Rous, Nathanaell Meade, Margery Lower, Loveday Lower, Richard Lower, Mary Lower, Bridgett Lower and John Abraham, Each two guinnies.

Item. I doe give to my grand children, Charles Fell, Issabell Graues, and Margarett Manwaring, Each one guinnie.

[1] Thirnbeck MSS. 25.

All the remainder and residue of my worldly estate whatsoever I doe give unto my deare and loueing daughter, Rachell Abraham, wife of Daniell Abraham aforesaide, who hath lived with mee many yeares in my old age, and hath dilligently and dutifully demeaned her selfe to me with a great deale of care & tenderness. And I doe make my said daughter, Rachell Abraham, sole executrix of this my last will and testament, Hereby revokeing all other wills and testaments whatsoever formerly made by mee.

In witness whereof I have hereunto sett my hand and seale, the sixth day of April, Anno Domin one thousand six hundred ninety and eight.

Margarett Fox

M.F.

her mark.

Signed, sealed, published, and declared by the said Margarett Fox to be her last will and testament in the presence of us.

Henry Phillips

Wm. Davis

William Meade

Sarah Meade

Proved at Richmond, Yorks., 3rd Oct. 1702.

An Inventory of the goods and chattels, rights and creditts of Margarett Fox, late of Swarthmoor hall in the County of Lancaster, Widdow, deced, taken and apprized by Joseph Sharpe, of Hollowintre, Yeom, Wm. Fisher, of Worstone, Mercer, Barnard Benson, of Swarthmoor, husbandman, and Thomas Hodgshon, Junior, the second day of October, Ano. Dmj 1702:

	£.	s.	d.
First her wearing apparell and purse	040.	00.	00.
Plate	030.	00.	00.
Her books	010.	00.	00.
Her credits	249.	00.	00.
Household Goods	171.	03.	08.
Total	500.	03.	08.

Joseph Sharpe
Wm. Fisher
Bernard Benson   Apprizos.[1]
Thomas Hodgshon

[1] Jnl. F.H.S. II, 104.

Appendix Fourteen

MARGARET FELL'S WRITINGS

Between 1653 and 1698 Margaret Fell wrote some twenty-seven Epistles, most of which were reprinted in her *Works* in 1710. These were chiefly addressed to Friends. In addition she wrote many times to Charles II, and in her *Works* is a summary of her letters to Cromwell, to Charles II, the Duke of York, the Duke of Gloucester, the Princess of Orange, the magistrates of London, the Mayor and Justices of London, the Queen Dowager Mary, and the Queen of Bohemia. She wrote a letter to Major-General Harrison and his companions, condemned to death early in Charles II's reign, and another to Charles himself begging him to exercise mercy in dealing with his enemies.

Her first book, *False Prophets, Antichrists*, etc., was published in 1655 together with a short essay pointing out the hypocrisy of Protestants in England helping persecuted Protestants on the Continent, when they themselves were persecuting Quakers. She mentions that the latter had joined in sending relief to these persecuted Continental Protestants.[1] In 1656 she made a cogent exposure of the teaching of the Ranters. This latter was omitted from her *Works*, possibly because by 1710 the Ranters were no longer a powerful or dangerous movement in the religious world.

She wrote sixteen books, of various lengths, between 1655 and 1677. Her most active years in her writing were from 1655 to 1660, and again from 1664 to 1668 during her imprisonment at Lancaster. The subjects of these books are varied, five were addressed to the Jews, some to the clergy, some for Friends themselves, and one advocated the spiritual equality of men and women in the Church.

Four of her books were translated into Dutch, two into Hebrew, one book and an Epistle into Latin.

She wrote one 44-line poem, in memory and praise of Josiah Coale, who died in New England in 1668. It is printed in the *Works of Josiah Coale*. (Bevan Naish Library, 216, Woodbrooke, Birmingham.)

The Writings of M. Fell's daughters and sons-in-law

John Rous wrote seven books between 1656 and 1694.

Isabel Yeamans wrote one book in 1679.

[1] *False Prophets* and this Essay are No. 43 in 2,210, Bevan-Naish Library, Woodbrooke, Birmingham.

William Meade wrote seven books between 1670 and 1712, usually in collaboration with other Friends.

William Ingram wrote three, in 1685, in collaboration with others. Sarah Fell was responsible for the *Household Account Book of Swarthmoor Hall*, and Thomas Lower wrote a great part of George Fox's *Journal* at dictation, and many Epistles and letters for him.

George Fox in his Journal recorded that the North took 600 of 'every sort of book that was printed, and continued for many years till the Truth was spread over the nation, and this was settled when we first began to print.' 'The North at the first bore the charges for all the printing for several years.' (Camb. Jnl. I, 266-7)

Appendix Fifteen

CHRONOLOGY OF MARGARET FELL'S LIFE

1598-9   Birth of (Judge) Thomas Fell.
1603   *Death of Queen Elizabeth. Accession of James I.*
1614   Birth of Margaret Askew at Marsh Grange, nr. Dalton.
1616   *Death of William Shakespeare.*
1624   Birth of George Fox.
1625   *Accession of Charles I.*
1632   Marriage of Thomas Fell to Margaret Askew.
c1633   Birth of Margaret Fell, Junior.
c1635   Birth of Bridget Fell.
c1637   Birth of Isabel Fell.
c1638   Birth of George Fell.
1640   *Long Parliament first met.*
1642   *Outbreak of the Civil War.*
1642   Birth of Sarah Fell.
1647   Birth of Mary Fell.
1649 (Jan.)   *Execution of Charles I.*
1650   Birth of Susannah Fell.
1651   *Battle of Worcester.*
1652 (June)   George Fox's first coming to Swarthmoor.
1653 (April)   *Cromwell dissolved Long Parliament.*
1653 (Oct.)   Birth of Rachel Fell.
1656   Margaret Fell wrote *To Manasseth-ben-Israel.*
1657   Margaret Fell wrote *A Loving Salutation*

1658 (Sept.) *Death of Oliver Cromwell.*
1658 (Oct.) Death of Judge Thomas Fell.
1660 (April) *Declaration of Breda.*
1660 (May) *Restoration of Charles II.*
1660 (May) Arrest of George Fox at Swarthmoor and imprisonment in Lancaster Castle till September.
1660 (June) Margaret Fell's first visit to London with Margaret Fell, Jr.
1660 (June) Margaret Fell's declaration against violence and war.
1660 (Dec.) Marriage of George Fell with Hannah Potter.
1661 (Jan.) *Rising of Fifth Monarchy Men.* Nation wide persecution of Friends.
1661 (Sept.) Margaret Fell and her daughter returned to Swarthmoor Hall, after freedom had been granted to Friends.
1662 (Jan.) Marriage of Margaret Fell, Jr., to John Rous.
1662 (March) Marriage of Bridget Fell to John Draper.
1662 (May) *Quaker Act passed.*
1662 (May) Margaret Fell's second visit to London.
1662 (Aug.) Quakers freed from prisons.
1662 (Sept.) Margaret Fell returned to Swarthmoor.
1662–3 (winter) Margaret Fell went to be with Bridget Draper at Headlam, Durham.
1663 (March) Death of Bridget Draper, and her baby, Isaac.
1663 (May–Aug.) 1,000-mile journey through England—Margaret Fell, Sarah Fell, Mary Fell, Leonard Fell, Thomas Salthouse, William Caton in S.W. (George Fox and Thomas Lower with them there), Yorks, Bishoprick, Northumberland, Westmorland.
1663 (Aug.) *Kaber Rigg Plot in the North.* Renewed persecution of Quakers.
1664 (winter) George Fox at Swarthmoor, arrested; examination of George Fox and Margaret Fell at Holker Hall.
1664 (Jan.) George Fox tried and imprisoned at Lancaster.
1664 (Feb.) Margaret Fell arrested, and imprisoned at Lancaster.
1664 (March) Trial and imprisonment of both George Fox and Margaret Fell.
1664 (July) Isabel Fell married William Yeamans at Bristol.
1664 (July) *First Conventicle Act.*
1664 (Aug.) Margaret Fell praemunired (wrote *A Call to the Universal Seed of God*).
1664–7 *War between England and Holland.*
1664 (Nov.–Dec.) Mary Fell ill, probably plague, in London.

1665 (Jan.)   Swarthmoor Estate of Margaret Fell granted to George Fell by Charles II.

1665 (March)   George Fox praemunired.

1665 (April)   George Fox moved from Lancaster to Scarborough Castle. John and Margaret Rous and Mary Fell returned to Swarthmoor.

1665   *The Plague in London.*

1665 (Nov.)   Death of William Caton in Holland.

1666 (Sept.)   George Fox released from Scarborough.

1666 (Sept.)   *The Great Fire of London.*

1666   Margaret Fell wrote *Women's Speaking*, etc.

1666 (Aug.)   Margaret Fell wrote *Epistle to Charles II*.

1666 (Sept.)   Margaret Fell wrote *A Touch-Stone*, etc.

1666   Margaret Fell wrote *Standard of the Lord Revealed.*

1666–7 (winter)   Mary Fell in Bristol with Isabel Yeamans.

1667   William Penn and Robert Barclay joined the Quakers.

1668   Margaret Fell wrote *A Call unto the Seed of Israel.*

1668 (June)   Margaret Fell released from Lancaster Castle.

1668 (Aug.)   Mary Fell married Thomas Lower. Margaret Fell travelled in North and Western England with Rachel, and to Bristol, Devon and Somerset.

1668–9 (winter)   Margaret Fell's third visit to London, with Rachel.

1669 (spring)   Margaret Fell and Rachel visited Friends in Kent.

1669 (summer)   Margaret Fell and Rachel in London.

1669 (Oct.)   Margaret Fell married George Fox at Bristol. George Fox travelled in the South and Midlands. Margaret Fox returned to Swarthmoor.

1669 (Dec.)   George Fell scheming in London to get his mother's estate and Swarthmoor. (Susannah and Rachel Fell at Swarthmoor, Sarah Fell in London. Thomas and Mary Lower living in London. John and Margaret Rous living in London.)

1670 (April)   Margaret Fox's second imprisonment, Lancaster.

1670 (May)   *Second Conventicle Act.*

1670 (summer)   Sarah Fell returned home.

1670 (Oct.)   Death of George Fell.

1670 (Sept. to spring '71)   George Fox very ill in London, nursed by Margaret Rous, etc.

1671 (April)   Margaret Fox released by discharge under the Broad Seal.

1671 (May–Aug.)   Margaret Fox's fourth visit to London.

1671–3   George Fox in America.

1672　Charles II's 'The Great Pardon' released 500 Friends and other Nonconformists.

1672 (April)　Margaret Fox and Rachel Fell travelled in Yorkshire (268 miles).

1672 (late)　Margaret Fox travelled again—district not known.

1673 (June)　Margaret Fox with Sarah and Rachel Fell and Thomas Lower went to Bristol to meet George Fox on his return from America. Margaret Fox's fifth visit to London.

1673　*Test Act passed.*

1673–85　Continuous and severe persecution of Quakers.

1673 (Dec.)　George Fox arrested at Armscott and imprisoned at Worcester. Margaret Fox and Rachel Fell returned to Swarthmoor. Thomas Lower stayed at Worcester.

1674 (Aug.)　Margaret Fox with Thomas Lower and Susannah Fell went to Worcester.

1674 (Oct.)　Margaret Fox's sixth visit to London and interviewed King.

1675 (Feb.)　George Fox discharged freely from Worcester.

1675 (June)　George Fox, Margaret Fox and Susannah Fell returned to Swarthmoor. George Fox stayed at Swarthmoor for twenty-one months.

1676 (April)　William Penn at Swarthmoor.

1676　Thomas and Mary Lower moved to Marsh Grange.

1677 (March)　George Fox left Swarthmoor for London.

1677 (summer)　Journey to Holland—George Fox, William Penn, Robert Barclay, George Keith and wife, Isabel Yeamans.

1678　Isabel Yeamans in Scotland with Robert Barclay and wife.

1678 **(Sept.**–March 1680) George Fox at Swarthmoor (last visit).

1680–90　Isabel Yeamans lived in various places, including London and Stockton-on-Tees.

1681–91　George Fox in or near London.

1681 (June)　Sarah Fell married William Meade in London.

1681 (May–July)　Margaret Fox's seventh visit to London.

1682　William Penn founded Pennsylvania.

1683–6　Thomas Lower in prison at Launceston, Cornwall (see p. 412).

1683 (March)　Rachel Fell married Daniel Abraham.

1683 (Sept.)　Margaret Fox, Rachel, and Daniel Abraham arrested and tried by Roger and William Kirkby in Lancaster.

1684 (June)　These three were fined heavily and imprisoned.

1684 (Nov.–March 1685)　Margaret Fox's eighth visit to London— Mary Lower and Leonard Fell with her, and Susannah Fell. Margaret Fox aged nearly seventy.

1685 (Feb.)   *Death of Charles II.* Margaret Fox interviewed James II.

1685 (May or June)   Robert Barclay visited Swarthmoor, on his way from London to Scotland.

1686 (March)   *James II's General Pardon and Royal Warrant* released Friends from prison.

1687 (spring)   *Declaration of Indulgence for all Nonconformists.*

1688   Swarthmoor Meeting House given by George Fox.

1689   *Fall of James II. Accession of William amd Mary.*

1689 (May)   *Toleration Act,* giving limited religious freedom.

1690   Isabel Yeamans married Abraham Morrice of Lincoln.

1690 (April–June)   Margaret Fox's ninth visit to London, now seventy-six years old.

1690   Death of Robert Barclay.

1691 (Jan.)   Death of George Fox in London.

1691   Marriage of Susannah Fell to William Ingram.

1694   Death of Gulielma Penn.

1696 (March)   Death of John Rous at sea, on returning from Barbados.

1697–8   Margaret Fox's tenth and last visit to London, aged eighty-three.

1698   Margaret Fox's Epistle to Friends *re* Oaths. Trouble in Society of Friends *re* Whigs and Tories.

1698 (May)   Margaret Fox attended Yearly Meeting.

1698 (June)   Margaret Fox sent a letter to William III by Susannah Ingram. Death of William Yeamans.

1698 (late June)   Margaret Fox's First Epistle against regimentation, etc.

1699   Second visit of William Penn to Pennsylvania.

1700 (April)   Margaret Fox's Second Epistle against regimentation.

1701 (Nov.)   Margaret Fox's last Testimony.

1702 (March)   *Death of William III. Accession of Anne.*

1702 (April)   Death of Margaret Fox, aged nearly eighty-eight, at Swarthmoor Hall.

An additional note by Isabel Ross records that Thomas Lower was temporarily released and at Swarthmoor in May 1684; that he was again released and in London and Kingston in February 1684/5 (*Short Journal* p. 102); and that he had returned to Launceston the following month.

INDEX

A BRIEF
COLLECTION

OF

Remarkable Paſſages and Occurrences

Relating to the

Birth, Education, Life, Converſion, Travels, Services, and *Deep Sufferings*

OF THAT

Ancient, Eminent, and Faithful

Servant of the Lord,

𝕸argaret 𝕱ell;

But by her Second Marriage,

𝕸argaret 𝕱ox.

Together

With Sundry of Her *Epiſtles, Books*, and *Chriſtian Teſtimonies* to Friends and Others; and alſo to thoſe in Supreme Authority, in the ſeveral late Revolutions of Government.

Mat. 5. 16. *Let your Light ſo ſhine before Men, that they may ſee your good Works, and glorifie your Father which is in Heaven.*
Luke 18. 7. *Shall not God avenge his own Elect, which cry Day and Night unto him, though he bear long with them?*

LONDON, Printed and Sold by J. Sowle, in *White-Hart-Court* in *Gracious-ſtreet*, 1710.

After her death, Margaret Fell's chief writings were included in this 1710 book, which is recommended for further study.

George Fell of Hawkswell,
owner of Osmotherley, near Ulverston

THOMAS FELL of Swarthmoor H
Ulverston, b.1598, m.1632, d.1658

Margaret=John Rous	Bridget=John Draper	Isabel=1.Wm.Yeamans	George=Ha
b.1633? of Barbados	b.1635? of Headlam,	b.1637? of Bristol,	b.1638? Po
m.1662 & Kingston-	m.1662 Durham	m.1. 1664 d.1674	m.1660 né
d.1706 on-Thames,	d.1663	2. 1689 2.Abraham	d.1670 Co
d.1696		d.1704 Morrice, of	
		Lincoln	

1. Lydia, b.1665, d.1666   Isaac, d. an
                              infant, 1663

2. Bethia, b.1666, m.1692,
   David English of Pontefract

3. Margaret, b.1667, m. — Manwaring

4. Nathaniel, b.1670, m. Hannah ?, d.1714

5. Anne, b.1672, d.1709
   m. Benjamin Dykes of Colchester

6. Thomas, b.1673, d.1674

7. Bridget, b.1675, d.1683

   and 1 or 2 others

1. William,
   d. an infant

2. Rachel, b.1666,
   d.1676

3. Margaret, b.1668,
   died young

4. William, b.1670?,
   d.1698

1. Sarah, b. ?
   d.1669

2. Hannah, b.
   1667

3. Isabel, b.166
   m. James G

4. Charles, b.1
   m. Mary Bre